COMMUNITIES of the LAST DAYS

The Dead Sea Scrolls, the New Testament & the Story of Israel

C. MARVIN PATE

InterVarsity Press
Downers Grove, Illinois

InterVarsity Press
P.O. Box 1400, Downers Grove, IL 60515
World Wide Web: www.ivpress.com
E-mail: mail@ivpress.com

InterVarsity Press® is the book-publishing division of InterVarsity Christian Fellowship/USA®, a student movement active on campus at hundreds of universities, colleges and schools of nursing in the United States of America, and a member movement of the International Fellowship of Evangelical Students. For information about local and regional activities, write Public Relations Dept., InterVarsity Christian Fellowship/USA, 6400 Schroeder Rd., P.O. Box 7895, Madison, WI 53707-7895.

Scripture quotations, unless otherwise noted, are from the Revised Standard Version of the Bible, *copyright 1946, 1952, 1971 by the Division of Christian Education of the National Council of the Churches of Christ in the U.S.A., and are used by permission.*

Grateful acknowledgment is made for permission to reprint excerpts from the following copyrighted works:

Responses to 101 Questions on the Dead Sea Scrolls, *by Joseph A. Fitzmyer, S.J. © 1992 by the Corporation of the Roman Catholic Clergymen, Maryland. Used by permission of Paulist Press.*

The End of the Ages Has Come, *by Dale C. Allison Jr. Copyright © 1985 Fortress Press. Used by permission of Augsburg Fortress.*

The New Testament and the People of God, *by N. T. Wright, copyright © 1992 Augsburg Fortress.*

Jesus and the Victory of God, *by N. T. Wright, copyright © 1996 Augsburg Fortress.*

The Dead Sea Scrolls Translated: The Qumran Texts in English, *by Florentino García Martínez. Leiden: E. J. Brill, 1994. Used by permission of E. J. Brill.*

Reclaiming the Dead Sea Scrolls *by Lawrence H. Schiffman. Copyright © 1994, 1995 by Lawrence H. Schiffman. Used by permission of Doubleday, a division of Random House, Inc.*

Epistles to the Colossians and to Philemon, *NIGTC. © 1996 by James D. G. Dunn. Wm. B. Eerdmans Publishing.*

Lord of the Banquet: The Literary and Theological Significance of the Lucan Travel Narrative, *by David P. Moessner. Copyright 1989. Published by Fortress Press.*

The Dead Sea Scrolls Today, *by James C. VanderKam. Copyright 1994. Published by William B. Eerdmans Publishing.*

Cover photograph: Erich Lessing/Art Resource, N.Y.

ISBN 0-8308-1597-X

Printed in the United States of America ∞

Library of Congress Cataloging-in-Publication Data

Pate, C. Marvin, 1952-
    Communities of the Last Days : the Dead Sea scrolls, the New Testament & the story of Israel/C. Marvin Pate.
      p. cm.
    Includes bibliographical references.
    ISBN 0-8308-1597-X (pbk. : alk. paper)
      1. Dead Sea scrolls—Criticism, interpretation, etc. 2. Dead Sea scrolls—Relation to the
    New Testament. 3. Bible N.T.—Criticism, interpretation, etc. I. Title.
    BM487 .P35 2000
    296.1'55—dc21
                                                             99-087490

17	16	15	14	13	12	11	10	9	8	7	6	5	4	3	2	1
14	13	12	11	10	09	08	07	06	05	04	03	02	01	00		

To Dr. Carol K. Stockhausen,
scholar and mentor par excellence

CONTENTS

Acknowledgments

The idea for this book was born almost four years ago, after a phone conversation with Daniel G. Reid, academic and reference editor at InterVarsity Press. I shared with Dan my love for the New Testament as well as my intrigue with the Dead Sea Scrolls, and he related to me that he had been searching for some time for an author who would be willing to tackle a project integrating the two. I put together a proposal for doing just such a study, and now that dream has become a reality. Not that the task was easy; it took three years and three revisions for the book to take its final form. But the effort was worth it to me personally, and I hope that the reader will also profit from the labor.

There are several groups of people without whom this work would have never seen publication. I am indebted to them for their acts of kindness. First, I am thankful for my teaching assistants who had a part in typing this manuscript: Susan Marsh, Greg Catlin and Erin Bonnell. Their diligence and cheerfulness greatly lightened the load of this task. In this connection I also wish to express my appreciation to Marty Hartley of the Moody Bible Institute, whose computer skills saved the day for this book numerous times.

Second, how encouraging and what a privilege to have worked with the fine staff of InterVarsity Press, including Jim Hoover, David Zimmerman and Dan Reid. Dan is an editor "in whom I am well-pleased." His insight, skills and perseverance made this manuscript possible. Thanks, Dan!

Third, I should like up front to offer my heartfelt thanks to those scholars, on whose research on the Dead Sea Scrolls and the New Testament this work is based: Michael Wise, Michael Douglas, Lawrence Schiffman, James Vanderkam, N. T. Wright, James M. Scott and Frank Thielman, to name only a few. Such an array of scholarship has taught me much about the story of Israel as portrayed in the Scrolls and in the New Testament, even though at times the evidence has led me down a different path of interpretation. And speaking of scholars, I offer here my profound gratitude to Carol K. Stockhausen, my dissertation director over a decade ago. Her expertise, meticulous argumentation and immense patience first guided me in my study of the Dead Sea Scrolls and the New Testament. It is only fitting, therefore, and it is with great joy, that I dedicate this book to her.

C. Marvin Pate

Abbreviations

WTJ	*Westminster Theological Journal*
WUNT	Wissenschaftliche Untersuchungen zum Neuen Testament
ZNW	*Zeitschrift für die neutestamentliche Wissenschaft*
ZThK	*Zeitschrift für Theologie und Kirche*

Commentaries

AB	The Anchor Bible
HNTC	Harper's New Testament Commentary
HTKNT	Herders theologischer Kommentar Neuen Testament
ICC	International Critical Commentary
NICNT	New International Commentary on the New Testament
NIGTC	New International Greek Testament Commentary
WBC	Word Biblical Commentary

Biblical Literature

Gen	Ezra	Joel	Jn	Philem
Ex	Neh	Amos	Acts	Heb
Lev	Esther	Obad	Rom	Jas
Num	Job	Jon	1 Cor	1 Pet
Deut	Ps	Mic	2 Cor	2 Pet
Josh	Prov	Nahum	Gal	1 Jn
Judg	Eccles	Hab	Eph	2 Jn
Ruth	Song	Zeph	Phil	3 Jn
1 Sam	Is	Hag	Col	Jude
2 Sam	Jer	Zech	1 Thess	Rev
1 Kings	Lam	Mal	2 Thess	
2 Kings	Ezek	Mt	1 Tim	
1 Chron	Dan	Mk	2 Tim	
2 Chron	Hos	Lk	Tit	

Extracanonical Literature
Apocrypha and Pseudepigrapha

2 Apoc. Bar.	*2 Apocalypse of Baruch*

Apoc. Abr.	*Apocalypse of Abraham*
Apoc. Zeph.	*Apocalypse of Zephaniah*
Asc. Is.	*Ascension of Isaiah*
Bar	*Baruch*
Ep. Arist.	*Epistle of Aristeas*
Jub.	*Jubilees*
Jdt	*Judith*
Macc	*Maccabees*
Pss. Sol.	*Psalms of Solomon*
Sib. Or.	*Sibylline Oracles*
Sim. Enoch	*Similitudes of Enoch*
Sir	*Sirach*
T. 12 Patr.	*Testaments of the Twelve Patriarchs*
T. Levi	*Testament of Levi*
T. Zeb.	*Testament of Zebulun*
T. Dan	*Testament of Dan*
T. Benj.	*Testament of Benjamin*
T. Abr.	*Testament of Abraham*
T. Job	*Testament of Job*
Tob	*Tobit*
Wis	*Wisdom of Solomon*

Qumran

CD	Damascus Document
1QApGen	Genesis Apocryphon
1QH	Thanksgiving Hymns, *Hôdāyôt*
1QpHab	1Q*Pesher* on Habbakkuk
1QM	The War Scroll
1QS	The Rule of the Community
1QSa	The Rule of the Congregation
1QSb	The Rule of the Benediction
4QdibHam	Words of the Luminaries
4QFlor	4Q174 Florilegium
4QMMT	Some Works of the Torah
4QpHos	4Q*Pesher* on Hosea
4QpIs	4Q*Pesher* on Isaiah
4QpNah	4Q*Pesher* on Nahum
4QpPs	4Q*Pesher* on Psalms/4Q171
4QShirShabb	Angelic Liturgy/Songs of Sabbath Sacrifice

4QTestim	4QTestimonia
4Q521	4QMessianic Apocalypse
4Q541	4QTestament Levi
11QMelch	11QMelchizedek
11QPs(a)	11QApocryphal Psalms
11QTemple	11QTemple Scroll

Babylonian Talmud

B. Bat.	Baba Batra
Pes.	Pesahim
Shab.	Shabbat
Sanh.	Sanhedrin

Midrashim

| Gen. Rab. | Genesis Rabbah |
| Deut. Rab. | Deuteronomy Rabbah |

Josephus

Ag. Ap.	Against Apion
Ant.	Antiquities of the Jews
J.W.	Jewish War
Life	Life of Flavius Josephus

Philo

Agric.	De Agricultura
Conf. Ling.	De Confusione Linguarum
Fug.	De Fuga et Inventione
Gig.	De Gigantibus
Leg. All.	Legum Allegoriae
Poster. C.	De Posteritate Caini
Quaest. in Ex.	Quaestiones in Exodum
Som.	De Somniis
Vit. Mos.	De Vita Mosis

Other Jewish Writings

| Mek. | Mekilta |
| Sifre Deut | Sifre Deuteronomy |

Translations

LXX	Septuagint
MT	Masoretic Text
Tg. Isa.	*Targum Isaiah*
Tg. Ps.-J.	*Targum Pseudo-Jonathan*
Tg. Neof.	*Targum Neofiti*

8

Introduction

Over fifty years have elapsed since the discovery of the Dead Sea Scrolls in 1947, the most celebrated, if not fortuitous, archaeological discovery of this century. In the spring of that year, three Bedouin shepherds were in the area called Qumran, which is on the northwest side of the Dead Sea, apparently tending their flock. The shepherds were cousins and members of the Ta'amireh tribe, one of whom, Jum'a Muhammad Khalil, amused himself by throwing rocks at a cave opening in the cliffs to the west of the plateau at Qumran. One of the stones went into the cave and made a shattering noise. The Bedouin did not enter the cave that day, but two days later one of them, Muhammad ed-Dhib, went back to it and, venturing in, found ten jars. One of those jars held three ancient manuscripts. The rest of the containers were empty, but later four additional scrolls were found hidden in that cave.[1] The discovery of those ancient documents and the hundreds more that nearby caves would later yield is regarded by many as the most significant archaeological finding in the twentieth century and as nothing short of providential.

It is no small coincidence that, in the same year the Dead Sea Scrolls were unearthed, the nation of Israel was reborn, creating an intriguing parallel between the two: The creation of modern Israel, like the ancient Dead Sea Scrolls, symbolized the culmination point of the Old Testament history of the Jews. Such a story moved from exile to restoration. For modern Israel, it meant that Jews came to their native land from all quarters of the Diaspora (a term used for Jews living outside of Israel since the fall of Jerusalem to the Babylonians in 587 B.C.). For the Dead Sea Scrolls, as chapter one of this work will detail, the story of ancient Israel manifested itself in terms of those documents' being held hostage for over forty years by a few non-Jewish scholars, who reluctantly relinquished them to their rightful owners only after public pressure was brought to bear on the situation. Ironically, the story of the Scrolls paralleled that of ancient Jews who returned from the Babylonian exile to their homeland in

539 B.C. only to realize that they were still held captive by foreigners.[2]

But how does the New Testament factor into this discussion? Two significant considerations quickly come to mind which motivate the writing of this book. First, the Dead Sea Scrolls (hereafter DSS) have emerged as a key player in the question of the origins of Christianity. Now that Gnosticism (and Hellenism[3] in general) has finally released its grip on the topic, the way has been paved for the DSS to step into the forefront of the discussion. This is so because both communities—Christian and Essene (most probably the people who wrote the Scrolls; see chapter two)—are rooted in Jewish apocalypticism[4] and therefore share a common legacy of ideas. This present work will focus on that dimension. While other Jewish apocalyptic groups were approximately contemporaneous with the New Testament (hereafter NT)—for example, the reading communities of 1 Enoch, 4 Ezra and 2 Apocalypse of Baruch—the large volume of material comprising the DSS makes it the leading candidate for comparison with the NT. Second, intimately related to the previous point, both the DSS and the NT utilize apocalypticism to tell the story of Israel, which unfolds in the topics of sin, exile and restoration, though each set of documents tells the story from its respective point of view.

These two factors combine to articulate the thesis of this study: The story of Israel is the metanarrative adapted by the DSS and the NT. In what follows, I introduce the subject by offering an explanation of the thesis, the methodology employed in developing that thesis in this book and an overview of the work.

The concern of this study centers on the story of Israel as recorded in the Old Testament (hereafter OT), especially the book of Deuteronomy. That writing promised the Jews long life and blessings in the land of Israel if they obeyed the Torah (Deut 1:8-11; 4:1-8; 5:29—6:25; 7:12—8:10; 11:1-15, 18-25; 28:1-14; 30:11-15; 33; cf. Lev 18:4-5; 25:18-19; 26:3-13). In the event, however, that Jews acted unwisely by disobeying the law of Moses, they could expect to experience the Deuteronomic curses, including their defeat by the nations and exile into foreign subjugation (Deut 4:9-28; 8:11-20; 11:16-17; 27:15-26; 28:15-68; 31:16—32:51; cf. Lev 18:24-30; 26:14-39). The alternative choices of life and death based respectively on obedience and disobedience to the Torah are succinctly interwoven in Deuteronomy 7:6-11; 11:26-28. Alas, however, the ominous warnings regarding the Deuteronomic curses upon Israel tragically turned into reality (cf. Deut 29:24-27 with 2 Kings 22:14-17 and Jer 22:9).

Nevertheless, the hope for a brighter tomorrow also informs Deuteronomy, as the restoration prophecies therein indicate, for according to Deuteronomy 4:29, 31; 30:1-10 (cf. Lev 26:40-45), the promise is held out to Israel that, if she will return to the Mosaic law in exile, then God will restore Jews, the chosen people, to their land and will exalt them above the nations (see Deut 7:6-7; 10:14-15; 14:2; 26:19; 28:1). The story of Israel, then, follows the trajectory of sin—exile—restoration.

The message of Deuteronomy came true, or so it would seem. Israel broke covenant with God and from 605 to 587 B.C. was sent into exile to Babylonia (the beginning of the Diaspora). In 539 B.C., however, Cyrus the Persian, the new ruler of the world, permitted the Jews to return to their land. Many thought the long-awaited restoration had arrived, but such a hope was soon dashed. The rebuilt temple paled in significance compared to the Solomonic temple with its pristine glory, the people of God did not yet obey the Torah fully from the heart, and foreign nations continued to run roughshod over the land of Israel: Greece, Egypt, Syria and Rome. A strange and foreboding reality therefore set in. Israel, though now returned to the Promised Land, was still in exile.

As is increasingly being recognized among scholars today, the problem of Second Temple Judaism (539 B.C.–A.D. 70), including the DSS and the NT, was how to resolve the dilemma of Israel's restoration.[5] Various responses to that quandary were formulated and vociferously presented as divinely sanctioned by different groups—Pharisees, Sadducees, Zealots, Essenes and Christians, to name some of the more well-known sects. In providing alternative answers, however, each circle rewrote, indeed subverted, the story of Israel, redefining its symbols (Torah, temple and racial ethnicity), rituals (feasts, sacrificial system) and beliefs (monotheism, election and eschatology).[6] The result was both continuity and discontinuity in retelling the story of Israel; the former because it was still the story of Israel, but the latter because different endings to that story were proposed.

This is where the relationship of the DSS to the NT enters into the

picture, for these two groups retold the story of Israel from a decidedly apocalyptic perspective, that is, they believed themselves to be
restored Israel living in the last days. It is this conviction that will
guide the comparative analysis of the two bodies of literature in this
study. To my knowledge such an undertaking has not yet been
attempted by Jewish or Christian scholars. The working assumption
and methodology being suggested here account for the similarities
and differences between the DSS and the NT. The similarities stem
from the fact that both are retelling the same story line, while the dissimilarities proceed from the dynamic that they are redefining the
symbols, rituals and beliefs of that story. This approach should
deliver us from the danger of parallelomania,[7] the presumption that
parallel ideas in two writings necessarily indicate literary dependence between them. When this has occurred in past studies of the
relationship between the DSS and the NT, the direction of borrowing
has been thought largely to proceed from the NT to the DSS, though
some scholars espouse the reverse (see chapter two). The type of
comparative analysis followed in this work, however, avoids the pit-
fall of that methodology by arguing that the similarities between the
DSS and the NT are due rather to their common parent tradition (the
story of Israel) but presented from antithetical perspectives, thus
accounting for their differences.[8]

My thesis—the story of Israel is adapted by the DSS and the NT—
will unfold as follows. Chapter one will detail the story of Israel as it is
related to the discovery and publication of the DSS. Chapter two will
attempt to demonstrate that the Essenes produced the DSS and that
they, like the early Christians, read the story of Israel to suit their own
worldview. Chapter three sketches the literature comprising the DSS
and from that argues that the Essenes at Qumran employed, like Matthew, an eschatological hermeneutic in portraying themselves as the
embodiment of the true Israel prophesied in the OT. Chapter four
examines messianic hope as espoused in the DSS and in the NT vis-à-
vis the restoration of Israel. Chapter five investigates the concept of the
people of God as operative in the DSS and in Luke-Acts. Chapter six
considers how it is one enters and remains in the new covenant of the
true Israel, according to the DSS and the apostle Paul. Chapter seven

analyzes the relationship of wisdom, law and the restoration of Israel as depicted in the Colossian heresy and in the DSS, centering on the role of angels in that discussion. Chapter eight highlights the beliefs, or building blocks, of the story of Israel (monotheism, covenant and eschatology) as presented in Hebrews and in the DSS. Chapter nine focuses on the topics of exile and eschatology in the DSS and in John.

As it turns out, these chapters basically correlate with the NT in the following way: After the introductory material in chapters one and two, chapter three explores Matthew; chapter four draws on the Synoptic Gospels, especially Mark; chapter five centers on the two-volume work of Luke-Acts; chapter six highlights a key concern in the Pauline letters; chapter seven addresses a significant topic in the Pauline tradition; chapter eight focuses on one of the later NT epistles, Hebrews; chapter nine deals with the Johannine writings, especially the Gospel of John.

These comments have presented the thesis to be developed in this study, its method of investigation and an overview of its outworking, all of which revolve around the story of Israel. Yet if this theme is so important, we must ask at this point, why has it gone unnoticed by so many DSS scholars? The answer to this question, which I will discuss in chapter one, is that only recently has the complete corpus of the DSS been released to the public. To that issue I now turn.

Chapter One

From Exile to the Return

The Story of Israel & the Publication of the DSS

Introduction

For many years the DSS, like Israel of old, though in their land, were still in exile; both Scrolls and nation found themselves in the hands of non-Jews. The purpose of this chapter, therefore, is to accentuate that aspect of the parallel stories of Israel and the DSS. A significant part of this chapter is devoted to describing the sin-exile-restoration pattern depicted in Jewish literature of the Second Temple period, particularly the five components of the Deuteronomistic view of Israel's history: disobedience, prophetic warning, rejection of the prophets, exile, restoration. Elements four (exile) and five (restoration) then serve as the focal points of comparison with the publication of the DSS.

I should offer at the outset of this chapter, however, a disclaimer: In drawing similarities between ancient Israel and the modern intrigue surrounding the Scrolls, one should not press the analogy too far. My purpose here is in no way to impugn the character of those early scholars on the DSS team; in fact, their efforts were noble and indefatigable. At the end of the day, the ensuing delay of the publication of the Scrolls owed more than anything to the sheer magnitude of the task, even though, admittedly, other motivations emerged along the way.

The Story of Israel

In his monumental study of OT, Jewish and NT sources regarding the role and fate of the prophets in Israel's history, Odil H. Steck argues at length that Second Temple Judaism (587 B.C. to A.D. 70) was dominated by the Deuteronomistic view of Israel's history.[1] Steck makes a compelling case that especially by the time of Antiochus IV and the Maccabean revolt[2] the Deuteronomistic tradition, though capable of a certain fluidity of expression, had become a relatively fixed conceptual framework containing essentially five constituent elements. (Particularly important are elements four and five because of their relevance to the publication of the DSS.)

1. Israel's perpetual disobedience to God. The Deuteronomistic view of the story of Israel[3] asserts, first of all, that the nation has been "stiff-necked," rebellious and disobedient during its entire existence (see Ex 33:3, 5; Num 22:14; Deut 29:4; 31:27; Is 63:10; Jer 9:26; CD 3). Using a different metaphor but pinpointing the same reality, Deuteronomy 32:5 characterizes Israel as a perverse generation, stretching across its history. "They have dealt corruptly with him [God], they are no longer his children because of their blemish; they are a perverse and crooked generation." Verse 20 concurs: "They are a perverse generation, children in whom is no faithfulness" (Deut 32:20; cf. Lk 7:31; 11:29 and par.; Phil 2:15). Later Jewish writings viewed their generations as continuing Israel's disobedience. Thus *Baruch* (c. 150 B.C.) 1:18-19 laments:

> [We] have disobeyed him [God], and have not heeded the voice of the Lord our God, to walk in the statutes of the Lord that he set before us. From the time when the Lord brought our ancestors out of the land of Egypt until today, we have been disobedient to the Lord our God, and we have been negligent, in not heeding his voice. (cf. 2 Kings 17:23; Neh 9:32; Ezek 2:3-4; 20:3-8; Dan 9:5; *1 Esdr* 8:73-74; *2 Esdr* 9:7)

These passages, in their usage of the first plural pronoun, indicate the collaboration of contemporary Jews with the hard-heartedness of ancient Israel.[4]

2. Israel and the prophets. Already in Deuteronomy there is the hint that God will raise up prophets to call Israel to repentance. We read in Deuteronomy 18:15, "The LORD your God will raise up for you a prophet like me [Moses] from among you, from your brethren—him you shall heed." God announces, "I will raise up for them a prophet like you [Moses] from among their brethren; and I will put my words in his mouth, and he shall speak to them all that I command him" (Deut 18:18). Here the prophet-like-Moses is being referred to as the prototype of God's future messengers to Israel.[5]

   3. Israel's rejection of the prophets. Alas, however, Israel rejected God's prophets, refusing to repent of disobedience. Speaking of the coming prophet-like-Moses, Deuteronomy 18:19 ominously signals such a storied rejection: "And whoever will not give heed to my words which he shall speak in my name, I myself will require it of him." Repeatedly thereafter Israel's malignment of the prophets is highlighted in Jewish literature:

> We have not listened to thy servants the prophets, who spoke in thy name to our Kings, our princes, and our fathers, and to all the people of the land. (Dan 9:6)

> Nevertheless they were disobedient and rebelled against thee and cast thy law behind their back and killed thy prophets, who had warned them in order to turn them back to thee, and they committed great blasphemies. (Neh 9:26)

> We did not listen to the voice of the Lord our God in all the words of the prophets whom he sent to us, but all of us followed the intent of our own wicked hearts by serving other gods and doing what is evil in the sight of the Lord our God. (*Bar* 1:21-22; see *Jub.* 1:13; *1 Enoch* 89:51; CD 3:4; 4QpHos 2:3b-6; 1QS 1:3; 8:15-16; 1QpHab 2:5-10; cf. Lk 13:34-35)

   4. Israel and the Deuteronomic curses. Deuteronomy is replete with warnings of divine judgment should Israel lapse into idolatry (Deut 27:1-26; 28:15-68; 29:19-28). Deuteronomy 29:25-28 succinctly summarizes the curses that would accompany the nation's disobedience to the law of Moses:

> It is because they forsook the covenant of the LORD, the God of their fathers, which he made with them when he brought them out of the land of Egypt, and went and served other gods and worshiped them, gods

whom they had not known and whom he had not allotted to them;
therefore the anger of the LORD was kindled against this land, bringing
upon it all the curses written in this book; and the Lord uprooted them
from their land in anger and fury and great wrath, and cast them into
another land, as at this day.

With the fall of the northern kingdom in 722 B.C. and the defeat of the
southern domain along with the destruction of the temple in 587 B.C.,
those threats came true as the Jews were displaced from their land.

Gerhard von Rad observes that texts like Daniel 9, Nehemiah 9,
Ezra 9 and *Baruch* 1:15—3:8 reflect the conviction that the catastrophe
of 587 B.C. was an undiminished reality, for although that date had
passed, the authors believed that Israel was still under divine judgment (cf., e.g., CD 1:3-2:4; 1 Thess 2:15-16; Acts 28:26-27).[6] Von Rad's
perspective has proven compelling to a growing number of scholars.[7]
Michael A. Knibb encapsulates this view of a protracted exile when he
writes of Jewish materials in the Second Temple period:

> Despite many differences in presentation, the writings . . . seem to share
> the view that Israel remains in a state of exile long after the sixth century,
> and that the exile would only be brought to an end when God inter-
> vened in this world order to establish his rule.[8]

Two reasons seem to have combined to give the impression to
most Jews approximately contemporaneous with the DSS and the NT
that the Deuteronomic curses and exile continued to abide on Israel.
First, the glorious OT expectations of national restoration had not yet
materialized. As Jacob Neusner points out, all Judaic systems emphasized the present experience of exile as a recapitulation of 587 B.C.
This was so because with the nonoccurrence of the restoration in the
sixth century as was expected on the basis of the Torah, all Jews continued to push their hopes into the future and view themselves as living in an exilic situation.[9] Second, related to the first reason, the
invasion and control of Israel by foreign rulers, especially Antiochus
IV (171 B.C.), Pompey (63 B.C.) and Titus (A.D. 70), reiterated to the
minds of many that divine judgment still resided on the nation.[10]
Thus Israel, though returned to her land, was still in exile, not unlike
much of the story of the DSS.

tential prayer tradition of the ancient synagogues based on passages like Daniel 9:4-19[17] and Nehemiah 9:5-37[18] and contributed to the formation of what Joseph Klausner has labeled the "messianic chain," consisting of sin—punishment—repentance—redemption, which was deeply embedded in Israel's self-identity.[19]

As Steck points out, however, it is not necessary for an OT or later Jewish text to contain all five elements as *Baruch* 1:15—3:8 does in order for that passage to be framed by the Deuteronomistic perspective. Indeed, some texts may emphasize certain elements more than others and may therefore omit one or more components; other passages may expand an element by including a related tradition. But all of this nevertheless takes place within the basic Deuteronomistic underpinning. As a result of this consideration, Steck is able to show the pervasiveness of such a tradition not only in Palestinian Judaism of about 200 B.C.—A.D. 200 but also in the NT.[20]

For our purposes the exile—restoration elements in the Deuteronomistic perspective of the story of Israel provide an intriguing point of comparison with the publication of the DSS, for the latter, though discovered in their native soil, remained in subjection to non-Jews for over forty years.

The Publication of the DSS

I begin this treatment of the publication of the DSS with two introductory comments. First, the term *Dead Sea Scrolls* is used today in two senses, one generic and the other specific. In the generic sense the DSS refer to ancient manuscripts unearthed in caves along the western shore of the Dead Sea between 1947 and 1956. The discovery is comprised of seven sites: Khirbet (Arabic for "ruins") Qumran, Masada, Wadi (Arabic for "dry river bed") Murabba'at (Bar Kokhba Caves), Naḥal (Hebrew for "dry river bed") Ḥever, Naḥal Ṣe'elim, Naḥal Mishmar and Khirbet Mird. (Perhaps also Wadi ed-Daliyeh to the northeast of the Dead Sea should be included.) Except for a tentative connection between Qumran and Masada, the sites are not related to each other, extending in time from the third century B.C. to the seventh or eighth centuries A.D. More specifically, the DSS refer to those eleven caves in the vicinity of Qumran in which were discovered 867 documents dating from the third or early second centuries B.C. to the early first century A.D. These materials are far and away the most significant findings relative to the Scriptures among the seven sites, setting in motion a flurry of activity and controversy. The renowned archaeologist W. F. Albright proclaimed the DSS "the greatest manuscript discovery of modern times."

Second, with regard to the discovery of the eleven Qumran caves and their manuscript treasures, Geza Vermes, expert on the DSS, provides a helpful summary:

> The first lot of documents, consisting of several biblical and non-biblical scrolls, was found accidentally by an Arab shepherd in the spring of 1947. In 1949, the place was identified and explored by archaeologists, and the authenticity and antiquity of the find was established. Then, between February 1952 and January 1956, ten more caves were located. For two of them (3 and 5), the archaeologists were responsible; workmen on the site discovered four others (7, 8, 9, and 10); and the indefatigable Ta'amireh tribesmen, who most of the time succeeded in outwitting their professional rivals, were able to uncover four more (2, 4, 6 and 11), two of them (4 and 11) containing extremely rich manuscript deposits. Finally, in 1967, the giant Temple Scroll emerged from clandestinity and joined the other documents in the Shrine of the Book in Jerusalem.[21]

Although the discoveries themselves occurred between 1947 and 1956, the disclosure of the manuscripts stretched over decades; hence the enormous controversy that came to surround them.[22] The publication of the DSS can be divided into three commonly recognized periods: 1947-1956, 1956-1967 and 1967-1991.

1947-1956: The publication of the first seven scrolls. The first phase of the publication of the DSS centered on the seven scrolls discovered by Bedouin shepherds in Cave 1: a complete copy of Isaiah, the Rule of the Community (governing the conduct of the DSS community), the commentary on Habakkuk, the collection of thanksgiving hymns, a partial copy of Isaiah, the War Scroll (an eschatological text describing the final war between the "sons of light" and "the sons of darkness") and the Genesis Apocryphon (an expanded commentary on Genesis).

The story behind the acquisition of these seven scrolls is as intriguing as it is suspenseful. Their journey to publication began when the Bedouin brought their chance finds to Kando (Khalil Islandar Shahin), a part-time antiquities dealer who lived in Bethlehem, in March 1947. Kando and the Bedouin struck a deal to sell the scrolls to Athanasius Yeshua Samuel, a metropolitan associated with St. Mark's Monastery in Jerusalem, which was a part of the Syrian Orthodox Church. (Samuel was contacted because Kando and the Bedouin thought the Scrolls were written in the Syriac language.) He purchased four of the scrolls—the larger Isaiah Scroll, the Rule of the Community, the commentary on Habakkuk, the Genesis Apocryphon—for about one hundred dollars.

At this point the plot thickens. The metropolitan attempted to get information from various experts about the nature of his newly purchased materials. One of those consulted was Professor Eleazar Sukenik from the Hebrew University of Jerusalem. At the time Palestine was a volatile place, caught between the declining rule of the British mandate and the indecision of the United Nations as to how to partition the land. These conditions naturally made travel dangerous. Nevertheless, when Sukenik learned that an antiquities dealer in Bethlehem was offering what appeared to be ancient scrolls for sale, he made a secret visit to that city on November 29, 1947, the very date on which the United Nations passed the resolution to create the state of Israel.

The coincidence was not lost on Sukenik (hence the justification for our seeing a parallel between the story of Israel and the publication of the Scrolls). Sukenik saw the three scrolls that the metropolitan had not purchased. These he bought—two (the Hymn Scroll and the War Scroll) on November 29 and the third (the second Isaiah scroll) in December—after becoming convinced of their antiquity. In January, an acquaintance showed him the four purchased by the metropolitan, and he was permitted to keep them for a short time. Sukenik was not aware that they had come from the same source as the three he had just obtained. Naturally he wanted to buy them as well, but Samuel decided against selling them at that time. Thus the seven scrolls from the first cave were separated into two groups and would be published by different individuals.[23]

To make a long story short, Samuel attempted to sell his four scrolls in America for the price of one million dollars, but to no avail. On June 1, 1954, he placed a now-famous ad in the *Wall Street Journal*: " 'The Four Dead Sea Scrolls' Biblical Manuscripts dating back at least to 200 B.C. are for sale. This would be an ideal gift to an educational or religious institution by an individual or group."

Interestingly enough, the celebrated Israeli war hero and archaeologist, and son of the by now deceased Sukenik, Yigael Yadin happened to be in the United States at the time. Through intermediaries Yadin bought the four scrolls from the metropolitan for $250,000, thus reuniting them with Sukenik's three scrolls. The seven manuscripts were placed in the newly built construction in Jerusalem—the Shrine of the Book—a part of the Israel Museum. They were published by 1956.

Thus while the path to publication of the initial findings of the DSS took various twists and turns, it nevertheless occurred at an early date.[24] At least the first seven scrolls were now returned to their rightful owners. Not so for the rest of the manuscripts.

1956-1967: The delay in publication of the rest of the Scrolls. From 1947 to 1952 Cave 1 was explored in conjunction with an initial investigation conducted at the nearby ruins of Qumran. The other ten caves were discovered between 1952 and 1956 in concert with three more excavations at Qumran itself. The result was that from 1947 to 1956 eleven caves containing written documents were found within a rather small area in the vicinity of Qumran. The Bedouin proved to be the big winners in the race to find manuscripts, locating the three richest caves (1, 4, 11) and two others (2 and 6), while the archaeologists found Caves 3, 5 and 7-10, none of which contained impressive manuscript remains.[25] Table 1.1 describes the more significant discoveries in caves 2-11.[26]

As is obvious from this list, Cave 4 yielded the biggest findings. The cave itself is the closest of all the caves to the ruins of Qumran and, judging from the holes in its walls, contained wooden shelves filled undoubtedly with the main library of the community. Such a treasure trove necessitated the formation of a scholarly team to work on its publication. James C. VanderKam provides a helpful summary of that undertaking:

> The real problem came with Cave 4, which yielded so many thousands of battered fragments. As the myriad pieces were being purchased by the Jordanian government and brought to the Palestine Archaeological Museum in East Jerusalem, it soon became evident that the task of handling them would be massive and that they would require extra time and special expertise. In 1952 G. Lankester Harding, the director of the

Cave 2	Eighteen fragmentary texts of the OT, including Leviticus 11:22-29 written in paleo- (old) Hebrew script.
	Fifteen fragmentary nonbiblical texts, including *Sirach* 6:14-15, 20-31 in Hebrew.[27]
Cave 3	Fourteen fragmentary texts, three biblical (Ezek 16:31-33; Ps 2:6-7; Lam 1:10-12; 3:53-62) and eleven nonbiblical, the most famous of which is the *pesher* (commentary) on Isaiah 1:1.
	The Copper Scroll, which contains a list of places where great treasure (the Jerusalem temple's?) had been buried.[28]
Cave 4	The most important cave discovered at the Dead Sea, containing some 584 fragmentary texts, including 127 biblical manuscripts. The nonbiblical texts include eleven copies of the Rule of the Community, eight copies of the Damascus Document, the *Testament of the Twelve Patriarchs*, *Jubilees*, a "Son of God" text and, perhaps the most significant of all, 4QMMT ("Some Works of the Torah").
Cave 5	Eight biblical fragments (e.g., Deut 7:15-24; Is 40:16, 18-19).
	Seventeen nonbiblical texts, including a copy of the Rule of the Community and the Damascus Document, and an Aramaic text on the New Jerusalem.
Cave 6	Seven biblical texts—two of them in paleo-Hebrew (Gen 6:13-21; Lev 8:12-13).
	Twenty-four nonbiblical texts, including liturgical and juridical writings.
Cave 7	Nineteen tiny fragments written in Greek, two of which are identified as Exodus 28:4-7 and the *Epistle of Jeremiah* 43—44 (the noncanonical *Baruch* 6:43-44).
Cave 8	Four biblical texts (e.g., Gen 17:12-19; 18:20-25; Ps 17:5-9, 14; 18:6-9, 10-13).
	One nonbiblical hymn.
Cave 9	One small papyrus fragment with six Hebrew letters on it.
Cave 10	An ostracon (a piece of broken pottery used in antiquity for writing short texts) with two Hebrew letters on it.
Cave 11	Leviticus (in paleo-Hebrew), a Psalms Scroll, the Targum (Aramaic translation) of Job, the Temple Scroll.
	Some nonbiblical texts.

Table 1.1. Contents of the caves

Jordanian Department of Antiquities, named [Father Roland] de Vaux as chief editor of the Judean desert texts. With more and more fragments pouring into the museum, those in charge determined that an international team of scholars should be appointed to work on the Cave 4 materials. The directors of archeological schools in Jerusalem (they sat on the board of the Palestine Archeological Museum) were asked for assistance in forming such a group; also, leading scholars in England and Germany were asked to name candidates. The experts who eventually constituted the Cave 4 team, their nationalities, and their religious affiliations were, in the order of their appointments: Frank Moore Cross, American, Presbyterian; J. T. Milik, Polish, Catholic; John Allegro, English, Agnostic; Jean Starcky, French, Catholic; Patrick Skehan, American, Catholic; John Strugnell, English, Presbyterian, later Catholic; Claus-Hunno Hunzinger, German, Lutheran. These seven, all appointed in 1953 and 1954, joined de Vaux, who had been elected chair by the museum board, as the international team responsible for the Cave 4 fragments. In 1958 Maurice Baillet joined the team, and Hunzinger eventually withdrew, leaving his material to Baillet.[29]

As can be seen from this digest, no Jewish scholar was invited to join the team, and this would eventually become a point of controversy. The Scrolls, in effect, though in their land, were in exile. Despite the erudition of the Scrolls Committee, publication of the Cave 4 manuscripts was at best meager.[30] From 1956 to 1967 only a handful of texts were made available to the public, most notably the Psalms Scroll and the Melchizedek text from Cave 11, the Copper Scroll from Cave 3 and manuscripts 158-86 from Cave 4. Why the delay? Lawrence H. Schiffman, a rabbinic and Qumranic scholar, answers the question rather bluntly:

> The answers are, in reality, rather prosaic. Those who were supposed to publish them failed for a variety of reasons: Their efforts were insufficiently funded. Some lost interest. Some succumbed to alcoholism. Some died. Some lacked sufficient linguistic skills to do the job in a reasonable amount of time. Selfishly, they continued to believe both that only they could do the job correctly and that they and the students they chose had rights to the material in perpetuity.[31]

1967-1991: The furor over the finds. With the Six-Day War of 1967, the DSS reached a turning point, for Jews now came into possession of them. Israeli officials, however, agreed to permit the Christian team to continue its work, with the proviso that the Scrolls would be published as soon as possible. Scholars outside the committee later came to rue that decision. Schiffman writes,

> In retrospect, this constituted a clearly naive decision. It was impossible for the scholars ever to finish their task, for their allotments were simply too large for publication within a reasonable time. Some were even assigned to publish more scrolls than any individual could handle in a lifetime. Some died, bequeathing their texts to their students, who themselves failed to publish them. Yet the editorial team refused anyone else access to the remaining unpublished documents. Like misers, they hoarded the scrolls as currency to enrich their careers and those of their students.[32]

For a decade (1967-1977) publications from Cave 4 were still forthcoming. Four significant moments, however, escalated the debate, bringing the matter to a head in 1991. Interestingly enough, and rightly so, Jewish influence was brought to bear on the issue.

Yigael Yadin published the Temple Scroll in 1977 (the Hebrew text was translated into English in 1983). This publication was a watershed moment in the disclosure of the DSS because its contents dealt extensively with *halakhah* (law). It therefore required Jewish expertise to be properly interpreted.

Miqsat Maase Ha-Torah from Cave 4 (the *Halakhic* Letter devoted to "Some of the Works of the Torah" and related to the Temple Scroll), a foundational document of the Qumran community, was revealed to twelve hundred scholars in Jerusalem by John Strugnell and Elisha Qimron (the former a member of the DSS official team of translators) in April 1984. It too contained significant statements about the Torah, therefore requiring Rabbinic expertise in order to grasp its meaning. Surprisingly, both manuscripts appeared to be Sadducean in perspective, which seemingly contradicted the claims of most Qumran scholars heretofore that the DSS were written by Essenes (more on this momentarily).

Later that year John Strugnell of Harvard was promoted by the Israeli Department of Antiquities (which now controlled the DSS) to the position of editor-in-chief of the Scrolls publication project. Strugnell expanded the team to include three Jewish scholars: Devorah Dimant, Elisha Qimron and Emanuel Tov. The enlargment of the committee and the promise of publication did not, however, calm the storm of criticism being raised by a host of scholars, including Morton Smith, Ben-Zion Wacholder, Hershel Shanks, Robert Eisenman and Philip Davies.

The final straw came in November 1990, when Strugnell, whose health was declining, made anti-Semitic remarks in an interview printed in *Haaretz* ("the land"), an Israeli newspaper. Strugnell was subsequently replaced by Emanuel Tov as head of the project, and the team was increased even more for the express purpose of hastening the publication process. But it was not fast enough. In September 1991, Ben-Zion Wacholder and Martin G. Abegg of Hebrew Union College in Cincinnati, Ohio, published the first fascicle of the unpublished DSS using a computer and, ironically, a concordance of the DSS circulating among the original editorial team. On September 22, Huntington Library in San Marino, California, shocked the scholarly community by revealing that it possessed an extra set of negatives of the photographs of the DSS (which had been distributed to it with the permission of the Israeli Department of Antiquities) and that it was now making those copies available to the public. At long last the hope for a full release of all the DSS was now a reality. The Scrolls were no longer in exile.

The Literature Comprising the DSS

In considering the types of literature that make up the DSS, it is wise to begin with some elementary observations such as the standard guide used in citing the Scrolls, the materials on which they were written, the languages in which they were inscribed and the date of the manuscripts. Regarding the guide used in identifying the Scrolls, the following pattern is usually adhered to: the cave in which the manuscript was found; an abbreviated title of the work; a superscript letter if there is more than one copy of the text; an Arabic number for the column; a colon (European writers use either a comma or a period); an Arabic number for the line(s).[33] Here are some examples:

☐ 1QapGen 2:18 = Cave 1 of Qumran, Genesis Apocryphon, column II line 18

☐ 1QpHab 7:15—8:3 = Cave 1, *Pesher* (commentary) on Habakkuk, column VII line 15 to column VIII line 3

☐ 11QPs[a] = Cave 11, copy "a" of the Psalms Scroll

The vast majority of the DSS are written on vellum or parchment (animal skin) because it was ritually clean and also durable. Some manuscripts are written on papyrus, a reed plant that flourished in the Delta area of lower Egypt, the Hula basin north of the Sea of Galilee in Israel and Byblos, an ancient port city located in Syria. One scroll is written on copper (hence its title: the Copper Scroll).

The greatest part of the DSS (both biblical and nonbiblical manuscripts) is written in Hebrew, but some have been preserved in Aramaic, a sister language of Hebrew, the spoken language of Israel in the last centuries B.C. and the first centuries A.D. Most of the Aramaic texts are translations of the OT (called Targumim). A few texts (about twenty) are in Greek, based on the Septuagint (the Greek translation of the OT, c. 250 B.C.).

Three methods have been used to date the DSS: paleography, the study of ancient scripts; carbon 14; and internal historical allusions. Together these methods indicate that the Scrolls come from the last two centuries B.C. and the first century A.D. (c. 170 B.C.—A.D. 68). The majority of them seem to have been produced in the Hasmonean period (152 B.C.—30 B.C.).[34]

Four types of literature were discovered in the eleven caves associated with Khirbet Qumran: OT books, apocryphal and pseudepigraphical works, commentaries on the prophets and writings about the DSS community itself.

OT books. Over two hundred OT manuscripts have been found in the eleven caves, representing every OT book except Esther. Table 1.2 by Schiffman summarizes the data. The order is that of the threefold division of the Jewish Bible: Law, Prophets, Writings.[35]

The Pentateuch is the division most represented in the DSS. This stands to reason, for the community was extremely devoted to the Mosaic Law. The Prophets (especially Isaiah) receive the next highest distribution of manuscripts, undoubtedly because the community applied these prophecies to itself as well as appealed to them as the basis for its messianic expectation. From these two observations already we begin to sense that the people of the DSS perceived themselves to be the restored Israel because they properly adhered to the Torah.

Canonical Section	Book	Number of Qumran Manuscripts
Torah	Genesis	18 + 3 ?
	Exodus	18
	Leviticus	17
	Numbers	12
	Deuteronomy	31 + 3?
Former Prophets	Joshua	2
	Judges	3
	1-2 Samuel	4
	1-2 Kings	3
Latter Prophets	Isaiah	22
	Jeremiah	6
	Ezekiel	7
	Twelve (Minor) Prophets	10 + 1?
Writings	Psalms	39 + 2?
	Proverbs	2
	Job	4
	Song of Songs	4
	Ruth	4
	Lamentations	4
	Ecclesiastes	2
	Esther	0
	Daniel	8 + 1?
	Ezra-Nehemiah	1
	1-2 Chronicles	1

Table 1.2. OT manuscripts found in the caves

Except for the Psalms and Daniel, the Writings are not heavily drawn upon. The Psalms were utilized in the sect's worship, and Daniel's predictions were believed to be actualized in the group. Beyond these examples the presence of the Writings is minimal. Esther is not even mentioned. Two alternative theories frequently are offered to explain this phenomenon: the Qumran community did not consider Esther canonical (inspired), possibly because the book extolled the holiday, Purim, the only biblical feast not celebrated by the DSS congregation; or, Esther's absence is due to chance, not its supposed noncanonical status. The latter suggestion seems to be more plausible, for a work related to Esther, Proto-Esther, has been found in Cave 4.

Two other comments are generated by the presence of the OT books in the DSS. The first has to do with the canon. Although it is widely held that the canon of the OT was not closed until A.D. 80-90 or later (at the meetings of the rabbis at Jamnia, Israel), the DSS seem to provide evidence to the contrary. For one thing, every OT book quoted in the DSS (except Esther) was later considered canonical in rabbinic tradition. Although we cannot assume from that equation that the OT was closed at the time of the writing of the DSS (especially since they also include noncanonical books), the evidence at least points in that direction. This is more or less confirmed by 4QMMT, which refers to the tripartite division of the Hebrew Bible:

> To you we have wr[itten] that you must understand the book of Moses [and the works of the] prophets and of David [and the annals] [of eac]h generation. (lines 95-96)[36]

This threefold delineation—Law, Prophets, David (or Writings; David is thought to have written the Psalms, the first book in the Writings)—seems to attest to a commonly held list of inspired books (other Jewish works at the time presume the same classification, e.g., prologue to *Sir; 2 Macc* 2:2-3, 13; cf. Lk 24:32, 44-45).[37]

Second, three text-types of the OT surface in the DSS: the proto-MT (the Hebrew text which later became the basis for the Masoretic text), the Septuagint (LXX) and the Samaritan Pentateuch (SP). Of these three, the Hebrew text constitutes 60 percent of the biblical manuscripts in the DSS, while the LXX and the SP amount to a combined total of 20 percent of the biblical texts. The other 20 percent consists of Qumran-style manuscripts and nonaligned texts.[38]

Apocryphal and pseudepigraphical literature. By apocryphal or deuterocanonical[39] literature we mean those Jewish works written after the close of the OT (400 B.C.). Although they most probably found a place in the LXX, these books have never been considered by official Judaism to be inspired. Nevertheless, Jews have rightly held the apocrypha in high regard, both for its historical and ethnic value. Christians would do well to follow suit. In any case, four apocryphal pieces were found in the DSS caves.

Tobit (c. third century B.C.) is a fanciful tale about a godly Jewish exile in Nineveh, Assyria, whose name, as the title indicates, is Tobit. During the course of the story, Tobit, who is sightless, is miraculously healed because of his obedience to the Law. The work's emphasis on the exile and sufferings of the righteous apparently appealed to the Qumran community, which perceived itself to be in a similar situation.

Sirach (Greek *Ecclesiasticus,* not the canonical Ecclesiastes), is a wisdom book that exalts the role of the Torah, God's incarnated wisdom (c. 180 B.C.). The DSS people enjoyed an obvious affinity with the work, for they believed that they possessed divine wisdom because they were following the true Torah.[40] The Hebrew text of this piece discovered in Cave 2 matched well with the medieval Hebrew copy of *Sirach,* thus confirming the accuracy of the latter manuscript.

Also identified among the DSS are the *Epistle of Jeremiah* (*Baruch* 6) and *Psalm 151,* both of which are included in our oldest copies of the LXX.

In addition to apocryphal literature, pseudepigraphical works[41] were discovered among the DSS. The pseudepigrapha are Jewish materials written in the last centuries B.C. and the first two centuries A.D. which are not considered canonical by Jews or Christians. Nevertheless they are valuable historically, ethnically and theologically in that they provide a window into the thought of early Judaism. Three especially call for comment.

First Enoch, a very popular Jewish writing in early Judaism, was unearthed in Cave 4. Comprised of five collections (the *Book of Watchers* 1—36; the *Similitudes* or *Parables of Enoch* 37—71; the *Astronomical Book*

72—82; the *Book of Dreams* 83—90; and the *Epistle of Enoch* 91—107), this material contains certain recurring themes that strike a chord in the DSS: the advent of sin through fallen angels (Gen 6); the revelation of the endtimes to the faithful; and the mystic ascent to heaven by the righteous, like Enoch of old. Of further interest is the fact that the *Similitudes of Enoch* portray the kingdom of God as devolving onto the heavenly Son of Man (cf. Dan 7 and the Gospels). The absence of this material from the DSS has occasioned a lively debate as to whether it in actuality was composed as early as the Scrolls (c. 171 B.C.—A.D. 68). The tendency among scholars these days is to hold that the *Similitudes* were written that early but that they circulated in a different strand of Judaism.

Jubilees, a rewriting of Genesis 1—Exodus 14 (c. second century B.C.), also extols the Mosaic law. Of particular value to the Qumran community is this work's claim that the solar calendar of 364 days is the correct one (cf. the Enochian *Astronomical Book*) over against the traditional Jewish lunar calendar of 354 days. Obviously, in espousing the former view the DSS observed biblical feasts on different days than did "normative" Judaism.

The *Testament of the Twelve Patriarchs* (c. second century B.C.) is attested to in the DSS. While some later Christian additions were made to this work, the majority of it is Jewish in origin, including the expectation of two Messiahs—a priestly one and a kingly one—a notion prominent among the Qumran sectaries, as will later be evident.

Other pseudepigraphical pieces are in the DSS,[42] but the aforementioned are among the most famous. An intriguing question surfaces with the presence of these and other nonbiblical materials in the DSS: Did the Qumran community regard this literature as canonical? Contrary to the view of many scholars, it is likely that the DSS did not. Schiffman pinpoints the heart of the matter:

> Much ancient and medieval Jewish literature was composed by the reuse of materials found in the canonical Scriptures. The most familiar example of this process can be found in the liturgical poetry of the synagogue that is made up of snatches of biblical passages often recast to express ideas found in later midrashic literature. The Qumran sect and many of the other Jewish groups of the Second Temple period composed their

texts in the same way. The reuse of material in this way is based upon the assumption that it is divinely inspired and that it has religious authority. Only texts accorded such canonical status served as the raw material for new sacred compositions. Determining which texts provided this raw material for derivative texts will reveal which books the authors considered authoritative. At Qumran all the biblical books, that is, those in our canon of the Hebrew Bible, are used in this way, but such is not the case with any other books. Therefore, it is highly probable that the biblical canon at Qumran was the same as that of the later Rabbis.[43]

A thematic tie seems to bind most of the apocryphal and pseudepigraphical materials together, one that well commended itself to the Qumran community: this literature is informed by the Deuteronomistic tradition—the sin-exile-restoration of Israel.[44]

Commentaries on the prophets. One of the fascinating discoveries that emerged in the DSS was the Qumran community's unique interpretation of the biblical prophets. Labeled *pesher* (derived from an Aramaic term meaning "interpretation"), this hermeneutical method contemporized OT prophetic oracles by applying them to current events relative to the Qumran people. Two assumptions informed this approach: (1) The biblical prophets ultimately referred not to their own time but to the latter days of history; (2) Qumran readers believed that they were living in the endtimes and that therefore the biblical prophecy pertained to the DSS sect. The spiritual acumen for grasping the meaning of the text was God's gift to the Qumran members. The method itself unfolds in the following steps: The biblical verse is quoted; the formulaic phrase occurs, "its interpretation concerns" *(pesher)*; the application to the day of the Qumran expositor is supplied. Here is a famous example in the *pesher* exposition of Habakkuk 6:12—7:4:

> I will stand firm in my sentry-post. I will position myself in my fortress to see what he says to me, what he answers to my allegation. YHWH answered me and said: Write the vision; inscribe it on tablets so that [he who reads it] takes it on the run. *Hab 2:1-2* [. . .]

> *Col VII* And God told Habakkuk to write what was going to happen to the last generation, but he did not let him know the end of the age. *[Blank]* And

as for what he says *[Hab 2:2]*: "so that the one who reads it/may run." Its interpretation concerns the Teacher of Righteousness, to whom God has disclosed all the mysteries of the words of his servants, the prophets.

The threefold procedure enumerated above is clear in this example, a text which claims that the leading figure at Qumran—the Teacher of Righteousness—was granted divine wisdom to interpret properly the Habakkuk prophecy by applying its endtime fulfillment to his own ministry.

The *pesharim* (plural of *pesher*) in the DSS divide into two basic groups of texts: continuous and thematic (though I will later introduce a third type—single quotation). The first is essentially a verse-by-verse interpretation of one of the biblical prophets, approximating a commentary. Examples of this category include the *pesher* on Habakkuk just cited and the *pesharim* on Nahum, Isaiah, Hosea, Micah, Zephaniah and Malachi.[45]

The second type of *pesher* assembles a number of biblical passages that relate to a theme. Three of the most well-known thematic groups are Florilegium (4Q174), a collection of texts based on the messianic Davidic King of 2 Samuel 7, Psalm 1—2 and Amos 9:1; the Testimonia (4Q175), which draws on OT passages describing some of Israel's past leaders—Numbers 24:15-17 (David), Deuteronomy 5:28-29 and 18:18-19 (Moses), and Deuteronomy 33:8-11 (Levi)—but recasting them eschatologically; and the Melchizedek Text (11QMelch), which combines Leviticus 25:13, Deuteronomy 15:2 and Isaiah 61:1 in order to portray Melchizedek as a messianic figure.

Here is a portion of 4QFlorilegium ("anthology") as an example of thematic *pesharim*:

> And *2 Sam 7:12-14* "YHWH de[clares] to you that he will build you a house. I will raise up your seed after you and establish the throne of this kingdom [forev]er. I will be a father to him and he will be a son to me." This (refers to the) "branch of David," who will arise with the Interpreter of the law who [will rise up] in Zi[on in] the last days, as it is written: *Amos 9:11*, "I will raise up the hut of David which has fallen," This (refers to) "the hut of David which has fallen," who will arise to save Israel. (1:10-13)

As will be shown later in this study, *pesher* hermeneutics is not a strange phenomenon to the NT. It should also be noted that the DSS *pesharim* disclose contemporary events and persons affecting the Qumran community (e.g., pNah 3-4.I.2-4—Demetrius IV Eukairos [95-88 B.C.]; pNah 3-4.I.5—Alexander Jannaeus [104-76 B.C.]; pNah 3-4.I.2-4—the Kittim or the Romans [63 B.C.]; and most interesting if not controversial of all, pHab 12:7-9—Jonathan the High Priest [152 B.C.]). In the next chapter I will dwell more on Jonathan the High Priest when I attempt to identify the people who produced the DSS. Moreover, chapter three of this study will investigate how *pesher* in both the DSS and in Matthew is intimately involved with the hermeneutic of Israel's restoration from exile.

Writings about the community. The fourth major type of literature in the DSS relates to writings concerning the Qumran community itself, which may be conveniently classified under four genres: legal, eschatological, liturgical and sapiential.

The legal type of literature in the DSS is basically composed of four foundational documents which stress the utmost importance of the law for the Qumran community: the Damascus Document, the Rule of the Community, the Temple Scroll and Some of the Works of the Torah. Because these writings provide critical information regarding the identity and the reason for existence of the group producing the DSS, each requires our attention.

The Damascus Document, or the Damascus Covenant, is so named because of its reference to "Damascus" as the place of exile of the community producing it (e.g., CD 6:4-5, 19; 7:18-19; 19:33-34; 20:11-12). Scholars differ as to whether Damascus is to be interpreted literally or, more likely, figuratively as an allusion to the Qumran site. Important historical data is given in this document as to the time of the sect's origin. Column I lines 5-7 read:

> And at the moment of wrath, three hundred and ninety years after having delivered them up into the hands of Nebuchadnezzar, king of Babylon he [God] visited them and caused the sprout from Israel and from Aaron a shoot of the planting.

Three pertinent observations can be made about this key text. First, the Damascus Document views its community to be in exile like Israel of old was in Babylon, in both cases due to the sinfulness of the Jewish rank and file. Second, the Qumran people identify themselves with the shoot of Israel and of Aaron, which anticipates the document's later treatment of the coming of the two Messiahs and the restoration of Israel (CD 19:10-11; 20:1; cf. 1QS 9:11-12). Third, the historical beginnings of the Qumran community date to the second century B.C.:

☐ the Babylonian Exile, 587/586 B.C.

☐ the continued exile in Damascus, 390 years later

☐ historical beginnings, c. 196-152 B.C. (allowing for uncertainty surrounding the Jewish chronology of the fall of Jerusalem to Babylonia and as compared with excavations at Qumran; see the discussion in chapter two)

All of this bespeaks the Deuteronomistic pattern of sin-exile-restoration.

A copy of the Damascus Document was discovered in the Ezra synagogue in Old Cairo, Egypt, in 1896 by the Jewish scholar Solomon Schechter (hence the name CD = Cairo Damascus). There in the *geniza* (the storage room of a synagogue where old, discarded sacred manuscripts are kept), Schechter found two copies of this manuscript which dated to the tenth and twelfth centuries A.D. Some entitle the document the Zadokite Fragments because of its allegiance to Zadok, high priest of Solomon (CD 3:21—4:3). The traditional theory informing this choice of title is that the DSS community rejected the Hasmonean priesthood established by Judas Maccabeus and his brothers because it departed from the Zadokite lineage. With the search of Cave 4, nine copies of the Damascus Document were unearthed that essentially matched the manuscripts Schechter discovered. Joseph Fitzmyer provides a helpful summary of the contents of this work:

> The text of CD contains two main parts: (1) *An Exhortation* (1:1-8:21 [+ 19:1-20:34]), which includes (a) a meditation on the lessons of the history of Israel (1:1-2:1); (b) on the predestination of the righteous and the wicked (2:2-13); (c) a second meditation on the lessons of history (2:14-4:12a); (d) the three nets of Belial in which Israel is ensnared (4:12b-6:1); (e) the community of the New Covenant (6:2-7:6); and (f) the diverse fates of those faithful to the Covenant and of apostates (7:9-8:17 [+ 19:5-

20:34]). (II) *Constitution: Life in the New Covenant* (15:1-16:20; 9:1-14:2), which includes (a) rules for entrance into the Covenant and for oaths (15:1-16:16); (b) regulations within the community (9:1-10:10a); (c) rites to be observed in the community (10:10b-12:18); (d) organization of the community (12:19-14:19); (e) a penal code (14:20-22).[46]

The Rule of the Community (1QS—Cave 1, also known as the Manual of Discipline or the *serek hayyahad*) was one of the original seven scrolls found in Cave 1 in 1947, though over ten copies of it also turned up in Caves 4 and 5. This document probably served as the constitution of the Qumran sect. It agrees remarkably with the descriptions of the Essenes provided by Josephus (c. 90 A.D.), one of the identifiable Jewish groups of pre-70 A.D. (*J.W.* 2.8.2-13 [119-61]). Fitzmyer's digest of the work is useful:

> The Manual of Discipline has an introduction, which states the aim and purpose of the community (1:1-15). It then describes the rite for entrance into the Covenant of the community (1:16-3:12), the theological tenets of the community, e.g. its doctrine about the two spirits, the spirit of truth and the spirit of iniquity which God has created to govern human life (3:13-4:26); again the purpose of the community and its rules for communal life, for the assembly of members, and for the admission of candidates (5:1-6:23). It gives the penal code of the community (6:24-7:25), a description of the model, pioneer community (8:1-9:26), and the text of a hymn, in which the community praises the creator, sings of God's righteousness, and gives thanks to him for his goodness (10:1-11:22).[47]

One can recognize in this description, as in the Damascus Document, that the DSS community believed itself to be the restored Israel; hence its emphasis on strict obedience to the Torah.

The Temple Scroll, discovered in Cave 11 in 1956, came into the hands of Yigael Yadin in 1967. He subsequently published the document in 1977. It is the longest Qumran manuscript, consisting of sixty-seven columns. Its disclosure introduced a new phase of DSS studies, demonstrating the central role that the law played in the community. Recently Michael O. Wise has concluded that the Scroll was intended to replace Deuteronomy 12—26, rewriting the laws of the land of Israel to apply to the future temple.[48] The portrait of the temple therein is unlike any other biblical or extrabiblical description, designed to emphasize the purity required before God will indwell it. The document most likely owes its origin in some way to the Teacher of Righteousness.

Although Schiffman has argued that the Temple Scroll was not written by the Qumran community, nevertheless there are telling connections between it and the DSS. Politically, the anti-Hasmonean polemic in the Temple Scroll matches the DSS on that point (cf. 11QTemple 56:12-19; 57:5-11; 59:17-19 with, e.g., CD 1:5-11; 4Q171 [4QpPs 37] 4:7-9; 1QpHab 11:2-8). Liturgically, the Temple Scroll envisions a temple complex to be built greatly different from any known temple, thus expressing the author's dissatisfaction with the current Jerusalem cultus, a theme hospitable to the DSS (cf. 11QTemple 46:9-12; 47:3-6 with, e.g., 1QS 9:4-5). Moreover, the Temple Scroll adheres to the solar calendar as did the Qumran sect (cf. 11QTemple 30—45 with Phases of the Moon [4Q317]). Scripturally, both the Temple Scroll and the DSS equate their respective writings with divine revelation (cf., e.g., 11QTemple 51:6-7 with the DSS *pesharim*). Legally, the authors of both materials view their regulations as constituting a second Torah, a supplement to Deuteronomy (cf. 11QTemple 2:1-15 with CD 5:2-5; Catena [4Q177]; the last two works are perhaps the equivalent of the sealed book of the law revealed when Zadok came). Textually, as Vermes has pointed out, the relationship between the Temple Scroll and the Damascus Document is striking in the cases of prohibitions of royal polygamy, marriage between uncle and niece, marital relations within the city of the sanctuary (cf. 11QTemple 57:16-18; 66:15-17; 45:11-12 with CD 4:20—5:5; 5:8-11; 5:6-7/12:1-2, respectively).[49]

Some Works of the Torah (4QMMT = *Miqsat Maase Ha-Torah*), or the *Halakhic* Letter, though known about since 1984, has only recently been published.[50] It consists of three parts: a liturgical section espousing the solar calendar; a list of twenty-two laws, over which the sectarians disagree with the addressee of the letter; and an epilogue. Three observations are in order at this point: *Miqsat Maase Ha-Torah* probably stems from the earliest stage of the sect's development, prior to the arrival of the Teacher of Righteousness; the *halakhic* statements in the document have been compared with other legal texts of the period of our investigation (in this regard *Miqsat Maase Ha-Torah* opposes Pharisaic views but coincides with the perspectives of the Essenes and the Sadducees); the document sheds significant light on the NT, especially the writings of Paul, even if by way of contrast with the apostle's pronouncement in Romans 3:20 and Galatians 2:16 that all who attempt to be justified by "the works of the law" are under the divine curse. In chapter six I will argue that Paul reverses the Deuteronomic blessings and curses as found in a document like *Miqsat Maase Ha-Torah*.

The eschatological (endtime) literature in the DSS reflects the community's apocalyptic self-understanding. That is to say, the Qumran sect viewed itself to be the true Israel, the righteous remnant with whom God was establishing his new covenant in the last days (see, e.g., 1QS 1:1; CD 4:2). As the faithful of God, the people of the DSS equated their suffering with the severe messianic woes which Judaism expected to test Israel before the advent of the Messiah (CD 1:5-11; 20:13-15; 1QH 3:7-10). The community's exile into the desert (Qumran) under the eventual leadership of the Teacher of Righteousness was understood to be the final preparation for the arrival of the messianic age.

Probably the sect's scrupulous observance of the Mosaic law was motivated by the belief that if Israel kept the Torah, the Messiah would come (cf. CD 4:1-17 with the following rabbinic literature [c. 200-500 A.D.]: *Pirke 'Abot* 2:8; *b. Sanh.* 97b; *Sifre Deut* 34). But by the same token, the period of trials to which the sect was exposed was predetermined by God (CD 1:5-11; 1QM [War Scroll, Cave 1]). The DSS harbor the hope for the two Messiahs of Aaron and Israel (CD 20:1; 1QS 9:11-12). At that time the sons of light (the Qumran members) will wage war against the sons of darkness (everybody else) and will prevail, thus ushering in the kingdom of God (1QM) and the New Jerusalem (4QFlor 1:11-12; New Jerusalem texts [5Q554-55]). In anticipation of that day, the Qumran sect observed a messianic meal (1QS 2:11-22), worked at overcoming the evil inclination within them by submitting to the law and the good inclination (the struggle between the two was expected to give way to the cosmic eschatological holy war; 1QS 3-4), and convened to worship God with the angels, which was a proleptic experience of the coming messianic age. Schiffman nicely summarizes the eschatological self-understanding of the DSS as reflected in its explicitly apocalyptic literature (e.g., 1QM; 1QS; New Jerusalem texts) as well as in its general conceptual framework:

> Equally important to the sectarians was the immediacy of the End of Days. They anticipated that the old order would soon die. The sect lived on the verge of the End of Days, with one foot, as it were, in the present age and one foot in the future. They were convinced that the messianic era would happen in their lifetime. Their move to the desert from the main population centers of Judaea and their establishment of a center at Qumran had marked the dawn of the new order. Their lives were dedicated to preparing for that new age by living as if it had already come.[51]

As will be seen in this work, such "inaugurated eschatology" (the initiation of the last days) is thoroughgoing in both the DSS and the NT. That is to say, the DSS and the NT view their respective communities as constituting the restored, eschatological Israel.

Besides the biblical Psalms, other DSS were utilized in a liturgical setting, notably the Thanksgiving Hymns (1QH = *Hôdāyôt* and the Angelic Liturgy (4QShirShabb; 4Q400-405; 11Q17). The former consists of some twenty-five psalms and takes its name from the verb that introduces these poems: *'odekah* ("Thank you [Lord]"). Form analysis of these hymns suggests that they fall into two categories. The first group is written in the first person singular, quite possibly by the Teacher of Righteousness. These lament hymns recount the author's struggles with his enemies and petition God to vindicate his servant. Consider *Hôdāyôt* 12:5-10, for example:

> I give you thanks, Lord,
> because you have brightened my face with your covenant
> and [. . .]I have looked for you.
> Like perfect dawn you have revealed yourself to me with your light.
> But (to) them, your people,
> [interpreters of deceit, with their wo]rds they lure them,
> sowers of fraud [misdirect them]
> and make them fall without them being aware.
> For in folly they carry out their deeds.
> Because I have been an object of ridicule for them,

and they do not esteem me
when you make yourself great through me.
For they evict me from my land
like a bird from the nest;
all my friends and my acquaintances have been taken away from me,
and rank me like a broken jug.
But they are sowers of deceit
and seers of fraud,
they have plotted evil against me [. . .]
to alter your Law, which you engraved in my heart,
by flattering teachings for your people.

The second group of hymns in the *Hôdāyôt* seems to articulate the experiences of the community. VanderKam identifies the key characteristic of these poems:

> (1) God is the creator before whom humans, mere creatures of clay, are painfully lowly and inadequate; (2) the wicked attack the righteous, who suffer intensely, but God saves them from their troubles and judges the evil; (3) he gives wisdom to the righteous, that is, knowledge of himself and his will, and with them he enters into a covenant; (4) the righteous in turn sing his praises.[52]

The lament form of the *Hôdāyôt* suggests that they served a liturgical purpose. This seems confirmed by the fact that they also express the notion that the congregation is united with heaven in a cultic setting to join the angels in worship.[53]

The last mentioned theme is central to the Angelic Liturgy or Songs of Sabbath Sacrifice (4QShirShabb), a collection of poems designed to be read on the Sabbath. These psalms give instruction on how and when to praise God, based on the solar calendar. One of their striking features is the correspondence of heavenly and earthly worship. These materials also borrow from the language of Ezekiel 1 and its presentation of the glorious throne of God. In doing so the Angelic Liturgy serves as an important witness to the pervasiveness of mysticism in early Judaism which, as will be clear in chapter seven, makes for an intriguing comparison with the Colossian heresy.

That wisdom is vitally important in the DSS is evident from the fact that they preserved the canonical wisdom books, fragments of the popular sapiential work *Sirach* (c. 180 B.C.) and approximately fourteen other wisdom texts (e.g., 4Q184-185; 4Q413-419; 4Q424; 4Q521; 4Q525). At least three traits of wisdom recur in these manuscripts.

☐ Wisdom is built into the order of creation; to embrace it therefore is to find life.

☐ Wisdom is manifested specifically in the Torah given to Israel.

One meets in these two aspects a harmonization of the apparently contradictory notions in Judaism that wisdom is universal and that wisdom is restricted to Israel.

☐ Wisdom is eschatological; it is a divine gift to the Qumran people that enables them to discern the signs of the endtimes and to prepare themselves accordingly. The association here of Wisdom and Torah will factor heavily in chapters seven through nine of this work in reaction to the following theme: Divine wisdom is embodied in the law, the adherence to which will effect Israel's restoration.

Conclusion

This chapter has highlighted the ironic parallel that exists between the story of ancient Israel and the publication of the DSS: the theme of exile-return. Finally the controversy surrounding the ownership of the DSS has been resolved. In addition, the types of literature which make up the DSS have been catalogued, recognizing that much of it draws on the Deuteronomistic tradition. Although the issue of the return of the Scrolls to their rightful owners is passed, a new challenge has taken its place, namely, the identification of the group producing those materials.

Chapter Two

Prelude to the Story

The DSS, the Essenes & the NT

Introduction

Jacob Neusner's definition of Judaism in the preface of the book *Judaisms and Their Messiahs at the Turn of the Christian Era*[1] sets the stage for the discussion in this chapter. He writes, "A Judaism comprises a world view and a way of life that together come to expression in the social world of a group of Jews. The 'Judaisms' of the title therefore constitute several such ways of life and worldviews addressed to groups of Jews."

While I will investigate the topic of messianism in the DSS and in the NT in chapter four of this work, here I am particularly concerned with the two constituent components of Neusner's definition. According to his understanding, the essence of Judaism is that a group of Jews manifests a common worldview and way of life. At the same time, however, this description obviously allows for the existence of *Judaisms*, because different groups of Jews, in fact, display contrasting worldviews and ways of life.

This idea captures the heart of the literature of Second Temple Judaism(s), for in that material we find various reconstructions of the story of Israel. This includes both the DSS and the NT, the former because they presented their community as true Jews who anticipated the restoration of the nation; the latter because, with the exception of Luke, its authors were also Jews retelling the story of Israel the way their master did.

Before pursuing their respective angles on the story of Israel, however, we must first wrestle with the issue of the authorship of the DSS, for if we can successfully identify the community producing the Scrolls, then we will find ourselves in a better position to grasp its worldview and proposed way of life. Having accomplished that, we will proceed to raise and answer the question of the relationship of the DSS to the NT.

The Identification of the Community Producing the DSS

Thus far in my comments on the DSS, I have not discussed the identification of the people composing the Scrolls. The dominant theory espoused by the majority of DSS experts is that Khirbet Qumran was associated with the ancient Essenes, though such a view has always had its share of critics. While we cannot enter here into a full-scale treatment of the issue, we need to at least present the contours of the debate by dividing the pertinent evidence into two types: internal and external. The internal evidence pertains to both the data contained in the DSS regarding the identity of its authors as well as the findings at Khirbet Qumran, the most recent of which would seem to confirm the connection between Qumran and the Scrolls.

From this internal evidence will emerge four fundamental criteria that will serve as the basis for evaluating the external data. The latter involves the four most well-known Jewish groups existing approximately during the period of our investigation: Pharisees, Sadducees, Essenes, and Zealots. These are the leading candidates as the originators of the Scrolls, according to the history of Qumran scholarship (the sensationalist hypothesis that Christians produced the DSS will be quickly dismissed in the second part of this chapter). Thus we will arrive at our conclusion as to who wrote the Scrolls by filtering the external data through the four criteria emerging from the internal evidence.

The internal evidence. I begin here because the internal evidence must be accorded pride of place in that it deals with the primary data. Carefully sorting through the morass of information regarding the identity of the community producing the DSS leads to four fundamental criteria. They represent the following areas of investigation: sociology, archaeology, paleography and history.

Sociologically, the authors of the DSS formed a sectarian movement. N. T. Wright asserts:

> If ever there was a sect, this was it: isolated from the rest of Israel geographically and theologically, claiming to be the true heir of all the promises and the scriptures, regarding even devout Jews of other persuasions as dangerous deceivers. They were the sons of Light, so they thought, and all others, not just the pagans, were the sons of darkness. This group is, in fact, one of the clearest examples known to us of what a sect looks like.[2]

Archaeologically, it seems now confirmed that the DSS are linked to Qumran. For two related reasons, it was natural for early interpreters of the Scrolls to connect those documents with Khirbet Qumran. First, the writings themselves portray their community as living in exile in the wilderness, most likely the Judean wilderness (see 1QS 8:14-25; CD 1:5-10). Second, the close proximity of the desert site of Qumran to the caves containing the Scrolls made it a logical choice to investigate. So it was that for five seasons archaeologists excavated Qumran under the leadership of Father Roland de Vaux, director of the *École Biblique* in Jerusalem. De Vaux identified the following periods of settlement at Qumran:

Israelite	8th-7th centuries B.C.
Hellenistic I	Ia before c. 134 B.C.
	Ib c. 134 B.C. - 31 B.C.
Roman (Herodian) II	c. 31 B.C. - A.D. 68
Roman III	after A.D. 68 - 73
Bar Kokhba Revolt	c. A.D. 132 - 135[3]

The outer periods—the Israelite and the Bar Kokhba occupations—
were not judged to fall within the parameters of the dating of the DSS,
leaving the other three settlements as the ones most pertinent to the
discussion. Period Ia seems to have begun during the Maccabean
Revolt (approximately 168-164 B.C.) and lasted until 134 B.C., with little
development occurring. Period Ib probably ran from the beginning of
the rule of John Hyrcanus (134 B.C.) until the destruction caused by an
earthquake in 31 B.C. During this settlement, Qumran experienced its
most significant growth. The buildings whose remains can now be
seen were constructed then, including: rooms and courtyards, storage
areas, workshops, the defense tower, a kitchen, pottery (over a thousand eating vessels) and kilns, a water system consisting of aqueducts
from the Wadi to cisterns to keep it (and to store the rain as well), ritual
baths (mikva'ot), an assembly hall, a dining room, a storage area for
grain, stables for livestock, hundreds of coins and a scriptorium with
inkwells and tables. Moreover, a nearby cemetery containing eleven
hundred graves accompanied this period.

During Phase II, the third period, Qumran was abandoned from 31
B.C. to 4 B.C., coterminous with the reign of Herod (was he more hospitable to the occupants than previous rulers?). Around the time of
Herod's death, the site was rebuilt and lasted until A.D. 68 when the
Roman troops overran it. Evidence of destruction by fire and Roman
arrowheads confirm this last observation. Qumran remained a Roman
military outpost basically thereafter (A.D. 68 until the second century).

Though some have disputed de Vaux's conclusions, it seems clear
now that his connection of the DSS to the site of Qumran stands.
Three pieces of archaeological evidence cumulatively establish this as
highly likely: (1) The periods of Qumran settlement (approximately
171 B.C. to A.D. 68) correspond with the dating of the DSS. Paleographical analysis (the study of ancient handwriting), carbon-14 dating, and pottery identification converge in agreement on this point.
(2) The type of cylindrical jars found in Cave 1 matches that excavated at Qumran, pottery not occurring elsewhere. (3) Most recently,
the term yahad (Hebrew for "the community"), a favorite self-designation of the authors of the DSS (e.g., 1QS = serek hayyahad), has
turned up at Khirbet Qumran on an ostracon (broken ancient pot-

tery), seemingly sealing the association between the two.[4]

In light of these considerations, we may eliminate three theories concerning Qumran and the DSS. First, Christian origin of the DSS must be ruled out. Although the two have much in common (as this work intends to show), the Qumran community was inhabited long before the rise of Christianity. Second, Norman Golb's theory that Qumran was the ruins of a military fortress and therefore had no integral connection with the DSS has now been seriously challenged with the aforementioned discovery of the *yaḥad* ostracon.[5] Third, archaeologists Pauline and Robert Donceel's theory that Qumran was built as a royal winter villa now also has to be questioned in the light of the *yaḥad* inscription. This is so because Qumran, linked to the DSS as it apparently was, proves to have been a sectarian community, hardly a fitting description of Israelite royalty, an observation confirmed by the fact that no evidence at this site survives of artifacts relating to luxurious living.[6]

Paleographically, of the hundreds of nonbiblical literary works in the DSS, 75 percent of them have multiple copies. Furthermore, the Scrolls as a whole give evidence of having been written by many different scribes. These realities, along with the previously mentioned point that Cave 4 housed the majority of the DSS (approximately 550 texts out of some 850), suggest that Qumran served as the central library for the group producing the manuscripts.

Recently some scholars, notably Golb, have attempted to use this information (that the DSS caves housed a library) against the Qumran theory, claiming instead that the Scrolls came from Jerusalem, being hidden there by mainline priestly Jews. But again the *yaḥad* ostracon connecting the DSS with Qumran argues forcefully that the latter and the nearby caves (especially Cave 4) did indeed house the library. As we will see in the next section, this datum admirably supports the reigning Essene hypothesis, particularly the theory that Qumran was the central headquarters of the Essene movement, which inhabited various other camps throughout Israel.

Historically, a few texts actually refer to individuals by name who lived in the first centuries B.C.: the Syrian King Demetrius Eukairos (*pesher* Nahum 1:2, 95-78 B.C.), King Alexander Jannaeus of

Israel (In Praise of King Jonathan, 103-76 B.C.), Queen Salome Alexandra of Israel (An Annalistic Calendar, 76-67 B.C.), King John Hyrcanus II (An Annalistic Calendar, 67-63 B.C.) and the Roman general Aemilius Scaurus (An Annalistic Calendar, active in Israel 65-63 B.C.). In addition, the *pesher* on Habakkuk makes a transparent reference to the Roman invasion of Israel in 63 B.C.[7]

The commentary on Habakkuk establishes 63 B.C. as a significant middle date for the DSS community. But can we identify its beginning point? The traditional theory holds that date to be about 171 B.C. A historical sketch of that view is provided here, using primarily the DSS themselves along with the testimony of the Jewish historian Josephus (c. A.D. 90).

171-152 B.C.: The pre-Teacher of Righteousness period at Qumran. Two texts in the DSS allude to the earliest period of its community, to which I would add a third passage that possibly pinpoints the reason for the sect's coming into being (CD 1:5-11; 4QMMT; 11QTemple 56:1-14). I had occasion earlier to comment on CD 1:5-11 to the effect that this text locates the starting point of the DSS sect in approximately 171 B.C. (1:5-8).[8] The passage goes on to say that the community in exile (presumably now settled at Qumran) operated without the needed leadership for twenty years. Therefore God sent them the Teacher of Righteousness at the end of that time to direct their paths (1:9-11).

It seems that 4QMMT was also written at the inception of the Qumran community before the arrival of the Teacher of Righteousness. The purpose of this foundational document was to list the twenty-two laws regarding temple practice in Jerusalem with which the authors disagreed:

> These are some of our regulations [concerning the law of G]od, which are pa[rt of] the precepts we [are examining and] they [a]ll relate to [. . .] and the purity of [. . .] . . . (3-6)

The contemptible practices of the Jerusalem priesthood prompted the authors of the *Halakhic* Letter to separate themselves from mainstream Judaism:

> [And you know that] we have segregated ourselves from the rest of the peop[le and (that) we avoid] mingling in these affairs and associating

with them in these things. And you [know that there is not] to be found in our actions deceit or betrayal or evil. (92-94)

It is relatively clear from the pronouns in the letter that the dispute is between "we" — the authors of 4QMMT but with no specific leaders yet — and "you" (in the singular) — most probably the High Priest of Jerusalem.

When we look for the period in history that best correlates with Damascus Document 1:5-11 and 4QMMT, the majority of scholars point to the rise of the Hasmonean dynasty. With the successful revolt of Judas Maccabeus against the Hellenistic onslaughts of Antiochus Epiphanes (c. 171-164 B.C.), the political tide changed in Israel, culminating in Jewish self-rule. The Hasmonean reign had now dawned and would remain in control until the Roman occupation of the land in 63 B.C. Following the Maccabean revolt, a crisis occurred in the Jewish priesthood that seems to have motivated the formation of the Qumran sect. In 152 B.C., Jonathan Maccabeus appropriated to himself the office of the high priest. VanderKam rehearses the events leading up to and including Jonathan's self-appointment:

> For centuries before this time, the leading native official among the Jews had been the high priest who was descended from the line of David's priest Zadok. That family had lost the high priesthood shortly before the events of the 160's B.C. and never regained it. Instead, the kings of the Seleucid Empire appointed several high priests for what appear to have been largely political and financial reasons. Josephus, who with the authors of 1-2 Maccabees is one of our few sources of information for the period in question, maintains that there was no high priest in Jerusalem between 159 and 152 B.C. In 152, Jonathan, one of the Maccabean brothers, was appointed high priest by another Seleucid king (Alexander Balas) because he needed Jonathan's military backing. In this way the Maccabean or Hasmonean high priesthood began. It lasted until 37 B.C., some 115 years in all.[9]

It is a reasonable conjecture that the Qumran community, composed as it was of pro-Zadokite priests (note, for example the title of one of its documents—the Zadokite Fragments), therefore grew suspicious of the early Maccabean movement. As tension mounted between the two

groups, separation became inevitable. 4QMMT appears to be a failed
attempt by the pro-Zadokites to persuade the Jerusalem priesthood to
return to the old tradition. With Jonathan's takeover of the high
priestly office, discussion between the two groups officially ended.
Although it is sometimes said that the DSS give no hint that its authors
were indeed anti-Hasmonean, on the contrary, an allusion to that effect
seems to be in Temple Scroll 56:1-14,

> [. . .] . . . [. . .] the word about you [. . .] they shall make known to you the
> sentence. You shall act in accordance with the word which they say to
> you from the book of the law. They shall explain it to you accurately
> from the place I shall select in which to install my name, and you shall
> take care to act in accordance with everything they tell you. You shall not
> deviate either to the right or to the left from the law which they explain
> to you. Whoever does not listen and acts with effrontery in order not to
> listen to the priest placed there to serve in my presence or the judge, that
> man shall die. Thus you shall eliminate the evil from Israel and all the
> people shall listen and fear and no one will behave insolently in Israel
> any more. *Blank* when you enter the land which I give you, and own it
> and live in it and say to yourself: I shall set a king over myself like all the
> peoples which surround me, then you shall set over yourself a king
> whom I shall choose. From among your brothers you shall set over your-
> self a king.

This passage applies Deuteronomy 17:14-15 to the Israel of its day,
spelling out the law that should govern the king's life. It is most significant that the text separates the spheres of kingship (56:1-7, 10-14) and
priesthood (56:8-9). Schiffman well-identifies the probable referent of
this allusion, "The requirement that a King be appointed is most likely
intended as a critique of the early Hasmonean rulers, who, while serving as high priests, arrogated to themselves the temporal powers of the
King. Our passage requires that the monarchy and the high priesthood
be two separate offices with two distinct incumbents."[10]

We see, then, that two events seem to have impacted early Qumran
history before the arrival of the Teacher of Righteousness. The machi-
nations of Antiochus Epiphanes that precipitated the Maccabean revolt
(171-164 B.C.) which, in turn, effected the reversal of fortunes of the
Zadokite priesthood, were the motivating factors in the formation of

the DSS community. This is attested to in Damascus Document 1:5-11 and 4QMMT. The second event is intimately related to the first, that of the usurping of the Jerusalem priesthood by Jonathan in 152 B.C., which finalized the separation of the two groups. This appears to be alluded to in TS 56:1-14.

152-134 B.C.: The leadership of the Teacher of Righteousness. Twenty years after the founding of the Qumran community, the Teacher of Righteousness arrived on the scene to provide much-needed leadership for the group (CD 1:5-11). Judging from a comparison of Damascus Document 6:4-5, 19; 19:33-34 and 1QS 8:12-16, the "Damascus" in which the community dwelled was the desert. In other words, *Damascus* was a code name not to be interpreted literally. Moreover, most likely the incident that brought the Teacher of Righteousness to that group was the action of Jonathan to appropriate the priesthood unto himself. If that is so, then we find in Jonathan (died 143 B.C.) or possibly in his brother Simon (died 134 B.C.), who later replaced him, the identity of "the Wicked Priest" mentioned in the Scrolls. That the Wicked Priest was a high priest has long been suspected by scholars. This is so because the epithet "the Wicked Priest" (*ha kōhēn hā-rāsā*) is a Hewbrew wordplay on the title "the High Priest" (*ha kōhēn hā-rō 'š*).[11] It seems reasonable that Jonathan or Simon was the target of such nomenclature because they were the first kings in Israel to call themselves high priests.

Yet there is more to go on in identifying Jonathan or Simon as the Wicked Priest. Certain passages in the DSS seem to allude to these two brothers. Temple Scroll 57:5-11 is interesting with respect to Jonathan. That text exclaims that the king

> shall select a thousand, a thousand from each tribe, to be with him: twelve thousand men of war who will not leave him on his own, so that he will not be seized by the hands of the nations. All those selected, which he selects, shall be men of truth, venerating God, enemies of bribery, skilled men in war; and they shall always be with him day and night and they shall guard him from every act of sin and from the foreign nations so that he does not fall into their hands.

Schiffman writes of this passage that the elaborate arrangements for

the royal guard only make sense against the background of the reign of
Jonathan Maccabeus (152-143 B.C.), who, while traveling with three
thousand guards, was captured by Trypho, a Seleucid pretender, and
later murdered.[12] This incident may well be related to 1QpHabakkuk
8:7-9:2; 9:8-12, passages that speak of the violent fate with which the
Wicked Priest met:

> They shall say: Ah, one who amasses the wealth of others! How long will
> he load himself with debts? *Blank* Its interpretation concerns the Wicked
> Priest, who is called by the name of royalty at the start of his office. How-
> ever, when he ruled over Israel his heart became conceited, he deserted
> God and betrayed the laws for the sake of riches. And he stole and
> hoarded wealth from the brutal men who had rebelled against God. And
> he seized public money, incurring additional serious sin. And he per-
> formed repulsive acts of every type of filthy licentiousness. *Hab 2:7-8*
> Will your creditors not suddenly get up, and those who shake you wake
> up? You will be their prey. Since you pillage many countries the rest of
> the peoples will pillage you. *Blank* The interpretation of the word con-
> cerns the Priest who rebelled [. . .] the precepts of [God].

> (Col. IX) being distressed by the punishment of sin; the horrors of terrify-
> ing maladies acted upon him, as well as vengeful acts on his fleshly body
> . . . *Hab 2:8b* For the human blood [spilt] and the violence done to the
> country, the city and all its/occupants/ *Blank* Its interpretation concerns
> the Wicked Priest, since for the wickedness against the Teacher of Righ-
> teousness and the members of his council God delivered him into the
> hands of his enemies to disgrace him with a punishment, to destroy him
> with bitterness of soul for having acted wickedly against his elect.

The handing over of the Wicked Priest to his enemies and their torture
of him coheres with the capture and murder of Jonathan mentioned
above.[13]

Alternatively, some scholars have identified Simon as the Wicked
Priest. One passage in particular appears to support this interpretation.
The Psalms of Joshua (a document included in 4QTestimonia 175) reads:

> *Blank* At the moment when Joshua finished praising and giving thanks
> with his psalms, he said *Jos 6:2* "Cursed be the man who rebuilds this
> city! Upon his first-born will he found it, and upon his Benjamin will he
> erect its gates!" And now/an/accursed/man, one of Belial, has arisen to

be a fowler's trap for his people and ruin for all his neighbors. [. . .] will arise, to be the two instruments of violence. And they will rebuild [this city and ere]ct for it a rampart and towers, to make it into a fortress of wickedness [a great evil] in Israel, and a horror in Ephraim and Judah. [. . . And they wi]ll commit a profanation in the land and a great blasphemy among the son of [. . . And they will shed blo]od like water upon the ramparts of the daughter of Zion and in the precincts of Jerusalem. (21-30)

Some argue that this piece alludes to the incident when Simon and his two sons attended a banquet at the newly built fortress of Jericho in 134 B.C. The three were murdered by the local commander, who attempted a coup. However, Simon's remaining son, John Hyrcanus I, eventually reestablished Hasmonean control in that same year.[14] Yet, on balance, Jonathan seems the most likely candidate for the Wicked Priest, especially since he first combined the offices of king and priest.

According to 1QpHabakkuk 11:2-8, the Wicked Priest attempted to kill the Teacher of Righteousness:

Hab 2:15 Woe to anyone making his companion drunk, spilling out his anger! He even makes him drunk to look at their festivals! Blank Its interpretation concerns the Wicked Priest who pursued the Teacher of Righteousness to consume him with the ferocity of his anger in the place of his banishment, in festival time, during the rest of the day of Atonement. He paraded in front of them, to consume them and make them fall on the day of fasting, the Sabbath of their rest.

Two observations can be gleaned from this passage. First, the Wicked Priest pursued the Teacher of Righteousness to "the place of his banishment," apparently to a spot within the jurisdiction of the high priest. This might exclude Damascus proper, which does not seem to have been a part of the Hasmonean empire. Assuming the accuracy of that observation, Qumran seems therefore to be the location intended. Second, as scholars have long noted, the two groups must have followed different calendars in their worship, for the Wicked Priest pursued the Teacher of Righteousness while the latter was observing the Day of Atonement. Had the former been following the same calendar, he would have had no time as a high priest over

Jerusalem to chase after his enemy on an extremely busy day. In other words, he must have commemorated the Day of Atonement on a different day. Whether or not the preceding conflict ended in the Teacher's death is debatable. Passages like Damascus Document 20:13-15 and 4QpPs[a] 2:17-19 may imply that he died at a later time.

Regarding the role of the Teacher of Righteousness, Fitzmyer provides a helpful summary:

> Môreh haṣṣedeq,"the Teacher of Righteousness" is identified in the QS as a priest (hakkôhēn, 4QpPsa 1:3-4 iii 15; 1QpHab 2:8), presumably a member of the Zadokite line, one whom God raised up to guide the groping community in its early days (CD 1:11). The community regarded him as one whom God endowed with a special understanding of Scripture, especially of "the words of his servants, the prophets" (1QpHab 7:5). Sometimes he is called môreh hayyaḥad, "teacher of the community" (CD 20:1), or simply "the Teacher" (CD 20:28; cf. 20:32; cf. 1QpMic [1Q 14] 8-10:4). He is never named, but details about him are given in 1QHab 1:13; 2:2; 5:10; 7:4; 8:3; 9:9-10; 11:5, so that he must have been a historical figure, even though we cannot yet identify him. He is often regarded as the author of those Thanksgiving Psalms of Cave 1 that are formulated in the first singular and refer figuratively to trials and troubles.[15]

While the Teacher of Righteousness is not equated with the Messiah in the DSS (more on this later), it would be fair to say that he was instrumental in shaping the community's apocalyptic vision, which formed the conceptual basis of the group's separatist mindset. To use the terminology of Max Weber (a German sociologist of two generations ago), the Teacher of Righteousness was the "charismatic" leader of the Qumran movement.

134-31 B.C.: The growth of the Qumran community. The most developed stage in the history of the Qumran community began with the rise of John Hyrcanus I to the throne in 134 B.C. and continued until 31 B.C., when an earthquake destroyed the settlement. This corresponds with the archaeological period entitled Ib. The majority of DSS scholars correlate the following key Hasmonean rulers with this era: John Hyrcanus I (134-104 B.C.), Alexander Jannaeus and his wife Salome Alexandra (104-67 B.C.), Salome's sons, Hyrcanus II and Aristobulus II (67-63 B.C.). It is necessary to offer a few comments about how the paths of these people intersected with the DSS community.

The numismatic evidence from de Vaux's excavations revealed a dramatic increase of Jewish coins at Qumran from the period of John Hyrcanus I to the Roman destruction: 134 B.C.- A.D. 68 (about 325 coins at that time contrasted to some ten before Hyrcanus I and five after the Roman destruction in A.D. 68). This coinage increase, along with the intensified building activity of the period, testify to the chasm in relationship that had developed between the Qumran sectarians and the Hasmonean dynasty, now focused on John Hyrcanus I. Most likely two indications of this hostility toward Hyrcanus are in the DSS, Temple Scroll 2:1-5 and 56:14-19:

> *Col 11* [fo]r what [I sha]ll do [to you will be dreadful.] [Behold, I evict before you] the A[morites, Canaanites,] [Hittites, Girgash]ites, Per[izzities, Hivites and] [Jebusites. Bew]are of making a covenant [with the occupants of the country] amongst whom you are going to come, so that they will not be a [trap in your midst]. (2:1-5)

As Schiffman points out in his comments on this text, one probably finds here an application of Exodus 34:10-16 to what was perceived by the authors to be the Hellenistic practices of John Hyrcanus. His adherence to the Hasmonean cultus, especially the "pagan" lunar calendar, was thought to continue the pollution of the Jerusalem temple and its priesthood (cf. e.g., 11QTemple 2:5-15; 46:9-12; 47:3-6, 17-18).[16]

A second text containing vitriolic language against the Hasmonean dynasty is Temple Scroll 56:14-19.

> From among your brothers you shall set over yourself a king; you shall not set a foreign man who is not your brother over yourself. But he is not to increase the cavalry or make the people go back to Egypt on account of war in order to increase the cavalry, or the silver and gold. *Blank* I told you "You shall not go back again on this path." He is not to have many wives or let his heart go astray after them. He is not to have much silver and gold; not much.

Schiffman interprets this text as follows:

> Josephus gives us a hint about the dating of this section. He reports that the unrest in Syria "gave Hyrcanus leisure to exploit Judaea undisturbed, with the result that he amassed a limitless sum of money." No

doubt Hyrcanus's extensive military campaigns outside the boundaries of Judaea also contributed to his wealth. It is likely that this text, in repeating here the Torah's law against the king's sending his people to war to increase his own wealth, is reacting to conditions during the period of John Hyrcanus.[17]

The most noticeable growth of the Qumran community took place during the periods of Alexander Jannaeus and (after his death) his wife Salome Alexandra, as is evidenced in the 144 Jewish coins discovered there dating to this time. Why the expansion? A perusal of some of the DSS, together with the testimony of Josephus, will reveal the answer, which has significant bearing on the issue of the identity of the Qumran sect.

There is a scholarly consensus concerning a historical reconstruction of the Jewish period from 104-67 B.C. First, some Pharisees tried to oust Alexander Jannaeus by joining forces with King Demetrius, a Seleucid (Syrian) monarch. The attack failed and, in revenge, Jannaeus crucified eight hundred Pharisees (c. 88 B.C.; cf. 4QpNah 1: 1-8; 11QPrayer for Jonathan B 1-9 with Josephus *Ant.* 13.14.1-2 [377-83]). All of this was obviously to the advantage of the Sadducees, the rival party to the Pharisees. It is important to observe that 4QpNahum 1:1-8 refers to the Pharisees as those "looking for easy interpretations" (1:2, 7), thereby expressing the Qumran community's contempt for the Pharisaic "loose" handling of the Torah. All scholars therefore rightly exclude this group from being the authors of the DSS.

Second, after Jannaeus' death his wife Salome Alexandra made peace with the Pharisees, a move that led to the party's dominance in the political arena. Consequently, those not of the Pharisaic persuasion, including the Sadducees and Essenes, now became the object of great persecution (see Josephus *J.W.* 1.5.1 [111]; cf. An Annalistic Calendar). Josephus' text is illuminating relative to the situation. He writes that the Pharisees

became themselves the real administrators of the public affairs; they banished and reduced whom they pleased; they bound and loosed [men] at their pleasure.

The majority of DSS scholars suggest that the resurgence of the

Pharisaic party at this particular time sent a large number of Essenes scurrying to Qumran for refuge, thus accounting for its burgeoning growth.[18] Some interpreters, however, disagree. Michael Wise argues that it is at this time, not earlier, that the DSS were written and that by proto-Sadducees.[19] While this is an intriguing reading of the data, its dependency on Norman Golb's theory that the DSS were not associated with the community at Qumran will prove to be a major hurdle to its acceptance, for the *yahad* inscription apparently connecting the two would seem to confirm the traditional dating of the DSS to a time before 134 B.C.

Lawrence Schiffman agrees with the connection of the DSS and Khirbet Qumran, but he disagrees with the prevailing hypothesis that the Essenes were the authors of those materials. A more thorough critique of this view will be offered in the next section, but here we may broach the subject by noting that the period of Salome Alexandra is the first time the Sadducees were officially dispossessed of their control over the Jerusalem priesthood (76-67 B.C.). The point is a telling one, because by then the Qumran community and the DSS were already a century old! The only way Schiffman can circumvent this difficulty is to divide the Sadducees into two groups: strict (Qumran Sadducees) and moderate (Hellenized, pro-Hasmonean Sadducees).

> In the aftermath of the revolt, a small, devoted group of Sadducean priests probably formed the faction that eventually became the Dead Sea sect. Unwilling to tolerate the replacement of the Zadokite high priest with a Hasmonaean, which took place in 152 B.C.E., they also disagreed with the Jerusalem priesthood on many points of Jewish law. . . . Other moderately Hellenized Sadducees remained in Jerusalem. It was they who were termed Sadducees, in the strict sense of the word, both by Josephus in his descriptions of the Hasmonaean period and by the later rabbinic traditions. They continued to play a key role in the Hasmonaean aristocracy, supporting the priest-kings and joining with the Pharisees in the governing council. After dominating that body for most of the reign of John Hyrcanus and Alexander Janneus, they suffered a major political setback when Salome Alexandra turned so thoroughly to the Pharisees. In the Herodian era, the Sadducees regained power when they made common cause with the Herodian dynasty.[20]

Because I will deal with this hypothesis later, I offer here only cursory remarks regarding Schiffman's statement. First, as mentioned before, there is no evidence that the Sadducees were ousted from political power before 76-67 B.C., while there is good indication that the Essenes were marginalized from society immediately after the Maccabean revolt (168-164 B.C.). The traditional view that the Essenes formed a part of the Hasidic reaction to the excesses of the Hasmonean dynasty matches well with what we know from other historical writings describing the conflict.[21]

Second, Schiffman's argument that Qumran was established by a strict Sadducean element is predicated on a flawed assumption. He presumes that the legal interpretations in 4QMMT and the Temple Scroll were embraced exclusively by the Sadducees, this despite the fact that *Essene halakhah* fit the interpretations just as well.

Hartmut Stegemann pinpoints the difficulty of the Sadducean hypothesis on this point:

> Many Essenic halakhot as well as many Sadducean halakhot may have been common halakhot of both groups from their common past, i.e., from the times before the Jewish priests split into antagonistic groups about the middle of the second century B.C. Only the Pharisees, becoming more and more laïqu [lay]oriented, abandoned this traditional conformity, afterwards becoming favoured by the Rabbis. Therefore most of the older pre-rabbinic halakhot, which did not conform to accepted Pharisaic-Rabbinic traditions, may have been just as well Essenic as Sadducean, without any difference.[22]

The upshot of this critique is that no solid evidence exists for dividing the Sadducees into two hypothetical groups: a strict, Qumranic following and a moderate, Hasmonean party.

Third, the main evidence we do have about the Sadducees from Josephus and others concerns that of an aristocratic priestly group who, except until 76-67 B.C., supported the Hasmonean dynasty. From what these writings tell us about the Sadducees, their cardinal doctrines are quite different from those in the DSS (e.g., affirmation of life beyond the grave, an anti-Hellenistic mindset).[23]

With the death of Salome Alexandra in 67 B.C., a rival relationship ensued between her two sons, Hyrcanus II and Aristobulus II, as they vied for political control over the nation. Eventually Aristobulus II prevailed but subsequently fell to the Romans (the Kittim, 1QpHab 2:12—3:15) in 63 B.C. (see An Annalistic Calendar for references to Salome, Hyrcanus II and Aemilius, the first Roman governor of Syria, 65-62 B.C.). After the Roman takeover, things seemed to calm down for a while.

In 31 B.C., Qumran was destroyed by an earthquake; it was not repopulated until after Herod the Great's death in 4 B.C. Apparently, the Qumran community posed no threat to the client king. Around the time of Herod's death, the site was rebuilt. Phase II began, then, in 31 B.C. and, after the interruption in settlement, was repopulated from 4 B.C. to the Roman destruction of the community in A.D. 68. When that attack came, members of the group probably hid their manuscripts in the caves nearby. Undoubtedly many in the sect perished in the onslaught of the Romans (see Josephus' description of their torture by the Romans at that time, *J.W.* 2.8.10 [152-53]).

2. The external evidence. Our goal in this section is to filter the external evidence relative to the four sects described by Josephus and Pliny the Elder through the preceding criteria: sociological, archaeological, paleographical and historical. Adhering to this procedure should lead to a fair conclusion regarding the identity of the group producing the DSS.

Josephus, a late A.D. first-century Jew who was a historian for Caesar, describes three main Jewish sects or philosophies active in Israel from the mid-second century B.C. until the destruction of Jerusalem by the Romans in A.D. 70: Pharisees, Sadducees, Essenes (*J.W.* 2.8.2-14 [119-66]; *Ant.* 13.5.9 [171-73]; 18.1.2-5 [11-22]; *Life* 1.2). Some would also add a fourth group to the list—the Zealots. (It could be argued that Josephus alludes to this sect in *Ant.* 18.1.6 [23-25], but most probably he does not; *J.W.* 7.8.1 [252-74] on the fall of Masada better fits the Zealot portrait.) Josephus claims to have spent time with the Pharisees, Sadducees and Essenes (*J.W.* 2.8.2-14 [119-66]; *Life* 1.2), thus providing firsthand information about them.

DSS experts agree that the Pharisees should be excluded as the group which crafted the Scrolls because it is they who are identified as the community's enemies. The Pharisees are the ones who interpreted

the Torah loosely and thus incurred the wrath of the DSS people (e.g.,
4QpNah 1:2, 7). Furthermore, from a sociohistorical perspective, the
Pharisees maintained a strong presence in Jerusalem, always exercis-
ing their clout in order to gain and maintain political dominance. They
were hardly a sectarian movement in the strict sense of the term. One
should not be surprised therefore that no archaeological or paleographical connections exist between them and the DSS of Qumran.

A second group, the Zealots, does meet the above sociological criterion, for they were sectarian even to the point of being revolutionary,
which was fed by apocalyptic fever. It is this group, in all probability,
that was the catalyst for embroiling the Jews in their revolt against
Rome in A.D. 66. The view that the Qumran covenanters were Zealots,
however, fails to meet the other criteria. No significant archaeological
and paleographical connections have been forged between Qumran
and Masada, the site of the last stand of the Zealots against the Romans
in A.D. 73. One work, the Songs of the Sabbath Sacrifice, was unearthed
in both places, but one writing is not sufficient evidence to establish a
direct association between the two locations. The probable explanation
for the presence of this work in both communities is that it espoused
the solar calendar, a conviction shared by a number of Jewish groups in
our period of investigation (cf., e.g., 1 Enoch, Jub.). From a historical
point of view, the Zealot movement did not seem to gather force until
the years just prior to the Jewish revolt in A.D. 66, long after the writing
of the DSS.[24]

The hypothesis that the DSS were written by the Sadducees,
though a minority view among scholars in the history of Qumran
research, has had erudite defenders in Solomon Schechter,[25] J. M.
Baumgarten,[26] and more recently Yaakov Sussman[27] and Lawrence
Schiffman.[28] The older argument for the Sadducean hypothesis was
based on the fact that both the authors of the DSS and the Sadducees
were priests. After all, it was said, the self-description of the Qumran
community was "Zadokite," a term seemingly derived from the word
Sadducee. Moreover, both the DSS authors and Sadducees were
priests who were anti-Pharisaic in disposition. The current defense of
the Sadducean theory rests primarily on the proposed legal parallels
between 4QMMT and the description of the Sadducees as presented

in the Mishnah (a rabbinic body of literature dating to around A.D. 200). The clearest similarity is in *Mishnah Yadayim* 46:7:

> The Sadducees say: "We complain against you Pharisees. For you declare pure the [poured out] liquid stream."[29]

Compare this statement with the ruling in 4QMMT 58-61:

> And also concerning flowing liquids: we say that in these there is no purity. Even flowing liquids cannot separate unclean from clean because the moisture of flowing liquids and their containers is the same moisture.

Schiffman points out the parallel between 4QMMT and the Mishnaic passage: Both agree that even though the water poured out from the upper vessel is pure, contact with the impure water in the lower vessel renders the upper impure. This ruling was in contrast to the teaching of the Pharisees, who declared that the water in the upper vessel was unaffected by the lower vessel. For Schiffman, this, and other similar regulations shared by 4QMMT and the Sadducees as presented in the Mishnah, convince him that the DSS possessed a substratum of Sadducean *halakhah*.[30]

Although the parallels between 4QMMT and the Sadducees referred to in the Mishnah at first blush look impressive, they are, however, not sufficient to establish a direct relationship between the two. We earlier registered Stegemann's criticism of the supposed commonalties shared exclusively between the Sadducees and the DSS. Essene and Sadducee *halakhah* intersected on a number of points as well. VanderKam concurs, offering an explanation for the agreements between the Sadducees and the Essenes: both groups had deep priestly roots. This seems to be indicated by the very names of the two communities; thus the Qumran group was founded and led by the sons of Zadok (the leading priest at the time of David and Solomon), while the term *Sadducee* seems to be derived from the name "Zadok." Both circles opposed the Pharisees, promoting a more rigid interpretation of the law. It would be understandable, therefore, that the two movements overlapped in their legal rulings.[31] In effect, then, the sociologically sectarian nature of some of the *halakhah* in the DSS would have been hospitable to both Sadducee and Essene.

A second criticism of the Sadducean theory is a historical one, namely, the rabbinic literature describing the Sadducean position is far removed from the era in which the DSS were written thus making it likely, as Stegemann remarks, that the later orthodox rabbis confused Sadducean teaching with Essene *halakhah*.[32] On the other hand, the information about the Sadducees which we have from Josephus, Pliny the Elder, Philo and others is both a century closer in time to the DSS than the Mishnah and more comprehensive in scope. And the portraits these authors paint of the Sadducees do not line up well with the profile of the Qumran community that emerges in the DSS. For example, VanderKam calls attention to two significant anti-Sadducean teachings occurring in the Scrolls: belief in angels and determinism.[33]

The date of the founding of the Qumran community constitutes a third serious difficulty for the Sadducean hypothesis, for archaeological and paleographical evidence confirm at least a pre-134 B.C. (more likely 171 B.C.) beginning for the DSS sect. But, as we saw earlier, no solid indication exists that the Sadducees were dispossessed of the Jerusalem priesthood before the reign of Salome Alexandra (76-67 B.C.). One could perhaps appeal to the few years the post of high priest was vacant during the Maccabean era (c. 159-152 B.C.) as a time when Sadducees were marginalized from society, but this was due to Seleucid control of that office, not a Pharisaic or Hasmonean anti-Sadducean campaign.

Furthermore, to argue that the Zadokite priests, the authors of the DSS (as ousted by the Hasmonean dynasty in about 152 B.C.), are to be equated with the Sadducees (as is repeatedly done by advocates of the Sadducean theory of authorship) is a non sequitur. As a matter of record, Schiffman himself admits that the predominant Sadducean tendency up until 76-67 B.C. was to support the Hasmonean priesthood. In order, therefore, to still claim Sadducean authorship of the DSS, which is anti-Hasmonean, he must posit the emergence of a fringe group of Sadducee priests who interpreted the Torah rigorously during the reign of Jonathan (152 B.C.), an assumption that has yet to be proved.[34] In actuality, the oldest and most thorough descriptions of the Sadducees that we possess, as we noted earlier, decidedly contradict the perspective of the DSS. All of this to say that the first time the Sadducees were assigned a sectarian role was 76-67 B.C. (and that apparently only temporarily), a century after the founding of the Qumran community. The two therefore simply cannot be connected.

The Essene hypothesis, first proposed by Sukenik, who came into possession of three of the Scrolls from Cave 1, has always been the prevailing view among scholars relative to the identification of the authors of the DSS. As we filter comments about the Essenes by Josephus and Pliny the Elder through the four criteria determined from the internal evidence above, this alternative will prove to be the best option.

First, sociologically the Essenes were a well-known wilderness sect dating back to approximately 150 B.C. In his work *Natural History* (A.D. 77) Pliny the Elder[35] refers to the reclusive setting and the unique lifestyle of the Essenes:

> On the west side of the Dead Sea, but out of range of the noxious exhalations of the coast, is the solitary tribe of the Essenes *[Esseni]*, which is remarkable beyond all the other tribes in the whole world, as it has no women and has renounced all sexual desire, has no money, and has only palm-trees for company. Day by day the throng of refugees is recruited to an equal number by numerous accessions of persons tired of life and driven thither by the waves of fortune to adopt their manners. Thus through thousands of ages (incredible to relate) a race in which no one is born lives on for ever; so prolific for their advantage is other men's weariness of life!
>
> Lying below the Essenes [literally: these] was formerly the town of Engedi, second only to Jerusalem in the fertility of its land and in its groves of palm-trees, but now like Jerusalem a heap of ashes. [36]

Next, with regard to their sectarian lifestyle, we turn to Josephus' descriptions of the Essenes, noting the similarities with the DSS. We simply list some of the more well-known comparisons:[37]

☐ Both emphasize the sovereignty of God over the freedom of the human will (cf. *Ant.* 13.6.9 [172] with e.g., 1QS 3:15-16; 21-23; 1QH 1:7-8, 18-20; 1QM 2:6-10). In this perspective the Essenes and the authors of the DSS decidedly differed from the Sadducees and the Pharisees (see again Josephus *Ant.* 13.6.9 [172]).

☐ Both point out the impurity of oil (cf. *J.W.* 2.8.3 [123] with 4QMMT 58-61; CD 12:15-17). The DSS texts explain that the nonuse of oil was because the community believed liquids were ready transmitters of ritual impurity. This view was substantially different from the practice of Jews in Israel who applied oil to their skin to protect themselves from the arid condition.

☐ Josephus' account of the Essenes' habit of sharing goods and property (*J.W.* 2.8.3 [122]) accords with the DSS (1QS 6:18-23; cf. 1:11-12; 5:2; more on this matter in chapter five).

☐ Josephus and the DSS record a number of requirements to be met before a person could participate in communal meals: membership in the community, premeal bath, sitting at the tables according to assigned rank (cf. *J.W.* 2.8.5 [129-30] with 1QS 6:13-23; cf. 5:13-14; 6:3-6). These particulars seem to be unique to the descriptions of Josephus and the DSS.

☐ Even the toilet habits of the two presentations match. Josephus writes that the Essenes

> are stricter than any other of the Jews in resting from their labors on the seventh day; for they not only get their food ready the day before, that they may not be obliged to kindle a fire on that day, but they will not remove any vessel out of its place, nor go to stool thereon. Nay, on the other days they dig a small pit, a foot deep, with a paddle (which kind of hatchet is given them when they are first admitted among them); and covering themselves round with their garment, that they may not affront the divine rays of light, they ease themselves into that pit, after which they put the earth that was dug out again into the pit; and even this they do only in the more lonely places, which they choose out for this purpose and although this easement of the body be natural, yet it is a rule with them to wash themselves after it, as if it were a defilement to them. (*J.W.* 2.8.9 [147-49])

Compare this testimony with the machete found in Cave 11 and the procedure for ritual cleanness regarding bodily waste given in War Scroll 7:5-7 and Temple Scroll 46:13-16.[38]

☐ The two descriptions agree even in the unusual detail of spitting. Both *Jewish War* 2.8.9 [147] and Rule of the Community 7:15 forbade spitting in the camp (possibly it was considered impure), a practice sufficiently unusual to which to call attention.

The preceding similarities are some of the more celebrated ones but, as Todd Beall has demonstrated, there are others as well. Beall's analysis identifies twenty-one probable parallels between Josephus and the Scrolls.[39]

Two major disagreements, however, are often said to pertain to Josephus' descriptions of the Essenes and the DSS. First, while Josephus writes that there was a three-year initiatory procedure for joining the Essenes (*J.W.* 2.8.7 [137-38]), the DSS seem to indicate a two-year probationary period (1QS 6:13-23). This is not an insurmountable problem, however, for, as VanderKam notes, the sources can be harmonized:

Josephus	1QS
(1) one year outside the group but living by its rules	(1) period from examination by the Guardian to examination by the Congregation
(2) tested for two more years	(2) in the Council of the Community but has limited rights to the meal for a year
(3) then he may be enrolled	(3) after another year, he is again tested and becomes a full member with full rights to the meal.[40]

Second, Josephus in his *Jewish Wars* 2.8.2 [120] and Pliny the Elder in his *Naturalis Historia* 5.73 describe the Essenes as being a male celibate group, which compares nicely with the Qumranic Rule of the Community yet, the fact that the Damascus Document and the Rule of the Congregation envision its members as married, coupled with the presence of a few skeletons of women and children in the nearby cemeteries (but note that over a thousand of the eleven hundred graves contained men), suggest to some that the Essenes are not to be equated with the DSS community.

These apparent contradictions, however, are not formidable. With regard to the first, Josephus also describes another order of Essenes that were married (*J.W.* 2.8.13 [160-61]). It may well be, then, that Josephus' different descriptions correlate with two types of Essenes, both of whom are represented in the DSS. The Qumran celibate community corresponds with the Manual of Discipline, while other Essenes living among non-Essenes and having families matches the Damascus Document and the Rule of the Congregation.

With regard to the graves of women and children, VanderKam offers a number of plausible explanations, none of which need negate the celibate nature of the Qumran camp:

> One could explain the presence of skeletons of women and children . . . in various ways. One is, of course, that the community was not celibate . . . at every stage of its existence. It is more likely, though, that the women and children were visitors to the Qumran community—either relatives who came to see their kinsmen or the curious who came to observe the unusual society. They could also have been travelers who died in the arid region.[41]

A third criticism (a minor one) voiced against the Essene hypothesis is that the name *Essene* does not occur in the DSS. But this objection flounders in light of the fact that *Essene* is not a Hebrew word but rather represents Greek and Latin spellings from various texts. That is to say, we do not know the etymology of the name *Essene*. Who is to say, then, that its Hebrew counterpart does not indeed occur in the DSS but in an unrecognizable form to moderns?[42]

Second, the archaeological evidence connects the DSS with Khirbet Qumran, a site that fits Pliny the Elder's geographical description of the Essenes (see above his *Natural History* 5.73). VanderKam assesses the situation, noting that Pliny's placement of the Essenes to the west of the Dead Sea, with En-gedi to the south, nicely fits Khirbet Qumran. This is all the more so since the area Pliny describes shows no archaeological evidence of having been inhabited by any other communal group besides the one at Qumran. Although some argue that Pliny's words *lying below* imply that the Essenes settled in the hills above En-gedi, most probably they mean "to the south of." The fact that no evidence exists that this community occupied those hills confirms this interpretation.[43]

Detractors from the Essene hypothesis, however, point out two problems with Pliny's description. One is that he apparently confuses the oasis of En-gedi with Jericho in terms of the latter's fertility and palm trees. Yet this minute mistake need not cast the whole of Pliny's report in doubt. Another criticism is that Pliny writes about the Essenes in the present tense, even though his work was written in A.D. 77 after the destruction of Qumran by the Romans in A.D. 68. But again the Essene theory is not really affected by this matter, for Pliny could have been using the "historical present," describing a past event in the present tense. Or, more likely, he may well have been utilizing a source dating to the Qumran era.[44]

Third, the paleographical evidence indicates that numerous duplicate copies of manuscripts as well as various styles of handwriting characterize the DSS. This strongly suggests that Qumran was the library or headquarters of a larger movement, which aligns well with Josephus' description of various branches within the Essene following (*J.W.* 2.8.4 [124]; *Ant.* 18.1.5 [22]).[45]

Fourth, historically, the period of Qumran existence, which ranged from the mid-second century B.C. to A.D. 68, is in agreement with the time frame mentioned by Josephus regarding the Essenes (*Ant.* 13.5.9 [171]; *Life* 1.2). Moreover, it is significant that the period when Qumran was not inhabited, 31-4 B.C., correlates with the reign of Herod the Great. Josephus specifically states that the Essenes were highly respected by that ruler (*Ant.* 17.13.3), implying a relationship between the two (the lack of occupation of Qumran and Herod's approval of the Essenes). It is a reasonable conjecture that the Essenes, because they enjoyed a positive relationship with Herod, felt no need to live in the desert at that particular time.

Surveying the internal evidence (the four criteria) and now the external data (the ancient descriptions of the four Jewish sects, especially the Essenes) leads one to the justifiable conclusion that the Essenes wrote the DSS and inhabited ancient Qumran. I close this section by affirming a now-famous statement made by one of the original scholars on the DSS committee, Frank M. Cross:

> The scholar who would "exercise caution" in identifying the sect of Qumran with the Essenes places himself in an astonishing position: he must suggest seriously that two major parties formed communistic religious communities in the same district of the desert of the Dead Sea and

lived together in effect for two centuries, holding similar bizarre views, performing similar or rather identical lustrations, ritual meals, and ceremonies. He must suppose that one, carefully described by classical authors, disappeared without leaving building remains or even potsherds behind; the other, systematically ignored by the classical sources, left extensive ruins, and indeed a great library. I prefer to be reckless and flatly identify the men of Qumran with their perennial house-guests, the Essenes.[46]

This assessment paves the way for a potentially fruitful investigation of the relationship between the DSS and the NT, especially since the latter is hospitable to the convictions and perhaps to some degree the lifestyle of the Essenes. While the bulk of this work addresses that association, I anticipate that subject in the next section.

The Relationship Between the DSS and the NT

Some of the greatest excitement and intense controversy attending the Scrolls has been their relationship to the NT. The fact that the DSS do not mention Jesus or any other NT person and the high probability that no NT book or early Christian text is included among the many scripts from the eleven caves has convinced most DSS experts that the NT and the Scrolls have no direct relationship between them.[47] With this assessment I concur. Rather, the similarities between the two bodies of literature, as I will argue throughout this study, stem from the fact that both groups are retelling the story of Israel from an apocalyptic point of view. A few notable exceptions apply to the preceding rule. Some scholars have made claims of direct contact between the DSS and the NT, causing a stir both in academic circles and in public opinion. We here summarize the more significant of those views.

1. Jesus and the Teacher of Righteousness. At the beginning of DSS research, assertions were made intimately connecting Jesus and the Teacher of Righteousness. The French scholar André Dupont-Sommer wrote a book in 1952 entitled *The Dead Sea Scrolls: A Preliminary Survey*, in which he asserted that the Teacher of Righteousness was an exact prototype of Jesus, particularly as a martyred prophet, who was revered by his followers as the suffering servant of the Lord in Isaiah but crucified by his enemies between 67 and 63 B.C. Dupont-Sommer made a controversial statement about these first and second "Christs":

> Everything in the Jewish New Covenant heralds and prepares the way
> for the Christian New Covenant. The Galilean Master, as He is presented
> to us in the writings of the New Testament, appears in many respects as
> an astonishing reincarnation of the Master of Justice (i.e., the Teacher of
> Righteousness). Like the latter He preached penitence, poverty, humility,
> love of one's neighbor, chastity. Like him, He prescribed the observance
> of the Law of Moses, the whole Law, but the Law finished and perfected,
> thanks to His own revelations. Like him He was the Elect and the Mes-
> siah of God, the Messiah redeemer of the world. Like him He was the
> object of the hostility of the priests, the party of the Sadducees. Like him
> He was condemned and put to death. Like him he pronounced judge-
> ment on Jerusalem which was taken and destroyed by the Romans for
> having put Him to death. Like Him at the end of time, He will be the
> supreme judge. Like him He founded a Church whose adherents fer-
> vently awaited His glorious return. In the Christian Church, just as in the
> Essene Church, the essential rite is the sacred meal, whose ministers are
> the priests. Here and there at the head of each community there is the
> overseer, the "bishop." And the ideal of both Churches is essentially that
> of unity, communion in love—even going so far as the sharing of com-
> mon property.[48]

Edmund Wilson popularized Dupont-Sommer's view in an article
he wrote for the *New Yorker*, "The Scrolls from the Dead Sea." According to Wilson, the relation of the Qumranic Essenes and the NT was
one of successive phases of a movement.

> The monastery, this structure of stone that endures, between the bitter
> waters and precipitous cliffs, with its oven and its inkwells, its mill and
> its cesspool, its constellation of sacred fonts and the unadorned graves of
> its dead, is perhaps, more than Bethlehem of Nazareth, the Cradle of
> Christianity.[49]

Elsewhere Wilson charged that Jewish and Christian Scrolls scholars
were reluctant to admit the close proximity between the Qumran materials and the NT because it would challenge their assumptions about
the uniqueness of Christianity.[50] Such a criticism initiated a line of reasoning that continues among some to this day.[51]

Perhaps the most notorious example of grandiose claims about the relationship between Jesus and Christianity and the Teacher of Righteousness and Qumran was made by one of the scholars on the original Scrolls team, John Marco Allegro. In a series of broadcasts on BBC Radio in January 1956, Allegro made sweeping generalizations about Jesus and the DSS. One of the more famous was quoted in the *New York Times* (February 5, 1956, p. 2):

> The origins of some Christian rituals and doctrines can be seen in the documents of an extremist Jewish sect that existed for more than 100 years before the birth of Jesus Christ. . . . The historical basis of the Lord's Supper and part at least of the Lord's prayer and the New Testament teaching of Jesus were attributable to the Qumranians, who called themselves the Sons of Zadok. . . . The "Teacher of Righteous"[sic], the leader of the monastic community in the first century before Christ was persecuted and probably crucified by Gentiles at the instigation of a wicked priest of the Jews.[52]

For Allego, therefore, the Teacher of Righteousness provided a pattern into which the early church placed Jesus, his arrest, crucifixion and resurrection.[53] Frustrated by Allegro's comments, the rest of the Scrolls team repudiated his statements in a letter printed by the *Times* of London (March 16, 1956, p. 11), denying the existence of any Essenic pattern into which Jesus of Nazaeth was fit.[54] The letter was signed by de Vaux, Milik, Skehan, Starcky and Strugnell. It made minimal impact, however, on Allegro's position.

Nevertheless, the majority of DSS scholars avoided thereafter tendentious connections between Jesus and the Teacher of Righteousness. Yet in 1991 Robert H. Eisenman revived the theory of direct contact between Jesus and the Teacher of Righteousness by calling attention to a fragment from Cave 4 (4Q285 7:4-5), the so-called "Pierced Messiah Text." His translation of that passage is as follows:

> (4) and they will put to death the leader of the community, the Bran[ch of David],

> (5) and with woundings, and the (high) priest will command . . .[55]

Scholars have been quick, however, to register their disagreement with Eisenman's translation, pointing out that he incorrectly reversed the subject and object of the verb in line 4. The text should rather read "the leader of the community will kill him," with reference to the Davidic Messiah's defeat of the leader of the Kittim (the Romans). Moreover, Eisenman's rendering of the Hebrew word *mehollot* (line 5) as "woundings" or "piercing" (supposedly under the influence of Isa 53:5) is inaccurate; it should be translated *dancings*. Schiffman's translation of 4Q285 is the more correct one:

> [. . . as it is written in the Book ofl Isaiah the prophet, "[The thickets of the forest] shall be hacked away [with iron, and the Lebanon trees in their majesty shall] fall. But a shoot shall grow out of the stump of Jesse, [a twig shall sprout from his stock (Isaiah 10:34-11:1) . . .] shoot of David, and they will be judged, the . . . and the Prince of the Congregation will kill him, the arm[y] of . . . [with drum]s and with dances. And the [high] priest commanded . . . [the c]orpse[s] of the Kittim . . . [56]

Subsequent scholarly discussion has rendered highly suspect the claim by Eisenman that this text refers to the execution of a messianic leader and thereby supposedly "puts to rest the idea presently being circulated by the scroll editorial committee that this material has nothing to do with Christian origins in Palestine."[57]

2. John the Baptist and the Essenes. From the beginning of comparative studies of Qumran and the NT, scholars have been impressed with the similarities between John the Baptist and the DSS.[58] In fact, no other person in the NT is as likely a candidate for being connected with the Qumran community as John the Baptist. We may note four commonly proposed parallels between the two. First, geographically, both lived in the Judean Desert (cf. Lk 1:80; 3:2 with 1QS 8:13). Second, textually, both based their ministries on Isaiah 40:3, "A voice cries: 'In the wilderness prepare the way of the LORD' " (cf. Mt 3:3; Mk 1:3; Lk 3:3-6 with 1QS 8:12-16). Third, both proclaimed their messages with an eschatological fervency (cf. e.g., Lk 3:1-20 with 1QS 3-4). Fourth, both adhered to a type of baptism of repentance for Jews (cf. Lk 3:16 with 1QS 4:20-21). In light of these similarities, it is possible that John the Baptist may have been associated with the Qumran sect at one time; nevertheless, he later separated from the group to pursue his own calling.[59]

Some scholars, however, have gone beyond the preceding opinion, holding that there is a more specific connection between John the Baptist and the DSS, notably Barbara E. Thiering of Australia. In four works, Thiering developed the thesis that the Teacher of Righteousness in the DSS was John the Baptist and that his main opponent, the man of lies, was none other than Jesus, the founder of Christianity![60] To support her theory Thiering obviously had to redate the DSS, which she did by arguing that all Qumran manuscripts written in semicursive style originated in the first century A.D. Thus works like 1Qp Habakkuk were interpreted to refer to the beginnings of Christianity. Fitzmyer's assessment, however, of Thiering's thesis, as well as other attempts to date the DSS to the time of Jesus (c. A.D. 30), expresses the conviction of the vast majority of DSS scholars:

> Such opinions, however, ride roughshod over the archaeological, palaeographical, and radio carbon dating of the evidence that clearly pinpoints most of the QS [Qumran Scrolls] to the pre-Christian centuries.[61]

Of those DSS that do date to the first century A.D., Fitzmyer writes that they usually come from so early a time in that century that there is again little likelihood that they mention Jesus.[62]

3. *James and the Teacher of Righteousness.* Another attempt to directly connect the NT with the DSS is that by Robert Eisenman, the author referred to above with regard to the so-called "Pierced Messiah Text." It is this scholar's contention that James, the brother of Christ, was the Teacher of Righteousness and that Paul the apostle was the man of lies of 1QpHabakkuk 2:2. To posit this theory, Eisenman, like Thiering, must argue that the DSS date a century later than what the majority of Qumran scholars claim.[63] But the same criticism pertaining to Thiering's misreading of the paleographical, archaeological, and radio carbon evidence applies to Eisenman's hypothesis as well.[64]

Conclusion

Having identified the Essenes as the most likely candidates to have produced the DSS, I then suggested that their relationship to the NT is an indirect, albeit vital, one. As we will see in the chapters that follow, the similarities between the two result from their concern to tell the story of Israel—sin, exile and restoration. But the fundamental differences between the DSS and the NT result from the fact that, in the case of the latter, Israel's story is radically reinterpreted in the light of Jesus' life, death and resurrection. Jesus presents and initiates a whole new way of being Israel and ultimately a new way of being human. The NT writers offer a multiperspectival response to that event but with a commonality amidst them. They share a different view of reality than that of the DSS. In fact, they subvert some of the important symbols and practices, as well as the story line of the worldview of the DSS. One of the advantages that the DSS afford Christians is that in them we can observe a fairly coherent Jewish perspective of the first century and, through noting similarities and dissimilarities, deduce how a particular type of Jewish thought would have been transformed by the gospel. To begin to address that topic, the next chapter examines how these two faith groups interpreted their OT.[65]

Chapter Three

The Hermeneutic of Restoration

Matthew, Pesher & the DSS

Introduction

This chapter will begin the comparative analysis of the DSS and the NT by investigating the key hermeneutical technique employed by the Essenes and Matthew in presenting their respective views of the restoration of Israel, namely, *pesher*. Matthew is viewed, since the discovery of the Qumran documents, as the most celebrated example of that interpretive method in the NT; hence the focus here on the First Gospel.

Earlier I surveyed the pervasive usage of *pesher* by the DSS. A number of components constitute that genre, as is shown, for example, in the *pesher* on Habakkuk 7:1-4. The biblical prophet's message (in this case Habakkuk) deals ultimately with the future, but its full comprehension was a mystery *(r'z)* to him (see 1QpHab 7:1). That mystery of prophecy is now being revealed or interpreted *(pesher)* to the Teacher of Righteousness (see 1QpHab 7:3-4). The fulfillment of the prophecy is occurring in the last days (note 1QpHab 7:1).

Although they are not spelled out in every instance, these components form the basic assumptions lying behind *pesher* hermeneutics,

and the overriding purpose driving the method is the concern to legitimate the Essenes' interpretation of the Torah. In doing so, the Essenes
laid claim to being the rightful guardians of the Mosaic law and
thereby constituted the restored Israel envisioned by the OT prophets.[1]
More on this later.

As mentioned above, with the publication of the DSS, Matthew's
Gospel quickly attracted attention as a leading candidate for comparison
with *pesher* hermeneutics. Thus Krister Stendahl argued that the
Matthean fulfillment quotations (see below) fit the pattern of *pesher* as
found in the *Pesher* on Habakkuk.[2] Two authors, however, begged to differ with such a theory. On the one hand, Bert L. Gärtner contested
Stendahl's claim, contending that the quotation-interpretation structure
of the DSS *pesharim* (1QpHab in particular) does not characterize Matthew's citations of the OT.[3] On the other hand, Joseph Fitzmyer demonstrated that the Matthean fulfillment quotations do not occur in the
pesharim of the DSS.[4] While these two authors' arguments are sound,
more recent scholarship has (rightly) entertained the possibility that
there is nevertheless a broad connection between Matthew and *pesher*
hermeneutics as espoused by the covenanters in terms of the way those
writers adapt and apply the OT to their communities, perceived by them
as eschatological in scope. Thus Michael Knowles observes:

> Whatever criticisms have been levelled on formal grounds against
> Stendahl's comparison of Matthew's exegetical methods and pesher exe-
> gesis at Qumran, it nonetheless remains true that both demonstrate an
> exegesis of accommodation, or, as Stendahl calls it, 'text interpretation of
> an actualizing nature.'[5]

We pursue such an association below by calling attention to the
presence of three types of *pesharim* in both the DSS and Matthew: single (cf. Mt 3:3; 1QS 8:12-16 with Is 40:3), continuous (cf. Mt 21:33-46;
4QpIs 1:1:1—2:2:1 with Is 5:1-7) and thematic (cf. Matthew's fulfillment
quotations with 4QTestim; and cf. Mt 11:25-30; 4QFlor with 2 Sam 7). In
identifying the OT basis of these texts shared by the Qumran community and Matthew, it will become clear that the same theme undergirds
their exegesis—the restoration of Israel. But before tackling that task
(the second section in this chapter), we first must take a step back by

grasping the overall importance of the story of Israel (sin-exile-restoration) for the DSS and Matthew.

The Story of Israel in the DSS and in Matthew

The story of Israel in the DSS. Odil H. Steck demonstrated that the Deuteronomistic tradition exerted its influence on Jewish literature between 200 B.C. and A.D. 100, with four tenets repeatedly surfacing in those materials:

1. The history of Israel is one long, persistent story of a "stiff-necked," rebellious and disobedient people.

2. God sent his messengers, the prophets, to mediate his will (i.e., the law), to instruct and admonish them in his will, and to exhort them to repentance lest they bring on themselves judgment and destruction.

3. Nevertheless, Israel en masse rejected all those prophets, even persecuting and killing them out of their stubborn "stiffneckedness."

4. Therefore, Israel's God had "rained" destruction on them in 722 and 587 B.C. and would destroy them again in the future in a similar way if they did not heed his word.[6]

Relevant to this discussion, David P. Moessner applies Steck's fourfold category to the DSS. The history of Israel is defined as a continuous story of disobedience to Moses' law (e.g., CD 3). God sent his prophets to call Israel to repentance, the epitome of whom for the DSS was the Teacher of Righteousness. The nation rejected this teacher (e.g., CD 3:4; cf. 4QpHos 2:3-6; 1QS 1:3; 8:15-16; 1QpHab 2:5-10). God's judgment came on Israel in 722 B.C. and again in 587 B.C. (e.g., CD 1:3—2:4). Only by divine grace is the Qumran community exempt from such punishment; it separated itself from the nation for the purpose of obeying God by adhering to the ways of the Teacher of Righteousness (e.g., CD 1:3-4; 1QS 1:3; 8:15-16; 1QpHab 7:5).[7]

Emerging out of the category of God's judgment is the conviction of the Essenes that their community constituted restored Israel. A quick glance at the noncanonical literature making up in the DSS readily reveals the importance of such a motif in that material. The legal works (e.g., 4QMMT; 1QS) establish the conceptual framework for the authors of the Scrolls: they viewed their community as the restored people of God. Those who entered it and obeyed its precepts were therefore the recipients of the covenantal blessings, while all others remained under the Deuteronomic curses. In that literature, as well as in the liturgical and astronomical writings (the former includes 1QH and the Songs of Sabbath Sacrifice [4Q400-405; 11Q17], while the latter involves Astronomical Enoch [4Q209-11] and the Calendrical Documents [4Q320-21, 327]), the divine law that is prescribed is different and more stringent than the OT Torah (e.g., espousal of the solar, not lunar, calendar; variant feast days; stricter purification rituals).

Justification for such reinterpretation (actually subversion) of the Torah and the prophets is offered especially in the the *pesharim*: The OT authors' knowledge of the things of God was incomplete, only to find its ultimate significance in the promulgations of the Teacher of Righteousness and those who followed him (see 1QpHab 7:1-15). The presence of apocryphal works like *1 Enoch* and *Jubilees* in the library of a sectarian community such as Qumran might seem puzzling, but these works actually follow a similar *halakhah* to that found in the Scrolls. Eschatological pieces such as the Messianic Rule (1Q28a), the War Scroll (1QM), Florilegium (4Q174) and Testimonia (4Q175) assure final victory for and vindication of the Qumran community's worldview over against all other contenders for the faith. The preceding categories of literature (legal, liturgical, astronomical, apocryphal, eschatological), then, attest to the importance of the restoration of Israel for the DSS.

Two examples futher illustrate the significance of the theme of the restoration of Israel for the DSS: the Damascus Document, a foundational document, and the *pesher* on Habakkuk 7:5—8:3 (mentioned above). The restoration motif occurs in both in the context of discussions of Israel's sin and exile.

That Deuteronomy is deeply ingrained in the Damascus Document has been demonstrated by Steck. Thus one is greeted in the opening statements of the document with the sin-exile-restoration pattern: Israel's sin (cf. CD 1:3 with Deut 28:15) has caused divine judgment and exile to fall on the Jews (cf. CD 1:3-4 with Deut 31:17), which is specified as the curses of the covenant (cf. CD 1:17 with Deut 28:16-35). Nevertheless God spared a remnant by raising up the Qumran community, which has repented and been restored to him. Consequently the promise of the Deuteronomic blessings of prosperity in the land is their inheritance (cf. CD 1:5-11 with Deut 4:29; 30:5, 9).

This twofold theme of Deuteronomic blessings on the Qumran community but curses on the rest of Israel continues in the Damascus Document. The former is attested to with the promise that the Essenes will fill the land with their posterity (CD 2:11-12), that those who obey the covenant will enjoy eternal life (CD 3:20), and that those who keep the covenant are assured long life in the land (CD 20:1-5, where Deut 7:9 is quoted; see also CD 7:5-10; 20:27-34). (For the motif of the covenantal curses abiding on non-Essenes, see CD 3:7-12, 17; 4:13-20; 5:21; 15:1-5.)[8]

This conceptual framework informs Damascus Document 3:15-16, which alludes to Leviticus 18:5 (perhaps the most important OT verse regarding obedience to the Torah), "his [God's] just stipulations . . . which man must do in order to live." The context in Damascus Document 3:13-16 specifies the nature of the stipulations required to produce the life of the covenant referred to in Leviticus 18:5. These consist of the "hidden matters"[9] divinely revealed to the Qumran community (CD 3:18), which redefine the Mosaic law in terms of its feasts, sabbaths and dietary regulations (CD 3:13-15).[10] In effect, Damascus Document 3:13-16 reinterprets the restoration of Israel by holding up its sectarian *halakhah* as the means for inheriting the Deuteronomic blessings of life.

The significance of the restoration of Israel for the *pesher* on Habakkuk 7:5—8:3 is highlighted by first summarizing the concern of the OT book of Habakkuk and then analyzing the DSS text's reinterpretation of Habakkuk 2:3-4. The prophet was deeply worried over the paradigm of Israel's sin—exile—restoration. In Habakkuk 1:1-4 he laments the fact that the nation has abandoned the law of Moses. God responds to Habakkuk's complaint by announcing that he will raise up the Chaldeans to punish Israel, judgment that recalls the Deuteronomic curses. This divine premonition proves to be too much for Habakkuk, who bemoans God's choice of instrument of discipline (Hab 1:5-17; 2:4-20). God, however, comforts the prophet with the news that Israel one day will be restored to the land (Hab 3:1-19). In the meantime, the righteous should manifest their trust in God's covenantal faithfulness (Hab 2:1-4). The focal point of the book, then, is Habakkuk 2:4: Those who shrink back from their confidence in God during the upcoming crisis will fail, while those who remain steadfast in their trust in God will live. N. T. Wright tracks this concept of faith as it is expressed throughout Second Temple Judaism. He delineates its components as follows:

> First, it is the appropriate stance of the covenant people before their rightful god (and, for that matter, of creatures before their maker). Second, it is the thing which marks out the true people of Israel at a time of crisis and judgment. Third, it will characterize the people who are restored after the exile. We may add to this a fourth point, from the literature on the conversion of proselytes: faith, in the sense of belief in the one true god and the rejection of pagan idols, was of course a vital characteristic for anyone seeking to join the people of Israel. "Faith" is thus not simply of religious interiority. Nor is the vital question the one which occupies so much twentieth-century writing on the subject, namely the shape of "faith" and its role within religious experience as a whole. What matters is that faith is a crucial part of the definition of Israel at her time of great crisis. Jesus' call for "faith" was not merely the offering of a new religious option or dimension. It was a crucial element in the eschatological reconstitution of Israel around himself.[11]

One gathers from these comments that the means for remaining in the covenant was faith/faithfulness.[12] Such an interpretation imprints 1QpHabakkuk 7:5—8:3 (cf. Rom 1:17; Gal 3:11; Heb 10:37-39), except that the DSS passage *reinterprets* the sin-exile-restoration pattern of ancient Israel to fit its own day.

> For the Vision has an appointed time, it will have an end and not fail. Its interpretation: the final age will be extended and go beyond all that the prophets say, because the mysteries of God are wonderful. Though it might delay, wait for it; it definitely has to come and will not delay. Its interpretation concerns the men of truth, those who observe the Law, whose hands will not desert the service of truth when the final age is extended beyond them, because all the ages of God will come at the right time, as he established for them in the mysteries of his prudence. See, [his soul within him] is conceited and does not give way. Its interpretation: they will double [persecution] at being judged.
>
> Its interpretation concerns all observing the Law in the House of Judah, whom God will free from punishment on account of their deeds and their loyalty to the Teacher of Righteousness.

The emphasis of this commentary regarding Habakkuk 2:3-4 is on the opposite reactions demonstrated toward the commandments of the Teacher of Righteousness. Those like the Wicked Priest and his followers, though once belonging to the new covenant community of the Essenes, apostatized by shunning the principles of the Teacher of Righteousness and persecuting him (cf. 1QpHab 7:15-16 with 1QpHab 1:11-15, 2:1-10). Elsewhere the author labels such people "traitors of the New Covenant" (1QpHab 2:3; cf. 1QpHab 2:6).

Thus the commentary redefines sin in terms of breaking the new covenant, the laws of the Teacher of Righteousness. Consequently the Wicked Priest was apprehended by his enemies,[13] and ultimately the Hasmonean dynasty fell to the Kittim[14] (the Romans), God's tool of judgment (1QpHab 8:14—9:16). The Wicked Priest's exile and death were proof that he was not a part of the remnant, those destined to participate in the restoration of the land (1QpHab 2:11—4:15). With poetic justice, the Essenes are promised that one day they will rule over Israel, including the others who abandoned the new covenant of the Qumran community (1QpHab 5:1-12; 6:1-16). In the meantime, the faithful are to uphold the laws of the Teacher of Righteousness. This is the true fulfillment of Habakkuk 2:3-4 and the key to the restoration of Israel (see 1QpHab 7:5-14; 8:1-3).

Thus Habakkuk 2:3-4 is interpreted in the Scrolls text in the following way: The time of the restoration of Israel forecast in Habakkuk 2:3 is now beginning to be accomplished (1QpHab 7:1-4). Those who betray the new covenant of the Essenes are the Wicked Priest and his followers. These shrink back from faith in God (cf. Hab 2:4 with 1QpHab 7:15-16), but those who are true to the Teacher of Righteousness will live (cf. Hab 2:4b with 1QpHab 7:5-14; 8:1-3).

It is clear, then, from the Damascus Document and 1QpHabakkuk 7:5—8:3 that the motif of the restoration of Israel was of vital interest to the Qumran community. The same theme is operative in the Rule of the Community and *Miqsat Maase Ha-Torah*, two other foundational documents of the Essenes, as will be shown later in this book. Moreover, a similar concern can be identified in other *pesharim* of the DSS, as will be seen later in this chapter.

The story of Israel in Matthew. Space does not permit here a detailed analysis of how the story of Israel influences the first Gospel, but N. T. Wright's insights allow us a thumbnail sketch of the subject. In the light of his work, I suggest the following outline for Matthew:

1:1-17: Introduction: Genealogy
1:18—2:23: The New Moses
3: The New Exodus
4: The New Israel
5—25: The New Covenant Described
26—27: The New Covenant Inaugurated
28: Conclusion

The overriding theme of these sections is the sin-exile-restoration paradigm of Israel, with the emphasis falling on the third of these components.

Wright has demonstrated that the threefold division of the Matthean genealogy centering on Abraham, Moses and Christ is designed to evoke the story of Israel.

> Abraham is the start…[which] is the story of Israel. The next focal point is . . . on Jesus as the true David, the Messiah. The third focal point is unexpected: the exile. This is not so regular a marker within Jewish schemes, but for Matthew it is crucial. As we saw, most Jews of the second-temple period regarded themselves as still in exile, still suffering the results of Israel's age-old sin. Until the great day of redemption dawned, Israel was still "in her sins," still in need of rescue. The genealogy then says to Matthew's careful reader that the long story of Abraham's people will come to its fulfilment, its seventh seven, with a new David, who will rescue his people from their exile, that is, "save his people from their sins." When Matthew says precisely this in 1:18-21 we should not be surprised.[15]

Looming behind the introduction and making his explicit appearance in Matthew 1:18—2:23 is Moses and in particular Jesus, the New Moses. As such, Jesus the deliverer inaugurates a new exodus, according to chapter 3.[16] More than this, in Matthew 4 we learn that Jesus is the true Israel who obeys God in the wilderness, whereas ancient Israel did not. One begins to sense from these early chapters in the first Gospel that Jesus' redemption of his people constitutes the fulfillment of the long-awaited restoration of Israel.

This is confirmed by the heart of the Matthean material, chapters

5—25, wherein Jesus presents the New Covenant to Israel, Deuteronomic blessings included. Wright correctly points out that the five
blocks of teaching material occuring in this major section are designed
by Matthew to elicit Deuteronomy 27—30 (especially Deut 30:15-20).
The first and last blocks draw on the Deuteronomic blessings, including the Beatitudes (Mt 5—7) and the curses on the Pharisees (Mt 23—
25). The dominant theme informing Matthew in all of this is the new
covenant.[17] Figure 3.1 shows a chiastic structure of the five teaching
blocks, along with brief comments on each, reflecting this understanding of Matthew.[18]

A-Deuteronomic blessings (5-7).
   B-Deuteronomic blessings and curses on those who follow or reject Jesus, respec-
     tively (10-11).
      C-The above two choices are by divine design (13).
   B'-Deuteronomic blessings and curses on those who follow or reject Jesus, respec-
     tively (18).
A'-Deuteronomic curses (23-25).

Figure 3.1. Chiastic structure of Matthew

Points A and A', as observed above with Wright, contrast the desti-
nies of those who follow Jesus and those who do not. Thus according
to A (Mt 5—7), those who obey Jesus' teaching are blessed and inherit
the kingdom of God, the epitome of the Deuteronomic blessings.[19]
Those who reject Jesus (most notably the Pharisees), however, bring on
themselves and the nation of Israel the Deuteronomic curses, as presented in A' (Mt 23—25).

Actually, the careful reader will detect in Matthew 23—25 the presence of the four tenets of the Deuteronomistic tradition: (1) Israel has
been continuously disobedient to God in the past and now in the
present due to the Pharisee's warped teaching (Mt 23:1-28); (2) God
sent his prophets to call Israel to repentance (Mt 23:29-30, 34); (3) Israel
has rejected God's messengers, culminating in its crucifixion of Jesus,
instigated by the Pharisees (Mt 23:31-34, 37); (4) God consequently will
judge the nation in the future, and the city of Jerusalem will be
destroyed (by the Romans) as it was in the past by the Babylonians (Mt
23:35-36; amplified in Mt 24—25). All of this bespeaks the actualization
of the Deuteronomic curses on those who reject Jesus.[20]

Points B (Mt 10—11) and B' (Mt 18) envision two responses. Those who accept Jesus' followers receive the Deuteronomic blessings, while those who reject them heap on themselves the covenantal curses. Point C (Mt 13), the central concern of the five blocks of Matthean teaching, presents the truth via parables that one's reaction to Jesus—acceptance or denial—is by divine design (cf. Mt 13:14-15 with Is 6:9). Such knowledge *(pesher?)* supplies the disciples the key to unlocking the mystery *(r'z?)* of the kingdom of God (Mt 13:11).

Having portrayed the new covenant (in Mt 5—25), Matthew then describes Jesus' inauguration of such through his death and resurrection (Mt 26—27). Chapter 28 (especially vv. 16-20) concludes Matthew's story of Israel. Comparing this to Deuteronomy 31—34 and Moses' final blessing on the people and his ascent of the mountain to see the land Israel would possess, Wright notes, "After his resurrection, Jesus, like Moses, goes up the mountain and departs from his people, leaving them with a commission to go in and possess the land, that is the entire world."[21]

Matthew, *Pesher* and the Restoration of Israel

The concern of this section is to examine the usage of *pesher* hermeneutics by Matthew and the DSS in terms of the theme of the restoration of Israel. The three types of *pesharim* occurring in the DSS—single, continuous and thematic—are also found in Matthew, as will be shown.

Single pesharim: Matthew 3:3; Rule of the Community 8:12-16 and Isaiah 40:3. It will be recalled from the introduction to this chapter that *pesher* hermeneutics in the DSS involves an eschatological reading of an OT text such that its fulfillment is thought to be taking place in the Qumran community, the true Israel of the endtime. Single *pesharim* focus on one OT verse, first quoting it and then interpreting it as applicable to the Qumran community. One of the most famous examples of single *pesharim* in the DSS is Rule of the Community 8:12-16 and its appropriation of Isaiah 40:3. Matthew, too, interprets that OT text eschatologically in similar fashion to the Scrolls text (see Mt 3:3; cf. Mk 1:3; Lk 3:4-6; Jn 1:23). Those passages read Isaiah 40:3 to mean that the restoration of Israel has been inaugurated in their own communities.

Among other things, the wilderness motif in the OT conveys the eschatological hope for a second exodus. This is especially the case in Isaiah 40:3-4 (cf. Is 41:18-19; 43:19-20; 48:20-21; Hos 2:14; 12:9; Mic 7:14-15).[22] Such a background explains why Jewish messianic claimants living in the late Second Temple period led their followers into the Judean wilderness and then, like Joshua of old, staged a new conquest, hoping that God would intervene by delivering Israel from the Romans. Thus Josephus reports, for example, the failed revolt of Theudas (c. A.D. 44-46; *Ant.* 20.5.1 [97-98]; cf. Acts 5:36), who attempted a coup of the Roman government by leading a band of four hundred devotees over the Jordan River. A similar incident is told by Josephus of an unnamed Egyptian Jew (*J.W.* 2.13.5 [261-63]; cf. Acts 21:38).[23] It is not surprising, therefore, that the writers of the DSS and John the Baptist appealed to Isaiah 40:3 in their announcements that the restoration of Israel had begun. Accordingly, Rule of the Community 8:14-16 says:

> As it is written: "In the desert, prepare the way of****, straighten in the steppe a roadway for our God." This is the study of the law which he commanded through the hand of Moses, in order to act in compliance with all that has been revealed from age to age, and according to what the prophets have revealed through his holy spirit.

In *pesher* fasion, this DSS text quotes the OT (cf. line 14 with Is 40:3) and then interprets it in lines 15-16 by applying the prophecy to the Qumran community. The resulting meaning is that the covenanters believed that the Isaianic passage predicted their departure to the desert for the purpose of preparing for the establishment of the New Covenant (see 1QS 8:1-13; 16-26). The means for accomplishing this was the congregation's unreserved commitment to the law of Moses, in particular the Essenes' stringent reinterpretation of the Torah (see again 1QS 8:11-13; 16—26). Moreover, the Qumran community expected that three eschatological figures would culminate the restoration of Israel: a prophetic forerunner, the messianic priest and the Davidic King (1QS 9:11).[24]

Matthew 3:3 does much the same in its use of Isaiah 40:3, "For this is he who was spoken of by the prophet Isaiah when he said, 'The voice of one crying in the wilderness: Prepare the way of the Lord, make his paths straight.'" Matthew 3:3, like Rule of the Community 8:14-16, interprets the Isaiah text in *pesher* fashion: quotation—Isaiah 40:3; interpretation—"This is John" the Baptist (Mt 3:1-2); except that it reverses the order of Rule of the Community 8:14-16, which first presents the interpretation, followed by the quotation.[25] Similar to the DSS identification of an endtime figure, Matthew 3:1-11 names the eschatological forerunner of Israel's renewal—John the Baptist—whose mission was to exhort Jews to enter into the wilderness for the purpose of preparing for the imminent arrival of the kingdom of God (Mt 3:2).

Two other resemblances between these passages surface in their utilizations of Isaiah 40:3, both of which also convey a New Covenant nuance. Matthew 3:1-12 portrays the need for repentance from sin, using the symbol of baptism (vv. 6-7, 11), as does the context of Rule of the Community 8:14-16 (namely, 1QS 4:20-21; 5:13-14). In each case a ritual washing was practiced as an expression of repentance and was demanded of fellow *Israelites* (not just Gentiles, as was typically the rule), something unheard of in the extant Jewish literature from that time. Most likely, the impetus for the two groups' message of baptism was the New Covenant text of Ezekiel 36:25: "I will sprinkle clean water upon you, and you shall be clean from all your uncleannesses, and from all your idols I will cleanse you."

Both communities connected the baptism of repentance with the purifying work of the Spirit (cf. Mt 3:11-12 with 1QS 4:20-21; cf. 1QH 16:11-12).[26] Remarkably, both of these texts intimately associate the concepts of "water (baptism), Spirit and fire"[27] in order to make the point that the Spirit's presence within their respective groups served to convict and cleanse them of sin. This too seems to proceed from Ezekiel 36:25-26, which conveys the expectation that the Spirit in the eschaton will be the agent for purifying disobedience.[28]

These two observations indicate, then, that the Essenes and John the Baptist went into the desert in conscious fulfillment of Isaiah 40:3, the place of the exile,[29] for the purpose of repenting of iniquity in order to prepare to participate in the conquest of the land upon the advent of the Messiah(s). They apparently differed, however, from other messianic movements of the period which did the same by embracing a spiritual rather than militant message for reclaiming Israel.

It should be noted, however, that John the Baptist was at odds with the Essenes in the matter of the restoration of Israel on two critical points. First, he did not isolate himself from the nation like the DSS people did; on the contrary, he reentered the land to call his country-men to repentance. Second, the message of John the Baptist did not focus on the observance of the Torah in the same manner as did Qum-ran. For him, the "way" of restoration was actualized by following Jesus.

Continuous Pesharim: Matthew 21:33-46; the **Pesher** *on Isaiah 1:1— 2:1; Isaiah 5:1-7.* When we refer to continuous *pesharim*, we mean those DSS passages that provide a verse-by-verse interpretation of a biblical text (most often one of the prophets), approximating a commentary. The standard "quotation-interpretation" formula accompanies the con-tinuous *pesharim*, even as it does the single *pesher*. The *pesher* on Isaiah 5:1-7 (and context) and Matthew 21:33-46 reinterpret those OT verses to say that their respective communities are the divine replacements of unfruitful Israel.

Isaiah 5:1-7 contains the famous parable predicting Israel's ominous future in exile because of spiritual unfaithfulness, thus creating the need for Israel's return to the land. As such, it is stamped by the Deu-teronomistic pattern of sin, exile and restoration. This parable is drawn on in the *pesher* on Isaiah of the DSS and in Matthew 21:33-44. *Pesher* on Isaiah 1:1—2:1 reads:

> *Frag. 1 col.* I   *Is 5:5* For now I will tell you what I am going to do with my vineyard: [. . . remove its fence so that it can be used for pasture, destroy] its wall so that you trample it. *Is 5:6* For [I will leave it flattened; they shall not prune it or weed it, brambles and thi[stles] will grow. The inter-pretation of the word: that he has deserted them [. . .] and as for what he says: "Brambles will grow, [and thistles": its interpretation concerns . . .] and what [it says . . .] of the path [. . .] his eyes.

> *Frag. 1 col.* II   The interpretation of the word concerns the last days, lay-ing waste the land through thirst and hunger. This will happen at the time of the visit to the land.

This commentary applies Isaiah's diagnosis of the spiritual unfaith-fulness of ancient Israel to the leaders in Jerusalem of its day who followed the Wicked Priest in the endtimes (cf. 4QpIs 1:2:1 with 1:2:2-7). These have disobeyed the law of the Lord and thereby incurred divine wrath on the nation of Israel (1:2:7-10). But as 4QpIsaiah 8-10:3:11-19 makes clear in its application of Isaiah 11:1-3 to the Qumran community, the Essenes, from whom the "Branch of David" will arise, constitute the restored Israel, the true vineyard of the Lord.[30] Matthew 21:33-44 similarly applies Isaiah 5:1-7 to the officials of Jerusalem (cf. Mt 21:33-34 with vv. 45-46; see also Mk 12:1-8; Lk 20:9-19), whose spiritual fruitlessness and repeated rejection of the prophets, especially Jesus, earmarked the nation of Israel for divine wrath.[31]

In fact, the four tenets of the Deuteronomistic tradition identified in Matthew 23—25 also occur here in Matthew 21:33-44: (1) Israel has been disobedient to God, now portrayed in terms of spiritual fruitlessness generated by the Pharisees (cf. Is 5:1-7 with Mt 21:33-34, 43, 45-46; see Mt 23—25); (2) God has sent his messengers to Israel (Mt 21:34); but (3) they were rejected, most notably Jesus (Mt 21:35-39); (4) consequently, God will judge the nation (Mt 21:40-44), which, for the first Gospel, would transpire at the fall of Jerusalem in A.D. 70 (recall Mt 23—25). Therefore, God has replaced unfaithful Israel led by the Pharisees with the Christian community (Mt 21:43).

Thematic pesharim. Thematic *pesharim* refer to those DSS texts that bring together various OT verses in tractlike form, the two most familiar of which are 4QTestimonia and 4QFlorilegium. Testimonia supplies OT verses without intervening comments, whereas Florilegium provides the phrase "this refers to" (*pesher* in Aramaic) accompanied by an interpretation after each quotation of an OT verse. Both of these DSS texts are deeply influenced by the theme of the restoration of Israel. Moreover, they find intriguing counterparts in the First Gospel (4QTestim and the Matthean OT fulfillment quotations; 4QFlor and Mt 11:25-30 and context).

Testimonia and Matthean OT fulfillment quotations. This discussion can be initiated by highlighting the debate over the relationship between the NT and testimonia collections. Rendall Harris put forth the hypothesis that a "Book of Testimonies" existed in the early church which brought together particular verses from the OT for devotional, liturgical and apologetic purposes. For Harris, such a book was compiled by

Matthew.[32] In the early 1950s, C. H. Dodd disagreed with Harris' testimonia theory, claiming instead that the NT draws not on isolated OT verses collected in one book but rather on blocks of OT material, clustered around three themes (eschatology, the new Israel and the suffering servant). For Dodd, if there were testimonia, they were the result, not the presupposition, of the work of early Christian biblical scholars.[33] But with the publication of the DSS Testimonia in the late 1950s, evidence had now been supplied from pre-Christian Judaism that testimonia did indeed exist. Thus with the third state of the debate, one reaches a compromise: Harris's theory was somewhat vindicated (though without following his argument that Matthew was the author of such a collection of texts), while Dodd's view continued to have much to commend itself as well (minus his contention that testimonia were the result, not the presupposition, of early Christian interpreters, which now has to be rejected).[34] What all of this means for this study is that in 4QTestimonia scholars now have an analog for understanding the Matthean OT fulfillment quotations. Here is the text of 4QTestimonia:

> *1* And****spoke to Moses saying: *Dt 5:28-29* "You have heard the sound of the words *2* of this people, what they said to you: all they have said is right. *3* If (only) it were given to me (that) they had this heart to fear me and keep all *4* my precepts all the days, so that it might go well with them and their sons for ever!" *5 Dt 18:18-19* "I would raise up for them a prophet from among their brothers, like you, and place my words *6* in his mouth, and he would tell them all that I command them. And it will happen that the man *7* who does not listen to my words, that the prophet will speak in my name, I *8* shall require a reckoning from him." *Blank 9* And he uttered his poem and said: *Num 24:15-17* "Oracle of Balaam, son of Beor, and oracle of the man *10* of penetrating eye, oracle of him who listens to the words of God and knows the Knowledge of the Most High, of one who *11* sees the vision of Shaddai, who falls and opens the eye. I see him, but not now, *12* I espy him, but not close up. A star has departed from Jacob, /and/a scepter/has arisen/from Israel. He shall crush *13* the temples of Moab, and cut to pieces all the sons of Sheth." *Blank 14* And about Levi he says: *Dt 33:8-11* "Give to Levi your *Thummin* and your *Urim*, to your pious man, whom *15* you tested at Massah, and with whom you quarreled about the waters of Meribah,/

he who/said to his father *16* [...] and to his mother 'I have not known you', and did not acknowledge his brothers, and his son did not *17* know. For he observed your word and kept your covenant. /They have made/your judgments/shine/for Jacob, *18* our law for Israel, they have placed incense before your face and a holocaust upon your altar. *19* Bless, ****, his courage and accept with pleasure the work of his hand! Crush/the loins/of his adversaries, and those who hate him, *20* may they not rise!" *21 Blank* At the moment when Joshua finished praising and giving thanks with his psalms, *22* he said *Jos 6:2* "Cursed be the man who rebuilds this city! Upon his first-born *23* will he found it, and upon his Benjamin will he erect its gates!"And now/ an/accursed/man, one of Belial, *24* has arisen to be a fowler's trap for his people and ruin for all his neighbors. *25* [. . .] will arise, to be the two instruments of violence. And they will rebuild *26* [this city and ere]ct for it a rampart and towers, to make it into a fortress of wickedness *27* [a great evil] in Israel, and a horror in Ephraim and Judah. *28* [. . . And they wi]ll commit a profanation in the land and a great blasphemy among the son of *29* [. . . And they will shed blo]od like water upon the ramparts of the daughter of Zion and in the precincts of *30* Jerusalem.

The logic behind this *pesher* seems to be that the authors consider the Qumran community, taught by the Teacher of Righteousness and anticipating the Davidic and Levitic Messiahs, to be true Israel, not the Hasmonean rulers. Four statements draw out this interpretation.

1. Deuteronomy 5:28-29 is quoted (lines 1-4) because the authors believe that Israel in large part did not obey the covenantal regulations (see Deut 5:1-29). Consequently, things did not go well for the nation; rather, its sin led to exile.

2. The promise of a prophet like Moses (cf. lines 5-8 with Deut 18:18-19) in the endtime was now beginning to be realized in the Teacher of Righteousness, who was leading the Essenes on the path of godliness.[35]

3. At the appointed time, God will send his two Messiahs—a Davidic prince (cf. lines 9-13 with Num 24:15-17) and a Levitic priest (cf. lines 14-20 with Deut 33:8-11)—for the purpose of rescuing the Qumran community.[36]

4. Therefore, the Hasmonean rulers are illegitimate leaders of Israel,

with their arrogation of the priesthood and kingship unto themselves; hence God's judgment on Simon and his two sons (lines 21-30 = the noncanonical Psalms of Joshua).[37]

A consideration of the Matthean OT fulfillment quotations uncovers a similar logic being utilized by the First Gospel, namely, that author wishes to make the point that Jesus is the true means for restoring Israel.[38] Space permits only the most cursory comments on these texts. In Matthew 1:22-23 and Isaiah 7:14 Jesus is called the Immanuel of God because he will save his people from their sins, (i.e., exile). Matthew the Evangelist (Mt 2:5-6; cf. Mic 5:1; 2 Sam 5:2) equates Jesus with the Messiah who will deliver his people. In Matthew 2:14-15 Jesus' return to Israel from Egypt after Herod the Great's death is portrayed as a type of exodus which, in light of Matthew 3:3, should be understood as his vocation to deliver Israel from the bondage of sin (cf. Hos 11:1). Matthew perceives in Jesus' ministry the fulfillment of Jeremiah's prophecy of Israel's restoration (Mt 2:17-18; cf. Jer 31:5).

The text of Isaiah 11:1 (cf. Is 4:2) envisions the coming of the Davidic deliverer, called the Branch. If *Nazarene* refers to *Nezer* (Branch),[39] then Matthew 2:23 can be viewed as equating Jesus with the Davidic Messiah, which would be in keeping with the DSS interpretation of its founder as a messianic figure (cf. 4QpIs 8-10:3:11-19; see also Mt 3:3; Is 40:3; 1QS 8:12-16). Isaiah 9:1-2 foretells of Israel's future restoration and the Gentiles' conversion, which the First Evangelist sees as resulting from Jesus' miracles (Mt 4:14-16). In both Matthew 8:17 and Isaiah 53:4 healing as a metaphor for Israel's restoration is applied to Jesus' dealings with the masses.

Obviously, the First Gospel perceives in Jesus the suffering servant who will be the catalyst for Israel's restoration to God (Mt 12:17-21; cf. Is 42:1-4). In Matthew 13:14-15 Israel's rejection of Jesus is interpreted as indicating that the nation's sin and exile persist (cf. Is 6:9-10). The overriding theme of Psalm 78 is the story of Israel—sin-exile-restoration—and for that reason is drawn on in Matthew 13:35. Isaiah 62:11 and Zechariah 9:9 predict that God will send a messianic deliverer to Israel, which is applied by Matthew to Jesus at his triumphant entry (Mt 21:4-5). The smiting of the shepherd and the scattering of the nation is applied in Matthew 26:56 (cf. v. 31) to Jesus' death and the disciples' subsequent departure, perhaps as an allusion to the continuing exile of Israel (cf. Zech 13:7). But possibly we are also to understand Matthew to be indicating that Jesus' crucifixion asborbed Israel's curse and exile.[40] The purchasing of a field by Jeremiah (Jer 32:6-15) was promissory of the coming restoration of Israel, even though that nation was about to go into exile. Perhaps Matthew (Mt 27:9-10; cf. Zech 11:12-13) understands the purchase of the field with Judas' blood, and at the expense of Jesus' death, to have conveyed a divine irony: that which cost Jesus his life (the cross and exile) was the basis for the true restoration of Israel.

The dominant theme, then, in all of these Matthean fulfillment texts is the restoration of Israel inaugurated by Jesus. Not to be overlooked in all of this is the situation in life necessitating the writing of Matthew's Gospel, which is commonly thought to have been the post-70 A.D. debates between the Matthean community and the Pharisees. Both of these groups (along with others as well) were touting their respective devotees as the true Israel to emerge after the fall of Jerusalem. Matthew portrays the Jesus movement as restored Israel over against the Pharisees; hence, his use of the OT as a witness to the truth of that message, not unlike what the DSS do vis-à-vis their debates with Pharisees, including the Hasmoneans.[41]

Florilegium and Matthew 11:25-30; 12:6. What follows is a significant portion of the 4QFlorilegium.

Frags. 1-3 *col.* I   *2 Sam 7:10 1* ["And] an enemy [will trouble him no mo]re, [nor will] the son of iniquity [afflict him again] as at the beginning. From the day on which *2* [I establish judges] over my people, Israel." This (refers to) the house which [they will establish] for [him] in the last days, as is written in the book of *3* [Moses: *Exod 15:17-18* "A temple of the Lord] will you establish with your hands. *YHWH* shall reign for ever and ever:" This (refers to) the house in which shall never enter *4* [...] either the Ammonite, or the Moabite, or the Bastard, or the foreigner, or the proselyte, never, because there [he will reveal] to the holy ones; *5* eternal [glory] will appear over it for ever; foreigners shall not again lay it waste as they laid waste, at the beginning, *6* the tem[ple of Is]rael for its sins. And he commanded to build for himself a temple of man, to offer him in it, *7* before him, the works of the law. And as for what he said to David: *2 Samuel 7:11* "I shall obtain for them rest from all *8* the sons of Belial, those who make them fall, to destr[oy them for their s]ins, when they come with the plans of Belial to make the s[ons] of *9* light fall, and to plot against them wicked plans so that they are trapped by Belial in their guilty error. *Blank 10* And *2 Samuel 7:12-14* "YHWH de[clares] to you that he will build you a house. I will raise up your seed after you and establish the throne of his kingdom *11* [for ev]er. I will be a father to him and he will be a son to me. This (refers to the) "branch of David," who will arise with the Interpreter of the law *12* [who will rise up] in Zi[on in] the last days, as it is written: *Amos 9:11* "I will raise up the hut of David which has fallen." This (refers to) "the hut of *13* David which has fallen," who will arise to save Israel. *Blank 14* Midrash of "Blessed the man who does not walk in the counsel of the wicked." The interpretation of this sa[ying: they are those who turn] aside from the path [of the wicked,] *15* as it is written in the book of Isaiah, the prophet, for the last days: *Isa 8:11* "And it happened that with a strong hand he turned me aside from walking on the path of *16* this people." And this (refers to) those about whom it is written in the book of Ezekiel, the prophet that *Ez 44:10* "[they should] not [defile themselves any more with all] *17* their filth." This (refers to) the sons of Zadok and to the men of his council, those who seek jus[tice] eagerly, who will come after them to the council of the community. *18 Ps 2:1* "Why do the nations [become agitated] and the people plo[t] nonsense? {the kings of the earth [ag]ree [and the ru]lers conspire together against YHWH and against *19* [his anointed one." Inter]pretation of the saying: the kings of the nations [become agitated and conspire against] the elect of Israel in the last days.

In its thematic approach, which collects together various OT texts, 4QFlorilegium is similar to 4QTestimonia. But it is different from 4QTestimonia in that intervening comments occur between the OT quotations. These editorial remarks begin with the formulaic phrase, "This refers to . . . ," and then offer an eschatological application of the OT texts to the Qumran community. In this regard, the overarching concern of 4QFlorilegium is to assert that the future, eschatological temple envisioned in the OT passage it quotes is now being actualized in the Qumran community, the endtime people of God. This is the true nature of Israel's rest. Table 3.1 shows the OT passages that make up 4QFlorilegium, along with their significance for the Essenes.[42]

4QFlorilegium	OT Passage	Qumran Interpretation
1-3.1:1-2	2 Samuel 7:10	The oracle predicting the Davidic dynasty and temple is applied to the Qumran community.
1-3.1:3-7	Exodus 15:17-18	A portion of the Hymn of Moses sung in commemoration of Israel's deliverance from ancient Egypt is applied to the Essenes, especially its promise of a future triumphant temple of the Lord. The Scrolls text envisions that such a prediction is being fulfilled in the Qumran community. The congregation, holy and separate from all those who are impure, constitutes the true temple because the Essenes truly obey the law of Moses.
1-3.1:7b-9	2 Samuel 7:11	Applies the Deuteronomic rest to the Qumran community, whose inheritance of the land will one day prevail over the sons of Belial, i.e., the Wicked Priest and his followers.
1-3.1:10-11	2 Samuel 7:12-14	The passage, with its hope of a Davidic seed/temple,[43] is thought to be realized in the Qumran community (the branch of David) and founded by the Teacher of Righteousness ("the Interpreter of the law"). Most probably, as George J. Brooke has argued, this indicates that the Essenes viewed themselves as the prophetic eschatological temple, with the Teacher of Righteousness serving as a type of the coming Aaronic Messiah.[44]
1-3.1:12-17	Amos 9:11	The passage, with its promise of the restoration of the Davidic line, is announced as being fulfilled in the DSS people. Moreover, though the reference to Psalm 1:1 has been lost, that verse, along with Isaiah 8:11 and Ezekiel 44:10 and their statements about God's election of pure Israelites, is perceived as pertaining to the sons of Zadok, the Qumran community.[45] These are the remnant of the last days.
1-3.1:18	Psalm 2:1	The passage pronounces judgment on the enemies of Israel, which includes all non-Qumranian Jews, because they oppose the Essenes, the elect of God in the last days. 4QFlorilegium 1-3:2:1—4:7 expands on this concept of the persecution of the Essenes in the endtimes, a period called the age of Belial, that is, the messianic woes. In other words the Essenes, not the Hasmonean leadership, constitute restored Israel.

Table 3.1. 4QFlorilegium and interpretation of OT passages

Matthew 11:25-30 is often thought to allude to *Sirach* 51[46] or possibly Exodus 33.[47]

> At that time Jesus declared, "I thank thee, Father, Lord of heaven and earth, that thou hast hidden these things from the wise and understanding and revealed them to babes; yea, Father, for such was thy gracious will. All things have been delivered to me by my Father; and no one knows the Son except the Father, and no one knows the Father except the Son and any one to whom the Son chooses to reveal him. Come to me, all who labor and are heavy laden, and I will give you rest. Take my yoke upon you, and learn from me; for I am gentle and lowly in heart, and you will find rest for your souls. For my yoke is easy, and my burden is light."

While I have argued elsewhere that Matthew 11:25-30 is indeed an allusion to *Sirach* 51,[48] Jon Laansma has expanded the semantical field of the Matthean passage by rooting it and Matthew 12:6 in 2 Samuel 7:1-16 and Psalm 2:7.[49] Laansma thoroughly demonstrates that Matthew 11:25-30 is dependent on both the rest motif in 2 Samuel 7:1 (see Mt 11:28-30) and the sonship theme in 2 Samuel 7:14 (cf. Ps 2:7; see Mt 11:25-27). As such, Matthew thereby presents Jesus as the Davidic Messiah, the Son of God, who is bringing to pass Israel's long-awaited rest(oration). Moreover, like 2 Samuel 7:1-16, Matthew 12:6 depicts Jesus as the new temple of God.[50] In doing so, the First Gospel seeks to exalt the way of Jesus over against the *halakhah* of the Pharisees.[51]

In light of Laansma's exegesis of Matthew 11:25-30 and 12:6, he is right to call attention to the remarkable parallels between those verses and 4QFlorilegium, and its use of the same OT texts.[52] Noteworthy also is that both the Scrolls text and the Matthean passages present the enemies of true Israel as being their opponents (the Pharisees; cf. 4QFlor lines 7-9, 18-19, 1-3:2:1-5; 4:1-7[53] with Mt 11:25-30; 23:1-39), who will be defeated at God's appointed time.

Conclusion

This chapter has been concerned to draw out the basic similarities in the way the DSS and Matthew reinterpreted the OT to present their communities as the fulfillment of the hopeful restoration of Israel, which is the final component of Israel's story. The investigation here focused on the use of *pesher* by these two writings, which make essentially three points:

☐ The restoration of Israel has been inaugurated by Jesus or the Teacher of Righteousness respectively (cf. Mt 3:3 with 1QS 8:12-16).

☐ This inauguration took place despite opposition from the nation's leadership (cf. Mt 21:33-46 with 4QpIs 1:1:1—2:2:1).

☐ The means for participating in Israel's rest(oration) is to follow the precepts of the Teacher of Righteousness or Jesus (cf. 4QTestim; 4QFlor with Matthew's OT fulfillment quotations and Mt 11:25-30; 12:6, repectively).

Although the First Gospel has proved to be fertile ground for comparing it with *pesher* hermeneutics, it should be noted that such an interpretive technique is not restricted to Matthew, for Paul's writings and Hebrews give evidence of being strongly influenced by a similar reading of the OT (e.g., Rom 3:10-18; 10:6-8; 2 Cor 6:14-7:1; Heb 1:5-14; 10:5-10, 37-39). But this should not occasion surprise, for those two authors were also heavily engaged in debating their opponents over who formed the true Israel. As such, *pesher* for them, as for Matthew and the DSS, can be understood to be the hermeneutic of legitimation. Ironically, however, at the end of the day Pharisaism won out over against the Essenes and the Matthean congregation in terms of the official reconstitution of Judaism after the fall of Jerusalem in A.D. 70.

Chapter Four

Messianism in the DSS & in the NT

Retelling the Story of Israel

Introduction

Modern scholarship has made it clear that there was no monolithic messianic expectation in Second Temple Judaism.[1] Nevertheless, as N. T. Wright argues, despite the diversity and unstandardized nature of the evidence, the idea of a Messiah was latent in several varieties of Judaism. Four types of sources in particular take the OT as their point of departure in presenting the hope of a Messiah: the DSS, *Psalms of Solomon*, Josephus and some Jewish apocalyptic works.[2]

The DSS provide unambiguous witness to the expectation of a messianic deliverer (cf., e.g., 4QFlor with 2 Sam 7:11-14; Ps 2:1; Amos 9:11; cf. 1QSa with Ps 61:2; Is 11:1-5; Mic 4:13; see also 1QSb). *Psalms of Solomon* 17:21-32 (c. 50 B.C.) explicitly mentions the arrival of a Messiah who will deliver Israel and crush that nation's enemies (cf. Ps 2; 18; 104; Is 42). Josephus refers to an unnamed prophecy in the OT of a coming savior that incited the Jews to revolt against Rome in A.D. 66. That passage merits quoting:

But what more than all else incited them to the war was an ambiguous oracle, likewise found in their sacred scriptures, to the effect that at the time one from their country would become ruler of the world. This they understood to mean someone of their own race, and many of their wise men went astray in their interpretation of it. The oracle, however, in reality signified the sovereignty of Vespasian, who was proclaimed Emperor on Jewish soil. For all that, it is impossible for men to escape their fate, even though they foresee it. Some of these portents, then, the Jews interpreted to please themselves, others they treated with contempt, until the ruin of their country and their own destruction convicted them of their folly. (J.W. 6.5.4 [312-15])

Two observations regarding this passage are pertinent to the concern of this chapter. (1) The text clearly roots the Jewish revolt in messianism, quite possibly based on a *pesher* reading of Daniel 2 (or Dan 7, 9).[3] (2) Josephus subverts the story of Israel by identifying the predicted ruler with the Roman general Vespasian. What Jews should have done, therefore (according to Josephus), was to submit to Rome, for only in that way could they be released from exile.[4]

Finally, the Jewish apocalyptic writings of *1 Enoch* 37-71; *4 Ezra* 11—12; and *2 Apocalypse of Baruch* 39—40 also refer to a coming messianic deliverer who will defeat the enemies of Israel.[5]

John J. Collins reaches a similar conclusion to Wright's regarding messianic expectation in late Second Temple Judaism. After discarding what he believes are two extreme scholarly positions relative to the subject—uniformity of messianism on the one hand, no commonality of ideas on the other hand—Collins argues that amidst the diversity there emerges in post-Hasmonaean Judaism four messianic paradigms: Davidic Messiah (king), priest, prophet and the Danielic Son of Man.[6] Collins then proceeds to analyze the DSS in terms of those personages.[7]

The concern of this chapter is to survey messianic hope as espoused in the DSS and in the NT by utilizing in particular the insights of Collins and Wright. Collins' fourfold category of messianic expectation operative in the DSS will prove to be a useful frame of reference for comparing the Scrolls with the evidence of the NT, while Wright's emphasis on Jesus' retelling the story of Israel as depicted in the Gospels will shed important light on how the Qumran community related its message to mainstream Judaism. Along the way, significant differences will also surface between the two bodies of literature vis-à-vis their understanding of messianism. Simply stated, the thesis of the ensuing discussion is that the respective messianisms of the DSS and the NT represent a retelling, actually subverting, of the story of Israel as understood by many Jews in late Second Temple Judaism.

Davidic Messiah

D. S. Russell's survey of the concept of Messiah in the OT provides a convenient point of entrance into the discussion of how the Davidic Messiah is presented in the DSS and in the NT.[8] *Messiah* (the Hebrew term) or *Christ* (the Greek word) means "anointed" with reference to one who is especially set apart for God's work. As such, this term is most often applied in the OT to the kings of Israel (e.g., 2 Sam 19:21; 23:1; Lam 4:20) and in the postexilic period to the priests of God (Ps 133:2; Zech 4:14). Emerging out of the prophetic material toward the close of the OT, however, is a more general messianic hope (though the word *messiah* is not actually used for the concept) of a future golden age, the kingdom of God, in which the fortunes of Israel will be restored and the surrounding nations judged (Is 40:66; Ezek 40:48; Joel 3; Zech 9:9). The conclusion Russell draws from the preceding data is that the role of the Messiah in the OT is restricted to a nontechnical sense; that is, there is not some single individual anticipated as the Messiah but rather a broad messianic expectation of the coming kingdom of God.

By the end of Second Temple Judaism (and beyond), however, that longing had solidified into the hope for a Davidic Messiah who would effect the overthrow of Israel's enemies and the restoration of Israel's land. Wright identifies four historical proofs from that period which demonstrate that such a conviction was widespread[9]:

☐ Despised though he may have been, Herod the Great's (37-4 B.C.) temple project was designed to present himself as the Davidic king.

☐ Josephus informs us that various messianic (Davidic) movements intensified after Herod's death from 4 B.C. to A.D. 70.

☐ The NT (1st century A.D.) portrays Jesus as the Davidic Messiah (see below).

☐ The Jewish revolutionary Bar-Kokhba (A.D. 132-135) was hailed by the venerable Rabbi Akiba as the "Son of the Star" and the "Son of David," in a rebellion that was crushed by the Romans. With this historical backdrop in mind, I now turn to the Davidic Messiah of the DSS and the NT. For both, note that this personage is employed to retell the story of Israel.

The Davidic Messiah in the DSS. A number of Scrolls texts allude to a Davidic Messiah, either as the "branch (or shoot) of David," the "prince of the congregation" or both, as well as the "Messiah of Israel." We summarize each category below.

Pesher on Isaiah 8-10:3:11-19 quotes Isaiah 11:1-5, a key OT promise about the coming Davidic deliverer. Lines 18-19 read: "[The interpretation of the word concerns the shoot] of David which will sprout [in the final days, since] [with the breath of his lips he will execute] his enemies and God will support him with [the Spirit of] courage." No doubt this passage envisions a coming Davidic king who will fight on behalf of the faithful in the eschatological war.

The 4QFlorilegium, as was discussed in the last chapter, expresses the conviction that a Davidic deliverer will come. Quoting passages like 2 Samuel 7:12-14 and Amos 9:11, 4QFlorilegium 1-3:1:10-19 speaks of the revival of the branch of David who will one day vindicate the Qumran community by destroying the enemies of God.

Pesher on Genesis (4Q252) 5:1-7 applies Genesis 49:10 (the promise of a continuous Davidic ruler) to the Qumran community:

> (1 Gen 4:9:10) A sovereign shall [not] be removed from the tribe of Judah. While Israel has dominion, (2) there will [not] lack someone who sits on the throne of David. For "the staff" is the covenant of royalty, (3) [the thou]sands of Israel are "the feet." Until the messiah of justice comes, the branch (4) of David. For to him and to his descendants has been given the covenant of royalty over his people for all everlasting generations, which (5) he has observed [...] the Law with the men of the Community, for (6) [...] it is the assembly of the men of [...].

Here the Essenes are associated with "the messiah of justice . . . the branch of David" (cf. lines 3-4 with Jer 23:5; 33:15) who will rule over Israel and the nations when he arrives.

Appendix B to the Rule of the Benediction (1QSb 5:21) utters a blessing on "the prince of the congregation, that God will raise up for him the kingdom of his people." As Collins observes, the blessing that follows is heavily indebted to Isaiah 11:

> "To dispense justice with [equity to the oppressed] of the land (Isa 11:4a). (May you smite the peoples) with the might of your hand and ravage the earth with your scepter; may you bring death to the ungodly with the breath of your lips! (Isa 11:4b) . . . and everlasting might, the spirit of knowledge and of the fear of God (Isa 11:2); may righteousness be the girdle (of your loins) and may your reins be girded (with faithfulness) (Isa 11:5)."[10]

Moreover, a subsequent statement (1QSb 5:27), "for God has established as the scepter," alludes to Balaam's oracle in Numbers 24:17.[11] In view of this, it is perspicuous that the prince of the congregation is a messianic figure, almost certainly to be equated with the branch of David.[12] Damascus Document 7:19 also connects the prince of the congregation with Numbers 24:17, thus implying messianic overtones:

> The Star is the interpreter of the law who shall come to Damascus, as it is written, "a star shall come forth out of Jacob and a scepter shall rise out of Israel." The scepter is the prince of the whole congregation, and when he comes he shall smite all the children of Sheth.

Two observations are in order about this text. First, the reference to Numbers 24:17 suggests that the prince of the congregation is a Davidic-type. Second, the prince will engage in holy war when he comes (cf. a similar use of Numbers 24:17, though without reference to the prince of the congregation, in 4QTestim 9:13; 1QM 11:6 [though 1QM 5:1 does mention the prince of the congregation]).

Further confirmation that the prince of the congregation in the DSS is a Davidic Messiah can be found in the Dying Messiah Text (4Q285), where the prince is explicitly equated with the branch of David: "the prince of the congregation, the bran[ch of David] will kill him."[13] Moreover, it should be noted that such a personage is associated with eschatological war. I mentioned above that 4QpIsaiah 8:10:3:18 contains a reference to the branch of David. It should now be noted that 4QpIsaiah 2:6.2:15 refers to the prince of the congregation, thus leading to the conclusion that the two figures are one and the same.

No doubt another personage in the DSS connected with the Davidic Messiah is the "Messiah of Israel" (CD 12:23—13:1; 14:19; 19:10-11; 1QS 9:16; 10:11; 1QSa 2:11-22). Leaving aside for the moment the question of whether the Messiah of Israel is separate from the Messiah of Aaron, the point to be made here is that such a figure is portrayed as a Davidic-like king who will engage in holy war on behalf of the Essenes. Collins draws together the preceding diverse strands in the Scrolls—branch of David, prince of the congregation, Messiah of Israel[14]—under the umbrella of the Davidic Messiah:

> The portrait of the ideal king that emerges from this corpus is sketchy but consistent. He is the scepter who will smite the nations, slay the wicked with the breath of his lips, and restore the Davidic dynasty. Hence his role in the eschatological war. He is also the messiah of righteousness, who will usher in an era of peace with justice. He is presumably a human figure, although he is endowed with the spirit of the Lord. He is expected to restore a dynasty rather that rule forever himself. Most of the passages we have considered, however, are brief and elliptic, and the picture could be filled out in various ways.[15]

In appropriating the tradition of the Davidic Messiah, however, the Qumran community altered the common interpretation at two critical points which served to subvert the prevailing telling of the story of Israel. First, the authors of the DSS react to the reigning Hasmonaean dynasty, criticizing it for replacing the Zadokite priesthood. In the OT, Zadok emerged as Solomon's high priest (the other, Abiathar, was banished; 1 Kings 2:26-27). Furthermore, Ezekiel 44:9-31 prophesied that the Zadokite priesthood would be instrumental in reestablishing the temple in the last days. These two factors—association with the Davidic/Solomonic dynasty and a future role in building the temple—legitimated the Zadokite lineage as the true priesthood. The wresting away of that authority by the Hasmonaeans, therefore, disqualified them to rule Israel and govern the temple cultus, according to the Essenes. Damascus Document 3:20—4:4 epitomizes this conviction:

> Those who remained steadfast in it will acquire eternal life, and all the glory of Adam is for them. As God established for them by means of Ezekiel the prophet, saying: *Ez 44:15* "The priests and the levites and the sons of *Col IV* Zadok who maintained the service of my temple when the

children of Israel strayed far away from me, shall offer the fat and the blood." The priests are the converts of Israel who left the land of Judah; and the "levites" are those who joined them; and the sons of Zadok are the chosen of Israel, "those called by name" who stood up at the end of days.

The meaning of this for the Qumran community is obvious: only they constituted the true Israel because only they continued the Zadokite lineage. Hence, when the Davidic Messiah comes, only the Essenes will be delivered by him, not the rest of Israel and certainly not the Gentile nations.

A second point emerges from the first in the DSS undermining of the conventional telling of the story of Israel, namely, not only would the rest of Israel not be delivered by the Davidic Messiah but, more than that, they would be destroyed by the Messiah and his army—the Qumran community (cf. 1QM with 1QS 1:23-24; 2:14-17; 9:16).

2. The Davidic Messiah in the NT. N. T. Wright's encapsulation of the story of Israel as told by many Jews approximate to the time of Jesus sets the stage for our discussion of the topic of the NT and the Davidic Messiah:

> Many if not most second-Temple Jews, then, hoped for the new exodus, seen as the final return from exile. The story would reach its climax; the great battle would be fought; Israel would truly "return" to her land, saved and free; YHWH would return to Zion. This would be, in the metaphorical sense, the end of the world, the ushering in at last of YHWH's promised new age. From the perspective of covenant history, this complex event would be climactic, and not merely a paradigmatic example of a general principle such as the importance of social justice. Moreover, this whole set of ideas and themes belongs together as a whole, not as a collection of abstract ideas, but precisely as a story. And the whole story clearly has to do with the kingdom of god, even when that phrase itself, or something like it, does not occur. This I suggest, is the proper and historically appropriate context in which to understand Jesus' sayings about the kingdom, or kingship, of Israel's god.[16]

In what follows I will utilize Wright's insights into the Gospels' portraits of Jesus as the Davidic Messiah. Three key aspects conveniently summarize such a presentation: the anointing of Jesus as the Davidic

Messiah; the confession of Jesus as the Davidic Messiah; the presence of the kingdom of God through the words and works of Jesus, the Davidic Messiah.

All four Gospels root Jesus' prophetic ministry in his baptism (Mt 3:13-17; Mk 1:9-11; Lk 3:21-22; Jn 1:29-34). It is commonly recognized that Psalm 2:7 ("you are my son") and Isaiah 42:1 ("with you [the servant] I am well-pleased") stand behind the voice heard at Jesus' baptism, thus attributing to him a messianic role.[17] Beyond this, Wright makes the case, two other OT passages inform Jesus' baptism—Isaiah 11:2 (the Davidic Messiah's anointing with God's Spirit) and 1 Samuel 16:13 (where the divine Spirit comes powerfully upon David after being anointed by Samuel). Taken together, the preceding four OT passages (1 Sam 16:13; Ps 2:7; Is 11:2; 42:1) give the impression that the Gospels portray Jesus' baptism as his anointing as the Davidic Messiah.[18]

The Synoptic Gospels report that early in his ministry at Caesarea Philippi, Jesus was perceived to be the Messiah and that, although he redefined the concept (see below), Jesus accepted the title (Mt 16:13-20; Mk 8:27-30; Lk 9:18-21). Moreover, Peter's confession of Jesus as Messiah precipitated the ensuing journey to Jerusalem. Wright draws two important conclusions from this: (1) Like David of old, Jesus was understood by his disciples to be the king-in-waiting; that is, he was anointed as the Davidic King (baptism and confession), but he was not yet enthroned as such. (2) Related to this, Jesus' journey to Jerusalem was initially interpreted by his followers as the goal of Jesus' ministry, at which point he was expected to be crowned as the Davidic Messiah.[19]

Jesus' words and works also bespeak the inauguration of the kingdom of God through him, both aspects of which are Davidic in orientation, as Wright points out. Under the category of Jesus' words are those sayings portraying him, like King David, as Israel's shepherd (cf. Mt 18:12-14; Lk 15:3-7; Jn 10; Mk 14:27; Mt 26:30; 10:6; Lk 10:3; 12:32; Mt 9:36 par. Mk 6:34 with 2 Sam 24:17; 1 Kings 22:17; Is 44:28; Ezek 34:23-24; Zech 11:4-17; 13:7).[20] Such OT imagery of the Davidic Messiah as the shepherd of Israel continued into the intertestamental period. The two are connected, for example, in *Psalms of*

Solomon 17:21; 39:42:

> See, Lord, and raise up for them their king,
> The son of David, to rule over your servant Israel
> In the time known to you, O God. . . . (17:21)

> His hope will be in the Lord.
> Then who will succeed against him,
> Mighty in his actions
> And strong in the fear of God?
> Faithfully and righteously shepherding the Lord's flock,
> He will not let any of them stumble in their pasture.
> He will lead them all in holiness
> And there will be not arrogance among them,
> That any should be oppressed.
> This is the beauty of the king of Israel
> Which God knew,
> To raise him over the house of Israel
> To discipline it. (39:42)

Moreover, the claim that in Jesus one greater than Solomon was present (Mt 12:41-42; Lk 11:31) signified that he was the Messiah who would build the eschatological temple and establish the Davidic kingdom.[21] Furthermore, Jesus' appeal to David's example of feeding his followers as an analog for Jesus' doing the same on the sabbath (Mt 12:3-4; Mk 2:25-28; Lk 6:3-5) conveyed his sense of Davidic royalty.[22] Added to this is Jesus' application of Psalm 110, a hymn associated with David, to himself (Mt 22:41-45; Mk 12:35-37; Lk 20:41-44).[23]

The second aspect of Jesus' ministry that displayed the kingdom of God was his works, which are programmatically set forth in Luke 4:18-21, a quotation of Isaiah 61:1-3.

> "The Spirit of the Lord is upon me,
> because he has anointed me to preach good news to the poor.
> He has sent me to proclaim release to the captives
> and recovering of sight to the blind,
> to set at liberty those who are oppressed,
> to proclaim the acceptable year of the Lord."
> And he closed the book, and gave it back to the attendant, and sat down;

and the eyes of all in the synagogue were fixed on him. And he began to say to them, "Today this scripture has been fulfilled in your hearing."

Wright is quite correct to argue that Isaiah 61 is an echo of Isaiah 11:1-10, a prophecy of the works of the coming Davidic king. Thus Luke 4:18-21 should be understood to present Jesus as the Davidic Messiah, who was anointed by God's Spirit to accomplish the supernatural purpose of restoring Israel from her exile.[24] The DSS also draw on Isaiah 61 (cf. Is 11) in delineating a similar list of miracles to be performed by the eschatological Messiah on behalf of Israel. Thus 11QMelchizedek 2:18-19 reads,

> The messenger [of Isaiah 52:7] is [the ano]inted of the spirit about whom Dan[iel] spoke . . . [and the messenger of] good who announces salv[ation is the one about whom it is written that] he will send him *Isa 61:2-3* "to comfo[rt the afflicted, to watch over the afflicted ones of Zion."]

Similarly, another text (4Q521 2:2:1, 7-14; 11—13) alludes to Isaiah 61:1-3 (cf. Is 11):

> For the heavens and the earth will listen to his Messiah. . . . For he will honour the devout upon the throne of eternal royalty, freeing prisoners, giving sight to the blind, straightening out the twisted . . . and the Lord will perform marvelous acts . . . for he will heal the badly wounded and will make the dead live, he will proclaim good news to the meek, give lavishly to the needy, lead the exiled and enrich the hungry.[25]

In summation, then, Jesus' anointing at his baptism, the disciple's confession of him as Messiah and the purported arrival of the kingdom of God through Jesus' words and works indicate that the Gospels perceived him to be the Davidic king who had come to restore Israel (see also Mt 1:1; 9:27; 12:23; 15:22; 20:30-34; 21:9, 15; Mk 12:35-37; Acts 2:29-31; 13:23; Rom 1:3-4; 2 Tim 2:8; Rev 5:5; 22:16).

Jesus' presentation of himself as the Davidic Messiah took an unfamiliar turn, however, which ultimately subverted the story of Israel's restoration. Wright's treatment of this retelling of Israel's story is insightful, three key points of which I here review.

First, returning to the subject of the inauguration of the kingdom of God through Jesus' words and works, it is noteworthy that both categories redefine the true Israel. Thus the parables about the restoration of Israel (Mt 13; Mk 4)[26] invite sinners and outcasts to join the ranks of the remnant, because they follow Jesus (e.g., Lk 15). Such a message certainly sounded strange to that nation which, at least since the Maccabean revolt, prided itself in obeying the Torah and thus separated itself from the ritually and morally unclean. The maimed, blind, lame, deaf and dumb were not recognized as full Israelites. Wright observes that for a first-century Jew, Jesus' healing would be viewed as restoring to membership in Israel those who, because of their physical illnesses, were thought to be ritually unclean.[27] Jesus' miracles reinforced his redefinition of those who constituted the true people of God. His healings in these categories, therefore, served not only a physical purpose but also a spiritual one. They reintegrated the marginalized into the worshiping community.[28]

Second, Jesus' retelling of Israel's story of sin-exile-restoration involved redefining the enemy. Israel's nemesis was not Rome but Satan. Three passages highlight this reality, as Wright points out.[29] The Beelzebul controversy (Mt 12:22-32; Mk 3:20-30; Lk 11:14-23) reflects the fact that the Jewish leadership, in attributing to Jesus' miracles the power of Satan, accused him of dishonoring the covenant with Yahweh, particularly in his dismissal of the boundary markers of the Torah (sabbath-keeping, dietary laws, circumcision) and later with his cleansing of the temple. This was perceived as nothing less than being in league with Israel's enemies, now personified in Rome—tantamount to being in cahoots with Satan. In effect, Jesus' refutation of such an accusation redefined Israel's real enemy: his miracles were by the power of God, not Beelzebul, and in actuality were defeating the evil one, the ultimate source of Israel's struggles. To miss this was to invite natural disaster because such a misperception would inexorably lead Israel into battle with Rome, the wrong opponent. Similarly, Luke 12:4-7 (cf. Mt 10:28-31) suggests that Israel's enemy was not Rome (the one who had the power to kill the body) but rather Satan (the one who had the power to cast the nation into Gehenna).[30] So also the story of the attempted exorcism and the returning of seven demons (Mt 12:43-45; Lk 11:24-26) makes the point that Israel's deliverance needed to be from Satan. That is, the nation's restoration would not come about by revolting against her physical enemies, something regrettably attempted since the Maccabeans, but rather by the expulsion of Satan.

The third aspect of Jesus' retelling of the story of Israel reaches the heart of the matter: Jesus came as the *suffering* Davidic Messiah (e.g., Mk 8:31; 9:31-32; 10:32-34). That such a portrayal amounted to a *reversal* of messianic Jewish expectation in Second Temple Judaism is indicated not only by the disciples' shock at Jesus' prediction of his affliction but also by the fact that there is no clear concept of a suffering Messiah in pre-Christian Judaism. Joseph Fitzmyer assesses the data:

> The notion of a suffering messiah is not found in the OT or in any texts of pre-Christian Judaism. Str-B (2.273-299) says that the "Old Synagogue" knew of "a suffering Messiah, for of whom no death was determined, i.e. the Messiah ben David" and a "dying Messiah, of whom no suffering was mentioned," i.e. the Messiah ben Joseph (ibid 273-274). Yet when it cites the passages from Rabbinic literature (ibid 282-291) that speak of the suffering Messiah ben David, they are all drawn from late texts, which scarcely show that the expectations of such a figure existed among Palestinian Jews in or prior to the time of Jesus. The same has to be said of the texts about the dying Messiah ben Joseph (ibid 292-299). Str-B rightly rejects the implication found at times in Christian commentators that Mark 8:31; Matt 16:21 refer to a "suffering Messiah," and the latter is not a "messianic" title without further ado. Where in pre-Christian Judaism does one find a "Son of Man" as an agent of Yahweh anointed for the salvation, deliverance of his people? True, in Tg Jonathan the "servant" of Isa 52:13 is identified as "the Messiah": "See, my servant, the Messiah, shall prosper; he will be exalted, great, very mighty", and 53:10c is made to read, "They will look upon the kingdom of their Messiah, many sons and daughters will be theirs." Yet no use of "Messiah" is made in the crucial verse, 53:12. It is not surprising that the "Servant" of Isaiah 52-53 was eventually identified with a messiah in the Jewish tradition; but it still remains to be shown that this identification existed in pre-Christian Judaism or in Judaism contemporary with the NT.[31]

Sometimes adherents of a pre-Christian origin of the suffering Messiah appeal to three texts thought to be important exceptions to the rule: *4 Ezra* 7:28-30; *Targum of Isaiah* 53; and the "Pierced Messiah" text in the

DSS (4Q285). The first mentions the death of the Messiah as the climax of the temporal messianic kingdom. However, it is important to note that there the Messiah does not suffer; rather, after having lived long and well for four hundred years, he simply dies with the rest of humanity. His death, therefore, has no apparent theological significance. Nor can the Aramaic translation (*Targum*) of Isaiah 53 be used as evidence for the concept of a suffering Messiah because it transposes (probably in reaction to Christianity) the afflictions of the suffering servant of Isaiah 53 *from* the Messiah *to* Israel or the surrounding Gentile nations (see again Fitzmyer's comments above). Moreover, both texts are dated after the birth of Christ and cannot be used as testimony for pre-Christian Jewish messianic understanding. With regard to the Pierced Messiah Text, it was noted earlier that this passage cannot for grammatical reasons be invoked to support the idea of a suffering Messiah.

Undoubtedly, although pre-Christian Judaism attributed righteous suffering to Jewish martyrs on behalf of Israel, as Wright observes, such persecution was thought to rally Israel to the Torah and thereby motivate God to overthrow the nation's enemies.[32] Yet Jesus' sufferings were an entirely different matter because his afflictions took place on a cross. This would have signified two things to Jews. First, Jesus' death on a cross indicated that he was accursed of God (Deut 21:23).[33] That is, he disobeyed the law of Moses and therefore suffered its consequences—the Deuteronomic curses. Second, Jesus' crucifixion by the Romans will have meant to Jews that God gave the disobedient Jesus[34] over to Israel's enemies to symbolize his defeat and "exile." Thus Jesus' self-portrait as a suffering Davidic Messiah will have subverted the story of Israel at its core.

The message of the early church, however, pointed to the paradox of the cross as the solution to Israel's plight of sin and exile. In his death Jesus embodied the Deuteronomic curses because of *Israel's* disobedience along with its exile and defeat at the hands of its enemies. But in his resurrection Jesus, now vindicated by God, offered to Israel the Deuteronomic blessings and restoration (e.g., Acts 2:22-40; 3:17-26). In essence, then, Jesus' defeat was actually the victory of God over sin.[35]

Priest
Another messianic figure occurring in both the DSS and in the NT is

the eschatological priest. As Collins notes, a priestly Messiah has its roots in the expression "the anointed priest" in Leviticus 4:3, 5, 16; 6:20. Moreover, after the Babylonian exile, the high priest Joshua, along with the Davidic heir Zerubbabel, shared the leadership of the Jewish community.[36] During the Hasmonaean dynasty, the roles of priest and king were combined into one office. With this background in mind, it is now important to turn to the presentation of the eschatological priest in the DSS and in the NT, especially relative to Hebrews.

The DSS and the eschatological priest. Two topics are here briefly addressed: the names of the messianic priest in the DSS and his purpose. Both of these aspects are involved in the retelling of the story of Israel in the Scrolls.

Two names are used by the Qumran community for the eschatological priest: "the Messiah of Aaron" and "the interpreter of the Law." Concerning the first of these, the discovery of the Damascus Document occasioned considerable interest among DSS scholars because of its reference to coming Messiahs: "until there arises the Messiah of Aaron and Israel" (CD 12:23—13:1); "[until there arises the Messiah] of Aaron and Israel" (CD 14:19); "when there comes the Messiah of Aaron and Israel" (CD 19:10-11); "until there arises the Messiah of Aaron and Israel" (CD 20:1). The singular noun *Messiah*, however, generated debate: Did one Messiah represent all Israel, or did the writer refer to two Messiahs, one from the priestly line of Aaron and another a Davidic deliverer? That issue was settled when the Rule of the Community surfaced, for it used the plural noun (see 1QS 9:16, 10:11, "Messiahs of Aaron and Israel"). These texts, along with others like appendix A of the Rule of the Congregation (2:11-22) and 4QTestimonia, have convinced most DSS experts that the Qumran community expected two Messiahs—a Levitic priest and a Davidic deliverer, with the former taking precedence over the latter.[37] The reason for this bifurcation of the Messiah into two personages undoubtedly was that the Essenes objected to the Hasmonaean combination of the two.

The second name for the eschatological priest in the DSS is the "interpreter of the law" which, as Collins demonstrates, is a synonym for the coming Messiah of Aaron (see e.g., 4QFlor 1:6-11; 4QTestim 13—

17; CD 7:18-19; 4Q541).[38] The Teacher of Righteousness is the prototype of such a personage (see 4QpPs [4Q171] 3:13-16; 1QpHab 2:8-9; cf. 7:4-5).[39]

Third, there is also evidence in the DSS that the eschatological priest was to be associated, if not equated, with Melchizedek. The primary document in this regard is 11QMelchizedek. That text reinterprets the Year of Jubilee (Lev 25:13) and the return from the Babylonian exile (Is 6:1-3) as ultimately finding their fulfillment in the Qumran community. Three points dominate the work:

1. The DSS people are the true inheritors of the land of Israel (11QMelch 2:1-4).

2. They have followed the true interpretation of the law (2:20-24); therefore Melchizedek, the heavenly priest, has made atonement for their sins (11QMelch 2:6-9).

3. When Melchizedek, the heavenly priest, wages eschatological war against those who follow Belial, which have departed from the true Torah (11QMelch 2-5; 11-13; 25), the Essenes will be vindicated and rule with him (11QMelch 2:10-11, 14-24; cf. 1QM 17:1-9, where Michael most likely is to be equated with Melchizedek).[40]

The purpose of the Essenes' aligning themselves with Melchizedek was, as the true descendants of Aaron (see CD 6:2-6; 1QSa 2), to legitimate their interpretation of the law of Moses over against the Jerusalem leadership's reading of the Torah. Thus to follow the Qumran community's *halakhah* was solely the means for entering the New Covenant and the Deuteronomic rest (see, e.g., CD 1:5-11; 1QS 1:16—2:25; 11QMelch 2:4-8).

2. Hebrews and Jesus, the eschatological priest. The book of Hebrews (especially Heb 3:1—7:28) provides the most extensive treatment in the NT of Jesus as the eschatological priest. I will devote a whole chapter later to a comparative analysis of Hebrews and the DSS, but for the current purpose I wish to make only two observations. First, in attempting to prevent his audience from regressing back to Judaism, the author of Hebrews demonstrates the superiority of Jesus to the Aaronic priesthood by revealing him to be of the order of Melchizedek. We may summarize the argument of Hebrews 4:14—7:28 using syllogistic logic:

Premise A: Melchizedek is greater than Aaron (Heb 7:1-19).

Premise B: Christ is of the order of Melchizedek (Heb 4:5-10; 6:20).

Conclusion: Therefore Christ, the Son of God, is superior to Aaron and his priesthood (Heb 7:20-28).

Second, Christ, the great High Priest, has provided the Deuteronomic rest which Judaism failed to achieve, and that apart from the law (see Heb 3:1-19).

Hebrews' use of the personage of Melchizedek in its presentation of Christ as the heavenly High Priest is similar to the three points that emerged in my survey of Melchizedek.

1. As noted above, Jesus offers the longed-for Deuteronomic rest (Heb 3:1—7:28).

2. He can do so because of his atonement for the sins of his followers (Heb 9:11-28). Those who depart from the faith, however, are subject to condemnation (e.g., Heb 2:1-4; 4:1-13; 5:11—6:8; 10:19-39).

3. Jesus, as the eschatological priest, has appeared in history to defeat disobedience (produced by the devil) and its consequence of death (Heb 2:14-18).

In the first two observations—Jesus' superiority over Aaron and Jesus' achievement of the Deuteronomic rest apart from the Torah—one finds a rewriting of the story of Israel.

The Prophet-like-Moses

Some Second Temple Jewish groups believed, based on Deuteronomy 18:15-19, that the end times would witness the arrival of a messianic prophet-like-Moses, who would lead Israel to a new exodus from bondage, reestablish the covenant and bring a better revelation of God, that is, a new law or more accurate interpretation of the old law.[41] The following remarks about the prophet-like-Moses as understood in the DSS and in the NT will focus on the roles attributed to him by those writings. This prophet is expected to conduct a new exodus into the wilderness in preparation for the conquest of "Canaan" (Israel), reestablish the covenant and provide new revelation concerning the Torah.

1. The DSS and the prophet-like-Moses. It is well known that the

DSS community attached paramount importance to the historical Moses. Its very reason for existence was to obey the Torah stringently, which the rest of Israel had failed to do (see, e.g., 1QS 1:1-11; 6:6-8; 4QMMT 93-118; CD 15:7-15). But according to Rule of the Community 9:11 and 4QTestimonia 5—8, the Qumran congregation also expected a prophet like Moses to appear on the scene at the end of history. The two—historical Moses and eschatological Moses—are of course conceptually related, the latter to reprise the roles of the former but in more profound ways. Rule of the Community 9:9-11 makes this clear:

> They should not depart from any counsel of the law [of Moses] in order to walk in complete stubbornness of their heart but instead shall be ruled by the first directives which the men of the community began to be taught until the prophet comes [the prophet like Moses], and the Messiahs of Aaron and Israel.

It is interesting that the aforementioned three roles expected of the prophet-like-Moses (which recall the functions of the historical Moses) occur in the Rule of the Community, one of the foundational documents of the DSS. In delineating those roles, I will also intersperse relevant corresponding texts from the other formative DSS works: the Damascus Document and *Miqsat Maase Ha-Torah*.

The prophet-like-Moses is associated with the Qumran community's exile in the wilderness in order to prepare for the eschatological conquest of Canaan (Israel). Rule of the Community 8:13-16 expresses it thusly:

> And when these exist/as a community/in Israel/in compliance with these arrangements/they are to be segregated from within the dwelling of the men of sin to walk to the desert in order to open there His path. As it is written: "In the desert, prepare the way of ****, straighten in the steppe a roadway for our God." This is the study of the law which he commanded through the hand of Moses, in order to act in compliance with all that has been revealed from age to age and according to what the prophets have revealed through his holy spirit. (cf. CD 1:4-11; 6:2-11; 4QMMT 92-93)

Comparing this passage with Rule of the Community 9:11 leads one to conclude that after duly preparing the community in the wilderness,

God will send the prophet-like-Moses along with the two Messiahs for the purpose of delivering Israel into the hands of the Qumran community.

The Rule of the Community also speaks of the annual renewal of the Mosaic covenant, invoking the Deuteronomic blessings or curses on those who respectively obey or disobey its precepts. Such a ritual receives extensive treatment (1QS 1:1—3:12; cf. CD 3:4-16; 4QMMT 99-118). Comparing Rule of the Community 1:1—3:12 with 9:11 leads to the observation that the Qumran community renewed the Mosaic covenant annually in expectation of the imminent appearing of the prophet-like-Moses.

Concerning the new revelation regarding the Torah, Rule of the Community 5:7-11 (cf. CD 3:12-16; 4QMMT 93-96) expresses the conviction that the Qumran community existed in order to interpret and obey the Torah's statutes properly:

> These are the regulations of behavior concerning all these decrees when they are enrolled in the Community. Whoever enters the council of the community enters the covenant of God in the presence of all who freely volunteer. He shall swear with a binding oath to revert to the Law of Moses with all that it decrees, with whole heart and whole soul, in compliance with all that has been revealed concerning it to the sons of Zadok, the priests who keep the covenant and interpret his will and to the multitude of the men of their covenant who freely volunteer together for this truth and to walk according to his will. He should swear by the covenant to be segregated from all the men of sin who walk along paths of irreverence. For they are not included in his covenant since they have neither sought nor examined his decrees in order to learn the hidden matters in which they err. (1QS 5:7-11)

Rule of the Community 8:10-16, a passage noted above, repeats this conviction. Schiffman's explanation of this aspect of Qumran exegesis is helpful:

> The notion of revealed and hidden laws discloses to us a system of sectarian legal theology. The revealed law—that is, the Torah and the words of the prophets—was known to all of Israel, who nonetheless, violated it. The hidden, on the other hand, was known only to the sect. These hidden laws constituted the very points of disagreement around which the

sect coalesced. The written Torah, originally revealed by God, had been modified later by His prophets through their divine visions. The hidden law, the *nistar*, had also developed over time and would continue to change, but it did not originate at the same time as the revealed Torah. Rather, it represented God's constant, ongoing revelation of Torah interpretation disclosed to the sectarians during and through their study sessions. These two types of law complemented each other and together made up the system of Jewish law as understood and practiced by the sect.[42]

According to Rule of the Community 9:9-11, maintaining this *halakhah* was the primary goal of the Qumran covenanters until the prophet-like-Moses should arise. Perhaps we are to see in this passage the idea, apparently prevalent in Judaism at the time, that if Israel will obey the Torah, the Messiah or the kingdom of God will come (cf. CD 4:1-17 with CD 12:23—13:1; 14:19; 19:10-11; *b. Sanh.* 97b-98a; *b. B. Bat.* 10a; *b. Yoma* 86b).[43] In any case, the expectations of the prophet-like-Moses executing a new conquest and reestablishing the covenant through renewed obedience to the properly interpreted Torah clearly point to the retelling of the story of Israel by the Essenes. It was another way for them to say that the current nation, though dwelling in its land, nevertheless lived in a state of sin and exile. Only those who joined the ranks of the Qumran community could hope to experience the promised restoration because only they truly followed the divine commandments.

   2. The NT and the prophet-like-Moses. Turning to the NT, we most probably encounter a Moses typology in 1 Corinthians 10:1-13; 2 Corinthians 3:1—4:6; Hebrews 3:1—4:10; and especially in Matthew. With regard to the First Gospel's presentation of Jesus as the prophet-like (more accurately, "greater than") Moses,[44] it is significant that the threefold role assigned to that eschatological figure in the DSS also occurs in Matthew. First, Matthew 3—4 seems to envision Jesus as the new Moses or the prophet-like-Moses, who reenacted the exodus at his baptism (Mt 3:13-17), overcame the temptations in the wilderness in a way Israel did not (Mt 4:1-11) and thereby prepared to enter "Canaan" to conquer Satan and his cohorts through his miraculous power (Mt 8—10).[45]

Second, in Matthew 5—7 Jesus issues forth his revelation regarding the Torah, calling for the fulfillment of the law of Moses (Mt 5:7-20) by the internalizing of it (Mt 5:21—7:29). The antitheses in the Sermon on the Mount ("you have heard that it was said . . . but I say to you") remind one, as VanderKam remarks, of the way in which *Miqsat Maase Ha-Torah* introduces disagreements between the Qumran sect and its opponents: "you know . . . we think/say."[46] This observation is in keeping with the view of numerous scholars that Matthew is presenting the Torah of Jesus over against the *halakhah* of the Pharisees (see the antitheses of Mt 5:21-48 together with the woes pronounced against the scribes and Pharisees in Mt 23:23-39). Indeed, I have argued elsewhere that the Matthean Jesus utters the Deuteronomic blessings on the followers of his Torah (see the Beatitudes, Mt 5:1-12) while reserving for the Pharisees the Deuteronomic curses (Mt 23:23-39).[47]

Third, according to Matthew 26:26-28, Jesus instituted the New Covenant, the basis of which would no longer be the shed blood of animal sacrifice (see Ex 24:6-8) but rather his own outpoured life on the cross.

It can be seen from these cursory remarks concerning Matthew that the First Gospel, like the DSS, is retelling the story of Israel. According to Matthew, the nation's sinful state and subsequent exile had only been exacerbated by the Pharisaic option. Indeed, such an approach may have even contributed to the destruction of Jerusalem (A.D. 70). Emerging as the only legitimate alternative in all of this was the Jesus movement which, empowered by the Spirit, constituted the true Israel.[48]

The Danielic Son of Man
Daniel 7:13-14 is a text that influenced late Second Temple Jewish messianic understanding.

> I saw in the night visions,
> and behold, with the clouds of heaven
>   there came one like a son of man,
> and he came to the Ancient of Days
>   and was presented before him.
> And to him was given dominion
>   and glory and kingdom,
> that all peoples, nations, and languages

should serve him;
his dominion is an everlasting dominion,
which shall not pass away,
and his kingdom one
that shall not be destroyed.

Influence of the Danielic Son of Man can be seen in the *Similitudes of Enoch*,[49] where that personage is implicitly equated with the Messiah (*Sim. Enoch* 46:1; 47:3)[50] and in *4 Ezra*,[51] where the Son of Man is explicitly called the Messiah (cf. 13 [cf. 12:11] with 7:28-29; 13:32), and also in the DSS (4Q246), the "Son of God" text, not to mention in Mark 13:26-27 (and parallels) as applied to Jesus' parousia.

Whatever the identification of the original heavenly Son of Man in Daniel 7:13-14 (collective entity, angelic personage, messianic individual),[52] factoring Daniel 9 into the discussion reveals that the author believed such a personage would effect the restoration of Israel. Actually, Daniel 9 encompasses the entire Deuteronomistic tradition: Israel's idolatry (Dan 9:4-5, 8-11); the prophets' denunciation (Dan 9:6); Yahweh's judgment via the covenantal curses (Dan 9:6, 12-14); Israel's repentance (Dan 9:15-23); and the nation's subsequent restoration, the Deuteronomic blessings, which are to be brought about by the anointed one of the Lord (Dan 9:24-27; cf. Dan 2; 7; 12).[53]

How do 4Q246 and Mark 13:26-27 (and context) make use of the Danielic Son of Man in order to retell the story of Israel? Drawing on the insights of Collins (for 4Q246) and Wright (for Mark 13), I will argue that these two texts introduce a critical reversal into the traditional telling of Israel's expected victory over her enemies, namely, the Danielic Son of Man is portrayed as fighting on behalf of the righteous (the Essenes and the followers of Jesus, respectively), whose enemies include the nation of *Israel*.[54]

1. 4Q246 and the Danielic Son of Man. 4Q246[55] reads as follows:

Col. I *1* [. . .]settled upon him and he fell before the throne *2* [. . .] eternal king. You are angry and your years *3* [. . .] they will see you, and all shall come for ever. *4* [. . .] great oppression will come upon the earth *5* [. . .] and great slaughter in the city *6* [. . .] king of Assyria and of Egypt *7* [. . .] and he will be great over the earth *8* [. . .] they will do, and all will serve *9* [. . .] great will he be called and he will be designated by his name.

Col. II   *1* He will be called son of God, and they will call him son of the Most High. Like the sparks *2* of a vision, so will their kingdom be; they will rule several years over *3* the earth and crush everything; a people will crush another people, and a city another city. *4 Blank* Until the people of God arises and makes everyone rest from the sword. *5* His Kingdom will be an eternal kingdom, and all his paths in truth and upright[ness]. *6* The earth (will be) in truth and all will make peace. The sword will cease in the earth, *7* and all the cities will pay him homage. He is a great God among the gods (?). *8* He will make war with him; he will place the peoples in his hand and cast away everyone before him. His kingdom will be an eternal kingdom, and all the abysses.

Most likely, as Schiffman[56] has observed, this manuscript is based on Daniel 7:13-14. Interpreted in the light of that OT passage, 4Q246 1:1-6 should therefore be understood as Daniel's[57] explanation of the dreams of a Babylonian ruler, to the effect that the end of history will witness an eschatological battle. At that time a final king, the Son of God, will arise and conquer the divine enemies and establish the kingdom of God (4Q246 1:7—2:8). Collins identifies the following similarities between Daniel and 4Q246, thus increasing the likelihood that the Danielic Son of Man figure is operative in this Scrolls text under the identity "Son of God":

☐ The words *eternal kingdom* are comparable between 4Q246 2:5 and Daniel 3:33; 7:17.

☐ The phrase "his kingdom will be an eternal kingdom" can be compared with 4Q246 2:9 and Daniel 4:31; 7:14.

☐ The conflict between the nations in column I of 4Q246 is reminiscent of Daniel 11.

☐ Both 4Q246 2:3 and Daniel 7:7 use the word *dwš* ("crush") with reference to the power of the kingdom of God and the beast, respectively.

☐ Both passages involve an interpretation before a king.[58]

It would seem, then, that the Danielic Son of Man surfaces in 4Q246 in terms of the Son of God.

Three alternatives vie for the identification of the Son of God referred to in 4Q246. First, based on the association with Daniel 7, some have interpreted the Son of God in 4Q246 as a collective entity.

While it is true that Daniel 7 suggests a parallel between the heavenly Son of Man (Dan 7:13-14) and the earthly people of God (Dan 7:18, 27),[59] Collins registers three problems with the corporate interpretation. First, there is no notion in the OT that the people of God will judge the earth. Second, the eschatological kingdom of Israel is usually connected with an individual ruler, whether an angel such as Michael in Daniel 10—12 and in the War Scroll (1QM) or a messianic figure. Third, although Israel is often called God's son (e.g., Ex 4:22-23; 36:17), it is not the titular usage such as one finds later in 4Q246.[60]

The second view of the identity of the Son of God in 4Q246 is that an angel, especially Melchizedek (see 1QM and 11QMelch),[61] is in the author's mind. If in fact the theology of 4Q246 is compatible with the War Scroll and the Melchizedek text (as it seems to be), Melchizedek becomes a strong candidate to be the Son of God. Indeed, Paul Kobelski has shown that the Danielic Son of Man figure in Daniel 7 corresponds to the presentation of Melchizedek in the Melchizedek text.

> Both Daniel 7 and 11QMelch describe the events of the final age in terms of a judgment and a military defeat of the enemy. Although the "one like a son of man" is not specifically presented as a judge of his opponents, he appears in a judicial context (Dan 7:10, 14; cf. Dan 7:24, 37) in which he is given the kingdom. In both cases, the "one like a son of man" (i.e., Michael in Dan 7:9-14) and Melchizedek are exalted to a place in the heavens (Dan 7:9, 13; 11QMelch 2:10-11), both triumph over the power of the enemy (Dan 7:23-27; Dan 12:1; 11QMelch 2:13-16; 2:25). The "one like a son of man" is given an indestructible kingdom (Day 7:14); Melchizedek is described as a king in the final age (11QMelch 2:7-8, 16, 23-25).[62]

Collins, however, points out two problems with the angelic reading of 4Q246. First, the title "Son of God" is not applied to Melchizedek elsewhere in the DSS. Second, it is unusual that God should be said to be the strength of an angelic being, for typically such a personage is portrayed as the divine agent.[63]

A third theory of identification suggests the Son of God in the Scrolls text is a messianic figure, especially the expected Davidic king. When one compares, for example, 2 Samuel 7:14 and Psalm 2:7-8; 89:26-27 with 4QFlorilegium 1:10-12 (cf. 1QSa; 4Q369; see also *4 Ezra* 7,

13—14), such an identification is preferable.[64]

The mission of the Son of God (probably the Davidic Messiah) as depicted in 4Q246 is perspicuous: He will wage eschatological war against the enemies of the righteous, thereby vindicating the remnant.[65] At that point, however, 4Q246 seems to depart from the story of Israel as traditionally told in Second Temple Judaism, for the similarities between the "Son of God" text and the War Scroll[66] suggest that 4Q246, like the War Scroll, is sectarian in orientation. Thus Collins writes of the Son of God text and the War Scroll that most scholars "would grant that the War Scroll is sectarian, whether it was originally composed at Qumran or not. The terminological echoes of the War Scroll here suggest that the Son of God text also comes from a sectarian milieu."[67] If this conclusion is correct, as it seems to be, then 4Q246, like the War Scroll, should be understood to reverse the story of Israel: The righteous, the Essenes, constitute the true Israel which will be defended by the coming Messiah in the eschatological battle, while the rest of Israel will be included with the Gentiles who will be destroyed.

2. Mark 13 and the Danielic Son of Man. Wright's arguments as summarized here highlight the influence of the Danielic Son of Man figure on Mark 13, especially Jesus' use of such a theme to subvert the traditional story of Israel. Wright divides the Olivet discourse in Mark 13 (cf. Mt 24; Lk 21) into two sections: Mark 13:5-23 and Mark 13:24-31, the latter of which especially focuses on Daniel 7:13-14. Concerning Mark 13:5-23, Wright uncovers three sets of OT passages informing that text. The first two deal respectively with the Babylonian and Maccabean crises, while the third set keys in on Jerusalem as not the victim of pagan aggression but the enemy of the people of God.

Wright demonstrates that the messianic woes[68] referred to in Mark 13:5-23 draw on those afflictions which attended the fall of Jerusalem to the Babylonians in 587 B.C. So it is that the theme of the destruction of Jerusalem in Mark 13:2 echoes Micah 3:12; Jeremiah 7:14; 46:8 and Ezekiel 24:21. More specifically, the idea of internecine strife in Mark 13:12 recalls Micah 7:2-10. The reference in Mark 13:17 to those fleeing with children should be compared to Hosea 13:16 [MT 14:1]. The shortening of the days for the sake of the elect in Mark 13:20 reminds one of Isaiah 65:8. Mark 13:22 and the presence of false prophets is rooted in

Deuteronomy 13 and Jeremiah 6:13-15. The warning to run to the mountains before the invasion of Jerusalem in Mark 13:14 hearkens back to Ezekiel 7:12-16.[69] In effect, then, Mark 13 is the apocalypticizing of the Deuteronomic curses.[70]

The second set of OT passages informing Mark 13:5-23 are related, according to Wright, to the Maccabean crisis in 171-164 B.C. (namely, Dan 9:24-27; 11:31-35; 12:10-11, which speak of the coming anointed one's victory over Antiochus Epiphanes).[71] Both of the previous crises, Babylonian and Maccabean, and the OT texts they spawned were obviously related to Israel's sin-exile-estoration.[72]

Wright observes that a third set of OT passages (Isa 6:9-11, 13; 12:15; 14:4; 34:3-4; 48:20; 52:11-12; Ezek 32:5-8; Joel 2:10-11, 30-32; 3:14-15; Amos 8:9; Zeph 1:15; Zech 2:6-8; 14:2-5, 9)[73] forms a part of the substructure of Mark 13:5-23 which reverses the story of Israel, namely, those texts accusing Jerusalem itself of being the enemy because of her idolatrous ways, thereby meriting her upcoming judgment.

From the preceding three sets of OT texts, Wright concludes:

> These passages, taken together and in their various parts, are clearly the intended background for several parts of the discourses in Mark 13 and parallels, before we even get to the Danielic allusions. They tell the story of Israel, her god, and the nations in ways that lend themselves perfectly to Jesus' redefinition of Israel around himself; to his announcement that the long-awaited release from exile (the "kingdom of god") was at hand; and to his identification of the forces opposing the true people of this god, not with Rome, but with present Jerusalem and its hierarchy. His retelling of the prophetic stories, like Susannah's addition to Daniel, has the force of turning the critique of pagan nations against the present Jewish rulers. Jerusalem's fall, and the disciples' flight and escape will be the final acting out of the predictions that Babylon would fall and Israel escape. This will be her vindication, the sign that her god is indeed king.[74]

So Mark 13:5-23 reverses the story of Israel: Israel is the enemy, while Jesus and his disciples are the true people of God. Mark 13:24-31 proceeds to make use of Daniel 7:13-14 in order to assure the disciples that Jesus' parousia will vindicate his followers.

I will offer three comments as a digest of Wright's interpretation of this Markan text. First, apocalyptic language is used therein to describe not the end of the world but the coming of Jesus, the heavenly Son of Man, to Jerusalem.[75] Second, like the Danielic Son of Man,[76] Jesus will arrive at the holy city to defeat the enemies of the people of God, which will bring true Israel's exile to an end (cf. Mk 13:24-31 with Deut 30:2-5; Ps 106:47; Is 27:13; Dan 7:2; Zech 2:6-12; 2 *Macc* 2:7).[77] Third, ironically, the OT promises of Jerusalem's deliverance and the nation's restoration are transferred in Mark 13:24-31 to Jesus and his followers, while Jerusalem has become the enemy whose destruction signals the vindication of the true people of God.[78]

Wright's exegesis of Mark 13 seems quite compelling, except for an important qualification, namely, he reduces apocalyptic language to the level of symbol, which when decoded emphasizes a historical reading of biblical prophecy. That is to say, Wright's treatment does not give due place to the futurity of the parousia, that is, the second coming of Christ. Elsewhere I have attempted to demonstrate that both the historical and eschatological approaches can be nicely integrated in one's interpretation of Mark 13.[79] But I certainly agree with Wright's overall concern to show that Mark 13 subverts the traditional telling of the story of Israel.

Conclusion

The task of this chapter was to address messianic hope as reflected in the DSS and in the NT. Four paradigms emerged therein: Davidic Messiah, eschatological priest, prophet-like-Moses and Danielic Son of Man. Undergirding the messianism attached to these personages was the story of Israel as retold by the authors of the DSS and the NT. Both argue that ethnic Israel ironically is aligned with the enemies of God and that only their own communities constitute the genuine people of God.

Beyond that agreement, however, the two present radically different means to the restoration of Israel. The DSS assert that only in adhering to the stringent interpretation of the Torah provided by the Teacher of Righteousness could one be incorporated into the remnant. By way of contrast, the Gospels present faith in Jesus the Messiah, whose words and work fulfill if not terminate the Torah as the exclusive solution to the plight of Israel. More specifically, Jesus the Christ took the Deuteronomic curses upon himself on the cross in order that the Deuteronomic blessings of forgiveness and life in the covenant might be offered to sinners.

Chapter Five

Story, Symbol & Praxis

Luke-Acts & the DSS

Introduction

N. T. Wright insightfully identifies the worldview of late Second Temple Judaism by raising and answering four crucial questions intimately related to the story of Israel:

☐ Who are we? We are Israel, the chosen people of the creator God.

☐ Where are we? We are in the holy land, focused on the temple; paradoxically, we are still in exile.

☐ What is wrong? We have the wrong rulers: pagans on the one hand, compromised Jews on the other, or halfway between, Herod and his family. We are all involved in a less than ideal situation.

☐ What is the solution? Our God must act again to give us the true sort of rule, that is, his own kingship exercised through properly appointed officials (a true priesthood; possibly a true king). In the meantime, Israel must be faithful to his covenant charter.[1]

For Wright these questions and answers can be encapsulated in three terms: *story, symbol* and *praxis*. The story of Israel is the metanarrative of sin-exile-restoration, which is reflected in the OT and in much of Second Temple Jewish literature.[2] That basic story line focused on key symbols which brought Israel's worldview into visible reality: temple, land, Torah and racial identity.[3] Those symbols in turn were reinforced through the daily life of Jews, which revolved around the major festivals and other key matters.[4]

In this chapter, using Wright's discussion as a point of departure, I will investigate how Luke-Acts and the DSS handle Israel's story, symbol and praxis. (Those two communities radically redefine the rather typical Jewish worldview of their day.) I do so by taking the three elements in reverse order—praxis, symbol and story—thereby tracking the increasing disagreement that existed between, on the one hand, Luke-Acts and the DSS, and on the other hand, traditional Judaism. By the third point, discord will be shown to have extended to Luke's congregation even relative to the Qumran community.

Praxis

It is well known that ancient Judaism (and probably modern Judaism as well) concentrated on "orthopraxy" as much as if not more so than it did on orthodoxy. At the heart of the matter, of course, was the deep-seated concern to properly adhere to the Torah. The communities of Luke-Acts and the DSS were no different in this regard, and they expressed that concern in their hymns, in their profession of having the Spirit, in their organization, in their rituals, in their attitude toward possessions and in their codes of conduct and discipline.[5] In what follows I will highlight each of these aspects, noting along the way two important considerations: all of these pragmatic interests centered on the restoration of Israel; and Luke-Acts and the DSS remarkably agree in their presentations of these concerns vis-à-vis their Jewish contemporaries.

Their hymns. Both sets of documents contain an impressive collection of hymns: Luke 1—2 with its infancy hymns surrounding the births of John the Baptist and Jesus,[6] and in the DSS the *Hôdāyôt* especially (the Psalms of the Righteous) as well as War Scroll 11—19 (a Divine Warrior Hymn envisioning the deliverance of the obedient at the end of the age) and others.[7] Amazingly, the four infancy hymns in Luke 1—2 (the *Magnificat,* the *Benedictus,* the Song of the Angels and

Nunc Dimittis) display striking similarities with their Qumranic counterparts (in particular 1QH and 1QM, which I will demonstrate). Moreover, a thematic thought ties together the Lukan infancy hymns and
the aforementioned DSS hymns: the deliverance of the righteous or the
redemption of Israel.

1. The *leitmotif* of the *Magnificat*, Mary's song of praise to God (Lk
1:46-53), is the divine reversal of the fortunes of the poor. *Ptōchoi* is
employed in Luke 1:46-53 with reference to God's exaltation of the status of the poor righteous ones whose trust is wholly in him (see 2 Sam
22:28; Ps 72:2, 4, 12; Is 26:6; 49:13; 62:2; Zeph 3:12; Lk 6:20-24; 12:13-21;
14:7-24; 16:19-31; 19:1-10).[8] In the *Magnificat* God's vindication of the
poor through Jesus the deliverer extends to Mary (Lk 1:48-49), those
who fear God (Lk 1:50-53) and even to Israel (Lk 1:54-55). *Ptōchoi* is the
Greek equivalent of the Hebrew *'nwm*, which is used in the OT passages mentioned above. After the OT, perhaps the most prolific usage
of the term occurs in the DSS, most notably in the *Hôdāyôt* (1QH 1:36;
2:34; 5:13-14, 21; 14:3; 18:14; cf. also CD 6:16, 21; 14:14; 19:9; 1QM 14:7;
1QSb 5:22; 4QpIs).[9] Furthermore, the common theme underlying the
designation in the Scrolls, like the *Magnificat*, is that of the deliverance
of the righteous, which is probably to be understood as the restoration
or redemption of Israel.[10]

2. The *Benedictus* (Lk 1:68-79), though an infancy hymn uttered at
the birth of John the Baptist, forerunner of the Christ, is no lullaby.
Quite the contrary, its theme of God's deliverance of Israel from her
enemies by the Davidic Messiah is reminiscent of the OT Divine Warrior hymns sung by Israel (e.g., Ex 15). It is most intriguing to note,
therefore, three parallels between the *Benedictus* and War Scroll 11—19,
a Divine Warrior hymn envisioning the eschatological vindication of
the Qumran covenanters. First, both refer to the Davidic Messiah star
prophecy of Numbers 24:17-19. War Scroll 11:6 reads, "A star will
depart from Judah, a scepter will be raised in Israel. It will smash the
temples of Moab, it will destroy all the sons of Seth." This text obviously alludes to the Davidic Messiah, who the Qumran community
believed would appear at the end of time on its behalf (cf. CD 7:19-20;
4QTestim 12). Numbers 24:17, as some commentators suggest, also
seems to inform Luke 1:78, "through the tender mercy of our God,

when the day shall dawn upon us from on high."[11] If indeed the allusion to the above OT text stands behind Luke 1:78, one finds here a remarkable parallel to War Scroll 11:6. Second, both the *Benedictus* and the War Scroll originated in circles identifying themselves as the "poor ones" (cf. 1QM 14:7 and the motif of the reversal of the fortunes of the righteous that also underlies Lk 1:68-79). Third, both hymns ground their deliverance in God's mercy, shown to them based on his covenant (cf. Lk 1:72-73 with 1QM 14:4; 19:4).

3. Until the discovery of the DSS, debate over Luke 2:14 (the Song of the Angels) centered on which translation was most accurate: "peace, good will among men" or "on earth peace among men of God's good pleasure."[12] But with the publication of the *Hôdāyôt*, that issue was virtually solved in favor of the latter reading. The Greek word *eudokias* (Luke 2:14) stands for the Hebrew word *ranson* ("good pleasure"), the exact word occurring in *Hôdāyôt* 4:32; 9:9 ("sons of good pleasure"). The context of these Qumran texts, as Ernest Vogt demonstrated, indicates that the phrase refers to people to whom God has chosen to confer his grace.[13] Vogt catches the significance of the verbal parallel between *Hôdāyôt* 4:32; 9:19 and Luke 2:14 in this regard:

> But the Qumran texts do more that lend decisive support to this reading. They also indicate that "God's good pleasure" here refers more naturally to the will of God to confer grace on those he has chosen, than to God's delighting in and approving of the goodness in men's lives. Thus neither "good will toward men" nor "peace among men with whom he is pleased" is an accurate translation, but rather "peace among men of God's good pleasure," i.e., his chosen ones.[14]

Thus both texts convey the notion that God will deliver his chosen people. For Luke 2:14, it is those who embrace Jesus that experience divine grace and redemption, whereas for *Hôdāyôt* 4:3; 9:19, such salvation belongs to those who join the Qumran community.

4. The theme of the deliverance of the righteous also informs *Nunc Dimittis* ("now dismiss"; Lk 2:29-35), Simeon's prayer-praise to God at the presentation of baby Jesus, as it does War Scroll 12 (cf. 1QM 19). Three conceptual similarities surface when one compares these hymns; both draw on the hope of the redemption of Israel (cf. Lk 2:30-31 with

the vindication theme of 1QM 12, cf. 19, itself a part of the Divine Warrior hymn). Both describe that redemption in terms of the glory of Israel (cf. Lk 2:32 with 1QM 12:12). Both speak of hope for the Gentiles (cf. Lk 2:32 with 1QM 12:14-15)—one because the nations will come to homage Christ, and the other because the nations will be required to pay honor to true Israel.

Their possession of the Spirit. It is clear that the early church perceived the outpouring of the Spirit on its community at Pentecost as a symbol of the arrival of the long-anticipated age to come (Acts 2:1-21; cf. Joel 2:28-32). The recognition of this reality is commonplace in biblical scholarship. Herman Ridderbos writes, "It is precisely the Spirit who is the great Inaugurator and the gift of the new aeon that has appeared with Christ."[15] George Ladd observes, "Life in the Spirit means eschatological existence—life in the new age. This is established by the fact that the presence of the Holy Spirit in the church is itself an eschatological event."[16] French Arrington notes that the Spirit was the sign to the early church that the end of time had arrived.[17] J. Christiaan Beker applies this perspective to Paul when he argues that the apostle's understanding of the eschatological nature of the Spirit rests in the "already/not yet" tension—the Spirit is the proleptic sign of the kingdom of God, the presence of the future. Thus the Spirit is proof that the age to come has dawned, though it is not yet completed.[18]

The early church, however, was not the only community of faith claiming possession of the eschatological Spirit; the Qumran covenanters did the same. Both the NT and the DSS commonly refer to the Spirit as the "Holy" Spirit (see, e.g., 1QS 4:20; 1QH 7:6; 16:12; Acts 1:2, 8; 2:4; 4:25; 5:3), a phenomenon rarely occurring in the OT (see the exceptions in Ps 51:11 and Is 63:10-11).[19] Moreover, the DSS, like the NT, asserted that God's Spirit had been poured out on their community. Thus 1QS 4:20-21 reads:

> God will refine with his truth all man's deeds, and will purify for himself the configuration of man, ripping out all spirit of injustice from the innermost part of his flesh, and cleansing him with the spirit of holiness from every irreverent deed.[20]

This discussion can be extended by calling attention to three significant similarities between the DSS and Luke-Acts concerning the topic of the Spirit, each of which conveys an eschatological nuance related to the restoration of Israel.

First, for both bodies of materials, the Spirit provides entrance into the salvific community. This is true with regard to the people at Qumran, for as H. W. Kuhn has persuasively argued, the *Hôdāyôt* expresses the conviction that the Spirit is granted to all members upon their association with that congregation (1QH 7:6-7; 9:32; 12:11-13; 13:18-19; 14:12-21; 16:6-7, 11-12; 17:26).[21] Acts 2:1-47 presents the same idea: Those who entered the church by faith in Christ, God's eschatological people, received the Spirit. For both, then, their respective communities constituted the beginnings of the restoration of Israel.

Second, both materials give the strong impression that to be identified with their groups is to experience the renewal of prophecy, which is an end-time gift reserved for true Israel. That ancient Judaism felt devoid of the Spirit and prophecy is rather obvious from the literary sources (e.g., *Sir* 49:10; *1 Macc* 4:46; 9:27; 14:41; *Sib. Or.* 1:386). Only at the end of history was God expected to restore his Spirit and the prophetic word to Israel (Joel 2:28-32). The DSS and Luke-Acts are exceptions to this rule that prophecy only belonged to bygone days.

On one hand, the DSS associate Moses and the prophets of old with the Spirit (1QS 8:15-16; CD 2:11-13), while on the other hand, they indicate that the Spirit of prophecy has been renewed in the Qumran community, particularly in the covenanters' insight into the Torah (e.g., 1QH 5:11; 12:11).[22] Prophecy is manifested in the DSS in at least two ways: inspired intelligible speech (1QH 1:27-29; 7:11; 8:36; 11:12) and inspired ecstatic speech, especially in worship (Songs of the Sabbath Sacrifice [4Q400-405, 11Q17]; Chariots of Glory [4Q286-87]). The emphasis in the last-mentioned works on *tongues of praise* and *knowledge* uttered by the righteous among the *angels* in heavenly worship is noteworthy (cf. 1 Cor 13:1; 14:1-39).

Luke-Acts also asserts that its community is a prophetic one whose reception of the Spirit marked it as the eschatological people of God (Acts 2:1-47), as Robert P. Menzies has carefully demonstrated.[23] Consequently, the Lukan church, like the DSS community, uttered inspired intelligible speech (e.g., Acts 1:8, 16; 2:4, 14, 17-18, 33; 4:8, 25, 31; 5:32;

6:10; 7:51; 9:31; 10:44-45; 13:9; 19:6; 28:5),[24] as well as inspired, ecstatic speech (Acts 2:1-13; 10:44-48; 19:1-7).

Third, both communities viewed themselves as the eschatological fulfillment of the Sinaitic covenant. There was a long-standing tradition in Judaism that connected the feast of Pentecost with Moses' giving of the law to Israel (*Jdt* 1:5; 6:11, 17; 15:1-4; *Tg. Ps.-J* 68:18; *Midrash Tehillim* on Ps 24:1 and Ps 106:2; *b. Shabb.* 88b; Philo [*Quaest. in Ex.* 2:40-43; *Vit. Mos.* 1:158; *Poster. C.* 14; *Som.* 1:186-88]). The *targum* (Aramaic translation) of Psalm 68:18 is especially germane in this regard: "You have ascended into heaven, that is, Moses the prophet; you have taken captivity captive, you have learned the words of the Torah; you have given it as gifts to men."[25] Thus Moses ascended Sinai to receive the divine law and descended to give the law to Israel. Andrew Lincoln and others call attention to the DSS and the association therein between Pentecost and Moses' giving of the law at Sinai.[26] Lincoln observes the following relationship between *Jubilees* and Qumran:

> The Book of Jubilees, which is usually dated between 135 and 105 B.C., makes Pentecost or the Feast of Weeks the most important of annual festivals in the Jewish liturgical year, associating it with the institution of the various covenants in Israel's history but above all with the covenant at Sinai (cf. 1:5: 6:11, 17; 15:1-24). The Qumran community followed the calendar of the Book of Jubilees which ordered an annual renewal of the covenant (16:17), and in all probability this was combined with the annual renewal of the members' own oath of entry into the community which took place in the third month of the year, the time of Pentecost's celebration. According to Exodus 19:1 the giving of the law took place in the third month also, as did the covenant renewal recorded in 2 Chronicles 15:10-12. The liturgy for the annual renewal at Qumran is given in the Manual of Discipline (cf. 1QS 1, 7-11, 19).[27]

More recently, Eisenman and Wise have called attention to a newly uncovered Scrolls text, The Foundations of Righteousness: An Excommunication Text (4Q266), which they believe originally formed the conclusion to the Damascus Document, one of the foundational documents of Qumran. Moreover, they connect it with Rule of the Community 8:15. Pooling together these texts leads those authors to conclude that the annual renewal of the Sinaitic covenant by the DSS community

occurred on Pentecost ("on the third month," 4Q266 17; cf. 1QS 1:7—
2:25). Furthermore, such an observance was associated with the Spirit,
whose presence in the community marked the true study of the Torah
accomplished by the faithful remnant in the end times (cf. 1QS 8:14-16
with 4Q266 18-19).[28] One might also mention that 4Q266 seems to
allude to the ascent of Moses on Sinai to receive and then give the law
to the people (4Q266 1-4, 11-12).[29]

It is very likely, as a number of commentators have suggested, that
Acts 2 and related passages should be interpreted as the reenactment
of Sinai.[30] All the components previously identified in the DSS are there
operative: Pentecost (Acts 2:1); the giving of the Spirit; (Acts 2:2-13);
the community of the last days (Acts 2:14-21); Christ (the new Moses;
cf. Acts 3:22-23 with Deut 18:15-19) ascending to God like Moses did on
Sinai (Acts 1:9-11), and sending back his Spirit; the power for obedience to God (Acts 2:1-13; v. 40, "Save yourselves from this crooked generation" [the theme of Deut 31:30—32:47]). And according to Acts
21:21-26, the accusation of the Jews that Paul disobeyed the Mosaic law
motivated the apostle to go to Jerusalem on Pentecost to demonstrate
his submission to the Torah.[31] Thus Acts 2, like the DSS, appears to
view its community as embodying the true Sinaitic covenant, enabled
by the Spirit. It was the Spirit therefore that guided their day-to-day
adherence to the Torah.[32]

Their organization. It is understandable that initial research on the
organizational pattern of the Qumran community should have created
excitement, especially when researchers compared Qumran to the
structure of early Christianity, particularly as expressed in Luke-Acts.
On this reading, the Teacher of Righteousness paralleled Jesus' ministry; the twelve representatives at Qumran corresponded to the twelve
apostles (cf. Lk 5; Acts 1 with 1QS 8:1-2; 1QM 2:2-3; 5:1-3; 11QTemple
18:14-16); the three priests of the covenant (1QS 8:1) were reminiscent
of the three innermost disciples of Jesus—Peter, James and John; and
the leaders of the Qumran community subsequent to the teacher's
death (cf. CD 13:9-19) were thought to anticipate the Christian bishop
(as depicted in the Pastoral Epistles). While one should avoid pressing
these parallels too far, similarity between Qumran and Luke-Acts does
seem to owe to more than speculation. This is especially the case for

the groups' appropriation of the number twelve. It seems clear that in both situations such a number was employed by the communities to convey the notion that their respective congregations comprised the restored, eschatological Israel.[33]

Their rituals. Like the NT church, the people producing the DSS celebrated two constitutive rituals: baptism and a sacral meal. With these two practices, significant differences in the telling of the story of Israel emerge between, on one hand, the DSS and Luke-Acts, and on the other hand, Second Temple Judaism.

John the Baptist and the DSS. I argued earlier in this work for some degree of relationship between John the Baptist and the DSS. Two key aspects characterize John's baptism as presented in Luke 3 and the ritual ablutions observed by the Qumran sectarians. First, both can be described as a "baptism of repentance." Luke 3:3 calls John's baptism "a baptism of repentance for the forgiveness of sins." Immediately following this is a description of the moral change of life that should accompany that act (Lk 3:4-14). VanderKam expresses how this ritual reminds one of Qumran.

> John's baptism for the purpose of repentance parallels the Qumran teaching about washing in water for cleansing and sanctification (Manual of Discipline 3:4-5, 9). The Manual also says: "They shall not enter the water to partake of the pure Meal of the saints, for they shall not be cleansed, unless they turn from their wickedness; for all who transgress His word are unclean" (5:13-14). As is well known, the Qumran complex is dotted with cisterns, some of which have stairways leading down into the water—a fact showing that they were used for regular ritual baths of those who belonged to the community. The baptism of John and the Qumran rituals probably differed in some ways. For example, John's baptism seems to have occurred just once for each penitent. The Qumran ablutions were almost certainly more frequent. Nevertheless, both types of washing—that of John and that of Qumran—are intimately connected with repentance and, unlike proselyte baptism, were meant for Jews.[34]

Second, expanding on the last comment, John's baptism, like Qumran and unlike other known Jewish groups of the time, demanded such a procedure not only of Gentile proselytes but also of the Jewish people themselves. Luke 3:7-8 is poignant in this regard, calling John's audience, the ethnic children of Abraham, "a brood of vipers" and warning them of impending judgment. The *Hôdāyôt* address national Israel as "serpents" (1QH 5:2), calling them "unclean and in need of the sprinkling of water" and "sanctification" (1QH 3:3-9). Here then is a retelling of the story of Israel to the effect that national Israel is not *ipso facto* the divinely intended recipient of restoration; only the repentant are.

The Lord's Supper and the messianic meal. Scholars have been quick to point out similarities between the Lord's Supper practiced by the early church and the "messianic meal" observed by the Qumran covenanters. First, both were *sacral* in character, due especially to the sacramental meaning attached to the elements of bread and wine. So it is that Luke 22:17-20 (cf. Mt 26:26-29; Mk 14:22-25) records that Jesus equated the wine of Passover with the blood of the New Covenant and the bread with himself, the Pascal Lamb, thereby rooting divine forgiveness in his sacrificial death. A similar meaning informs the meal practiced at Qumran. Thus Rule of the Community 6:1-6 reads,

> *Col.* VI *1* And in addition, no-one should raise a matter against his fellow in front of the Many unless it is with reproof in the presence of witnesses. In this way *2* shall they behave in all their places of residence. Whenever one fellow meets another, the junior shall obey the senior in work and in money. They shall eat together. *3* Together they shall bless and together they shall take counsel. In every place where there are ten men of the Community council, there should not be a priest missing amongst them. *4* And when they prepare the table to dine or the new wine for drinking, the priest shall stretch out his hand as the first to bless the first fruit of the bread {or the new wine *5* for drinking, the priest shall stretch out his hand as the first *6* to bless the first fruits of the bread} and of the new wine.

The sacramental nature of this meal becomes clear when we remember that the Essenes abandoned the sacrificial system of the Jerusalem Temple because they believed the Hasmonaean priesthood had become corrupt. In its place, the Qumran covenanters viewed themselves as the true priests who had now replaced the temple cultus (see the discussion below). As such, they perceived that their actions were sacred in import, providing true forgiveness of sins. Hence the very observance of their meals, presided over by the priests who blessed the

bread and wine and partaken of by the community, constituted a sacer-
dotal act.[35] Furthermore, to treat the sacred meal lightly, especially by
disturbing the harmony of the community, invoked divine judgment
(cf. 1 Cor 11:27-30 with 1QS 7:16).

Second, both meals were *continual* in practice. The Lord's Supper
was commemorated often, perhaps weekly (Acts 2:46), and the messianic meal at Qumran was also observed regularly, "and in accordance
with the regulation they shall act at each me[al, when] at least ten m[en
are gat]hered" (1QSa 2:21-22).

Third, both meals were *eschatological* in orientation. We may deduce
from Luke 22:14-20 and the other Gospel parallels, together with 1
Corinthians 11:23-26, that the Lord's Supper was understood by the
early church as eschatological in scope. Fellowship with God and his
Messiah makes one a participant in the kingdom of God. The most
extended description of a meal at Qumran, the Rule of the Congregation 2:11-20, makes a similar point:

> 11 This is the assembly of famous men, [those summoned to] the gather-
> ing of the community council, when [God] 12 begets the Messiah with
> them. [The] chief [priest] of all the congregation of Israel shall enter, and
> all 13 [his brothers, the sons] of Aaron, the priests [summoned] to the
> assembly, the famous men, and they shall sit 14 befo[re him, each one]
> according to his dignity. After, [the Me] ssiah of Israel shall ent[er] and
> before him shall sit the chiefs 15 [of the clans of Israel, each] one
> according to his dignity, according to their [positions] in their camps
> and in their marches. And all 16 the chiefs of the cl[ans of the congre]
> gations with the wise [men and the learned] shall sit before them, each
> one according 17 to his dignity. And [when] they gather at the table of
> 18 community [or to drink] the new wine [is mixed] for drinking, [no-
> one should stretch out] his hand to the first-fruit of the bread 19 and of
> the [new wine] before the priest, for [he is the one who bl]esses the first-
> fruit of bread 20 and of the new wine [and stretches out] his hand
> towards the bread before them. Afterwards the Messiah of Israel shall
> stretch out his hand towards the bread and after, he shall bless all the
> congregation of the community.

VanderKam pinpoints the messianic eschatological orientation of this
meal:

The meal is messianic in the most literal sense because it is eaten in the presence of the Messiah of Israel and his priestly colleague (who is called a Messiah in the Manual). The text stresses that the meal is only for those who are ritually pure. It is also explicitly eschatological, as the first words state: *"This is the Rule for all the congregation of Israel in the last days"* (1:1). One might think that the meal described in this text is unusual, one celebrated rarely; yet the last words of the document indicate otherwise: "It is according to this statute that they shall proceed at every me[al at which] at least ten men are gathered together" (2:21-22).[36]

From this it can be seen that the Qumran covenanters, like the early Christians, celebrated their regular community meals as if the Messiah were already there; that is, they observed them in anticipation of the future consummation and the restoration promised to Israel.

Their attitude toward possessions. The theme of material possessions is a major concern to Luke and not of little importance to the DSS as well. Four similarities regarding the topic surface in the literature.

1. For both groups, possessions served as a spiritual barometer of one's faith. One gets the distinct impression from reading Luke-Acts that a disciple's commitment to follow Jesus was expressed in terms of sharing one's material possessions with others (e.g., Lk 3:10-14; 4:18-19; 6:20-23; 8:1-3; 9:1-3, 23-27, 57-58; 12:22-34; 16:1-13; 18:28-30; 19:1-10; 21:1-4; Acts 2:44-45; 4:32-37). The same principle seems to have pertained to Qumran, for the more initiates progressed in purity, the more their property was pooled together for the community, or conversely, the less spiritual the initiates, the less their goods were made available to others (1QS 1:11-13; 2:25-33; 5:14-26; 6:18-24; 7:24-27). Moreover, as in Luke-Acts, in the DSS the selfish use of possessions invited punishment (cf. 1QS 6:4-25 with Lk 6:24-25; 10:10-12, 19-31; 18:18-26; Acts 5:1-11).

2. Both groups advocated communal sharing (cf. 1QS 5:1-5; 9:3-11 with Acts 2:44-45; 4:32-37).[37]

3. Both communities were committed to benevolent giving, especially to the poor and needy (cf. Acts 6:1-3 with CD 14:5-11).

4. The voluntary surrendering of one's possessions in Luke-Acts and in the DSS was probably eschatologically motivated. This was so for at least two reasons. First, both groups believed that the end of

times was upon them and, therefore, that they had no need to be concerned about the future. Second, both communities expected a reversal of the fortunes of the poor and the rich when the kingdom of God fully arrived. To give their possessions away, then, placed them in the category of the "poor," whose status was to be changed in the future. Better, therefore, to be poor now and rich later than the opposite.[38]

Their codes of conduct and discipline. A final matter of praxis related to the communities of Luke-Acts and the DSS is the high premium placed on discipline by those groups. Three considerations accentuate the importance of this quality for the congregations. First, both required the disciplines of repentance and self-denial in order to be a part of their faith communities. Luke 3:4-8, like Rule of the Community 8:12-16, bases membership in its group on Isaiah 40:3 and its call to repentance from sin in order to be pleasing to God. Furthermore, Luke 9:23-27 sets out the path for being faithful to Christ: self-denial leading to holiness. The same progress in purity born out of self-denial characterized the Qumran community in its initiation procedures (1QS 6:13-24).

Second, both groups exercised discipline in maintaining the spiritual health of their congregations, which included interpersonal confrontation. Luke 17:3-4, along with Matthew 18:15-17, 21-22, delineates a three-step procedure in reconciling recalcitrant offenders within the church:

☐ An individual exhorts the guilty party in private.

☐ That failing, witnesses then confront the individual in private.

☐ If those measures prove to be unsuccessful, then the offender is to be rebuked before the whole congregation.

Intriguingly, a similar three step "recovery" program was followed by the Essenes. Thus Rule of the Community 5:25—6:1 (cf. CD 9:2-8) reads:

> No-one should speak to his brother in anger or muttering, 26 or with a hard [neck or with passionate] spiteful intent and he should not detest him [in the stubbornness] of his heart, but instead reproach him that day so as not *Col.* VI 1 to incur a sin for his fault. And in addition, no-one should raise a matter against his fellow in front of the Many unless it is with reproof in the presence of witnesses.

Third, both groups resorted to punishment in the event of serious breaches of discipline by members of their communities. Thus the penalty for misbehavior at Qumran (e.g., lying, complaining, insulting others) included a reduction of food rations, while disputing the teaching of the sect or misuse of the divine name resulted in expulsion from the group. Interestingly, dealing deceitfully with the property of the group is listed under deeds of misbehavior.[39]

Luke also lists similar activity in the church, along with the punishment it brought about (Acts 5:1-10). It is not surprising, then, that the Lukan congregation generated fear in outsiders (Acts 5:11-13). Probably the stringent reaction displayed toward disobedient members within the early church proceeded from the belief that those individuals were apostates. A similar conviction informs the DSS regarding those who departed from the new covenant community (e.g., 1QpHab 1:1-10; CD 8:20-21; 19:34; 20:11-13; cf. Heb 3:12-13; 4:11; 6:4-6; 10:26-31; 12:15-17, 29). One is reminded here of the punishment unleashed on Achan at a critical point in ancient Israel's history (Josh 7:1-26).

The preceding matters of praxis—hymns, following the Spirit, organization, rituals, possessions and discipline—provide windows into the life setting of the communities of Luke-Acts and the DSS. Each of these practical concerns points to the assumption on the part of these respective groups that they constituted true Israel. The next section—symbols of the communities of Luke-Acts and the DSS—reveals a deep division between the perspective of these two groups and that of late Second Temple Judaism.

Symbol

Wright delineates four symbols reflecting the story of Israel in late Second Temple Judaism: temple, Torah, land and ethnicity. Luke-Acts and the DSS deal with each of these but in subversive fashion. Again, I will take them in reverse order.

Ethnicity. The story of Israel focused on the deliverance and restoration of the nation, i.e. ethnic Jews. As was shown earlier, however, John the Baptist and the Qumran community rejected the common presumption that ethnic Israel per se constituted the redeemed. Rather ethnic Israel was branded "a brood of vipers," that is, satanic, and was judged to stand under divine wrath (cf. Lk 3:7-8 with 1QH 3:12, 18; 5:2), hence the typical Jew's need to submit to the "baptism of repentance." Contrasted to mere ethnic Judaism were the communities of Luke-Acts and the DSS, which viewed themselves as the restored Israel.

Interestingly enough, these two groups share at least a fourfold terminology regarding the nomenclature of the people of God. First, both apply the designation *way* to themselves with reference to Isaiah 40:3 (cf. 1QS 8:14 with, e.g., Lk 3:4; Acts 9:2; 24:14). Second, as observed above, each community associates itself with the *'nwm* ("poor ones") tradition (cf., e.g., 1QH 1:36; 2:34; 5:13-14; 1QM 14:7 with, e.g., Lk 1:48-53; 6:20-24; 12:13-21; 14:7-14), thereby presenting themselves as people solely dependent on God. Third, the unusual description "men of God's good pleasure" is used in both writings (cf. Lk 2:14 with 1QH 4:32; 11:9), expressing their belief that they were divinely appointed. Fourth, both understand their respective communities to be participants in the New Covenant (cf. Lk 22:20 with, e.g., CD 8:21; 1QpHab 2:3).

Land. If the first divine promise to Abraham was that of a people for Yahweh's name, the second pertained to the gift of the land of Canaan (see especially Gen 12:1-3; 15:18). Rooted in these assurances were the exodus, wilderness and conquest traditions. Wright captures the significance of the land of Israel in all of this:

> If we are to understand first-century Judaism we must rank Land, along with Temple and Torah, as one of the major symbols. It was YHWH's Land, given inalienably to Israel. The Romans had no more right to be ruling it than did any of their pagan predecessors. The Land was, of course, not only a symbol: it was the source of bread and wine, the place to graze sheep and goats, grow olives and figs. It was the place where, and the means through which, YHWH gave to his covenant people the blessings he had promised them, which were all summed up in the many-sided and evocative word *shalom*, peace. It was the new Eden, the garden of YHWH, the home of the true humanity.[40]

But the question that was uppermost in the minds of many late Second Temple Jews was, If we are restored to our land, why are we still under the thumbs of foreign rulers? Luke-Acts and the DSS provide parallel answers to that quandary, namely, Israel is still in exile and therefore is in desperate need of a new exodus and conquest. Note how the complex of exodus, wilderness and conquest traditions factor heavily into the thinking of these two groups.

1. Both Luke-Acts and the DSS present their communities as participating in a new exodus by virtue of repentance from sin. We are surely to interpret Luke 3:3, 21-22 and parallels as portraying the baptisms of John the Baptist and Jesus as such. Most probably Rule of the Community 4:20-21; 5:13-14, with their references to baptism and forgiveness (see above), are intended to be understood similarly.

2. The new exodus is confirmed by Rule of the Community 8:12-16, which equates the DSS community's trek into the Judean desert with the inauguration of the Isaianic new exodus (see Is 40:3-4). W. D. Davies has shown that in ancient Judaism a return to the wilderness demonstrated the conviction that preparation was being made there for Israel's redemption.[41] More recently, Daniel G. Reid and Tremper Longman III have highlighted the fact that although the association of desert with testing, murmuring and disobedience is common in the OT, Second Temple Judaism maintained the more positive tradition of regarding the desert as preparation for Israel's restoration (Is 35:1-2; 40:3-5; 63:11-14; Ezek 20:33-44; Hos 2:14-23).[42] Rule of the Community 8:12-16, along with Luke 3:3-6; 4:1-13, is well explained against that background.

3. Related to the themes of the exodus and the wilderness, it is also clear that the DSS and Luke-Acts understand their people as participating in a new conquest of the land. This was the case for the War Scroll and 11QMelchizekek (recall chapter four in this study). Longman and Reid have insightfully suggested this also to be for Luke's presentation of both Jesus and the seventy-two disciples. Thus Jesus' exorcisms and healings should be perceived as the conquest of Satan who, with his demonic hordes, inhabits the land of Israel.[43] Similarly, the role of the seventy-two disciples in announcing the salvation of Israel is remarkably parallel to the Deuteronomic instructions for warfare against cities outside the land of inheritance (cf. Lk 10 with Deut 20:10-15) which immediately precede the guidelines for conquest of the promised land (Deut 20:16-18).[44]

At this point, however, the presentations of the DSS and Luke-Acts take a dramatic turn in the story of the Jews, for each in its own way subverts the traditional understanding of Israel's exodus, wilderness and conquest traditions. According to them, the enemy in the land needing to be expelled is none other than Israel itself! I earlier noted this to be the case for the DSS from a document like the War Scroll, which applies the label of Israel's "enemies" (*Kittim*) to the nation itself. I also made mention of Wright's argument that the Gospels reinterpret Israel's enemy to be not Rome but Satan. Along this line, undoubtedly Luke's emphasis on Jesus' exorcisms and healings (see above) communicated the reality that Israel required deliverance from a spiritual, not political, foe (cf. Eph 6:10-18).

Torah. The Torah was the covenant charter of Israel, establishing that people's relationship with God. Nowhere is the covenantal character of the law more evident than in the book of Deuteronomy. Patterned after the Hittite Suzerainty-vassal treaty (second millennium B.C.), Deuteronomy highlights the centrality of the Torah to ancient Judaism: preamble (Deut 1:1-5), historical prologue (Deut 1:6—3:29), stipulations (Deut 4—26), blessings and curses (Deut 28), public display (Deut 31:9, 24-26) and appeal to witnesses (Deut 31:26—32:47). These features accentuate the importance of the Torah for Israel's relationship to God. To obey it was to invite divine blessings for both people and land; to disobey it was to invoke God's curses in the form of defeat and exile suffered at the hands of foreign powers.

The Deuteronomistic tradition emerges out of all of this, as Steck has demonstrated, exerting its influence on Jewish literature between 200 B.C. and A.D. 100,[45] including the DSS. (Recall from chapter three Moessner's application of this tradition to the Qumran community.)[46] Undoubtedly, the same background significantly influences Luke-Acts as well. More than thirty years ago Christopher F. Evans proposed that Luke's central section (Lk 9:51—18:14; Jesus' journey to Jerusalem) is patterned after the content and order of Deuteronomy 1—26 (LXX).[47] Recently, Moessner has thoroughly shown that the fourfold tenet of the Deuteronomistic tradition is the dominant influence on that section. Figure 5.1 presents his summary chart (Moessner extends it to Lk 19:44):

A "This generation" "stiff-necked" like their "fathers"	B Jesus sent as a voice to mediate God's will, instruct, admon- ish, warn	C "This generation" rejects Jesus/ prophet and kills him	D Therefore God will rain destruc- tion on the whole crooked nation
	9:51, 52-56, 57-62	9:51, 52-56, 57-58	
	10:1-12, 13-15, 16, 17-20, 21-24, 25- 28, 29-37, 38-42	10:3, 10-11, 13, 16, 25	(10:12, 14-15)
11:29-32, 49-52	11:1-4, 5-8, 9-13, 14-23, 24-26, 27- 28, 29-32, 33, 34- 36, 37-54	11:14-23, 24-26, 29-32, 47-54	11:31-32, 50-51
12:54-56, 57-59	12:1, 2-9, 10, 11- 12, 13-15, 16-21, 22-32, 33-34, 35- 48, 49-53, 54-56, 57-59	12:49-50, 54-56	12:57-59
13:1-9, 22-30, 34	13:1-9, 10-17, 18- 19, 22-30, 31-33, 34-35	13:1-9, 14-17, 25- 30, 31-33, 34	13:24-30, 35
	14:1-6, 7-14, 15-24, 25-33, 34-35	14:1, 24	14:24
	15:1-7, 8-10, 11-32	15:1-2	
16:27-31	16:1-9, 10-12, 13, 14-15, 16-17, 18, 19-31	16:14-15, 16, 27-31	(16:27-31)
17:25-30	17:1-4, 5-6, 7-10, 11-19, 20-21, 22-37	17:25-30	17:26-30
18:8	18:1-8, 9-14, 15-17, 18-23, 24-30, 31- 34, 35-43	18:8, 31-34	
19:41-42, 44	19:1-10, 11-27, 28- 40, 41-44	19:7, 14, 39-40	19:27, 41-44

Figure 5.1. Table of contents of the central section of Luke and its Deuteronomistic prophetic tenets[48]

Furthermore, Moessner demonstrates that the same fourfold Deuteronomistic tradition undergirds the majority of Acts, beginning with Stephen (Acts 7) and focusing on Paul (Acts 9:3—28:9).[49] Little wonder, therefore, that Luke concludes his story of the church by applying Isaiah 6:9-10 (Acts 28:26-27), a classic encapsulation of the Deuteronomistic pattern, to Israel. We see then that a (perhaps *the*) key tradition informing Luke-Acts and the DSS is the Deuteronomistic paradigm.

While such a pattern is pervasive in late Second Temple Judaism, the DSS and Luke-Acts (and also the NT) distinguish themselves from contemporary Jewish literature in that they (1) redefine the Torah and (2) pronounce judgment on all who do not embrace their redefinitions. Concerning the first of these differences, the DSS provide a stricter interpretation of the law of Moses as promulgated by the Teacher of Righteousness, whereas Luke-Acts offers a greatly reduced summary of the law (love of God and neighbor, Lk 10:25-28) in the gospel of Jesus Christ. Concerning the second difference, the authors of the DSS and Luke-Acts pronounce the covenantal curses on those who reject the Teacher of Righteousness and Jesus respectively, because these are held up as God's final prophetic voices to Israel (hence the ensuing destruction of Jerusalem in A.D. 70). Those who accept them, however, will receive the Deuteronomic blessings.

Temple. The temple was the central symbol of ancient Israel, touching on key areas of Jewish existence: spirituality, politics and economics. It is rather dramatic, therefore, that the DSS and the NT decidely differ with Second Temple literature by rejecting or at the very least redefining such a vital institution, offering in its place their own communities as the true dwelling place of God (see 1QS 8:4-10; 4QFlor 1:1-16; Mk 14:58; Jn 2:19-21; 1 Cor 3:16-17; 69-20; 2 Cor 6:16-18; Heb 9; 1 Pet 2:5-10). Such a view extended beyond just the temple; it included the spiritualization of the whole cultus. Thus Richard A. Horsley can say of the DSS people,

> Their own community was now making atonement for Israel, their own prayers being "an acceptable fragrance of righteousness," their "perfection of way" a "delectable free-will offering," and their own deeds of Torah the true "smoke of incense" (e.g., 1QS 5:5-7; 8:4-10; 9:3-6; 4QFlor 1:1-13). This is a very understandable interpretation of their situation by a priestly dominated community alienated from the Jerusalem Temple.[50]

This proclivity to spiritualize temple and cultus is also operative in the NT (see my chapter eight regarding Hebrews), especially in Stephen's speech (Acts 6—7), which has been called the most sweeping repudiation of the temple and its worship in the entire NT.[51] The climax of Stephen's testimony comes in Acts 7:42-53, where three of the great symbols of ancient Israel are, for all practical purposes, jettisoned.

1. The sacrificial system is declared to be no substitute for heart-felt service to God (Acts 7:42-43).

2. The tabernacle and the temple are declared to be inadequate to house God (Acts 7:44-45).

3. The law does not engender obedience to God (Acts 7:53).

Thus despite these symbols, according to Stephen, Israel remained a "stiff-necked," hard-hearted people. In other words, Acts 6—7 verifies that Israel's past sins, which have culminated in the rejection of Jesus the Messiah, continued to subject the nation to the covenantal curses.

The symbols of Second Temple Judaism—ethnicity, land, Torah and temple—represent major points of dissension between the DSS and Luke-Acts, on one hand, and the majority of ancient Judaism, on the other hand. Those two bodies of literature reinterpreted such aspects so as to subvert the story of Israel. What was needed, they asserted, was remnant theology, not just ethnicity; a purified land, accomplished by repentance rather than revolt; obedient hearts, not mere lip service to Torah; and a holy congregation preserved for the presence of God, not simply a religious base of operations. But in the end the congregations of the DSS and Luke-Acts themselves disagree in their particular understanding of the story of Israel.

The Story of Israel

The story of Israel as told by the DSS community is familiar by now: Non-Qumranic Jews (and of course Gentiles as well) are sinners who are unfaithful to the law of Moses, not to mention the *halakhah* of the Teacher of Righteousness. Consequently, they are sinners and will remain under the covenantal curses. Roman occupation of the land is proof positive that the exile is still intact. In utter contrast to all of this is the Qumran congregation, whose adherence to the truth of God identifies it as the vanguard of the restoration of faithful Israel. Luke-Acts turns the preceding story topsy-turvy at its three crucial points.

Sin. Approximately one-third of the Gospel of Luke is unique material[52] and is informed by at least two themes:

☐ Salvation is being offered to Jews in the person of Jesus Christ.

☐ Christ's love and salvation are available also to the outcasts of Judaism: Gentiles, women, sinners, the poor, Samaritans and the like.

A logical connection exists between these two Lukan concerns which, in effect, reverses the story of Israel: sinners (the second theme), more so than mainstream Jews (the first theme), are the ones who participate in the restoration of Israel in that they accept Jesus as the Messiah. This surely was an affront to law-abiding Jews in Jesus' day.

Exile. Here recall the earlier observation that Jesus, in typical Deuteronomistic fashion, was rejected by Israel as God's most authoritative prophet (Lk 9:51—19:44). But, as Wright argues (recall chapter four), Jesus embodied Israel's fate, thereby embracing on the cross the Deuteronomic curses so that by his resurrection he might offer the covenantal blessings to those who follow him (cf. Lk 20-24).[53] For our purposes it is sufficient to point out that the association Jesus forged between himself and the Deuteronomic curses amounted to a reversal of messianic expectation in most Jews' minds. They anticipated a political conquering Messiah, not a crucified one.[54]

Restoration. Luke's second volume (Acts) bears out the twofold concern of the special material in his Gospel. Because the majority of the nation of Israel has rejected the good news of restoration (e.g., Acts 7:51), salvation has now gone to the Gentiles (e.g., Acts 13:46; 15:16-17; 22:21; 26:16-17). To put it another way, while the OT envisioned the conversion of the Gentiles to occur *after* the restoration of Israel (Is 2:2-3; 56:6-7; 60:1-7; cf. *Tob* 13:11-13; 14:6-7; *Pss. Sol.* 17:26-46; *T. Zeb.* 9:8; *T. Benj.* 9:2; *Sib. Or.* 3:767-95), Acts states the opposite: Gentiles are being restored first.[55] We are not left to our imagination as to how such a retelling of the story of Israel impressed ancient Jews. When Paul gave his testimony in Jerusalem, his Jewish audience listened until he reported his obedience to the divine call to go to the Gentiles. The crowd's immediate response is given in Acts 22:22: "Then they lifted up their voices and said, 'Away with such a fellow from the earth! For he ought not to live.'" The audience knew well that the conversion of the Gentiles, as Paul presented it, subverted the story of Israel.

Neither does one need to speculate on how the DSS people would have responded to Paul's message. Scot McKnight summarizes the anti-Gentile mentality (along with the antagonism toward non-Qumranic Jews) which characterized that community:

> The Essenes of Qumran are known for sectarian nationalism and social separation, not only from Gentiles but also from unfaithful Israelites (CD 6:14, 15; 7:13; 8:4, 8, 16; 11:4-5; 12:6-1; 13:14; 16:9; 19:17-29; 1QS 1-4; 5:1-2, 10-11; 6:15; 9:5, 8-9, 20-21; 1QH 14:21-22; 11QTemple 48:7-13; 60:16-21). Separation emerges as a sociological rule in order to avoid sin and idolatry (CD 11:15; 12:6-9). The scrolls, especially the War Scroll, seem to assign the Gentiles to the wrath of God (1QM 2:7; 4:12; 9:9; 11:9, 15; 12:11, 14; 14:5, 7, *et passim*; 1QpHab 5:4; 1QSa 1:21).[56]

Conclusion

This chapter has been concerned to show that the DSS and Luke-Acts attempted to restructure ancient Judaism's worldview by retelling the story of Israel through a recasting of its symbols and praxis. I conclude this discussion with an observation: Beyond all the stringency of the Qumran message, Luke-Acts makes an even more radical proclamation in its retelling of the story of Israel. On this point Wright insightfully draws parallels between Luke and Josephus:

> Luke's framework for Acts provides an analogue to that of Josephus. In both cases, the writer claims that this is the true reading of scriptural prophecy. In both cases, the new story radically subverts the old one: neither Josephus nor Luke suggests that there will be a fulfillment along the lines expected by militant Jews. In both cases, Israel's god is responsible for the royal progress from Jerusalem to Rome. Vespasian, and Jesus, are proclaimed king, first in Judaea, then in Rome. In each case, Jerusalem is left in ruins, the rebellious counter-kingdom.[57]

The Qumran community would not have agreed with Luke and, for that matter, with Josephus, for the rubble and cemetery at that site are eloquent witnesses today to that group's last stand against the Romans in A.D. 68.

Chapter Six

The Reverse
of the Curse

Justification According to the DSS & Paul

Introduction

The following quotations from Paul and the DSS highlight the importance of justification by faith in the soteriology of the apostle and of the Qumran community. The first is Paul's programmatic statement on the subject:

> For in it [the gospel] the righteousness of God is revealed through faith for faith; as it is written, "He who through faith is righteous shall live." (Rom 1:17)

The apostle's declaration obviously expresses the idea that the righteousness of God is given to sinners because of his grace. One might be surprised, therefore, to discover that a similar understanding of justification and salvation appears in the DSS. For example, Rule of the Community 11:12-15 reads,

> *12* the mercies of God shall be my salvation always;
> and if I fall in the sin of the flesh,
> in the justice of God, which endures eternally, shall my judgments be;

13 if my grief commences,
he will free my soul from the pit
and make my steps steady on the path;
he will draw me near in his mercies,
and by kindnesses set in motion my judgment;
14 he will judge me in the justice of his truth,
and in his plentiful goodness
always atone for all my sins;
in his justice he will cleanse me
from the uncleanness of the human being
15 and from the sin of the sons of man,
so that I can extol God for his justice
and The Highest for his majesty,
Blessed be you, my God,
Who opens the heart of your servant to knowledge!

Statements like these led Qumran scholar Millar Burrows to posit a connection between the DSS and Paul in this matter: "The point of prime importance here is that while man has no righteousness of his own, there is a righteousness which God, in his own righteousness, freely confers."[1] In a later study, Siegfried Schulz pursued the topic further by analyzing at length the doctrine of justification in Paul and in the Qumran community. He concluded that the apostle's view of justification *sola gratia* is derived from the DSS.[2] More recently, E. P. Sanders's watershed work calls attention to the idea of "covenantal nomism" present in early Judaism, including the DSS. According to Sanders, Jewish writers of the Second Temple period believed that salvation, or entrance into God's covenant, was based on God's justifying grace and that remaining in this status was accomplished by obeying the Mosaic law.[3] In his judgment, especially relative to the DSS, Sanders builds on an earlier study by Jürgen Becker. That author contended, somewhat differently from Burrows, that passages like Rule of the Community 10:9—11:22 do speak of *sola gratia* but only with regard to the Qumran sect, and that its members were not thereby freed from the law. Thus while the law does not bring righteousness ($ṣ^e dāqâh$), it is still a factor in the way to salvation.[4]

The discussion in this chapter takes as its point of departure the research of Sanders, especially his theory that covenantal nomism characterizes the DSS. Accordingly, two components can be perceived as informing the Qumran community's understanding of salvation:

☐ Entrance into the covenant is by God's justifying grace.

☐ Remaining in the covenant is accomplished by obeying the Torah.

This twofold concept invites comparison with Paul's doctrine of justification. The thesis that will be developed in the ensuing material is that the first aspect of covenantal nomism—God's justifying grace—is quite hospitable to the apostle's thinking, whereas the second is categorically rejected by Paul. According to him, no one can be saved (or kept) by the works of the law.

To conduct this comparative analysis I will divide the discussion into two parts. I will first identify four related strands of teaching on justification in the DSS, which are conceptually shaped by the Deuteronomic curses and blessings. From this it will be seen that the heart of the Scrolls' doctrine of justification pertains to obedience to the community's *halakhah*. This alone is the means for experiencing the covenantal blessings; not to do so is to invoke upon oneself the Deuteronomic curses.

I will then demonstrate from key passages like Romans 1:16—3:21; 5—8; 9:30—10:8; Philippians 3; and Galatians 3:10-14, that Paul *reverses* such teaching. Those who attempt to obey the law in any form in order to be justified ironically remain under the Deuteronomic curses. Only those whose faith is in Christ alone, apart from the works of the Torah, experience the Deuteronomic blessings.

Justification According to the DSS

With the help of Sanders, we may cull four ideas from the DSS regarding justification, each of which is rooted in the covenant.[5]

The righteousness of God versus human sinfulness. Sanders identifies one of the principal uses of the terms *righteousness* and *justification*[6] in the DSS; namely, God is righteous and humans are not.[7] Thus Rule of the Community 10:23 contrasts the *ṣidqōt* of God with the faithlessness of humans. In *Hôdāyôt* 1:26 the hymnist asks what reply can be offered concerning a person's sins and iniquities in the presence of God's "righteous judgment" (*mišpāṭ ha-ṣedeq*). The psalmist continues by saying, with a characteristic formula of ascription ("thine, thine"), that to God belong "deeds of righteousness" (ma'aśe ha-ṣᵉdāqâh), while to humanity belong the works of iniquity. Rule of the Community 11:9-10 powerfully captures the preceding contrast:

> 9 However, I belong to evil humankind,
> to the assembly of wicked flesh;
> my failing, my transgressions, my sins, {. . .}
> with the depravities of my heart,
> 10 belong to the assembly of worms
> and of those who walk in darkness.
> For to man (does not belong) this path,
> nor to a human belongs the steadying of his step;
> since judgment belongs to God.

The same sentiments are expressed in Hôdāyôt 12:29-30, where the depravity of humans are by implication contrasted to God's righteousness:

> 29 What is flesh compared to this?
> What creature of clay can do wonders?
> He is in sin from his maternal womb,
> 30 and in guilty iniquity right to old age.
> But I know that justice does not belong to man
> nor the perfect path to the son of man. (cf. 1QH 7:17-18; 9:14-17)[8]

Especially relevant to the polarity between the righteousness of God and the sinfulness of humanity is the covenantal framework into which such a contrast is placed. So it is that Rule of the Community 1:21—2:5 has the priests recite the righteous (ṣidqōt) deeds of God along with the subsequent Deuteronomic blessings that rest on those who, by his grace, obey him, while the Levites utter the iniquities of all non-Qumranians as well as the consequent Deuteronomic curses abiding on them:

> Blank 21 Blank The priests shall recite the just deeds of God in his mighty works, 22 and they shall proclaim all his merciful favours towards Israel. And the levites shall 23 recite the sins of the children of Israel, all their blameworthy transgressions and their sins during the dominion

of *24* Belial. [And all] those who enter the covenant shall confess after
them and they shall say:
"We have acted sinfully,
25 [we have transgressed,
we have si]nned, we have acted irreverently,
we and our fathers before us,
inasmuch as we walk
26 [in the opposite direction to the precepts] of truth and justice
[. . .]his judgment upon us and upon our fathers;

Col. II   1 but he has showered on us his merciful favour
for ever and ever."
And the priests will bless *2* all the men of God's lot who walk
unblemished in
all his paths and they shall say:
"May he bless you with everything good,
3 and may he protect you from everything bad.
May he illuminate your heart with the discernment of life
and grace you with eternal knowledge.
4 May he lift upon you the countenance of his favour
for eternal peace."
And the levites shall curse all the men of *5* the lot of Belial. They shall
begin
to speak and shall say:
"Accursed are you for all your wicked, blameworthy deeds."[9]

The righteousness of God and divine mercy. A possibly surprising
element that surfaces in discussing the Scrolls' understanding of righteousness is, as Sanders observes, that God's righteousness is often
synonymous with his mercy. More particularly, the writers of the DSS
praise God for having cleansed them by his righteousness/mercy. Rule
of the Community 11:3-15, especially lines 12-15, makes this clear:

12 the mercies of God shall be my salvation always;
and if I fall in the sin of the flesh,
in the justice of God, which endures
eternally, shall my judgment be;
13 if my grief commences,
he will free my soul from the pit

and make my steps steady on the path;
he will draw me near in his mercies,
and by kindnesses set in motion my judgment;
14 he will judge me in the justice of his truth,
and in his plentiful goodness
always atone for all my sins;
in his justice he will cleanse me
from the uncleanness of the human being
15 and from the sin of the sons of man,
so that I can extol God for his justice
and The Highest for his majesty.
Blessed be you, my God,
who opens the heart of your servant to knowledge!

It is hard to resist the conclusion here that mercy and justification/ righteousness are parallel. (Other passages basically make the same point: see, e.g., 1QH 4:37; 7:29-31; 9:34; 11:29-31; 16:9.)[10] How this is related to the covenant is demonstrated by the next consideration.

God's righteousness/mercy manifested through membership in the Qumran community. Though Sanders does not develop this aspect of righteousness in the DSS, it is nevertheless the logical consequence of the previous observation. Specifically stated, God's righteousness and mercy are extended to individuals in the sense that they are the objects of predestination, namely, that those who have been chosen to join the New Covenant community of the Essenes. Thus Rule of the Community 11, a text earlier shown to equate divine righteousness and mercy, associates righteousness and mercy with God's selection of the members of the Qumran community, beginning with the Teacher of Righteousness:

There is support for my right hand,
the path of my steps goes over firm rock,
it does not waver before anything.
For the truth of God is the rock of my steps,
5 and his might the support of my right hand.
From the spring of his *justice* is my judgment
and from the wonderful mystery is the light in my heart.
My eyes have observed what always is,

6 wisdom that has been hidden from mankind,
knowledge and understanding (hidden) from the sons of man,
fount of *justice* and well of strength
7 and spring of glory (hidden) from the assembly of flesh.
To those whom God has *selected* he has given them
as everlasting possession;
until they inherit them
in the lot of the holy ones. . . .
11 . . . By his knowledge everything shall come into being,
and all that does exist
he establishes with his calculations
and nothing is done outside of him.
As for me, if I stumble,
12 the *mercies* of God shall be my salvation always;
and if I fall in the sin of the flesh
in the justice of God, which endures eternally, shall my judgment be.
(1QS 11:5-7, 11-12, emphasis added)

A similar combination of righteousness, mercy and election occurs in
Rule of the Community 4:2-8, which is a part of the classic text in the DSS
detailing the divine predestination of the two spirits/ways (3:13—4:26):

2 *Blank* These are their paths in the world: to enlighten the heart of man,
straighten out in front of him all the paths of justice and truth, establish
in his heart respect for the precepts 3 of God; it is a spirit of meekness, of
patience, generous compassion, eternal goodness, intelligence, understanding, potent wisdom which trusts in all 4 the deeds of God and
depends on his abundant mercy; a spirit of knowledge in all the plans of
action, of enthusiasm for the decrees of justice, 5 of holy plans with firm
purpose, of generous compassion with all the sons of truth, of magnifi-
cent purity which detests all unclean idols, of unpretentious behavior
6 with moderation in everything, of prudence in respect of the truth concerning the mysteries of knowledge. These are the counsels of the spirit
for the sons of truth in the world. And the visitation of those who walk
in it will be for healing, 7 plentiful peace in a long life, fruitful offspring
with all everlasting blessings, eternal enjoyment with endless life, and a
crown of glory with majestic raiment in eternal light.

Thus those who have been chosen to be members of the Qumran community are the ones who have definitively experienced God's righ-

teousness/mercy (see especially lines 2-5).

Important to this discussion is the influence of Deuteronomy on the framework of the Rule of the Community. To enter the Qumran community is to embrace the Mosaic covenant as now reconstituted by true Israel (1QS 1:3, 6-7, 16; 2:18-25)—the ones who faithfully follow the divine stipulations (1QS 1:9) and therefore do not walk in that hardness of heart which characterized Moses' generation and beyond (e.g., 1QS 1:6). To the Qumran covenanters belong the Deuteronomic blessings of life, forgiveness and peace (1QS 1:19—2:4; 4:7-8; 5:5-6; 11:7-8). The Deuteronomic curses, however, are pronounced by the members of Qumran, the community of priests, on those outside it or who insincerely join their ranks (1QS 2:4-17; 4:9-13; 5:10-13).

Obeying the **halakhah** *of the Qumran community to maintain one's covenant status.* Sanders pinpoints the ultimate concept of righteousness which drove the DSS sect:

> Human righteousness *is* works of law being equivalent to perfection of way (cf. 1QS 11:17) and the opposite of transgression (1QH 7:28-31). A man is elect by God's predestining grace and thus classed as *tsaddiq*. The only way, however, is to do the commandments of God as specified by the sect's covenant and not to sin . . . being *tsaddiq* involves doing the law, while salvation comes by God's election. That is, doing the law is the *condition of remaining elect.*[11]

Similarly, Mark A. Seifrid notes that Scrolls passages connecting righteousness with "perfection of way" (1QS 1:8; 2:2; 3:9, 20, 22; 4:22; 8:1, 9-10, 18, 20-21; 9:2, 5, 14, 19) and with "holiness" (1QS 2:25; 5:6, 13, 18, 20; 8:5, 6, 8, 17, 20-21, 23; 9:2, 6, 8) attest to the community's definition of *justification*: it is faith plus works.[12] That is to say, obeying the sect's *halakhah* is the means for maintaining one's status in the New Covenant. Conversely, to demonstrate *genuine* faith by remaining true to the Essenes' interpretation of the law necessitates continued segregation from non-Qumranic people. As Sanders observes, the members of the DSS sect considered themselves to be priests[13] of whom ritual purity was required, and all who did not follow the Essenes' *halakhah* were unclean; therefore, contact between the two groups was unacceptable (e.g., 1QS 3:3-6; 5:14; 1QH 11:11; 16:10; 1QM 13:2, 5). One is reminded here of Rule of the Community 1:21—2:4, where the priests pronounce the Deuteronomic blessings on those faithful to the New Covenant of the Qumran community, while the Levites utter the Deuteronomic curses on those who are not.

Two foundational documents especially illustrate the covenantal nomist perspective of the Scrolls: the 1QpHabbakkuk and *Miqsat Maase Ha-Torah*. *Pesher* on Habakkuk 8:1-3 reveals the essence of the DSS concept of justification by faith in the way it interprets Habakkuk 2:4 ("the righteous shall live by his faith"): "Its interpretation concerns all observing the law in the house of Judah, whom God will free from punishment on account of their deeds and of their loyalty to the Teacher of Righteousness." In other words, one is justified by remaining true to the precepts of the Teacher of Righteousness, which means to depart from all other perspectives on the Torah. This is the way to maintain one's status in the new covenant.

The other significant document related to this particular discussion is *Miqsat Maase Ha-Torah*. Martin Abegg has convincingly demonstrated that the correct rendering of the title of this work, as reflected in lines 2 and 113, is "Some Works of the Torah."[14] As the document indicates, the works of the Torah are the *halakhah* of the Qumran community (lines 1-9) which separate that group from "normative Judaism," probably the Jerusalem leadership (lines 92-96). Those who are faithful to the sect's way of life will experience the Deuteronomic blessings, while those outside will remain under the Deuteronomic curses (lines 97-117). Significantly, line 117 assumes that those who are faithful to the community's interpretation of the works of the Torah are the ones who shall "be reckoned… in justice [righteousness]." Thus, like 1QpHabakkuk 8:1-3, *Miqsat Maase Ha-Torah* maintains that *justification* means to express one's faith by being true to the group's stance on the law.[15]

The preceding four statements, then, capture the essence of the DSS teaching on justification/righteousness: God is righteous, but humans are unrighteous; God's righteousness/justification is intimately related to his cleansing mercy; God's righteousness is demonstrated through his election of the Qumran community; obeying the community's *halakhah* is the means for remaining in the covenant. Furthermore, such covenantal nomism was deeply influenced by the Deuteronomic blessings and curses; blessings belong to those within the DSS sect, but curses abide on those who do not.

Paul's Reversal of the Deuteronomic Curses and Blessings

The point may be stated bluntly: in contrast to the DSS, Paul reverses the Deuteronomistic tradition. Its curses abide on those who attempt to keep the Mosaic law, whereas its blessings rest on those who do not; rather their faith is in Christ, who took on himself the curse of the law in order to bring it to its conclusion. Frank Thielman nicely encapsulates this reversal motif in Paul's writings with his concept of the "double paradox":

☐ First, the OT warns Israel that disobeying God's law will lead to experiencing the covenant curses (Lev 26:3-39). Indeed, Israel's exile is viewed by the prophets as divine judgment for not obeying the law and being faithful to the covenant (Ezra 9:6-15; Jer 2:9 [cf. Deut 29:24-27]; Ezek 5:6; 11:12; Dan 9:4-19; etc). Passages like Jeremiah 31:31-34 and Ezekiel 36:25-28, however, envision a future day when Israel, empowered by the Spirit of the messianic era, will obey God's law from the heart. Thielman convincingly shows that Paul believed Israel's subjugation to the Romans of his day was continuing evidence that Israel was still under the covenant curses and was not obeying the divine law.

☐ Second, according to Thielman, ironically Paul believed that Gentile Christians were now incorporated into the restored, eschatological people of God, which was anticipated by prophets such as Jeremiah and Ezekiel.

Succinctly stated, the double paradox was that while nonbelieving Jews were under the curses of the old covenant, believing Gentiles were incorporated into the blessings of the New Covenant.[16] This reversal motif can be illustrated as in table 6.1.

Deuteronomistic Tradition	Paul's Reversal
Curses on those who disobey the law	Curses on those who attempt to obey the law
Blessings on those who obey the law	Blessings on those who do not attempt to keep the law but rather put their faith in Christ, who fulfilled the law

Table 6.1. Pauline reversal of the Deuteronomistic tradition

The reversal of the Deuteronomic blessings and curses informs key Pauline texts dealing with justification: Galatians 3:10-14; Romans 1:16-3:31; 5-8; 9:30-10:8; Philippians 3. I proceed now to summarize each of these passages with that perspective in mind.

Galatians 3:10-14. The logic of Galatians 3:10-14 unfolds verse by verse: verse 10 quotes Deuteronomy 27:26, asserting that those who do not obey the Mosaic law will suffer the curses of God. But for the apostle, this is not a challenge designed to motivate people to obey the Torah; rather, it is a warning that no one is capable of keeping the law perfectly. This is why the apostle draws on the Septuagint of Deuteronomy 27:26; it adds the word *all* to the Masoretic text, thereby accentuating the criterion necessary to escape the divine curse—one must abide by *all* the things written in the law. Thomas Shreiner expresses the essence of Galatians 3:10 in a syllogism:

☐ Those who do not keep everything in the Law are cursed (3:10).

☐ No one keeps everything in the Law (implicit premise).

☐ Therefore, those who rely on the works of the Law for salvation are cursed (10).[17]

Galatians 3:11 confirms the inability and undesirability of attempting to keep the Torah by invoking Habakkuk 2:4, which Paul interprets to mean that a person lives—is justified—by faith (cf. Rom 1:16-17). This prophetic principle, according to Galatians 3:12, is at odds with Leviticus 18:5 and its teaching that one must obey the law in order to live. Galatians 3:13 seems to harmonize the two statements by in effect indicating that Christ alone has kept the law and has taken on himself humanity's curse for breaking the Torah.[18] Christ thereby both fulfilled and ended the law for all who trust in him, which according to Galatians 3:14 includes Gentiles.

Romans 1:16—3:31. As Richard B. Hays and James M. Scott have observed, the wrath texts in Romans 1:16—3:31 are informed by the theme of the Deuteronomic curses, such that Paul there announces that divine judgment rests on Israel because it continues to disobey the law of Moses (cf. Rom 2:9 with Deut 28:53, 55, 57; Rom 2:5 with Deut 31:27; Rom 2:8 with Deut 27:27-28).[19] I would add Romans 1:18-32 to this list, thus also including Gentiles in the purview of the Deuteronomic curses.[20] One group, the Jews, is under judgment for disobeying God's written law, the Torah. Another group, the Gentiles, is also under God's wrath for disobeying his law expressed in natural revelation. One is reminded here of a work like *Wisdom of Solomon*, which employs natural "law" to condemn Gentiles because they do not in fact live up to its light (*Wis* 13:1—15:17). Thus Paul places both Jew and Gentile under the Deuteronomic curses in Romans 1:18-32 (cf. Rom 2:9; 3:9). The driving force behind their rebellion, according to the apostle Paul, is surprisingly the law itself, which stirs up disobedience within the individual (Rom 3:19-20; 4:15; cf. Gal 2:15; 3:10-12). In effect, then, Paul here reverses the Deuteronomic curses: both Jew and Gentile are under divine wrath because the law within them has become the catalyst for sin.[21]

While the Deuteronomic curses abide on Jews and Gentiles because they do not obey the Torah, according to Romans 1:16—3:31 the Deuteronomic blessings abide on Christians because of their faith in Christ alone. Hays has pointed out that Romans 1:15-17 is informed by the OT promise of the restoration of Israel, the Deuteronomic blessings (cf. Rom 1:15-17 with Ps 24:2; 43:10; 97:2-3 (LXX); Is 28:16; 51:4-5, 10; Hab 2:4).[22] Furthermore, according to Paul in Romans 3:21-31, the divine means for actualizing this promise was the atoning death of Christ (Rom 3:24-25), which is to be received by faith (Rom 3:21-24, 27-31). Looking at the total picture of Romans 1:16—3:31, then, we can see Paul's logic: the righteousness of God, which includes the Deuteronomic blessings and the prophetic promise of restoration, is available to both Jew and Gentile exclusively through faith in Christ, whose death and resurrection brought an end to the Torah and its curses (cf. Rom 1:16-17 with Rom 3:21-31). The role of the law was therefore temporary; it served to convict both Jew and Gentile of sin (see Rom 1:18—3:20) in order to drive them to the gospel (Rom 3:21-31). Because the Torah is now terminated, both Jew and Gentile can be saved, but by faith alone (Rom 1:16—2:10; 3:30).

Romans 5—8. Two recent articles situate Romans 5—8 in the context of the story of Israel. N. T. Wright's study "The Vindication of the Law: Romans 8:1-11"[23] offers a helpful synopsis of Paul's logic in Romans 5—8:

> It should not come as a surprise, then, to find that the Torah and the covenant are still central categories in Romans 5-8. It could even be argued

that Romans 5.20 is the climax of the whole Adam-Christ passage, explaining the position of the law within the entire scheme of divinely ordered history: . . . ("but the law entered that the transgression might abound"). Certainly it is to that verse that the discussion of Torah in 7.1—8.11 looks back quite obviously, via the hints—which fit happily into the same scheme of thought—in 6.14-15. The position Paul is arguing, just as in Galatians 3, is that the Torah has not alleviated, but rather has exacerbated, the plight of Adamic humanity. This can only mean that the recipients of Torah, i.e., Israel, have found themselves to be under its judgment because of their participation in Adamic humanity. Since therefore Christians have left the realm of the . . . (old man) in baptism, they have also left the realm of Torah, coming out from the place where it could exert a hold over them.[24]

For Wright, then, Paul's solution to the human inability to obey the Torah is Christ, who as Israel's representative has drawn sin to himself on the cross and thereby defeated it (Rom 5:12-21; 7:7-25; 8:3). Because Christians are in Christ via baptism (Rom 6:1—7:6), they now possess the life of the covenant, which was the purpose for which the law was given in the first place (Rom 8:1-11).

Similarly Frank Thielman's article "The Story of Israel and the Theology of Romans 5—8"[25] locates the background of Paul's comments in that unit in the Deuteronomistic tradition. Table 6.2 lists some summary statements of Thielman's exegesis of those sections making up Romans 5—8.

5:1-11	The hope of Israel's restoration is being fulfilled in Christ.
5:12-21	Christ is God's answer to Adam's sin and Israel's violation of the covenant.
6:1—7:25	Through identification with Christ's death and resurrection, Christians are delivered (Deuteronomic blessings) from Adam's disobedience, which are continued in Israel's sin (Deuteronomic curses).
8:1-39	Paul restates the promise of Israel's restoration, which is now occurring through Christ.

Table 6.2. Thielman's exegesis of Romans 5—8

Romans 5—8 can be summarized from the argumentation of Wright and Thielman that the story of Israel is the key background of that unit. My own contention is that Paul reverses the Deuteronomic curses and blessings therein. For our purposes, Romans 5—8 can be divided into four sections: 5:1-11; 5:12-21; 6:1—7:6; 7:7—8:11.

Romans 5:1-11. Romans 5:1-11 should be understood as making the following statement: Christians now experience the Deuteronomic blessings because Christ has absorbed the Deuteronomic curses. That Paul intends to say as much is evident in the covenantal benefits which he believes accrue to Christians because they are justified by faith in Christ. "Peace" (Rom 5:1), as James D. G. Dunn has indicated, is a covenant concept. It refers to the prophetic hope of the return of God's favor to Israel now realized in Christ.[26] "Life" (Rom 5:10), the goal of the covenant, is now available to Christians because the wrath of God—the Deuteronomic curses—has been removed (Rom 5:9). "Reconciliation" (Rom 5:10-11) bespeaks the renewal of God's covenant with Israel but now applied to the church. Whereas *justification* deals with the legal aspect of the covenant, *reconciliation* addresses its relational side.[27]

All of this is made possible because Christ embraced the Deuteronomic curses at the cross (Rom 5:6-11). That Jesus' death is here portrayed against the canvas of covenantal thought becomes clear when we compare this text with the description of the Jewish martyrs in *2 Maccabees* and *4 Maccabees*, the purpose of whose deaths was to restore Israel to God by vicariously suffering for the nation's sins. Note the following three commonalities: *hyper* is found in Romans 5:8 and in *2 Maccabees* 7:9; 8:21 with reference to the martyr's death for the people. "By his blood" specifies the violent nature of the martyr's death (cf. Rom 5:9 with *4 Macc* 6:29; 17:22). Like Romans 5:10-11, *2 Maccabees* 1:5; 5:20; 7:33; 8:29 contain the infrequent word group *reconcile.*[28]

Major disagreement emerges between Romans 5:6-11 and *2 Maccabees* and *4 Maccabees,* however, with Paul's assertion that Christ died for the *ungodly* (Rom 5:6), which distinguishes his death from that of the Maccabean martyrs, whose deaths were offered on behalf of the covenant and the law (*2 Macc* 7:9; 8:21; *4 Macc* 1:8, 10). Dunn pinpoints this significant contrast: "His [Paul's] contemporaries were familiar with this thought of dying for the law(s) or for the nation, but the . . . (ungodly) were precisely those whose conduct put them outside the scope of such covenant faithfulness and concern."[29]

Romans 5:12-21. Probably the best background for interpreting the Adam-Christ antithesis presented in Romans 5:12-21 is the Deuteronomic blessings and curses. Adam's sin (of coveting) was tantamount to breaking the Torah before it was promulgated by Moses (cf. Rom 5:13-14; 7:7 with *4 Ezra* 7:11; *Tg. Neof.* 2:15; *Gen. Rab.* 16:5-6; 24:5; *Deut. Rab.* 2:25; *b. Sanh.* 56b). Therefore, if Adam's sin was perceived as committed against the Torah, then most likely we are to understand the ensuing judgments pronounced on Adam, Eve and the serpent (Gen 3:14-19) as anticipating the Deuteronomic curses.[30] This idea would help explain Paul's association of Adam and Moses in Romans 5:12-14.

However, as Wright has insightfully argued, the goal of Romans 5:20 ("Law came in, to increase the trespass") is to assert that Israel, though commonly thought to be the divinely intended replacement of Adam, has by breaking the Torah demonstrated itself to still be *in* Adam. Wright says of this:

> The place "where sin abounded" (v. 20b) is undoubtedly Israel, the "place" where "the law came in that the trespass might abound." Adam's trespass, active though unobserved until Sinai (vv. 13-14, cf. 7.9a), found fresh opportunity in the arrival of the Torah. Again it could display its true colours as trespass, the flouting of the commands of God.[31]

Thus if Adam's sin anticipated the Deuteronomic curses, Israel's disobedience became the focal point of that judgment.

All of this was according to the divine plan which, as Romans 5:15-21 makes clear, was that Christ—Israel's representative—by his obedient death would bring the covenantal curses to their climax (see especially Rom 5:20, "but where sin increased, grace abounded all the more"). Consequently, Christ's acceptance of the death that humanity deserved made it possible for God to offer to others the life of the covenant (Rom 5:21).

Romans 6:1—7:6. The preceding background enlightens Paul's logic in Romans 6:1—7:6, which can be simply put. Through baptism Christians have been united with Christ's death, and by that death the curse of the law over them has been dismissed; through Christ's resurrection they now participate in the Deuteronomic blessing of life.[32]

Romans 7:7—8:11. Thielman and Wright have (correctly) suggested that the phrases in Romans 8:2—"the law of the Spirit of life" and "the law of sin and death"—correspond to the Deuteronomic blessings and curses, respectively. Regarding the latter, those authors argue that "the law of sin and death" (see Rom 7:10-11; 8:2) alludes to the Deuteronomic promise of life based on the law but which, according to Paul, actually provoked the opposite effect, namely, death (Lev 18:5; Deut 4:1; 30:15, 19-20; 32:47). This ironic turn of events took place because of the law's inability to check sin (see Rom 4:15; 7:5; 8:3; cf. Gal 2:14; 3:21). The culprit, however, is not the divine law but sin, which distorts it (see Rom 7:13).[33] Thus Paul reverses the Deuteronomic curse in Romans 8:2: Whoever attempts to find life by obeying the Torah will suffer death.

Thielman and Wright also call attention to the New Covenant nuance that informs the phrase "the law of the Spirit of life." Thus those whose faith is in the atoning death of Christ (cf. the context of the words "the law of faith" in Rom 3:27) now experience the New Covenant, which has inaugurated the Deuteronomic blessings. Such a reality has occurred for Christians because they died to the law through Christ's death (Rom 7:1-6) and now share in his resurrection life (Rom 8:10-11; cf. Rom 6:1-14).[34] So we see from Romans 7:7—8:11 that Paul reverses the Deuteronomistic tradition; its curses abide on those who attempt to keep the Mosaic law while its blessings rest on those whose faith is in Christ, who took upon himself the judgment of the law in order to bring it to its conclusion (cf. Rom 8:1-11; 10:14; Gal 3:10-14). This powerfully alternates, like the Jews antiphonally responding to each other from Gerizim and Ebal, between presenting life (the Deuteronomic blessings) and death (the Deuteronomic curses), based on the choice to either believe Christ or follow the law.

Romans 9:30—10:8. By way of introducing 9:30—10:8, we should take note of the rather recent studies that call attention to the Deuteronomistic underpinning of Romans 9—11 as a whole. The first is by Richard B. Hays, who emphasizes the importance of Deuteronomy 32 for Romans in two respects. Deuteronomy 32 contains the salvation-historical scheme appropriated in Romans: God's election and care for Israel (Deut 32:6-14), Israel's rebellion (Deut 32:15-18; cf. Deut 32:5),

God's judgment on them (Deut 32:19-35) and ultimately God's final deliverance and vindication of his own people (Deut 32:36-43). Here are contained both the prophecy that God would stir Israel to jealousy through the Gentiles, cited in Romans 10:19 (cf. Deut 32:21) and the invitation to the Gentiles to join with God's people in praise, cited in Romans 15:10 (cf. Deut 32:43).[35]

The second author investigating the Deuteronomistic influence on Romans 9—11 is James M. Scott, who applies Odil Steck's sixfold description of the Deuteronomistic tradition to that material:[36]

1. Israel has been disobedient to the law of God throughout its history (Rom 9:31; 10:21; cf. Rom 2:1-29).

2-3. God has sent his prophets (including Paul) to call Israel to repentance, but they have been repeatedly rejected (Rom 11:2-5; cf. Rom 10:16; 15:31).

4. The Deuteronomic curses now rest on Israel in the form of foreign suppression (Rom 9:1-3; 10:3; 11:1, 5, 10, 16-25; cf. Rom 2:6-8; 3:5).

5. It is still possible for Israel to repent (Rom 9:22; 10:16, 19; 11:11, 14; cf. Rom 2:4-5).

6. Israel will repent and be restored (Rom 11:26-27).

I concur with these conclusions, except that neither of the above authors takes the next step to detect whether Paul's reversal of the Deuteronomic curses and blessings is operative in Romans 9—11. In failing to do this, Hays comes close to pitting Romans against Galatians 3:10-13 (which, as shown earlier in this chapter, does utilize that reversal):

> One might expect this book of conditional blessings and curses to bear witness—as it apparently does in Gal 3:10, 13—to precisely the sort of performance-based religion that Paul wants to reject. In fact, however, none of Paul's other references to the book is pejorative in character; nowhere else is Deuteronomy disparaged as a retrograde voice of legalism. Instead, … the words of Deuteronomy become [in Romans] the voice of the righteousness from Faith [and] a prefiguration of Paul's gospel.[37]

While I agree with the sentiment of this statement, especially Hays's concern to rescue Deuteronomy from a legalistic reading, such a comment does not take into account Paul's *reversal* of the Deuteronomistic

tradition both in Galatians 3:10-13 and here in Romans 9:30—10:8. Neither does Scott identify this dynamic in his analysis of Romans 9—11.
Romans 9:30—10:8 does, however, establish my thesis.

There are three indications which combine to show that in Romans
9:30—10:8 Paul reverses the Deuteronomic curses and blessings. First,
as was noted previously, the Deuteronomistic tradition is embedded in
the overall argument of Romans 9—11. Second, more specifically, we
have also seen that Romans 8:1-11 (cf. Rom 7) is well understood as
Paul's reversal of the Deuteronomic curses and blessings. Third,
Romans 9:25-29 continues Paul's thought along these lines when, in
quoting Hosea 2:23 (Rom 9:25), Hosea 1:10 (Rom 9:26), and Isaiah
10:22-23 (Rom 9:27), he draws on the themes of the exile (Deuteronomic curses on the unfaithful Jew) and the remnant (Deuteronomic
blessings on the faithful).

In light of these considerations, therefore, it can be understood that
Romans 9:30—10:8 reverses commonly held Jewish expectations.
According to Paul, those who do not attempt to be justified by the
works of the law but rather place their faith in Christ alone (Gentile
believers) experience the Deuteronomic blessings, whereas those who
attempt to be saved through adherence to the Torah (non-Christian
Jews) are under the Deuteronomic curses. This ironic contrast surfaces
when one observes the parallels in Romans 9:30—10:8 (see table 6.3).

9:30	the acquisition of salvation/righteousness	10:1
9:31	Israel's failure to obey the law	10:2
9:32-33	Israel's misunderstanding of the law	10:3-4

Table 6.3. Parallels between Romans 9 and Romans 10

With regard to the first proposed parallel, Romans 9:30 and Romans
10:1, both statements speak of acquiring the righteousness of God or
salvation. The former attests to the ironic fact that Gentiles, who do not
pursue God's righteousness via the Mosaic law, have actually received
that righteousness by faith (implied—through faith in Christ). The latter verse expresses Paul's deep desire that Israel also will receive God's
salvation or righteousness (implied—like the Gentiles already have).

The second parallel, Romans 9:31 and Romans 10:2, addresses

Israel's failure to obey the Torah. The first part of each verse speaks of Israel's commitment to keep the law ("pursued the righteousness which is based on law"; "have a zeal for God"). The second part of each verse laments Israel's nonachievement of that objective ("did not succeed in fulfilling that law"; "it is not enlightened").

The third parallel, Romans 9:32-33 and Romans 10:3-4, exposes Israel's misunderstanding of the law. Each text presents two aspects of that confusion—one general, the other specific. In general, Israel failed to perceive that the divine intent was that the law should be pursued by faith, not by one's meritorious works (cf. Rom 9:32 with Rom 10:3). More specifically, Israel perpetuates that mistake in its rejection of Jesus Christ, the fulfillment of the law and the only means of acquiring God's righteousness (cf. Rom 9:33 and Rom 10:4).

Paul concludes his argument in Romans 9:30—10:8 by explicitly contrasting obedience to the law (cf. Rom 10:5 with Lev 18:5) with the righteousness that comes by faith in Christ (cf. Rom 10:6-8 with Deut 30:12-14). In doing so, he essentially reverses the Deuteronomic curses and blessings by replacing the law with faith and particularism with universalism.[38]

Philippians 3. Paul's comments in Philippians 3 rank as some of his most polemical statements regarding the nomistic message of the Judaizers (cf. Gal 1:6-10; 3:10-13; 4:21-31; 6:12-15).[39] In effect, Paul's remarks reverse the Deuteronomic curses and blessings: those who rely on the Torah are under the divine curse, while those whose faith is in Christ, apart from the works of the law, enjoy God's acceptance. Thus the Judaizers are labeled "dogs," nomenclature normally applied to Gentiles (Phil 3:2). Peter T. O'Brien says of this remark, "In an amazing reversal Paul asserts that it is the Judaizers who are to be regarded as Gentiles, they are 'the dogs' who stand outside the covenantal blessings."[40]

The next description, "evil workers" (Phil 3:2), is even more forceful. The language echoes the Psalter's characterization of the enemies of God (e.g. Ps 5:5 [LXX 6]; 6:8; 14 [13]:14; 36 [35]:12). Paul undoubtedly used this epithet because of his conviction that the Judaizers' confidence in the works of the law was misplaced. Rather than stimulating a person to obedience before God, the Torah ironically was the catalyst for their becoming his enemies through disobedience (see again Rom 3:20; 5:20-21; 7:7-13; Gal 3:10). In this concept we meet Paul's reversal of the Deuteronomic curses.

According to Philippians 3:3, the Judaizing message of circumcision only mutilates the flesh; it does not change the heart.[41] Those whose faith is in Christ apart from the Torah are the true circumcision, the ones in whom the Spirit dwells and produces genuine godliness. All of this bespeaks the actualization of the New Covenant. Here, then, the apostle reverses the Deuteronomic blessings: not the works of Moses but faith in Christ is the means for ensuring divine acceptance. O'Brien catches the irony of the apostle's comments in Philippians 3:3: "Circumcision, their [the Judaizers'] greatest source of pride, is interpreted by the apostle as a sure sign that they have no part in God's people at all."[42]

If Paul in the past placed utmost importance on the Torah (Phil 3:4-6), since encountering Christ on the Damascus road he can no longer do so, according to Philippians 3:7-11.[43] The righteousness of the law is eternally inferior to the righteousness which comes through Christ (v. 7). Through the knowledge of Christ, Paul had been justified, thereby participating in the divinely intended restoration of Israel—not the earthly renewal of Jerusalem, the temple and the law but the prospect of resurrection and heaven had become the focus of the apostle's hope. This was made possible because of Christ's death on the cross, which embraced the curses of the law (vv. 8-11). But according to Philippians 3:12-16, the complete realization of the heavenly promise had not yet occurred; it awaited the parousia (Phil 3:20-21).[44] Until then, Paul would have to press on in faith.

In the meantime, Paul warned the Philippian church of the activities of the Judaizers, whose nomistic platform contradicted the message of the crucified Christ. These people were enemies of the cross (Phil 3:18) for two reasons. First, they failed to perceive that their law-keeping message was self-refuting; it stirred up disobedience rather then obedience. That is, they did not comprehend Paul's proclamation of the reversal of the Deuteronomic curses. Second, the Judaizers did not understand that the law misjudged Jesus (who perfectly obeyed God) and thereby rendered itself obsolete in the divine plan.[45] Stated another way, Paul's opponents did not grasp the truth that the cross of Christ, in ending the role of the law, opened up all the Deuteronomic blessings. Instead, the message of the cross scandalized the Judaizers (cf. 1 Cor 1:18—3:23). Consequently, they remained under the curse of the law ("their end is destruction," Phil 3:19). The Torah in which they boasted, with its dietary laws ("their god is the belly"),[46] observance of circumcision ("they glory in their shame")[47] and commitment to the national restoration of Israel ("with minds set on earthly things"),[48] paradoxically secured their judgment.

Finally, Philippians 3:20-21 continues Paul's theme of the reversal of the Deuteronomic curses and blessings, about which two comments are in order. First, verses 20-21 are in chiasm with Philippians 3:18-19, thereby contrasting Paul and his followers with the Judaizers:

A Enemies of the cross, v. 18
  B Their destruction, v. 19
    C Their earthly mentality, v. 19
    C' Paul's and his followers' heavenly origin, v. 20
  B' Their deliverance, v. 20
A' Their victory over their enemies, v. 21

The resulting nuance of verses 18-21 would then be

☐ C-C': The Judaizers' nomistic/particularistic message is earthbound, whereas Paul's message of faith is of heavenly origin.

☐ B-B': The end of the Judaizers is destruction (the Deuteronomic curses), but Paul and his followers will be delivered by the coming of the Savior (the Deuteronomic/covenantal blessings of restoration).

☐ A-A': The enemies of the cross, the Judaizers, will be defeated by the sovereign Christ, while Paul and those who believe his proclamation will be the victors.[49]

Second, as has been often noted, Philippians 3:20-21 enjoys a number of verbal correspondences with Philippians 2:6-11.[50] Morna D. Hooker claims, therefore, that 3:20-21 continues the line of thought begun in 2:6-11: Christ became human (vv. 6-8, which culminated in the Deuteronomic curses, poured out on the cross [v. 8]); he is presently exalted (vv. 9-11, Deuteronomic blessings). In 3:20-21, humans are offered the hope of becoming like Christ. In short, Christ became like us so that we can become like him. Hooker calls this the theology of interchange.[51]

If this Deuteronomistic underpinning of Philippians 2:6-11 and Philippians 3:20-21 stands, then we do indeed have a profound connection between the two texts centering on the concept of interchange. Christ took the Deuteronomic curses of the law by taking upon himself human nature and obeying God to the point of the death of the cross (Phil 2:6-8) so that believers might receive the Deuteronomic blessings Christ won at the resurrection (Phil 2:9-11; 3:20-21).

Whereas the Judaizers are portrayed in Philippians 3 as being under the Deuteronomic curses, Christian Gentiles are presented as enjoying the covenantal blessings. This last point is made clear in two passages conveying Paul's positive attitude toward Gentiles—Philippians 2:14-15 and Philippians 3:3. Both of these texts promote the idea that Gentiles are now incorporated into the people of God. In 2:14-15 Paul tells the Philippians, "Do all things without grumbling or questioning, that you may be blameless and innocent, children of God without blemish in the midst of a crooked and perverse generation, among whom you shine as lights in the world." As Thielman observes, these words echo the biblical record of Israel's wilderness wanderings. Philippians 2:15 in particular recalls the song of Moses (Deut 32:4-5 [LXX]). Thielman writes of this parallel.

> The theme of the song, then, is that despite God's faithfulness, Israel severed its filial ties with him through its disobedience and became a blemished, crooked and perverse generation. In contrast, Paul describes the Philippians as "children unblemished" (tekna amōma) who live "in the midst of a crooked and perverse generation" (meson geneas skolias kai diestrammenēs). Paul's language seems intentionally formulated to signal the Philippians' status as the newly constituted people of God who, unlike Israel of old, as "unblemished" and who, rather than constituting "a crooked and perverse generation," stand in contrast to it. . . .
>
> Paul then says that as this newly constituted and unblemished people, the Philippians "shine as stars in the world," a phrase that echoes the descriptions of Israel's vocation in Isaiah 42:6-7 and 49:6 as a "light to the Gentiles." With this comment Paul implies that the Philippians not only have taken over biblical Israel's role as the unblemished people of God but have been assigned Israel's vocation as "light to the Gentiles" as well.[52]

Thus Gentile Christians now enjoy the Deuteronomic/covenantal blessings against the backdrop of Israel's current state of disbelief and judgment.

Philippians 3:3 also conveys the thought that Gentiles are now incorporated into the people of God through faith in Christ, "for we are the true circumcision, who worship God in spirit, and glory in Christ Jesus, and put no confidence in the flesh." Paul here applies the language of the OT to the Philippian believers (who of course were composed of Gentiles and Jews). As was shown earlier, the phrase "true circumcision" refers to the biblical hope that Israel's heart would one day be circumcised for the purpose of obedience (Deut 10:16; Jer 4:4). Similarly, the word *worship* or *serve* adopts the language the LXX employs for Israel's service to God as his chosen people (Ex 3:12; Deut 10:12). Moreover, the phrase "in spirit" recalls the prophetic description of the restored Israel as a place where God's Spirit will dwell (Ezek 11:19; 36:27; 37:1-14).[53] In effect, then, what Paul does in Philippians 3:3 is to spiritualize language once applied to ancient Israel by now ascribing it to the Gentiles. The concluding words of 3:3 point in that direction as well: "glory in Christ Jesus and put no confidence in the flesh." The descriptions in Philippians 3:3, then, indicate that Gentile Christians are true Israel, to whom belong the covenantal blessings, while the Judaizers remain under the curses of the Torah.

Conclusion

I will bring this discussion of justification in the DSS and in Paul to closure by returning to E. P. Sanders's *Paul and Palestinian Judaism*. It will be recalled from the introduction to this chapter that Sanders identified "covenantal nomism" as an underlying motif in the DSS (along with much of Second Temple Judaism):

☐ The Essenes attributed their entrance into the New Covenant to God's grace.

☐ Their responsibility for preserving that status was obedience to the Torah as they interpreted it.

Sanders went on to indicate that Paul disagreed with the concept of covenantal nomism but not because the apostle viewed Judaism as a legalistic religion having a problem. Rather Paul, according to Sanders, encountered Christ and then proceeded to offer participation in him (the solution) as infinitely more desirable that adherence to Judaism.[54]

Frank Thielman and N. T. Wright came to a different conclusion than Sanders in their research on Paul. They agreed that Paul rejected covenantal nomism but for a different reason. Thielman's first book on the subject, *From Plight to Solution: A Jewish Framework for Understanding Paul's View of the Law in Galatians and Romans,*[55] as well as his second study, *Paul and the Law,* argue forcefully that the apostle's perspective on the subject was greatly influenced by the story of Israel: sin-exile-restoration. In other words, Paul, like many of his Jewish contemporaries, wrestled with the plight of Israel's continuing exile. His own solution was that Christ brought an end to the Deuteronomic curses by his death so that he could now offer in his resurrection the covenantal blessings (restoration).[56] Wright's *What Saint Paul Really Said*[57] provides a similar answer.[58]

The findings in this chapter confirm Sanders's conclusion that Paul rejected covenantal nomism. For Paul, covenantal nomism, in that it relied on the Torah, is doomed to fail as an entrance or maintenance requirement of the covenant. However, my research, with Thielman and Wright, also demonstrates from key Pauline passages on justification that the story of Israel accentuates that apostle's emphasis on the plight of the Jews; namely, the law, though promising life, ultimately brings about death. The only solution to such a dilemma is faith in Christ apart from the works of the Torah.

In terms of the DSS, therefore, while Paul would agree with the Essenes' first two teachings about divine righteousness (humans are sinful while God is alone holy; God's mercy conveys his righteousness to sinners), the apostle of grace would surely disagree with the Essenes' last two tenets (righteousness is to be found only in the Qumran community; there the law is properly practiced). For Paul, divine righteousness is experienced through faith in Christ alone.

Chapter Seven

The Agony
of the Ecstasy

*The Colossian Heresy,
the Angelic Liturgy
& the Story of Israel*

Introduction

Thus far in this comparative analysis of the DSS and the NT, I have
focused on the apocalyptic aspect of the restoration of Israel. That is,
the Deuteronomic rest associated with the age to come was perceived
as having been inaugurated in those two faith communities. But
another dimension influenced these bodies of literature—mysticism.

In the past, these two experiences—apocalypticism and mysticism—were thought by scholars to be at odds with each other. The
former, with its eschatological dualism of this age and the age to come,
was viewed as very different from the spatial dualism of the latter—
earth below and heaven above. The solution to eschatological dualism,
according to Jewish apocalyptic works, was to be found in the Messiah
or the kingdom of God, the arrival of which was expected to transition
history from this age into the age to come. The answer to spatial dualism, according to early Jewish mystical writings, was ecstatic ascent by
the righteous, which thereby bridged the chasm between earth and
heaven.[1]

In recent years, however, scholarship has come to no longer pit apocalypticism against mysticism. Alan F. Segal writes of the removal of this barrier:

> Apocalypticism and mysticism have rightly remained separate catego-
> ries in scholarly parlance because they refer to two different, easily dis-
> tinguishable literatures. But that does not necessarily mean that they
> were totally unrelated experiences. Jewish mystical texts are full of apoc-
> alypses. This suggests that scholars have without sufficient warrant car-
> ried a distinction in literary genre into the realm of experience. For
> instance, it may be misleading to distinguish strictly between ecstatic,
> out-of-the-body mystical visions of heaven which are found in apocalyp-
> ticism.[2]

Thus the current trend in scholarly interpretation of early Jewish mystic texts is to view ecstatic ascent to heaven by the righteous as participation in the age to come, which has already dawned in heaven but not yet descended to earth (e.g., *1 Enoch* 14; *Sim. Enoch* 37—71; *2 Enoch* 1—42; *3 Enoch*; *Asc. Is.* 9; *Adam and Eve* 37; *Apoc. Abr.* 29).[3]

Perhaps the most vivid expression of mystic ascent as constituting a foretaste of the age to come is to be found in the *merkabah* [chariot-throne] literature dating from approximately 150 B.C. to A.D. 500 (*1 Enoch* 14; *Sim. Enoch* 37—71; *2 Enoch*; *3 Enoch*; *Hekalot* [palaces] Rabbati). Culling together these sources, F. F. Bruce provides a helpful summary of Jewish *merkabah* mysticism: This teaching emphasized ascetic-mystic visionary experiences of the throne of God, patterned somewhat after Ezekiel 1:15-26. In order to achieve this "beatific vision," the worshiper was required to observe scrupulously the OT law, especially rituals of purification. Furthermore, the seeker engaged in a period of asceticism (estimated to be twelve or forty day periods). Then the heavenly mystic ascent was attempted, all the while showing deference to the angels who guided the mystic along the journey. The path to the abode of God led through some seven heavens, each controlled by an archon or angel. Within the seventh heaven, the mystic had to pass through seven halls or palaces (*hekalot*), each one of which was guarded by an angelic gatekeeper. Only after negotiating this heavenly maze could the worshiper view the glorious divine throne and participate with the angels in the worship of God. This emphasis on angels in *merkabah* mysticism, however, too easily moved from wor-shiping *with* angels to actually worshiping the angels. Also, it was inevitable that the seven heavens or the seven palaces would be corre-lated with the seven planetary spheres ruled by their respective lords, which was quite popular in ancient astrology.[4]

It is popular these days in scholarly circles to interpret the DSS and some of Paul's opponents as being heavily influenced by *merkabah* mysticism. This is especially the case for the Songs of Sabbath Sacrifice (4Q400-405, 11Q17), which describe the angelic liturgy as followed by the Qumran sectaries. John Strugnell, the publisher of these fragments, identifies the standard form of these songs:

> The first line of a typical section runs, "By a sage. The song of the Sab-bath sacrifice for the seventh Sabbath on the 16th of the 2nd month. Praise God, all ye angels . . . " and then the *Maskil* (sage) exhorts the angels, under numerous names, to various forms of praise. These then are elements in the liturgy of the Sabbath offering, composed by a *Maskil* for every Sabbath of the year according to the Essene calendar; according to one's judgment on another disputed issue one will see in them songs which accompanied the sacrifice schematically performed at Qumran or songs by which these sacrifices were spiritually replaced.[5]

Neil S. Fujita provides a useful summary of the *merkabah* compo-nents occurring in these liturgical songs: Essenes join the angels in worshiping God via the sabbath liturgy, with the angels serving as priests in the heavenly temple (which itself enshrines seven sanctuar-ies) and the Torah as the means for encountering the heavenly throne.[6]

More and more scholars also perceive *merkabah* mysticism to be an important backdrop to the Colossian heresy, particularly as it is por-trayed in Colossians 2:8-23. That passage affords striking similarities between *merkabah* mysticism and the Colossian error: mysticism (Col 2:2-3, 18), legalism (Col 2:13-14, 16-17), asceticism (Col 2:18, 21-23), angelology (Col 1:16-18; 2:8, 18, 20) and the glorious throne of God (Col 3:1-4).[7]

It should be noted that a common theme occurring in Jewish *merka-bah*, especially the Angelic Liturgy (4QShirShabb) of Qumran and the Colossian heresy, is angelology.[8] Such a topic provides an intriguing point of comparison between the DSS and Paul's refutation of the aberrant teaching in the Colossian church.[9] I will therefore devote this chapter to an investigation of three aspects of angelology found in the DSS, especially in the Angelic Liturgy, which also surface in Colossians 2:8-23 and its context: mysticism—angelic worship; legalism—angelic revelation; and asceticism—angelic purity. Each of these is related to the story of Israel, particularly its restoration.

Mysticism: Angelic Worship

The mystical nature informing the Colossian heresy is highlighted by two phrases, *thrēskeia tōn angelōn*—"worship of angels"—and *ha heoraken embateuōn*—"the things which he had seen upon entering" (Col 2:18). The meanings of both phrases have been debated but something of a scholarly consensus is now being reached in rooting them in Jewish *merkabah* mysticism.

"The worship of angels." This phrase in the past was interpreted to mean the worship or veneration of angels. Three pieces of data were often appealed to in support of this viewpoint[10]:

☐ Grammatically, the phrase in the Greek is an objective genitive—the angels are the objects of worship.

☐ Colossians 2:15, with its declaration that Christ triumphed over the rulers and authorities (presumably fallen angels)[11] is enlisted as evidence that the Colossian Christians were tempted to worship hostile angels, despite the fact that they were defeated at the cross.

☐ Extrabiblical literature approximately contemporary with Paul's day is drawn on in support of the theory that angelic veneration existed in Judaism: *Kerygma Petrou*; *Apology of Aristides* 14:4; Celsus (in Origen *Contra Celsum* 1:26; 5:6); *Pseudo-Philo* 13:6; *1 Enoch* 48:5; 62:6, 9 (which envisions the worship of the heavenly Son of Man, assuming that such a personage was an angel) and *Tosefta Hullin* 2:18.

The other interpretation of Colossians 2:18 is that it refers to humans joining—not worshiping—the angels in their adoration of God, particularly in mystic ascent. Four pieces of evidence convince most recent scholars that this is the correct rendering:[12]

☐ Grammatically, it is more likely that the phrase "worship of angels" is a subjective genitive, thus denoting worship offered by angels to God (cf. *4 Macc* 5:7).

☐ While Colossians 2:15 almost certainly alludes to evil angels triumphed over at the cross, good angels which worship God need not be ruled out in Colossians 2:18.

☐ While the aforementioned texts may point to the worship of angels in some Jewish circles,[13] more characteristic of ancient Judaism was the warning precisely against such type of activity (Deut 4:19; 17:3; Jer 8:2; 19:13; Zeph 1:5; *Apoc. Zeph.* 6:15; *Apoc. Abr.* 17:2; Philo *Fug.* 212; *De Somnis* 1.232, 238; *Asc. Is.* 7:21; *Pseudo-Philo* 34:2; cf. Rev 19:10; 22:9).

☐ Early Jewish-Christian literature is replete with references to angels worshiping God (e.g., Is 6:2-3; Dan 7:10; *1 Enoch* 14:18-23; 36:49, 39-40; 61:10-12; *2 Enoch* 20-21; *Apoc. Abr.* 17-18; *T. Levi* 3:3-8; Lk 2:14; Phil 2:10-11; Rev 4—5; *Asc. Is.* 7—9). More germane to Colossians 2:18 is the evidence from apocalyptic and mystical Jewish circles which attests to a desire on the part of humans to join angels in worshiping God (Ps 29:1-2; 148:1-2; *T. Job* 48—50; *Apoc. Abr.* 17; *Asc. Is.* 7:13-9:33; *Apoc. Zeph.* 8:3-4.)[14] Most interesting of all is the evidence that such worship was coveted in the Qumran community. James D. G. Dunn writes of this:

According to 1QSa 2:8-9 the rules for the congregation of the last days would have to be strict, "for the Angels of Holiness are [with] their [congregation]." But the implication of other references is that these rules were already in operation, indicating that the Qumran community saw itself as a priestly community whose holiness was defined by the presence of the angels (cf. particularly 4QCD[b] and 1QM 7:4-6 with Lev. 21:17-21). So explicitly in 1QH 3:21-22: "thou hast cleansed a perverse spirit of great sin . . . that it may enter into community with the congregation of the Sons of Heaven" (similarly 1QH 11:10-13). More to the immediate point, in 1QSb 4:25-26 one of the blessings of the priest is: "May you be as an Angel of the Presence in the Abode of Holiness to the glory of the God of [hosts] . . . May you attend upon the service in the Temple of the Kingdom and decree destiny in company with the Angels of the Presence." Most interesting of all are the recently published complete (but often fragmentary) texts of the Songs of the Sabbath Sacrifice (4Q 400-405), which contain songs of praise to be offered to God by angels in the heavenly temple during the first thirteen Sabbaths of the year and in which it is clear enough (since the Songs presumably belonged to the community's liturgy) that the community itself (or at least its priests) joined with the angels in reciting these songs of heavenly worship.[15]

Thus the most plausible background for the phrase in Colossians 2:18, "the worship of angels," is Jewish *merkabah* mysticism, in particular the variety expressed in the DSS.

"The things which he had seen upon entering." The same can be said of the other disputed phrase in Colossians 2:18. While these words were linked earlier this century to the mystery religions by William Ramsay[16] and later forcefully reiterated by Martin Dibelius,[17] since the research of Fred O. Francis, such a derivation has been all but discarded[18] for a number of reasons.

☐ The mystery religions did not proliferate until the second century A.D., thus making that background basically inoperative in Paul's day.[19]

☐ The word *embateuōn* does not really convey the technical nuance Dibelius claimed it did in terms of the initiate's "entrance" into the mystery religion. Rather, as Francis and others have shown, the word, especially in Judaism, meant to enter the Promised Land (Josh 19:49, 51 [LXX]; cf. Col 1:12-13). Moreover, the Apollo inscription at Klaros (a few miles northwest of Ephesus) identified by Ramsey and invoked by Dibelius, is itself not a technical term for initiation into the mystery sect but rather a word simply connoting a person's entrance into the sanctuary to consult the oracle.[20]

☐ The best background of the phrase "which things he had seen upon entering," as Dunn and Thomas J. Sappington demonstrate, is the mystic ascent of the righteous leading into the heavenly temple portrayed in Jewish apocalyptic materials. There the worshiper joined the angels in praise to God (*1 Enoch* 14:8-13; *2 Enoch* 3; *3 Enoch* 2:2; 3:1-2; *T. Levi* 2:5-7; cf. Rev 4:1-2).[21] The words "the things seen," a prominent way to refer to the heavenly vision of angels during the course of mystic ascent in apocalyptic texts (*1 Enoch* 14; *T. Abr.* 10; Rev 4—5; cf. 2 Cor 12:2-4), confirm this suggestion. And as was the case for the phrase "the worship of angels," so here the most viable background is the *merkabah* mysticism evident in the DSS. Dunn calls attention to this aspect of the Songs of Sabbath Sacrifice, noting that heaven therein is depicted as a temple into which the angels entered for the purpose of worshiping God. Thus 4Q405 14:1—15:3-4 exclaims, "Their wonderful praise is for the God of gods . . . and they sing . . . the vestibules by which they enter, the spirits of the most holy inner Temple." Similarly, 4Q405 23.1:8-10 says, "When the gods of knowledge enter by the doors of glory, and when the holy angels depart towards their realm, the entrance doors and the gates of exit proclaim the glory of the King, blessing and praising all the spirits of God when they depart and enter by the gates."[22]

In light of the discussion above, the best background of the phrases "worship of angels" and "the things which he had seen upon entering" seems to be *merkabah* mysticism, in particular the kind espoused in the Songs of Sabbath Sacrifice. It is quite reasonable, therefore, to imagine a Jewish synagogue in Colossae claiming that its sabbath worship participated in the worship of angels and thereby making inroads into the church. Paul, however, criticizes such mysticism with four comments in Colossians 2:18-19:

☐ Such humble worship is, in actuality, idle self-deceit ("puffed up without reason").

☐ Rather than taking them on a mystic heavenly journey, such teaching is to be characterized as the "sensuous mind." According to Hellenism, the mind was the higher part of the human being—the medium for entering heavenly realms—whereas the body was inferior and earthbound. In essence, Paul equates such "higher reason" with the flesh. Dunn notes, "To speak of the 'mind of flesh' was therefore in effect to deny that this Colossian worship with angels could ever have 'lifted off' from earth: even his mind was 'flesh' fast bound to earth."[23]

☐ Such an aberrant belief diminished the supremacy of Christ, the head of the church and world (cf. Col 1:15-20), and destroyed the unity of the church with its division of Christians into the categories of those who had mystic experiences and those who did not.

☐ It should also be noted in this connection that the Angelic Liturgy describes the angels as guarding "the temples of the King [. . .] in their territory and in their inheritance" (4Q400 1:1:13). It may well be, therefore, that the Songs of Sabbath Sacrifice identify mystic experience under the supervision of angels as the means for entering into heaven, the spiritualized rendition or possibly a foretaste of the end-time possession of the land of Israel, the Deuteronomic rest. Indeed, according to Joshua 5:13-15, the angelic warrior—the "commander of the army of the Lord"—guided the Israelites in their conquest of Canaan. The War Scroll applies that motif to Michael, the Essenes' apocalyptic advocate (1QM 1:1-14, 11:11; 13:10-12; 17:7). It is most interesting in this regard to read of the inheritance of the saints in Colossians 1:9-14. In light of Paul's polemic against angels in Colossians 1:16; 2:8, 14-15, 20 (if, as I propose is the case, angels should be included in the category of the "elements of the world"; see below) perhaps we are to understand the apostle as detracting attention from the role of angels in acquiring the heavenly rest. Rather, the Colossian church should focus on Christ. This interpretation is in keeping with Francis' finding that "entrance" (*embateuōn*, Col 2:18) occurs in Judaism with reference to possessing Canaan.

Legalism: Angelic Revelation

A mirror-image reading of Colossians has suggested to a number of commentators that the Colossian heresy emphasized the capacity of humans to receive angelic, heavenly revelation via mystical experiences. Two components of that supposed divine disclosure surface in Paul's letter to the church at Colossae: wisdom (Col 1:9, 15-20, 26-27; 2:3, 23) and law (Col 2:8-23).[24] More particularly, Paul seems to refute the prevalent Jewish notion that heavenly wisdom comes through obeying the Mosaic law (cf. *Sir* 24:23-26; *Bar* 3:36—4:1; *1 Enoch* 42; *4 Ezra* 4:5—5:13; *2 Apoc. Bar.* 38:1-4; 44:14; 48:24; 51:3-4; 77:15-16; 1QH 4:9-12; 6:10-12; 11:7-10; 12:11-13; 16:11-12; 1QS 5:8-10; 9:13; 11:15-18; Demons of Death 2:1-4; 4QMMT 113-14). My own analysis of these texts in another study demonstrates that there is a strong Deuteronomistic connnection between wisdom and law therein: If Israel wants to be restored to the land, it must follow God's wisdom, which is manifested through the Torah.[25]

The DSS are especially relevant to this discussion, for writings such as *Hôdāyôt* and the Rule of the Community, which equate divine wisdom with the Mosaic law, do so in the context of worship with the angels.[26] Also of special interest in this matter are the Songs of Sabbath Sacrifice or the Angelic Liturgy (4Q400-405; 11Q17), which envision the Qumran covenanters as joining in the angelic worship of God, who is seated on the glorious chariot throne (cf. 4Q405 20-22:1-4; 11Q17).[27]

Interestingly enough, the themes wisdom and law repeatedly occur in the Angelic Liturgy. To encounter the heavenly presence of God is to be made privy to his wisdom (variously called "knowledge and council" [e.g. 4Q400 1.1:5]; "wondrous mysteries" [4Q401 14.2:2]; "plan" [4Q402 4.6]; "hidden things" [4Q402 4.11]; "wonderful revelations" [4Q402 4.14]; "wonderful words" [4Q403 1:1-46]), which involves obeying God's law based on Qumran sectarian interpretation and labeled "precepts which are engraved ordinances" (e.g., 4Q400 1.1.4-6); "stipulations" (e.g., 4Q202 1.3); and "commandments" (4Q402 4.2).[28] To do this is to participate in the inheritance, the heavenly rest (4Q400 1:1-13).

Those DSS texts associating wisdom and law, especially *Hôdāyôt*, the Rule of the Community and the Angelic Liturgy, provide a very plausible backdrop against which to interpret Paul's letter to the church at Colossae. Two rejoinders to the Colossian heresy can therefore be culled from the apostle's comments:

☐ Divine wisdom is revealed in Christ, not mystic experience.

☐ Christ, God's wisdom, is received by faith, not by the works of the law.

Divine wisdom is revealed in Christ, not mystic experience. In several key texts in the epistle to the Colossians, Paul presents his belief that Christ is the wisdom of God, probably to counter the notion that the Torah is the locus of divine wisdom (Col 1:9, 15-20, 26-27; 2:3). It is valuable to summarize those passages here in light of the preceding debate.

Colossians 1:9. Most probably, as a number of scholars have suggested, Colossians 1:9 is a statement made in contrast to the Jewish belief that divine wisdom is revealed through the Torah (see Deut 4:6; *Wis* 15:2-3; *4 Ezra* 8:12; as well as the references already mentioned above). The DSS strengthen this hypothesis, especially since these documents, in associating wisdom and law, root obedience to the New Covenant in the eschatological reality of the Spirit, who is the medium for mystic experience (e.g., 1QH 4:9-12; 6:10-12; 1QS 5:8-10; 9:13).[29] Paul's prayer for the Colossian Christians as specified in 1:9 can be understood, therefore, as contradicting claims like those made in the DSS. Only through Christ can one access divine wisdom and true

understanding of the Spirit, "that you may be filled with the knowledge of God's will in all spiritual wisdom and understanding."
According to Colossians 1:9-14, this is the only legitimate way to gain
the heavenly inheritance.

Colossians 1:15-20. It has long been thought by scholars that Colossians 1:15-20 is a hymn, however one may delineate its structure.[30] Furthermore, it is safe to say that the majority of interpreters of this
passage identify personified/hypostatized wisdom as the best conceptual background for understanding the hymn. They rightly point to the
following descriptions: *eikōn tou theou tou aoratou* (Col 1:15; cf. *Wis*
7:26); *prōtotokos pasēs ktiseōs* (v. 15; cf. Prov 8:22; *Sir* 1:4; *Wis* 9:9; Philo
[*Conf. Ling.* 146; *Agric.* 51; *Som.* 1:215]); *en autō ektisthē ta panta* (Col 1:16;
cf. Prov 8:27-30; Irenaeus *Haer.* 189, 199) and perhaps *archē* (Col 1:18; cf.
Gen 1:1 as mediated through Prov 8:22).[31]

It seems that in presenting Christ, God's wisdom, as cocreator and
redeemer, Paul is severing the Jewish connection between wisdom and
law. First, according to Colossians 1:15-17, Christ was preexistent with
God and cocreator of the universe. This statement is a frontal assault
on those Jewish texts which predicated preexistence and cocreatorship
of the Torah (e.g., *Jub.* 16:29; 31:32; 39:7; *Sir* 16:29). Second, according to
Colossians 1:18-20, Christ is the means for humans to be reconciled to
God, not the law. Such denigration of the law would have been antithetical to much Jewish thinking (e.g., *Bar* 51:7; *Sir* 15:15; 45:5; 1QS
3:17—4:26). According to Colossians 2:13-14, the law alienated people
from each other and from God; yet Christ's death on the cross has
removed the enmity of the law (more on this passage later).

As Wright has perceptively argued, the wisdom background of
Colossians 1:15-20 is itself deeply influenced by the story of Israel's
sin—exile—restoration.[32] On this reading, the first part of the hymn
(Col 1:15-17) is steeped in the Jewish concept that God's wisdom is
manifested through the Torah, the cocreator of the world and the special possession of Israel. This is intimately related to the prevalent idea
among Jews that the world was made for Israel (see, e.g., *4 Ezra* 6:54-
59; 7:11; *2 Apoc. Bar.* 14:18-19; 15:7; 21:24; *Pirke Aboth* 6:11-12; *Pss. Sol.*
18:4). The second part of the hymn (Col 1:18-20) draws on the notion
that Israel's reconciliation with God and deliverance from sin and exile

is conditioned on her obedience to the Torah. Indeed, the same idea is latent in Colossians 1:9-14: adherence to the Torah, God's wisdom, is the means for implementing the restoration and deliverance from exile. Paul's take on the matter, however, is rather that Christ is divine wisdom, not the Torah, and he, not Israel, is the cocreator and goal of creation (Col 1:15-17). His death alone, not following the law, is the means for the forgiveness of sin and the end of spiritual exile from God. Furthermore, such reconciliation applies to the cosmos, not just the nation of Israel (Col 1:18-20).

Colossians 1:26-28 contains significant vocabulary which also occurs in the DSS: *mystery, hidden, revealed, wisdom, mature.* For Paul, however, these terms center on Christ, whereas for the DSS they focus on the law. Those contrasts can be summarized as follows:

☐ Both Paul and the Qumran community share the same conceptual world informing the term *mystery* (*mystērion,* Col 1:26; cf. Rom 11:25-26; 16:25-26; Eph 1:9-10; 3:3-6; *r'z,* 1QS 3:23; 4:18; 1QpHab 7:5; 1Q27), which is the apocalyptic notion that the divine plan for the end times is now being revealed to the righteous.[33] But the context of that mystery differs for Paul and Qumran. For the Essenes, the eschatological mystery is that the DSS sectaries are true Israel, while all outside that community are lost. For the apostle, however, the divine mystery is that God is forming his new people from both Jew and Gentile (Col 1:26-27). And for the Qumran community, the law is the fence that protects it from the contamination of the world, while for Paul it is a barrier between people groups that God removed through the cross of Christ (Col 2:13-14).

☐ Related to the last point, both Paul and Qumran employ the words *hidden-revealed* but with reverse intent. The DSS understand the terms *hidden-revealed (nistar/nigleh)* to refer to the law, as was discussed in chapter four of this study. While the Mosaic law had been revealed to (but spurned by) all Jews, the hidden meaning of the law (the sectarian interpretation of the Torah by the Teacher of Righteousness and the Qumranic leadership) is the exclusive property of the DSS covenanters (1QS 5:7-11; CD 3:12-16). This, of course, is a message of particularism. In utter contrast to the preceding understanding of the terms, for Paul the mystery of the inclusive nature of the people of God (composed of both Jew and Gentile) was hidden *(apokekrymmenon)* in past ages but now has been revealed *(ephanerōthē)* in Christ, not the law (Col 1:26; 2:3). This is a message of universalism.

☐ Both writings utilize the term *wisdom* (*sophia* [Col 1:28]; *ḥokmâh* [e.g., 1QS 4:3, 18, 24; CD 2:3]) but from differing vantage points. As we noted above, according to the DSS, divine wisdom resides in the law, but according to Paul, it indwells Christ (Col 1:15-20; 2:3) who inhabits his people (Col 1:27-28).

☐ Both Paul and the DSS describe the status of the righteous as "mature" (*teleion* [Col 1:28]; *tāmîn* [1QS 2:2; 3:9-11, 9:9-10, 19, 1QpHab 7:1-5]),[34] but the means for arriving at that position is at odds. For the DSS, perfection is achieved by obeying the sectaries' interpretation of the law; for Paul, however, it is received by faith in Christ alone.

Colossians 2:3 speaks of treasures of wisdom and hidden knowledge, a concept that appears in Jewish apocalyptic texts which describe wisdom as hidden away in heaven (*1 Enoch* 42; *4 Ezra* 4:5—5:13; *2 Apoc. Bar.* 48:33-36; cf. Job 28; Prov 1:20-33; *Sir* 1:1-10). Because such wisdom is in heaven, it requires mystic experience to be grasped. In the preceding apocalyptic works, mystic ascent for the purpose of gaining divine wisdom goes hand in hand with God's revelation of that wisdom through the law. The one—mystic ascent—is the means for better understanding the other—God's law, the embodiment of wisdom (e.g., *2 Apoc. Bar.* 44:14-15; 54:13-14). As noted earlier, a similar combination informs the DSS, especially the Rule of the Community, *Hôdāyôt* and the Angelic Liturgy. It may well be, therefore, that as J. Dupont argued, Paul's statement in Colossians 2:3 that the treasures of wisdom reside in Christ alone was designed to counter the above thinking associated with writings like the DSS (cf. Col 2:23).[35]

Christ, God's wisdom, is received by faith, not the works of the law. Paul's disassociation of wisdom and the law continues to occupy our attention as this section highlights the legalistic aspects of the Colossian heresy. At least four considerations in this epistle point to the law of Moses as factoring into the problem.

The three nationalistic marks of Judaism are criticized by Paul in Colossians 2:8-23: circumcision (vv. 11-12); dietary laws (vv. 16, 21); sabbath keeping (v. 16). Thus Dunn writes:

None of the features of the teaching alluded to in 2:8-23 resist being understood in Jewish terms, and several can only or most plausibly be understood in Jewish terms. To be more precise, the division of the world into "circumcision and uncircumcision" (2:11-13; 3:11) and the observance of the Sabbath (2:16) would generally be recognized in the ancient world as distinctively Jewish, as indeed also food and purity rules (2:16, 21) when set alongside circumcision and Sabbath (see on 2:11, 16, 21); so distinctively Jewish are they, indeed, that any non-Jew adopting them would be said to be "judaizing" (adopting a Jewish way of life).[36]

Similarly, W. Schenk observes that calendar piety, food laws and circumcision cannot be regarded as random elements of some syncretistic cult but are the very norms that provide and confirm the identity of Israel.[37]

The phrase "festivals, new moons, or sabbaths" was the typical Jewish language for the main festivals of Judaism (1 Chron 23:31; 2 Chron 2:3; 31:4; Neh 10:33; Is 1:13-14; Ezek 45:17; Hos 2:11; *1 Macc* 10:34).[38] Interestingly enough, the Qumran community claimed to have received special revelation regarding "the holy sabbaths and glorious feasts" and also of the new moon (CD 3:14-15; 1QS 9:26-10:8; 1QM 2:4-6).[39]

The two terms in Colossians 2:14—the *bond* or record *(cheirographon)* and the *decrees* or legal demands *(dogmasin)*—contribute to the theory that it is the law of Moses that Paul criticizes in his exposé of the Colossian heresy. The word *bond* is most probably to be identified with the Jewish idea of a heavenly book or record of good and evil deeds performed by humans while on earth, to be assessed at the final judgment (Ex 32:32-33; Ps 69:28; Dan 12:1; Rev 3:5; 20:12; *1 Enoch* 89:61-64, 70-71; 108:7; *Apoc. Zeph.* 7:1-8; *T. Abr.* (rescension A) 12:7-18; 13:9-14; (rescension B) 10:7—11:7; *2 Enoch* 53:2-3; *Apoc. Paul*).[40] According to Colossians 2:14, such a heavenly record serves to condemn humans.

The word *decrees* is the criterion against which to evaluate a person's deeds, which most likely is the law of Moses (*3 Macc* 1:3; Philo [*Leg. All.* 1:55; *Gig.* 52; Josephus *Ag. Ap.* 1:42).[41] That this interpretation is on target is demonstrated by the verbal form *dogmatizō* in Colossians 2:20, which alludes to the Jewish regulations of the law (cf. Eph 2:15). Thus the decrees intended by Paul are the *halakhic* rulings denounced in Colossians 2:11-12, 16, 21-22: circumcision, dietary laws and sabbath observance.

The enigmatic phrase "the elements of the world" or "the elemental spirits of the universe" (Col 2:8, 20; cf. Gal 4:3, 9) has generated three competing interpretations, as Andrew Bandstra has documented:
☐ the "principle" interpretation
☐ the "cosmological" view
☐ the "personalized-cosmological" interpretation[42]

The second view, that the *stoicheia* are the four basic components of the universe (earth, water, air and fire),[43] has been essentially abandoned in the twentieth century. This is so because, among other reasons, the elements of the world almost certainly are to be equated with the rulers and authorities over whom Christ triumphed at the cross (Col 2:15). The first view, that the *stoicheia* are the rudimentary principles of learning, the alphabet (cf. Heb 5:12), is a viable interpretation,[44] but again because of the personal nature of the rulers and authorities referred to in Colosians 2:15 it is a minority position.

The majority view today is the third perspective, the "personalized-cosmological" reading. There are primarily two variations within this approach, both of which associate the "elements" with angels.

One interpretation is that the elements are the angels that served as mediators of the Mosaic law.[45] Dunn observes of this view that precisely the same phrase is used in Galatians 4:3, 9, where it is clearly linked into the Jewish law, understood as itself a kind of power set in charge over Israel like a slave-custodian or guardian (Gal 3:23-25; 4:1-3, 9-10) and given "through angels" (Gal 3:19). The close association of the thought here with talk of Jewish festivals (Col 2:16; cf. Gal 4:10) and the "worship of angels" (Col 2:18) strongly suggests the same connotation of the phrase for Colossians 2:8, 20.[46]

This understanding accords well, as will be seen in the next chapter, with a comparative analysis of Hebrews and the DSS, relative to the giving of the law through angels (contrast Heb 1:5—2:18 with 4Q400-405).

The other variation within the personalized-cosmological view is that the elements of the world refer to angelic beings associated with the planetary bodies that exert control over humans[47] (e.g., *Jub.* 2:2; *1 Enoch* 75:1; *2 Enoch* 4:1; *T. Abr.* 13:11).[48] It is again noteworthy that the Qumran community espoused such thinking connecting, as it did, angels with the courses of the stars and their calendar. Thus horoscope texts have been discovered among the DSS (4Q186; 4QMess ar). Moreover, Josephus described the Essenes as believers in fate (*Ant.* 13.6.9 [172]) and could even claim that they prayed to the sun (*J.W.* 2.8.5 [128]). The preceding views need not, therefore, be mutually exclusive, for in the DSS one finds a combination of the two: The law was mediated through angels, and following that law (that is, the sectarian interpretation of it) harmonizes one with the heavenly bodies which are directed by the angels. Thus the law—angelic revelation—is the means for joining the heavenly host in worship of God, which anticipates the restoration of true Israel. Paul, however, refutes such thinking. Christ, as divine wisdom, alone should be the object of the Colossians' worship, not some heavenly trip based on scrupulous observance of the Torah.

Asceticism: Angelic Purity

The last key component of the Colossian heresy is asceticism—"Do not handle, Do not taste, Do not touch" (Col 2:21). These regulations have to do with Jewish laws of purity. *Handle* and *touch* refer to physical contact with impure objects or people (e.g., Lev 5:2-3; 7:19, 21; 11:8; Num 19:11-13) while *taste* applies to food taboos (cf. Mt 27:34; Lk 14:24; Jn 2:9; Acts 10:10-14; 20:11; 23:14). The word *tapeinophrosynē* in Colossians 2:23 suggests that such prohibitions were taken to great lengths. Francis' research on the term shows that while the word includes fasting, it encompasses a still broader range of bodily disciplines such as abstinence and stations.[49]

Such asceticism characterized the Colossian errorists' understanding of worship, which Paul pejoratively labels having "an appearance of wisdom in promoting rigor of devotion." Most probably, therefore, the Colossian heresy taught that mystic ascent leading to worship with the angels was accomplished through severe treatment of the body. Sappington's study demonstrates that a prominent feature of mystic ascent as portrayed in Jewish *merkabah* texts was asceticism, including fasting (e.g., for three weeks) and sexual abstinence.[50]

With the DSS, however, we reach the epitome of asceticism in order to achieve heavenly worship with the angels. Dunn expresses the point well, calling attention to passages like Rule of the Community 6—7, which emphasizes the purity of the Essenes, and Temple Scroll 47:3-5: "The city which I will sanctify, causing my name and sanctuary to abide [in it], shall be holy and pure of all impiety with which they can become impure. Whatever is in it shall be pure. Whatever enters it shall be pure." Likewise the Songs of Sabbath Sacrifice asserts "there is no unclean thing in their holy places" (4Q400 1:1:14).[51]

It is significant that a number of terms Paul employs in Colossians to describe Christians are also used in the DSS with reference to certain qualities Qumran members shared with angels: *saints* (cf. Col 1:2 with 1QM 3:5); *inheritance* (cf. Col 1:12 with 1QS 11:7-8); *light* as opposed to *darkness* (cf. Col 1:12-13 with 1QS 3:20-24; cf. 1QM 1:1; 8:14; 13:5-16).[52] It should be noted in this context that the Angelic Liturgy presents the Essenes as priests (Zadokites?) probably under the influence of Ezekiel 44:10-16, whose outstanding characteristic of ritual purity (see again, e.g., 4Q400 1:1:14) qualified them to participate in the heavenly inheritance (4Q400 1:1:13).

Taken together the preceding data suggest that the Colossian error was similar to the DSS teaching that ascetic observance of the law admitted one into the presence of angels and the heavenly inheritance. More than that, the initiate apparently achieved the level of purity the angels enjoyed. Paul, of course, begged to differ with such a view on two counts. First, for the apostle, the true people of God include Gentiles (see Col 1:2, 12-13, 24-29), whereas the Qumran community excluded all Gentiles and even nonobservant Jews. Second, for Paul, Christ was received by faith, not the works of the law, as promoted by Essenes.

Conclusion

This chapter, then, has displayed parallels between the Colossian heresy and the worship practices of the Qumran community. For Paul, however, Christ is the true wisdom of God who is to be received by faith. Sappington nicely summarizes this message as it confronted the Colossian teaching:

Paul affirms that it is not on the basis of ascetic observances or mystical experiences or legal obedience that individuals participate in the glorious hope of the revelation of Christ from the heavenly realm. Rather, it is simply by means of a present union with Christ through faith that men and women come to anticipate their future union with Christ at his coming in glory.[53]

In this regard, one is reminded of Paul's words in Galatians 1:8: "But even if we, or an angel from heaven, should preach to you a gospel contrary to that which we preached to you, let him be accursed [with the Deuteronomic curses]."[54]

Chapter Eight

Monotheism, Covenant & Eschatology

Hebrews & the DSS

Introduction

N. T. Wright's paradigm for grasping Second Temple Jewish belief—monotheism, covenant and eschatology—provides the conceptual framework for this chapter.[1] The conviction, so entrenched in ancient Israel, that there was but one God whose name is *Yahweh* goes back at least to the *Shema*—"Hear, O Israel, *Yahweh* our God, *Yahweh is one*" (Deut 6:4, emphasis added)—and is repeated manifold times thereafter. Thus Psalm 96:4-5, 10 exclaims,

> Great is YHWH, and greatly to be praised;
> he is to be revered above all gods.
> For all the gods of the peoples are idols,
> but YHWH made the heavens. . . .
> Say among the nations, "The LORD reigns!"[2]

As Wright further observes, such monotheism was threefold in nature:
☐ It was *creational*, asserting that God made the world but was distinct from it.

□ It was *providential*, promoting the assurance that God controlled history and events and was therefore intimately involved with the world. Israel's monotheistic faith was rooted in the covenant, which means that God's plan for dealing with the existence of sin precipitated by Adam and permeating the earth was to create Israel for the purpose of restoring humanity to its intended purpose (see, e.g., Gen 1:28; 12:2-3; 17:2, 6, 8; 22:16-17; Ex 1:7; 32:13; Lev 26:9; Deut 1:10; 7:13; 8:1; 28:63; 30:5, 16; Is 2:2-5; 42:6; 45:6; 51:4; Ezek 40—47 [47:7-12] Mic 4:1-5).[3] As *Genesis Rabbah* 14:6 later put it, " 'I will make Adam first,' proclaims Israel's God, 'and if he goes astray I will send Abraham to sort it all out.' " Wright concludes,

> The creator calls a people through whom, somehow, he will act decisively within his creation, to eliminate evil from it and to restore order, justice and peace. Central to this ongoing plan of action, then, is the call of Israel. When the creator acts to restore and heal his world, he will do so through this people.[4]

Thus Israel's monotheistic faith was rooted in the belief that it was the elect people of God appointed to right the wrong with the world by obeying the divine law—the charter of the covenant—thereby becoming a witness of the one true God to the nations. The book of Deuteronomy showcases this conviction, as was noted earlier in this study. Alas, however, Israel like Adam sinned and incurred the wrath of God (the Deuteronomic curses). All this because Israel broke covenant with Yahweh.

□ But, as Wright documents, Jewish monotheism and covenantal theology was also *eschatological*: it held the conviction that in the last days God would restore his people to himself and empower them to obey the New Covenant. As Wright observes, such an assertion was fundamental to the different movements and currents of thought within Second Temple Judaism. He writes:

> The Maccabaean crisis was all about the covenant. The setting up of Essene communities took place in the belief that Israel's god had renewed his covenant at last (but secretly, with them alone). The book of *Jubilees* celebrated this special status of Israel in virtue of the covenant. The later wisdom literature, for all its borrowings of ideas and idioms from

Israel's neighbours, stressed the Jewish covenant if anything more strongly than the biblical wisdom tradition had done. The apocalyptic writings looked in eager expectation for their god to fulfill his covenant, and thus to vindicate Israel. The later rabbis examined ever more carefully the obligations through which Israel was to act out her part in the divine covenant. It was the covenant which meant that Israel's oppression was seen as a theological as well as a practical problem, and which determined the shape which solutions to that problem would have to take. It was the covenant that drove some to "zeal" for Torah, others to military action, others to monastic-style piety. The covenant raised, and helped to answer, the question as to who really belonged to Israel. Covenant theology was the air breathed by the Judaism of this period.[5]

The problem one finds in this period of investigation, however, is that various groups made rival claims to be the one true people of God, virtually discounting all other contenders for the faith. Most likely, as J. Julius Scott has effectively argued, these counterclaims resulted from the destruction of Israel by the Babylonians in 587 B.C., along with the later threat to the Jewish nation posed by the onslaught of Greco-Roman culture (c. 300 B.C.—A.D. 70). In the aftermath of the disintegration of the temple and the dispossession of their land, numerous Jews were left in bewilderment as to the nature of their identity. Hence Judaism splintered into groups clamoring to legitimate themselves as the true Israel, the elect people of God who would be the catalyst for restoring divine blessing: Pharisees, Sadducees, Zealots, Essenes and even Christians.[6]

The preceding comments prepare the way for the thesis of this chapter: A comparative study of the DSS and the letter to the Hebrews affords a clear example of how two early Jewish-based groups on one hand are committed to the foundational beliefs of monotheism, covenant and eschatology but on the other hand do so from fundamentally different perspectives.[7] That is to say, both groups believed themselves to be the true Israel, who represented the one God and whose communities constituted the New Covenant of the last days. Their perceptions of why that was so, however, differed dramatically. According to the DSS, the Teacher of Righteousness, who continued the line of the Zadokite priesthood, had instituted the true Torah and regulations for the temple, whereas according to Hebrews, Jesus now fulfilled that role, whose gospel replaced the Torah and whose atoning work on the cross redefined priesthood and temple. To those similarities and differences I now turn. For convenience's sake, I will use Hebrews as a grid for discussing the DSS. In doing so, the emphasis will be on eschatology, particularly three end-time blessings that were expected to characterize those who represented the one true God: obedience to God (Heb 1:1—4:13), the New Covenant (Heb 8), and true worship (Heb 4:14—7:28; 9:1—10:39).

Obedience to God: Hebrews 1:1—4:13

Hebrews 1:1—4:13 has to do with obedience to God, which unfolds in terms of one's proper response to divine revelation in the last days (Heb 1:2). Three crucial components factor into such obedience: the content of revelation (Heb 1:1-4); the origin of revelation (Heb 1:5—2:4); and the goal of revelation (Heb 2:5—4:13). Positing a running contrast between the DSS and the author of Hebrews makes for a fascinating study of what constitutes obedience to God, which is intimately related to these two groups' retelling of the story of Israel.

The content of revelation: The wisdom of Christ versus the law of Moses (Heb 1:1-4). From *Sirach*[8] on it was common for Jewish works to equate divine wisdom with the Mosaic law, the content of God's revelation, and thereby to claim that wisdom/law indwelled Israel. *Sirach* 24:8-12, 23-24 makes this clear:

> Then the Creator of all things
>   gave me a commandment,
>   and the one who created me
>   assigned a place for my tent.
> And he said, "Make your dwelling in Jacob,
>   and in Israel receive your inheritance."
> From eternity, in the beginning,
>   he created me,
> and for eternity, I shall not cease to exist.
> In the holy tabernacle I ministered
>   before him

and so I was established in Zion.
In the beloved city likewise he
   gave me a resting place,
  and in Jerusalem was my
   dominion.
So I took root in an honored people,
   in the portion of the Lord, who
    is their inheritance. . . .

All this is the book of the covenant
   of the Most High God,
  the law which Moses
   commanded us
as an inheritance for the
   congregations of Jacob.[9]

The DSS people inherited such a view, except that they believed that their community was the true Israel through whom God's wisdom/ law was now manifest. At least three texts combine to establish this point: Demons of Death 2:1-4, which explicitly equates wisdom with law, and Rule of the Community 4:2-6 and Damascus Document 6:2-7, which build on that association by locating wisdom/law exclusively in the Qumran community.

These are their paths in the world: to enlighten the heart of man, straighten out in front of him all the paths of justice and truth, establish in his heart respect for the precepts of God; it is a spirit of meekness, of patience, generous compassion, eternal goodness, intelligence, under- standing, potent wisdom which trusts in all the deeds of God and depends on his abundant mercy; a spirit of knowledge in all the plans of action, of enthusiasm for the decrees of justice, of holy plans with firm purpose, of generous compassion with all the sons of truth, of magnifi- cent purity which detests all unclean idols, of unpretentious behavior with moderation in everything, of prudence in respect of the truth con- cerning the mysteries of knowledge. These are the counsels of the spirit for the sons of truth in the world. And the visitation of those who walk in it will be for healing. (1QS 4:2-6)

But God remembered the covenant of the very first, and from Aaron raised men of knowledge and from Israel wise men, and forced them to listen. And they dug the well: *Num 21:18* "A well which the princes dug, which the nobles of the people delved with the staff." The well is the law. And those who dug it are the converts of Israel, who left the land of Judah and lived in the land of Damascus, all of whom God called princes, for they sought him, and their renown has not been repudiated in anyone's mouth. *Blank* And the staff is the interpreter of the law. (CD 6:2-7)

Numerous other passages in the DSS reiterate this theme (e.g., 1QS 2:2-3; 9:9-11; 1QH 1:1-20; 4:9-11; Aramaic *T. Levi* [4Q213-14] 4:1:8-9; 4:1-11; 4:2:5-9; 4QMMT line 28).[10] These texts, along with Demons of Death 2:1-4, Rule of the Community 4:2-6 and Damascus Document 6:2-7, combine to make the point that the Qumran community possesses in its *halakhah* divine wisdom; to follow it is to obey God.

It is fascinating to compare this concept in the DSS with Hebrews 1:1-4. Three observations about the latter text are relative to the subject of wisdom and law: the sapiential influence on Hebrews 1:1-4, its chiastic structure and consequently the disassociation of Christ, the divine wisdom, from the Mosaic law.

Sapiential influence. Recent commentators of Hebrews 1:1-4 rightly call attention to the influence of the Jewish wisdom tradition on that passage. For example, "Whom he appointed heir of all things" (Heb 1:2) reminds one of the notion that Israel, as the intended ruler over humanity, inherited divine wisdom/law (*Sir* 24:23; 1QS 11:7-9; 11QMelch 2:5).[11] "Through whom [Christ] also he created the world" (Heb 1:2) draws on the concept of preexistent wisdom as cocreator with God (Prov 8:27; *Sir* 24:1-12; *1 Enoch* 42; *Wis* 7:12, 21; 8:1). "He reflects the glory of God and bears the very stamp of his nature" (Heb 1:3) recalls similar statements made about wisdom in *Wisdom* 7:25-26, as does "upholding the universe by his word of power" (cf. Heb 1:3 with *Wis* 7:24, 27). "He sat down at the right hand of the Majesty on high" (Heb 1:3), a quotation of Psalm 110:1, is reminiscent of wisdom's exaltation to the throne of God (*Wis* 9:4; 9; 18:15).[12]

Chiastic structure. Recent interpreters also recognize that a chiastic structure informs Hebrews 1:1-4. Typical of this is the outline proposed by Philip E. Hughes and D. W. B. Robinson (see table 8.1). Its significance will become clear in what follows.[13]

vv. 1-2a	A	God's revelation in Christ
v. 2b	B	God's inheritance in Christ
v. 2c	C	God's creation in Christ
v. 3a	C'	God's creation in Christ
v. 3b	B'	God's inheritance in Christ
v. 4	A'	God's revelation in Christ

Table 8.1. Chiastic structure of Hebrews 1:1-4

Disassociation of divine wisdom from Mosaic law. Taking into account the sapiential influence on Hebrews 1:1-4, as well as its chiastic structure, sheds light on the meaning of this text: The author of Hebrews wishes to refute the notion common in Judaism, especially present in the DSS, that God's wisdom is manifested through the Mosaic law, which resides in Israel.[14] Three counterarguments can then be seen to surface in this preface statement of Hebrews.

☐ While God's revelation used to be conveyed through the prophets (A/Heb 1:1-2) and in the Mosaic law as mediated by the angels (A'/Heb 1:4),[15] it is now fully and finally disclosed through Christ, his Son, who is the embodiment of divine wisdom.

☐ God's wisdom no longer manifests itself through the law, Israel's inheritance, but rather through Christ and his community, the true believers (B/Heb 1:2b; B'/Heb 1:3b).

☐ The law is not the agent of creation nor its sustainer; instead Christ, as divine wisdom, is both creator and sustainer of the universe (C/Heb 1:2c; C'/Heb 1:3a).[16]

All of this to say that, according to Hebrews 1:1-4, Christ is the true residence of divine wisdom (not the law) and, as such, the true content of revelation. To follow him is to obey God.

The origin of revelation: Angels as mediators versus Christ as direct revealer (Heb 1:5—2:4). It was commonly understood in Judaism that the law had been mediated to Moses through angels (*Jub.* 1:29; Josephus *Ant.* 15.5.3 [136]; *Mek.* on Ex 20:18; *Sipre* 102 on Num 12:5; cf. Acts 7:38-39; Gal 3:19).[17] The author of Hebrews shares this conviction, according to Hebrews 1:4; 2:2-3, as did also, in all probability, the Qumran community with its elevation of the angels to an exalted position.[18] It may well be that Hebrews 1:4 (and especially Heb 2:2-4) draw on the belief that angels mediated the law in order to attribute an inferior status to that law. Hughes is correct when he says,

> The message spoken by God through "angels" at Sinai (v. 2) is exactly balanced here by the declaration that the gospel was "spoken by God through the Lord." From this reminder, and in the light of the context, it may be inferred that among the letter's recipients some had been saying in effect: "Our forefathers received the law through angels; we received the Gospel only through men," and were accordingly disposed to suggest that the gospel was inferior to the law—a judgment that could well have been influenced by teaching similar to that of the Dead Sea Sect, in which angels were assigned so elevated a position. This erroneous conclusion is corrected by our author's assertion that, even though it was human evangelists who brought them the saving message, the true mediator of that message is the Son himself, whom he has already shown to be incomparably superior to all angels.[19]

Thus the point being made in Hebrews 1:5—2:4 is that angelic mediation of the law attests to the indirect divine origin of the Torah contrasted to the direct revelation from God of Christ's gospel. That being the case, the author of Hebrews appends a caveat: If people in the OT who rejected the mediated law suffered punishment, how much more so would those who now spurn Christ (Heb 2:1-4)?

The goal of revelation: Renewed humanity (Heb 2:5—4:13). I began this chapter by noting Wright's comments on creational, providential and covenantal monotheism. The end result of that discussion was that the OT and Second-Temple Judaism shared the conviction that Israel was the divinely intended replacement of Adam and, as such, constituted the true humanity. This idea informs Hebrews 2:5—4:13, which I divide into two sections: 2:5-18 and 3:1—4:13. The first has to do with Adam, the second with Israel. Precipitating this juxtaposition of ideas is the Jewish belief that Israel replaced Adam as the true humanity, except that the DSS and the author of Hebrews redefine Israel in terms of their respective communities. In doing so they subvert the traditional telling of the story of the nation.

Hebrews 2:5-18. That this passage contains an Adam Christology has been argued by a number of commentators, especially the notion that Christ, the last Adam, is restoring to his followers the first Adam's lost domain (cf. Heb 2:6-8 with Ps 8:4-6, a commonly recognized *midrash* on Gen 1:26-28) and life (cf. Heb 2:14-15 with Gen 2:17).[20] I concur with this line of thinking and have elsewhere argued that another Adamic theme informs Hebrews 2:5-18, that of the apocalyptic belief that righteous suffering in this age recaptures the lost glory of Adam in the age to come (cf., e.g., Heb 2:5-18 with *2 Apoc. Bar.* 51:3-14; *4 Ezra* 7:1-98; *T. Levi* 18:2-14; Rom 5:1-21; 8:17-39; 2 Cor 4:7—5:21; Col 1:15-29).[21] Such an idea wonderfully explains the intricate relationship between the concepts of suffering and glory occurring in Hebrews 2:5-18. This conviction is also attested to in the DSS, notably Rule of the Community 4:22-23, Damascus Document 3:18-20, *Hôdāyôt* and their contexts, as I have mentioned on other occasions.[22] But there the similarity between the DSS and Hebrews ends, for over against the former's claim that its community was the inheritor of Adam's glory because of the path of righteous suffering it tread, Hebrews 2:5-18 presents Christ and his community as the true eschatological humanity (see Heb 2:10), whose afflictions will perfect the community eschatologically.[23]

Hebrews 3:1—4:13. The rationale for the linkage of the house or temple of God theme described in Hebrews 3:1-6 and the concept of rest presented in 3:7—4:13 is most probably to be sought in the idea that the true, heavenly temple of God is to be equated with the eschatological rest long awaited by God's people. This notion originated from OT passages like Deuteronomy 12:9; 29:9 and Joshua 21:44 that portray the historical possession of Canaan as divine rest which, according to 1 Kings 8:54-56, is associated with the Solomonic temple.[24] The notion emerging from the preceding texts is interpreted eschatologically in Jewish apocalypticism to the effect that the true, heavenly temple or some similar metaphor is linked with the coming eschatological rest (see, e.g., *T. Dan* 5:12; *4 Ezra* 8:52; *2 Apoc. Bar.* 78:86; *1 Enoch* 45:3-6; *T. Levi* 18:9).[25]

The DSS are particularly interesting relative to this idea, especially 4QFlorilegium 1:1-10, 4QTestimonia 1:5-8 and Rule of the Community 8:5-25. It will be recalled that the first of these passages connects the

coming true temple (of which the tabernacle was a type) with eschatological rest, especially Israel's victory over her enemies. According to
4QTestimonia 1:5-8, the eschatological prophet-like-Moses will play a
key role in Israel's future obedience to the Torah. Rule of the Community
8:5-15 contains a constellation of Mosaic concepts: tabernacle of God,
covenant, law, wilderness and (implied) rest. The impression given in
the last passage (1QS 8:5-15) by this complex of ideas, along with the
other texts mentioned, is that the Qumran community viewed itself as
the true temple of God whose obedience to the law of Moses qualified it
to participate in the long-awaited eschatological rest. As such, it constituted the eschatological humanity, the replacement of Adam.

Comparing the aforementioned three DSS passages with Hebrews
3:1—4:13 reveals both continuity and discontinuity of convictions.
Regarding the former, both materials present their respective communities as the true heavenly temple to come which participates in eschatological rest. But on two counts Hebrews 3:1—4:13 takes exception to
DSS texts like those specified above. First, whereas the DSS elevate
Moses in their eschatological expectation (he is the builder of the tabernacle, the type of the heavenly temple [4QFlor 1—10], making him the
prototype of the coming prophet at the end of time [4QTestim 1:5-8]),
according to Hebrews 3:1-6, he is only a *servant* in God's house,
whereas Christ is the *Son*. Second, the DSS pinpoint the means for
membership in the true temple—the eschatological rest of God—as
being the observance of the law of Moses (as they reinterpreted it), but
according to Hebrews 3:7—4:13, it is faith in *Christ* that does so. One
even detects in the Hebrews passage the innuendo that the reason for
the Israelites' failure to enter Canaan was due to the inferiority of the
Mosaic law, contrasted to the superior way of faith in Christ with its
sustaining power of obedience.

Hebrews 3:7-19 and 4:7 draw on Psalm 95:7-11 and the pronouncement there of divine judgment on the wilderness generation due to its
hardness of heart. This description is very similar to the Song of Moses
in Deuteronomy 32, which brands the wilderness generation as "perverse and crooked" (Deut 32:5), a label that tragically continued to
characterize the nation. From this quotation, we may gather that the
author of Hebrews considered the Judaism of his day as continuing the

Deuteronomistic tradition of sin and exile. Only those who joined and maintained membership in the Christian community could experience the long-awaited restoration. No doubt the Essenes felt the same way about their group. In this assertion, both the DSS and Hebrews were engaged in retelling the story of Israel, for only their communities were perceived as obeying God. As such they constituted the replacement of Adam, the renewed humanity.

The New Covenant in the DSS and in Hebrews 8

One of the three theological pillars of early Judaism was the covenant,[26] which affords an interesting point of comparison between the DSS and Hebrews. Susanne Lehne has conducted such a study, which notes the following similarities between those authors' understanding of the New Covenant of Jeremiah 31:31-34. First, both believe their respective groups are the inheritors of the OT covenants, beginning with Abraham (cf. CD 3:10 [also CD 1:4; 6:2]; 8:16-17 with Heb 4:2, 6; 9:1). Second, both consider themselves to be divinely elected to participate in the covenant (cf. Heb 3:1, 14; 6:4; 9:15 with various passages in the DSS). Third, both interpret the New Covenant eschatologically, believing it to be now operative in their communities in the last days. Fourth, both reserve their harshest criticism for apostates from their covenantal communities (cf. 1QpHab 1:16-210; CD 8:20-21; 19:34; 20:11-13 with Heb 3:12-13; 4:11; 6:4-6; 10:27-31; 12:15-17, 29).[27] In terms of the story of Israel the preceding comparison may be put this way: Both groups believed themselves to be the restored Israel, inheritors of the covenant with Abraham and participants in the New Covenant. Simultaneously, they viewed all others as still in sin and exile. To leave their groups, therefore, was to leave true Israel; such action was considered a threat because it undermined their subversion of the story of the nation.

Two key aspects of the new covenant, however, are viewed differently by the Qumran sectaries and the author of Hebrews: the nature of the New Covenant and the stipulation to be met in order to enter and maintain it. Regarding the first of these, the DSS people perceived their experience of the New Covenant to be in continuity with the other OT covenants. Concerning the second issue, the Essenes emphasized the Mosaic law as the means for accomplishing those ends. Lehne touches on these two aspects in the DSS by calling attention to the sectaries' custom of annually renewing the covenant. This tradition confirmed the true intentions of the law given at Sinai, as redefined by the Teacher of Righteousness.[28]

Things are much different, however, for the author of Hebrews, who understands the New Covenant as making a break with the other OT covenants and who rejects the law as the means for entering and maintaining the covenant, replacing it with the sole requirement of faith (Heb 8; see Heb 7:11-28; 11:1-40).[29] Such a conviction amounted to a radical departure from the traditional telling of the story of Israel, one with which neither Judaism in general nor the Essenes in particular would have agreed.

True Worship: Hebrews 4:14—7:28; 9:1—10:39

There is in postexilic Judaism an intensification of the connection between temple or true worship and the Mosaic law; namely, Jews believed the reason they lost their temple in 587 B.C. to the Babylonians was because of their disobedience to the divine law. Conversely, therefore, when they returned to their homeland, they embraced the Mosaic law with a new vigor. This explains why the Qumran people formed their community, for in adhering to the *halakhah* of their congregation they perceived themselves as participating in heavenly worship. And those earthly worshipers who joined their assembly became a part of such a spiritual cultus. Similarly, the writer to the Hebrews envisioned his community as experiencing true worship, the rest for which Israel longed but now based on the atonement of Christ rather than the Mosaic law. We can unpack this topic by centering on three interlocking ideas: priesthood, sacrifice and spiritual worship. Once again, Hebrews operates as the grid for discussing the DSS.

The priesthood: Hebrews 4:14—7:28. As was noted earlier in this study, Melchizedek is a key topic of discussion when comparing Hebrews 4:14—7:28 and the DSS,[30] especially 11QMelchizedek (cf. 1QM 17:1-9; CD 6:2-6; 1QSa 2). But the differences between the two, particularly as they relate to the story of Israel, are more impressive. Three contrasts quickly come to mind.

First, as mentioned before, comparing 11QMelchizedek with War Scroll 17:1-9, Damascus Document 6:2-6 and Messianic Rule 2 indicates that the Qumran community, the replacement of Adam, claimed Melchizedek as its champion and eagerly awaited his eschatological deliverance on their behalf. Hebrews 4:14—7:28, however, disassociates Melchizedek from the Aaronic priesthood because the author views the OT priesthood as obsolete since the coming of Christ.

Second, the restoration the Essenes anticipated was still future; only after the end-time holy war when Melchizedek/Michael prevailed with them would the DSS people fully enter the Deuteronomic rest. Quite the contrary for the author of Hebrews, who asserts that Christ's atoning death and triumphant resurrection befitted him as high priest to offer paradisical rest now to his followers (cf. Heb 4:14-16 with Heb 4:8:13; 2:14-15). This assurance stems from the reality that the age to come has dawned in heaven through the coming of the Messiah (see, e.g., Heb 6:5; 9:11).

Third, whereas the preceding DSS texts define the enemy to be fought in the eschatological holy war as both supernatural (Belial) and human (all non-Qumranians), according to Hebrews (and here we must move outside Heb 4:14—7:28) the enemies are death and the devil, not humans (Heb 2:14-15).

Sacrifice and atonement: Hebrews 10. As the true priesthood, the Qumran community viewed its distinctive observance of the sacrificial system as the only means for atonement. Rule of the Community 8:1-10 vividly expresses this particular nuance of the Essenes' concept of sacrifice:

1 In the Community council (there shall be) twelve men and three priests, perfect in everything that has been revealed about all *2* the law to implement truth, justice, judgment, compassionate love and unassuming behavior of each person to his fellow *3* to preserve faithfulness on the earth with firm purpose and repentant spirit in order to atone for sin, doing justice *4* and undergoing trials in order to walk with everyone in the measure of truth and the regulation of time. When these things exist in Israel *5* the Community council shall be founded on truth, *Blank* like an everlasting plantation, a holy house for Israel and the foundations of the holy of *6* holies for Aaron, true witnesses for the judgment and chosen by the will (of God) to atone for the earth and to render 7 the wicked their retribution. *Blank* It (the Community) will be the tested rampart, the precious cornerstone that does not *Blank 8*/whose foundations do not/shake or tremble in their place. *Blank* It will be the most holy dwelling 9 for Aaron with total knowledge of the covenant of justice and in order to offer a pleasant/aroma/; and it will be a house of perfection and truth in Israel 10 {. . .} in order to establish a covenant in compliance with the everlasting decrees./And these will be accepted in order to atone for the earth and to decide the judgment of the wicked {. . .} and there will be not iniquity/.

It is clear from this text (especially lines 3, 4, 6) that the Qumran community, while believing itself to be in continuity with the Aaronic priesthood, nevertheless spiritualized the sacrificial system by designating their holy lifestyle and the persecution which it elicited from non-Qumranians as the true means of forgiveness of sins, an action that was ongoing. In direct opposition to such a claim, however, Hebrews 10:11-12 asserts that atonement is based exclusively on Christ's completed work on the cross:

And every priest stands daily at his service, offering repeatedly the same sacrifices, which can never take away sins. But when Christ had offered for all time a single sacrifice for sins, he sat down at the right hand of God.

Spiritual worship: Hebrews 9. Both Hebrews and the DSS portray their congregations as participating in spiritual worship and therefore as corresponding to the heavenly tabernacle (cf. Heb 9 with 1QS 8:5-9; CD 7:13-18; cf. 1QH 7:7-9; see also the Jerusalem texts). But beyond that, there is an important distinction between the two. The DSS authors, as Lehne argues, view their congregation as corresponding to the heavenly tabernacle. This, however, was an interim status, expected to give way to an earthly, eschatological divine dwelling place. For Hebrews, however, the joining of Christians with God in worship forms the heavenly, nonmaterial tabernacle (Heb 9). Thus Lehne writes:

In a way that appears paradoxical, but which is characteristic of the genius of our author, he uses cultic language throughout to describe the Christ event and its import, while clearly rejecting a continuation of the old Levitical cult. The sectaries' hope in a purified *material* cult of the future is not shared by Heb. Forced by their circumstances, the people at Qumran developed an interim worship style that can be likened to the 'sacrifice of praise' prescribed in Heb (13.15). For the latter document this nonmaterial form of worship becomes the only legitimate cultic activity during the earthly pilgrimage of the citizens of the "lasting city that is to come."[31]

Thus the heavenly tabernacle, entered in by faith in the atoning work of Christ alone—the high priest par excellence—has become for the author of Hebrews the final resting place for believers and the goal of their worship (cf. Heb 4:14-16; 10:19-25). Such a conviction relativizes the importance of the land of ancient Jews as well as their physical temple and in so doing undermines the telling of the story of Israel.

Conclusion

This chapter has been concerned to grasp how two Jewish-oriented writings, the letter to the Hebrews and the DSS, understood the paradigm of monotheism, covenant and eschatology. Both communities claimed to be the elect people of God who represented *Yahweh*. As the true Israel, each asserted that key eschatological blessings accompanied membership in their respective groups: obedience, the New Covenant and true worship.

There is another similarity between the DSS and Hebrews which has heretofore (to my knowledge) gone undetected. N. T. Wright has called attention to an intriguing parallel between *Sirach* 44—50 and Hebrews 11—12. The former work presents a hall of faith of heroes who were true to God in Israel's history, culminating in the greatest example of all—Simon ben Onias, the high priest (c. 170 B.C.). *Sirach* 50:5-7, 11 presents this splendorous and faithful priest:

How glorious he was, surrounded by the people,
As he came out of the house of the curtain.
Like the morning star among the clouds,
Like the full moon at the festal season;
Like the sun shining on the temple of the Most High,
Like the rainbow gleaming in splendid clouds; . . .

When he put on his glorious robe
And clothed himself in perfect splendor,
When he went up to the holy altar,
He made the court of the sanctuary glorious.

Wright goes on to point out a similar presentation in Hebrews 11—12 but by way of contrast with *Sirach* 44—50:

This is where Israel's history has been leading: a great high priest, magnificently robed, splendid in his liturgical operations, coming out of the sanctuary after the worship to bless the people. It is clear that this provides a close echo of a theme that characterizes Hebrews all through: Jesus is the "great high priest who has passed through the heavens," who is "holy, blameless, separated from sinners, and exalted above the heavens," who is "seated at the right hand of the throne of the Majesty in the heavens," and who, having finished his own performance of ritual duties (offering his own blood in the heavenly sanctuary) "will appear a second time . . . to save those who are eagerly waiting for him." What is not so often seen is that the list of "heroes of faith" in Hebrews 11 is *designed to make the same point*, by means of its clear subversion of the story in Ben-Sirach 44-50. Instead of the present high priest in the Temple being the point towards which all Israel's history was tending, it is Jesus, the true High Priest: Hebrews 12:1-3 stands to 11:4-40 as Sirach 50.1-21 does to 44.1-49.16.[32]

Another Jewish work portrays the same pictures—heroes of the faith, culminating in the high priest who resides in the true temple: Damascus Document 2—7. Thus the summary of Israel's history in Damascus Document 2—6 extols the righteous "men of renown" (CD 2:11-13) as examples to emulate: Abraham (CD 3:2), Isaac and Jacob (CD 3:3), Zadok and his lineage (CD 4:1-19). The unrighteous people mentioned in Damascus Document 2—6 serve as a foil to these godly role models. The climax of the presentation of the heroes of Israel's faith is the Teacher of Righteousness (CD 6:2-11), the star of Jacob and the scepter of Israel (CD 7:18-21). He and his followers came to restore the tabernacle of David by instituting true worship (CD 7:14-18).[33]

Here then are three different tellings of the story of Israel. *Sirach* 44—50 offers a traditional presentation, Damascus Document 2—7 provides a sectarian revision of that narrative, and Hebrews 11—12 redefines the story of Israel's restoration by portraying Jesus as the ultimate expression of that reality. The presentations of Israel's heroes (and in the case of the DSS, its villains as well) give evidence of the values and self-definitions of these three claimants to God's coming kingdom.

Chapter Nine

Exile &
Eschatology

*The Gospel of John
& the DSS*

Introduction

Now that supposed Gnostic, Hermetic and Philonic parallels with John have fallen on hard times in scholarly discussions regarding the background of the Fourth Gospel,[1] Palestinian Judaism in general and the DSS in particular have emerged as the most likely influence on that writing[2] and indeed as well on the remainder of the Johannine corpus—1-3 John and Revelation. This is the case in terms of the eschatologies of the two groups, particularly the idea that the age to come has been or is about to be inaugurated. According to early Judaism, time is divided into two consecutive periods: this age and the age to come. *This age* is characterized by sin and suffering as a result of Adam's fall. *The age to come* will be inaugurated when the Messiah comes and with him righteousness and peace. In effect, the age to come is synonymous with the kingdom of God.[3]

But according to the Gospels, the life, death and resurrection of Jesus Christ marked a paradigmatic shift resulting in the overlapping of the two ages. The age to come, or the kingdom of God, was inaugurated within this age. In other words, the two ages are coterminous, and Christians live in the intersection of the two. This idea is commonly referred to as the *already-not yet* eschatological tension. That is, the age to come has already dawned because of the first coming of Christ, but is not yet complete; that awaits his second coming. Gordon D. Fee rightly calls this already-not yet eschatological tension "the essential framework . . . of primitive Christianity."[4]

A similar concept seems to have informed the Qumran community, of which Schiffman writes,

> Important to the sectarians was the immediacy of the end of days. They anticipated that the old order would soon die. The sect lived on the verge of the end of days, with one foot, as it were, in the present age and one foot in the future. They were convinced that the Messianic era would happen in their lifetime. Their move to the desert at Qumran had marked the dawn of the new order. Their lives were dedicated to preparing for that new age by living as if it had already come.[5]

Related to the preceding is the concept of the signs of the times, events associated in Judaism with the transition of this age into the age to come: the messianic woes (wars, earthquakes, famines, etc.); the rise of the antichrist and apostasy; the arrival of the kingdom of God; judgment of the wicked and the resurrection of the righteous; and the new creation. These events were subsumed under the category of the "day of the Lord" or the last days. I do not wish to give the impression that all of these attendant circumstances were treated with equal interest in the pertinent Jewish writings; in actuality, some were of more concern to certain authors than others. But in general these happenings were equated with the signs of the times; hence their occurrence in a number of Jewish works. For the current purpose I wish to point out that the DSS and the Johannine literature both attest to the dawning of the signs of the times, the overlapping of the two ages. Table 9.1 encapsulates the eschatological similarities between the two bodies of materials in this matter.

The thesis of this chapter is that another, perhaps *the*, key similarity in the eschatologies of the DSS and the Johannine material relates to

Signs	Johannine Literature	DSS
Messianic woes	Jn 15:18—16:11 (cf. 1 Jn 2:18); Rev 6—18	1QH 3:7-10; 5:30; 7:20-21; CD 1:5-11
Antichrist, apostasy	Jn 6:70; 13:2; 17:12; Rev 6:2; 13:1-18; 17:8-13 (cf. 1 Jn 2:18, 22; 4:3)	CD 1:5-11; 20:13-15; 1QS 3:17—4:22; 1QM
Resurrection	Jn 5:24-30; Rev 7, 14 (20:1-6)	1QH 3:5—6; 7
The two spirits	Jn 14:16-17; 15:26; 16:13; 1 Jn 4:1-6; etc.	1QS 4:2-26; etc.
Sons of light, sons of darkness	Jn 3:3-8; 8:12; 12:36, 46; 1 Jn 1:5-7; 2:8-11; Rev 21:23-25; 22:5	1QM 1:1; 13:1-18; 14:12-18; 1QS 1:9-10; 3:1—4:26
New creation	Rev 21—22	The New Jerusalem texts; 1QH[6]

Table 9.1. Signs of the times in the DSS and the Johannine literature

those communities' retelling of the story of Israel, particularly their end-time perspectives on the exile and restoration. Using the Gospel of John as a test case, I will offer two major points in this chapter. First, the DSS (especially 1QH and CD) and John portray the founders of their congregations (the Teacher of Righteousness and Jesus, respectively) as having suffered the messianic woes—the culmination of the covenantal curses of the exile—and that through their exaltations the Deuteronomic blessings of the restoration are offered to their followers. Second, however, the DSS and John retell (actually subvert) the story of Israel by changing the expected means for ending the exile and activating the restoration. Whereas mainstream Judaism posited that observance of the Mosaic law was the remedy for Israel's sin, the DSS and John redefine that solution. For the DSS the answer lies in adhering to their unique *halakhah*; for John it centers on faith in Jesus, apart from the Torah.

The Teacher of Righteousness and Jesus
The thesis of this section is that the DSS and John present the founders of their movements as embracing the messianic woes—the culmina-

tion of the covenantal curses—as well as initiating the Deuteronomic blessings of the restoration. I will begin with the Teacher of Righteousness.

The Teacher of Righteousness. The DSS texts pertinent to this thesis are *Hôdāyôt* 3:7-10; 5:30; 7:20-21 and their contexts, as well as Damascus Document 1:20. The former work identifies the afflictions of the Teacher of Righteousness as the messianic woes,[7] while the latter equates that suffering with the Deuteronomic curses.

Hôdāyôt 3:7-10 is the key text of the three passages mentioned above dealing with the sufferings of the Teacher of Righteousness. It supplies the dominant metaphor symbolizing those afflictions—the birth pangs of a woman:

> 7 like a besieged city positioned opposite [its enemies].
> I was in distress
> like a woman giving birth the first time
> when her birth-pangs come on her
> 8 and a pain racks her womb
> to begin the birth in the "crucible" of the pregnant woman.
> Since sons reach the frontiers of death
> 9 and the woman expectant with a man is racked by her pains,
> for from the shores of death
> she gives birth to a male,
> and there emerges from the pains of Sheol,
> 10 from the "crucible" of the pregnant woman
> a splendid counselor with his strength,
> and the man is freed from the womb.

Dale C. Allison's treatment of the text is perceptive, meriting full quotation:

> Although this passage has received much discussion, little consensus has been reached. Some have thought that 1QH III, 7-10 foretells the advent of the Messiah in the period of eschatological distress; the mother in the hymn is the community at Qumran, the child is the Messiah, and the latter will come forth from the former. Most scholars have rejected this messianic interpretation. It is problematic, among other reasons, because (1) the "I" of line 7 seemingly indicates that the psalmist is describing his own troubles, not those of a group; (2) the plurals in lines 8 and 11 ostensibly

exclude reference to an individual (the Messiah); and (3) the birth-pangs are clearly a simile (line 7: "as"), not a reference to the birth of a historical person. Elaborating on the second point, the use of "children" [sons] in line 8 especially indicates that the hymnist probably has a collectivity in view. If so, then presumably this collectivity should be identified with the community of Qumran. On this reading, in line 9 both "man-child" and "man" stand for a group (cf. Isa 66:7; 1QS III, 20-23). On the other hand, the one who labors to bring forth the group must be an individual, and probably none other that the so-called Teacher of Righteousness, whom many hold to be the author of much of the *Hôdāyôt*, including 1QH III, 3-18. So just as Paul likened his relationship with the Thessalonians to that between a nurse and a child (1 Thess. 2:7; cf. 2:11), and just as he thought of himself as in "travail" with the Galatians, his "children," until Christ be formed in them (Gal. 4:10), so the Teacher of Righteousness evidently could declare that he had given birth to a community (cf. CDI, 11 and 4QpPs[a] III, 15-16). 1QH VII, 20-22 offers a parallel. Here the hymnist—again, probably the Teacher—cries out to God, "Thou has made me a father to the sons of grace, and a foster-father to marvelous men. They have opened their mouths like little infants . . . like a child playing in the lap of its nurse" (au. trans.).[8]

Allison, concurring with previous interpreters of this text, concludes that *Hôdāyôt* 3:7-10 portrays the afflictions of the Teacher of Righteousness as having initiated the messianic woes, a period in which the Qumran community continues to suffer. This can especially be seen in the way the image of birth pangs—together with related apocalyptic motifs like the earthquake (1QH 3:12-13), flood (1QH 3:14), disturbances in the heavens (1QH 3:13) and end-time judgment on the wicked (1QH 3:14-18)—are associated with the afflictions of the DSS community.[9]

Matthew Black had earlier reached the same opinion about *Hôdāyôt* 3:7-10: "The eschatological setting of the hymn suggests that its subject is the 'birth-pangs of the Messiah' in the sense of the emergence through trial and suffering of the redeemed Israel."[10] Two other passages in the *Hôdāyôt* utilize the same metaphor of birth pangs to describe the messianic woes that the Teacher of Righteousness experienced and which his followers continued to endure: *Hôdāyôt* 5:30; 7:20-21. The first passage presents the afflictions of the Teacher of Righteousness which initiated the messianic woes as symbolized by the metaphor of birth pangs:

> They announce the charge against me with the harp,
> their grumblings with verses in harmony,
> with demolition and destruction.
> Resentment has taken hold of me
> and torments like the pangs of giving birth. (1QH 5:30)

The second passage (1QH 7:20-21) presents the idea that the sufferings of the Teacher of Righteousness gave birth to the DSS community, which in light of *Hôdāyôt* 3:7-10; 5:9 must be interpreted as the initiation and continuation of the messianic woes:

> You have make me like a father for the sons of favour,
> like a wet-nurse to the men of portent;
> > they open their mouth like a child [on the breast of its mother,]
> > like a suckling child in the lap of its wet-nurse.

Allison sets the preceding *Hôdāyôt* passages in the eschatological scheme of things by connecting them with Damascus Document 1:5-11; 20:13-15 and the War Scroll, noting that Damascus Document 1:5-11 states that 390 years passed between the captivity under Nebuchadnezzar and the emergence of a remnant. This remnant, the precursors of the sectaries at Qumran, wandered and groped in the wilderness for twenty years. Then God raised up for them a guide, the Teacher of Righteousness. Damascus Document 20:13-16 states that forty years must elapse between his death and the dawn of the messianic epoch. Positing that the Teacher's ministry lasted forty years and adding that to the prior figures of 390 years plus twenty years plus forty years brings one to 490 years, the classic seventy weeks of Daniel. This may be coincidence, but it is consistent with the sectarians' belief that they were living in the last generation, just prior to or at the beginning of the great messianic war (1QM).[11] All that to say the Teacher of Righteousness' afflictions were perceived by the Qumran community (especially according to CD, 1QH and 1QM) as having begun a forty-year period of great tribulation, at the end of which the Messiahs were expected to come and, together with the sons of light, engage and defeat the sons of darkness in eschatological holy war.

Allison's mention of Damascus Document 1:5-11; 20:13-15 prompts another point regarding the afflictions of the Teacher of Righteousness, one that seems to have gone unnoticed by scholars; namely, those texts equate the period of affliction experienced by the Teacher of Righteousness and the group he formed with "the curses of his [God's] covenant" (CD 1:17; cf. CD 20:13-33). Such a time of divine wrath began with the Babylonian exile and was protracted for some 490 years (CD 1:5-6). The reason for God's judgment on Israel was its breaking of the divine law as the Essenes interpreted it (CD 1:18-21). Combining the two works (1QH 3:7-10; 5:30; 7:20-21 and CD 1:20) permits one to interpret the messianic woes the Teacher of Righteousness embodied as the beginning of the culmination of the exile (at least for his community). One might object that the messianic woes signify something positive— suffering for righteousness' sake as the true people of God—but the covenantal curses indicate something negative—God's judgment for disobedience. But this poses no real difficulty for our theory because the righteous sufferers in Israel's history often did so on behalf of the nation and in order to motivate it to repentance (see Is 52—53; *2 Macc*; *4 Macc*).[12]

To leave the matter there, however, is to miss the other half of the DSS perspective on the afflictions of the Teacher of Righteousness, which is that he was divinely delivered from them, whether through a dramatic rescue from his enemies or, more likely according to Damascus Document 20:15, by his death and resurrection ("the gathering in of the unique teacher").[13] I will now examine the aforementioned texts (1QH 3:7-10; 5:30; 7:20-22; CD 1) in light of the Teacher's deliverance, noting especially that such a theme is portrayed in terms of Israel's long-awaited Deuteronomic blessings.

Hôdāyôt 3:7-10, as was shown above, depicts the afflictions of the Teacher of Righteousness as those associated with the messianic woes. Interspersed with this description, however, is a song of praise by the Teacher to God for having rescued him from the troubles of this age. Such divine deliverance consists of having been snatched from the jaws of death (line 19) and given glory (line 4), forgiveness of sins (line 21) and joy (line 23). The same idea occurs in the context of *Hôdāyôt* 5:30: deliverance from the messianic woes in terms of forgiveness (1QH 6:8-9), recovering paradise (1QH 6:15-26) and, interestingly enough, recapturing the inheritance of the land (1QH 6:8). *Hôdāyôt* 7:20-21 and following proceeds along the same path of thought:

> 20 You have made me like a father for the sons of favour,
> 21 like a wet-nurse to the men of portent;
> they open their mouth like a child [on the breast of its mother,]
> like a suckling child in the lap of its wet-nurse.
> 22 You have exalted my horn above all those who denounce me,
> [you have scattered] those who fight me,
> 23 and those who bring a complaint, like straw in the wind,
> and those who dominate me [. . .]
> You have saved my life,
> and lifted my horn to the heights.
> 24 I am radiant with sevenfold light,
> in the light prepared for your glory,
> 25 for you are my everlasting luminary,
> and have established my foot on the right path.
> *26 Blank*
> I give you [thanks, Lord,]
> because you have taught me your truth,
> 27 you have made me know your wonderful mysteries,
> your kindness with [sinful] men,
> your bountiful compassion with the depraved of heart.

Once again, eschatological acts of salvation are clearly perceived by the writer as present possessions of the Teacher of Righteousness: paradise regained (Adam's dominion recovered; line 23); glorious resurrection (shining with a sevenfold light; lines 24-25); and forgiveness of sins (mercy to replace a perverted heart; line 27).[14] Furthermore, these eschatological acts of deliverance should be identified as the blessings of the covenant. Thus:

☐ The inheritance referred to in *Hôdāyôt* 6:8 is described in Damascus Document 1:7-8 in terms of the land (of Israel) being given to the sons of Aaron (the Qumran community) so that the land will become "fat with the good things of his [God's] soil."

☐ Forgiveness of sins (1QH 3:21; 6:8-9; 7:27) is the means for receiving the inheritance of the land belonging to the Essenes, which indicates the presence of the New Covenant (cf. CD 2:4-5).

☐ The paradisical blessings and the glory of Adam, as was shown earlier, are another way of saying that true Israel, now redefined as the Qumran community, has become the new humanity which will inhabit the restored land, the new Eden (cf. 1QH 6:15-26; 7:23; CD 3:20 with Is 11:1-16; 45:8; Jer 3:16; 23:3; Ezek 36:11; Zeph 3:20).

☐ Life to replace death in the land recalls a passage like Deuteronomy 30:15, 19-20 (cf. 1QH 3:19).

☐ Resurrection was also a metaphor in the OT for Israel's restoration to the land (cf. Ezek 37 with 1QH 3:4; 7:24-25).

Jesus' death in John. Recent research into the provenance of the Gospel of John locates that work in the Jewish-Christian debates in the synagogues (c. post-A.D. 70 and the fall of Jerusalem).[15] A key controversy generating those discussions was the death of Jesus, particularly this question: If Jesus was truly the Messiah, why did he die, and on a cross, no less? We are not left to our imagination as to the scandal surrounding Jesus' death for Jews. Justin Martyr's (A.D. 140) debating partner, Trypho, expresses it poignantly:

> Be assured that all our nation awaits the Messiah; and we admit that all the Scriptures which you have quoted refer to him. Moreover, I also admit that the name of Jesus by which the son of Nun was called, has inclined me very strongly to adopt this view. But we are in doubt about whether the Messiah should be so shamefully crucified. For whoever is crucified is said in the Law to be accursed, so that I am very skeptical on this point. It is quite clear, to be sure, that the Scriptures announce that the Messiah had to suffer, but we wish to learn if you can prove it to us whether by suffering he was cursed. (*Dial. Tryph.* 89.1)[16]

The Fourth Gospel's answer to that query, as Craig A. Evans has demonstrated, was that Jesus' death was in keeping with scriptural expectation. Evans identifies a twofold apologetic in John concerning the matter: Israel's rejection of Jesus the Messiah was predicted in the OT (see especially Jn 12:38 [Is 53:1] and Jn 12:39-40 [Is 6:10]); Jesus' death paradoxically was his moment of glory (Jn 12:23, 28; 13:31-32; 17:5), the background of which is the exaltation of the suffering servant of Isaiah (cf. Jn 12:41 with Is 52:13 [cf. 53:12]).[17]

It is also important to understand that according to the evangelist this "glory" is the glory which the prophet Isaiah saw and of which he spoke (Jn 12.41). The coordination of the quotations of Isa. 53.1 (Jn 12.38) and Isa. 6.10 (Jn 12.40) suggests that what was seen was the "glory" which the prophet beheld in his famous vision of Isaiah 6 and what was *spoken* were the words of the Suffering Servant Song. That is to say, when (or because) Isaiah saw God's *glory* he spoke about God's *servant*, who is none other that the *logos* who became flesh and tabernacled among us (Jn 1.14).[18]

One can move this discussion a step further by arguing that John[19] understands Jesus' death and resurrection as fulfilling the Jewish expectation of the coming messianic woes, the culmination of the exile,[20] much like the DSS portray the death and exaltation of the Teacher of Righteousness. The eschatological and exilic aspects of Jesus' death, therefore, will be addressed in what follows.

Eschatology. Dale C. Allison's perceptive study demonstrates that the Fourth Gospel stamps Jesus' death on the cross with the motif of the messianic woes. The key text in this regard is John 16:16-22. Allison adduces the evidence for this conclusion:

> The terminology of John 16:16-22 recalls eschatological doctrine. *Thlipsis* denotes the eschatological tribulation elsewhere in the New Testament (e.g., Mark 13:19, 24; Rom. 2:9; Rev. 7:14) and is also so used in Dan. 12:1 LXX. The image of a woman in pain bringing forth her child was a well-known symbol for the eschatological transition in Judaism and the early church, and it is used in the Tanach in connection with the coming of the Day of the Lord. The statement that the disciples will again see Jesus recalls to mind several Synoptic passages concerning the Parousia of the Son of man (for example, Mark 13:26 and 14:62); and "to see" the Messiah or the days of the Messiah was presumably a stock phrase (note Luke 17:22; Rev. 1:7; Justin, *Dialogue with Trypho* 14:8; 64:7; and *b. Sanh.* 98). In view of all this, John 16:16-22 evidently offers yet one more instance of a peculiar use of eschatological language. The passion is as the great tribulation, the resurrection as the arrival of the age to come.[21]

Allison concludes his comments on John 16:19-22, writing that this passage is based on a complex of sayings that originally had reference to the end, and that the prospect of tribulation turned into joy was at one time a prophecy of the coming eschatological woes and the subsequent salvation. In John, however, this has become obscured because the passion has drawn to itself language descriptive of the messianic travail, whereas the resurrection has drawn to itself language descriptive of the parousia.[22]

In other words, John 16:16-22 showcases the belief that Jesus has undergone the messianic woes but his resurrection has enthroned him in glory (see Jn 20—21 for the latter notion). For Jesus, therefore, deliverance from the eschatological tribulation is an accomplished fact.

John 12:23-36—a passage considered by commentators to be the crucial text on Jesus' death in John's Gospel—bears this out.[23] Three eschatological themes emerge in this passage, leading one to conclude that John portrays Jesus' death as stamped by the motif of the messianic woes.

First, the paradox of Jesus' death as simultaneously being his moment of glory (Jn 12:23-29) is imbued with apocalyptic significance: The suffering of the righteous in this age will lead to the glory of the age to come.[24] For John, the transition between the two occurred at the cross. Second, more specifically, Jesus' death as the Son of Man/ Davidic Messiah and concomitantly his glorious resurrection (Jn 12:34) draw on Daniel 7:13-14 and the theme there of the messianic woes, which the heavenly Son of Man and earthly people of God were expected to suffer and over which they were promised victory.[25] Third, as Judith L. Kovacs has shown, John 12:30-33 understands Jesus' defeat of the prince of this world (Satan) to be the triumph of the Messiah over evil in the eschatological holy war, which transpired at the cross.[26] It is striking to observe that the contrast between the sons of light and the sons of darkness delineated in John 12:35-36 matches the portrait of the end-time battle in the DSS (see 1QM), one which will secure victory for the saints because they have faithfully endured the messianic woes.

Exile. The Evangelist, in quoting Isaiah 53:1 (Jn 12:38) and Isaiah 6:10 (Jn 12:40) and in his statement that Isaiah saw Jesus' glory (Jn 12:41), indicates that Jesus was the suffering, exalted servant whose death atoned for the sin of Israel. Furthermore, as N. T. Wright has carefully demonstrated from Isaiah 40—45, the servant's suffering was expected to bring an end to the exile and the return to the land.[27] Wright well concludes his study of that section in Isaiah, together with its influence on subsequent related texts:

There was no such thing as a straightforward pre-Christian Jewish belief in an Isaianic 'servant of YHWH' who, perhaps as Messiah, would suffer and die to make atonement for Israel or for the world. But there was something else, which literally dozens of texts attest: a large-scale and widespread belief, to which Isaiah 40—55 made a substantial contribution, that Israel's present state of suffering was somehow held within the ongoing divine purpose; that in due time this period of woe would come to an end, with divine wrath falling instead on the pagan nations that had oppressed Israel (and perhaps on renegades within Israel herself); that the explanation for the present state of affairs had to do with Israel's own sin, for which either she, or in some cases her righteous representatives, was or were being punished; and that this suffering and punishment would therefore, somehow, hasten the moment when Israel's tribulation would be complete, when she would finally have been purified from her sin so that her exile could be undone at last. There was, in other words, a belief, hammered out not in abstract debate but in and through poverty, exile, torture and martyrdom, that Israel's sufferings might be, not merely a state *from* which she would, in YHWH's good time, be redeemed, but paradoxically, under certain circumstances and in certain senses, part of the means *by* which that redemption would be affected.[28]

All this to say that Jesus' death, like the Teacher of Righteousness of the DSS, was perceived as embodying the messianic woes, the culmination of Israel's exile. Thus the DSS and John present their respective messages against the backdrop of the story of Israel: sin-exile-restoration. That is, they combine the themes of exile and eschatology. But their presentations do more than repeat the traditional telling of the story of Israel; they subvert it.

The Subversion of the Story of Israel by the DSS and John
The typical telling of the story of Israel involved the call to obey the Mosaic law; only in doing so could the nation's restoration be accomplished. The DSS and John radically differ from this part of Israel's narrative by, in the case of the DSS, redefining the law, or in the case of the Fourth Gospel, discarding it altogether and replacing it with faith in Christ.

The DSS reinterpretation of the law. As was shown earlier, the DSS redefine the Mosaic law in terms of the Essenes' *halakhah*, particularly concerning the feasts, sabbaths and dietary regulations (see, e.g., CD

6:14-21; 4QMMT 1-92; cf. 1QS 5:7-13). Such a rigid reinterpretation of the Torah falls under the category of the "hidden" matters rather than the "revealed" Torah (the Mosaic code), the result of which is that the former undermines the latter.[29]

John. Building on the research of others, James D. G. Dunn and his student Martin Scott have pinpointed a key aspect of the Gospel of John: It presents Christ as the wisdom of God in opposition to the law of Moses.[30] This is to redefine the means for Israel's restoration. Dunn's and Scott's argumentation posits that three critical places in John are indebted to the wisdom tradition, but the evangelist uses that tradition to demonstrate that Jesus Christ is divine wisdom: the prologue, the "I am" sayings and the descent-ascent revealer motif.

Prologue. A number of parallels surface between John's prologue (Jn 1:1-18) and the figure of wisdom in Jewish literature (see table 9.2 for a partial list).

John	Wisdom
The Word was in the beginning (Jn 1:1)	Wisdom was in the beginning (Prov 8:22-23; *Sir* 1:4; *Wis* 9:9)
The Word was with God (Jn 1:1)	Wisdom was with God (Prov 8:30; *Sir* 1:1; *Wis* 9:4)
The Word was cocreator (Jn 1:1-3)	Wisdom was cocreator (Prov 3:19; 8:25; *Wis* 7:21; 9:1-2)
The Word provides light (Jn 1:4, 9)	Wisdom provides light (Prov 8:22; *Wis* 7:26; 8:13; *Sir* 4:12; *Bar* 4:1)
The Word as light is in contrast to darkness (Jn 1:5)	Wisdom as light is in contrast to darkness (*Wis* 7:29-30)
The Word was in the world (Jn 1:10)	Wisdom was in the world (*Wis* 8:1; *Sir* 24:6)
The Word was rejected by its own (Jn 1:11)	Wisdom was rejected by its own (*Sir* 15:7; *Bar* 3:12; cf. *1 Enoch* 42:1-2)
The Word was received by the faithful (Jn 1:12)	Wisdom was received by the faithful (*Wis* 7:27; *Bar* 3:37)
The Word became flesh (Jn 1:14)	Wisdom indwelled Israel (*Sir* 24:8, 23; *Bar* 3:37-42)

Table 9.2. The Word in John and the wisdom tradition[31]

Elsewhere I have argued that the common denominator underlying the wisdom motif in the Jewish literature mentioned in table 9.2 is that God's wisdom is embodied in the Mosaic law, the obedience of which is the means for Israel's restoration.[32] It can be seen, then, that John wishes to relocate wisdom; it dwells no longer in the law but in Christ.

"I am" sayings. Martin Scott uncovers the wisdom motif informing the Johannine "I am" sayings (see table 9.3).

John	Wisdom
Christ is the bread of life (Jn 6:35)	Wisdom is the bread, the substance of life (Prov 9:5, *Sir* 15:3; 24:21; 29:21; *Wis* 11:4)
Christ is the light of the world (Jn 8:12)	Wisdom is light (*Wis* 7:26-30; 18:3-4)
Christ is the door of the sheep and the good shepherd (Jn 10:7, 11, 14)	Wisdom is the door and the good shepherd (Prov 8:34-35; *Wis* 7:25-27; 8:2-16; *Sir* 24:19-22)
Christ is life (Jn 11:25)	Wisdom brings life (Prov 3:16; 8:35; 9:11; *Wis* 8:13)
Christ is the way to truth (Jn 14:6)	Wisdom is the way (Prov 3:17; 8:32-34; *Sir* 6:26)

Table 9.3. "I am" and the wisdom motif[33]

The major point to be gleaned from these parallels is that whereas in the Jewish texts, wisdom, embodied in the Mosaic law, is the means for receiving light, the truth, substance and so on, for John such can be found only in Christ.

The descent and ascent of the revealer. The Johannine emphasis on Jesus (rather than the Torah) as the revealer who descends from the Father to impart truth and then ascends back to his divine origin (cf. Jn 1:47-51; 3:12-13; 6:61-62) is steeped in the wisdom tradition. Thus, like wisdom, Jesus descends or is sent from God (thus implying his preexistence, see *Sir* 24:3-17; *Wis* 9:10, 17). But like wisdom, he is removed from the unbelieving and ascends to the Father (*1 Enoch* 42).

The preceding places, then—the prologue, the occurrences of the "I am" sayings and the references to Jesus as the descending-ascending revealer—and other locations in John[34] are imbued with sapiential themes, replacing the Torah with Christ.

The law of Moses. In opposition to Christ the wisdom of God is John's negative portrayal of the law of Moses. Dunn provides three principal examples of this in the Fourth Gospel:

☐ John 1:14-18 (cf. Jn 1:47-51) contrasts Christ, God's full revelation, with the Torah of Moses.

☐ John 3:1-14 (cf. Jn 3:31-36) polemicizes against any means of divine revelation other than Christ, including Moses.

☐ John 6 exalts Jesus the true bread, the Word of God, over against the manna of Moses.

Dunn concludes from these three texts, "In this way John's gospel attempts to anticipate one of its chief claims: That revelation from God, revelation of the heavenly mysteries is to be found in its fullest and clearest and final form in the fleshliness of Jesus, rather than in the Torah of Moses."[35] This assessment is confirmed by the wisdom theme present in the previous three passages, especially the descent-ascent motif therein (Jn 1:17-18, 47-51; 3:12-13; 6:61-62).[36]

Conclusion

The DSS and the Fourth Gospel are deeply concerned with the story of Israel, which for them centers on two primary concerns. First, their respective founders, the Teacher of Righteousness and Jesus, embraced the messianic woes (the culmination of the exile), yet consequently their exaltations have opened the flow of blessings of the restoration. Second, the means for actualizing such renewal is to follow the teachings of their leaders: for the DSS, their founder's *halakhah*; for John, faith in Jesus rather than the Mosaic law.

One of the key results of this retelling of the story of Israel in the DSS and John is that the recipients of the restoration are redefined: not ethnic Jews but those faithful to their founders, the Teacher of Righteousness and Jesus. The Fourth Evangelist is even more radical in this regard than the DSS, for the Gospel of John envisions Gentiles to be a part of the true people of God (Jn 1:10-13; 12:20-24, 32; 17:18-23; 20—21), something unthinkable to the Qumran community.

Conclusion

The Real Story
Behind the Story
of Israel

It is time now to bring this study to a conclusion by pondering the question, What is the real story behind the story of Israel as depicted in the DSS and the NT? That the two bodies of literature take the narrative of Israel's sin-exile-restoration as the point of departure for relating their messages is apparently undeniable. Both agree that Israel, though returned to the land, is nevertheless still in exile (see chapter one). Each offers an apocalyptic answer to Israel's plight by presenting its founder as an end-time personage who was forming the true people of God (chapter two), and the method for maintaining such a stance is *pesher* hermeneutics (chapter three). But the respective founders/redeemers of these two communities are unlike what "normative" Judaism expected (chapter four). Likewise the new way of life called for by each (chapter five) stands in contrast to traditional Judaism. Moreover, both the DSS and the NT emphasize the importance of justification by faith as the means for entering the New Covenant, though significantly different perspectives inform their understanding of how that salvation related to the Torah (chapters six through eight).

Finally, both communities looked to the death and exaltations of their founders as the focal points of the Deuteronomic curses and blessings (chapter nine).

Having said that, however, is there a deeper dynamic at work in the ways the DSS and the NT retell the story of Israel? In other words, is there a story behind the story of Israel to be told? I believe there is (and here let the reader be alerted that my faith perspective will become explicit in my answer to this query): the DSS message is impacted by cognitive dissonance. Elsewhere I have applied this aspect of the sociology of religion to millenarian groups that incorrectly predicted the date of the return of Christ,[1] and though to my knowledge scholars have not capitalized on such an approach relative to the DSS, this theory explains the dynamic informing the Scrolls remarkably well.

Leon Festinger[2] is considered the leading expert and pioneer in applying cognitive dissonance to millenarian movements. In his *A Theory of Cognitive Dissonance* Festinger explains that human beings usually strive for consistency (or consonance) in their beliefs (cognition). If one then acknowledges or does something that is inconsistent with personal beliefs, one usually tries to rationalize the inconsistency (or dissonance) as being consistent with those beliefs instead of accepting the inconsistency at face value. If the rationalization process does not work and the inconsistency persists, discomfort sets in. To alleviate this feeling, the person will work hard to reduce the dissonance, avoiding anything that would increase the tension.[3]

For example, members of a millenarian movement may set a date for the end of the world and the return of Christ. When the date passes and the prediction has not come true, they experience dissonance. The reality of things is inconsistent with their belief. They also feel victimized by those who mock them for holding to such a seemingly odd belief. These circumstances create great distress. They may accept that the prediction has failed and become greatly disillusioned. On the other hand, if they cannot accept that conclusion, they may atttempt to relieve the uncomfortable feeling by rationalizing away the failure of the predicition. They may set a new date, explain why the first one was incorrect or claim that the prediction was fulfilled and provide an alternative interpretation to what happened. They also tend to ignore or condemn anything that forces them to deal with the reality of the situation.

Festinger further claims that people who have made a commitment to a certain conviction to the point of taking action that cannot be reversed will, ironically, become even more convinced of the correctness of their conviction when presented with evidence that it is absolutely wrong.[4] He discusses five conditions under which this phenomenon occurs:

1. A belief must be held with deep conviction, and it must have some relevance to action, that is, to what the believer does or how he or she behaves.

2. The person holding the belief must have committed to it; that is, for the sake of one's belief, one must have taken some important action that is difficult to undo. In general, the more important such actions are and the more difficult they are to undo, the greater is the individual's commitment to the belief.

3. The belief must be sufficiently specific and concerned with the real world so that events may unequivocally refute the belief.

4. Such undeniable disconfirmatory evidence must occur and must be recognized by the individual holding the belief.[5]

Given these four conditions, we might expect that individuals would surrender their conviction. This will occur in many instances, but one further condition must be in place before people will hold on to a belief proved false.

5. The individual believer must have social support. If the believer is a member of a group of convinced persons who can support one another, we would expect the belief to be maintained and the believers to attempt to proselyte or to persuade nonmembers that the belief is correct.[6]

In the case of millenarian movements, the group must have set a date or a period of time within which Christ would return, giving details as to just what would take place. The commitment to the date must be held as important and is usually stated publicly.

I propose that the preceding components of cognitive dissonance are applicable to the DSS community, proceeding from the foundational prophecy made about the Teacher of Righteousness, namely, that during his life the restoration of Israel was inaugurated and would be culminated *forty years* after his death (CD 20:13-16). The community held this as well as the other teachings of their leader with deep fervor. It is the dynamic driving the Scrolls, whose writers believed themselves to be the vanguard of eschatological Israel living in the last generation. Such a cherished tenet motivated numerous followers to join the sectarian Essenes. The prediction was a matter of public record, at least to the Qumran covenanters, who knew well its prophecy. The prediction failed to materialize, however; forty years after its utterance (c. 100 B.C., assuming the death of the Teacher occurred about 150-140 B.C.), the world continued basically unchanged. Indeed, the Essenes inhabited Qumran long after the Teacher's death (until A.D. 68), all the while providing a spiritual support group for its followers.

But how did the Essene covenanters rationalize away the failed prophecy? There does not seem to be any evidence in the Scrolls that its authors recalculated the date of the end of the last generation, as some millenarian groups are wont to do. Rather, the DSS redefined the nature of the deliverance associated with the end time—specifically the culmination of the messianic woes/Deuteronomic curses—by promulgating the notion that they were *already* spared such when they gathered for worship. It was in that setting that they were joined with their beloved teacher and angels before the heavenly throne. There they experienced the Deuteronomic blessings and restoration of Israel in spiritual form until the final holy war would be waged (recall 1QH 3:7-10; 5:30; 7:20-21).

If this sounds bizarre to us moderns, a nineteenth-century analogy indicates that recourse to the spiritualization of failed prophecy is available to those who seek such. As was documented in my work *Doomsday Delusions*, probably the most spectacular failed prediction uttered regarding the date of Christ's return was that by William Miller.

Miller's theory was quite elaborate, but central to it was his interpretation of two verses in the book of Daniel, which he tied together to calculate the Lord's return: Daniel 8:14, "And he said to him, 'For two thousand and three hundred evenings and mornings; then the sanctuary shall be restored' " and Daniel 9:24, "Seventy weeks of years are decreed concerning your people and your holy city, to finish the trans-gression, to put an end to sin, and to atone for iniquity, to bring in ever-lasting righteousness, to seal both vision and prophet, and to anoint a most Holy place." Miller's basic reasoning can be outlined as follows:

1. The sanctuary cleansing mentioned in Daniel 8:14 referred to the return of Christ, which would eradicate all evil on the earth.

2. A prophetic day equaled one year, so one could correctly calculate the numbers in the passages as 2,300 years and 490 years (seventy times seven).

3. Using Bishop Ussher's popular OT chronology, the 2,300-year period began with the return of the Jews to Jerusalem to rebuild the city in 457 B.C. (Christ's crucifixion, A.D. 33, marked the end of Daniel's seventy weeks. Moving back 490 years from A.D. 33, one comes to the year 457 B.C.).

4. Two thousand three hundred years forward from 457 B.C. was A.D. 1843.[7]

There are two noteworthy examples of cognitive dissonance dis-played by the Millerites when Miller's prediction failed. The first was that his followers recalculated the date of the parousia to October 22, 1844 (Miller himself agreed).[8] When that prophecy failed, the second form of rationalization was drafted by Millerite Hiram Edson. Accord-ing to him, the "cleansing of the sanctuary" referred to in Daniel 8:14 actually did take place on October 22, 1844, *but in heaven.* Christ's entering the heavenly sanctuary symbolized how he was "blotting out" sins, not just forgiving them. With this last task accomplished in heaven, the stage was set for Christ's return to earth.[9] Such spiritual-ization of prophecy gone awry vividly reminds one of the similar stance taken by the DSS authors (noted above).

How does this phenomenon of cognitive dissonance that informs the story of Israel as adopted by the Qumran community relate to the NT? To answer that question, I return to N. T. Wright's study *Jesus and the Victory of God,* which insightfully demonstrates that the historical Jesus did indeed prophesy he would go to Jerusalem, die and then be resurrected. Such a death would absorb the Deuteronomic curses, while his life beyond the grave would dispense the covenantal bless-ings. Israel would be reconciled to God by accepting this message, but if not, the fate of Jerusalem would thereby be secured. Both predictions, in fact, came true, the one in A.D. 30 and the other in A.D. 70.

In the end, therefore, the resurrection of Jesus legitimates the NT's retelling of the story of Israel in a way unparalleled by all other contenders for the faith in Second Temple Judaism. Little wonder too that the NT's shaping of the story of Israel was truly unique: it offered restoration to God on the basis of faith in Christ apart from the law to Gentile and Jew alike. This was indeed the only way to become the humanity God intended.

More than just a "historical winner," the church succeeded where the Qumran community failed because it devoted itself to becoming God's witness of Christ's love and forgiveness to all peoples of the world. Furthermore, Christianity's message of grace offered deliverance from the obsessive-compulsive relationship with the law that had enslaved individuals such as the DSS authors. It may have been these spiritual realities of the gospel that caused Christianity eventually to triumph, even over mighty Rome.

Notes

Introduction

[1]This description of the discovery of the first seven Dead Sea Scrolls comes from John Trever, one of the scholars on the original team of translators. It is nicely summarized by James C. VanderKam, *The Dead Sea Scrolls Today* (Grand Rapids, Mich.: Eerdmans, 1994), pp. 2-10.

[2]This is not to suggest, however, that the rebirth of Israel in 1947-1948 began the last generation before the return of Christ, which has been a popular theme in those contemporary works taking a sensationalist approach to biblical prophecy. For a critique of that mentality, see C. Marvin Pate and Calvin B. Haines Jr., *Doomsday Delusions: What's Wrong with Predictions About the End of the World* (Downers Grove, Ill.: InterVarsity Press, 1995).

[3]*Gnosticism* is a term derived from the Greek word for knowledge, *gnōsis*, referring to what is generally believed by scholars these days to have been a second- to third-century A.D. aberration of Christianity. It taught that the spirit was good but the body was evil, and the awareness of such a duality brought deliverance to a person. *Hellenist* is basically synonymous with the term *Greek*, often with reference to the pervasive cultural influence on the ancient world brought about by the conquest of Alexander the Great (c. 330 B.C.).

[4]The word *apocalypticism* has as its etymological root *apocalypse*, which means "revelation" or "uncovering" with reference to the future. Thus apocalypticism, like eschatology, has to do with events at the end of time. Apocalypticism was at a fever pitch during the period of the DSS and the NT. Many Jews firmly believed that the age to come, or the kingdom of God, was poised to descend to earth from heaven. Judaism expected certain events to precede the coming of the kingdom of God, or God's rule on earth, especially the great tribulation (a time of unparalleled suffering which God's faithful were expected to endure at the hands of their enemies immediately before the arrival of the Messiah and the kingdom). Often called the messianic woes, it was thought that Israel's suffering, like birth pangs, would give birth to the Messiah (see Dan 12:1-3; *1 Enoch* 80:4-5; 91:7; *Jub.* 23:14-23; *4 Ezra* 7:3) and religious apostasy (a large-scale turning away from God in the face of persecution; see, e.g., *1 Enoch* 91:7; *Jub.* 23:14-23; *4 Ezra* 5:1-2). The Messiah, or God's anointed one, would then come to earth to establish the kingdom of God, or the age to come. (While many Jewish works anticipate the arrival of the Messiah—e.g., *T. Jud.* 17:5-6; *Pss. Sol.* 17:23-51; *T. Levi* 18:2-7; 1QSa 9:11; CD 14:19—not all do; see *Jub.* 31:18). At that time the resurrection of the righteous dead (Dan 12:2-3; *1 Enoch* 51:1-2; *4 Ezra* 7:32; *2 Apoc. Bar.* 21:23), the judgment of the wicked (Dan 2:7; 12:2; *4 Ezra* 7:113; *2 Apoc. Bar.* 85:12) and cosmic renewal, or a

new creation (Is 65:17-25; *1 Enoch* 45:4; *Jub.* 1:23; *4 Ezra* 7:75; *2 Apoc. Bar.* 32:6), were expected to occur. The controlling factor behind all these events was the belief that this age would give way to the age to come.

Two other matters relative to apocalypticism need to be sketched out: the origin of Jewish apocalypticism and the relationship between that genre and the motifs of apocalypticism. Concerning the former, four suggestions have been made: Old Testament prophecy, the wisdom movement, Hellenistic-Oriental syncretism and Canaanite religion. Of these four possibilities, the first seems the most likely option. French L. Arrington includes a good discussion of this issue along with a helpful bibliography in his *Paul's Aeon Theology* in *1 Corinthians* (Washington, D.C.: University Press of America, 1977), pp. 5-6. Regarding the latter concern, it needs to be kept in mind that, although an author's writing may not take the form of an official apocalypse (similar, for example, to that of Daniel or Revelation), it may still be indebted to apocalyptic motifs. Thus although the DSS and the NT may contain only a few explicitly apocalyptic works—for the former, the War Scroll, the Rule of the Community, the New Jerusalem texts; for the latter, the Olivet Discourse, 2 Thessalonians 2, Revelation—they are nevertheless greatly impacted by some of the fundamental themes of apocalypticism.

[5]For the general application of this thesis to the OT, the Intertestament (Jewish literature written from 400 B.C. to A.D. 100), and the NT, Odil H. Steck's work has proved to be programmatic: *Israel und das gewaltsame Geshick der Propheten: Untersuchungen zur Überlieferung des deuteronomistischen Geshichtsbildes im Alten Testament, Spätjudentum und Urchristentum*, Wissenschaftliche Monographien zum Alten und Neun Testament 23 (Neukirchen-Vluyn, Germany: Neukirchener, 1967). It is important to note the nuance distinguishing the terms *Deuteronomic* and *Deuteronomistic*: the former applies to the book of Deuteronomy itself while the latter pertains to the tradition developing out of Deuteronomy encompassing early Judaism. N. T. Wright has pursued this avenue of thought in his *The New Testament and the People of God* (Minneapolis: Fortress, 1992). His earlier work briefly applied the concept to Paul, *The Climax of the Covenant: Christ and the Law in Pauline Theology* (Edinburgh: T & T Clark, 1991). Wright will develop this theme relative to Paul in a forthcoming volume. Others who apply the story of Israel (the Deuteronomistic tradition) to Paul include Richard B. Hays, *Echoes of Scripture in the Letters of Paul* (New Haven, Conn.: Yale University Press, 1989); James M. Scott, "Paul's Use of Deuteronomic Tradition(s)," in *JBL* 112 (1993): 645-65; and Frank Thielman, *Paul and the Law: A Contextual Approach* (Downers Grove, Ill.: InterVarsity Press, 1994). The same theory has been utilized by David P. Moessner with regard to Luke-Acts in his *Lord of the Banquet: The Literary and Theological Significance of the Lucan Travel Narrative* (Minneapolis: Fortress, 1989), while its relevance to Matthew has recently been highlighted by Michael W. Knowles, *Jeremiah in Matthew's Gospel: The Rejected Prophet Motif in Matthean Redaction*, Journal for the Study of the New Testament Supplement Series 68 (Sheffield,

U.K.: Sheffield Academic Press, 1993). N. T. Wright's *Jesus and the Victory of God* (Minneapolis: Fortress, 1996) applies the theme of the story of Israel to the Gospels. For the theme of the exile in the DSS, see Martin G. Abegg, "Exile and the Dead Sea Scrolls," in *Exile: Old Testament, Jewish and Christian Concepts,* ed. James M. Scott (Leiden: Brill, 1997), pp. 111-26.

[6]See Wright, *New Testament and the People of God,* as well as later discussion in this book.

[7]Samuel Sandmel first coined the term *parallelomania* in his article "Parallelomania," *JBL* 81 (1962): 1-13, and thereby rightly warned scholars of positing a direct literary relationship between two writings just because they are parallel. Nevertheless, Joseph A. Fitzmyer perceptively issues a countercaution in the matter: "Again one often sees quoted E. R. Goodenough's famous dictum about literary parallels: A parallel by definition consists of straight lines in the same plane which never meet, however far produced in any direction. But the definition is derived from mathematics and applied to literature. To repeat the dictum as if it closes the discussion or absolves one from investigating the literary relationship of authors is only a form of obscurantism—something little better than parallelomania or pan-Qumranism. Moreover, it enables one to avoid asking the question when a *literary* parallel might cease to be such and actually prove to be a 'contact'" (Joseph A. Fitzmyer, *Essays on the Semitic Background of the New Testament,* Sources for Biblical Study 5, SBL [Missoula, Mont.: Scholars Press, 1974], p. 205 n. 1).

[8]This theory of common parentage but divergent perspectives is not to deny, however, that one might occasionally find NT texts that demonstrate literary dependence on the DSS (e.g., 2 Cor 6:14—7:1).

Chapter 1: From Exile to the Return

[1]Odil H. Steck, *Israel und das gewaltsame Geshick der Propheten: Untersuchungen zur Überlieferung des deuteronomistischen Geshichtsbildes im Alten Testament, Spätjudentum und Urchristentum,* Wissenschaftliche Monographien zum Alten und Neun Testament 23 (Neukirchen-Vluyn, Germany: Neukirchener, 1967). See my discussion of sin-exile-restoration in the introduction; compare also James Scott's useful summary and application of this pattern to Paul's writings in his "Paul's Use of the Deuteronomic Tradition(s)," *JBL* 112 (1993): 645-65.

[2]171 B.C. and following, the time frame into which the beginnings of the DSS should be placed; see chapter two.

[3]Ever since the works of Martin Noth, *Überlieferungsgeschichtliche Studien* 1 (Halle: Niemeyer, 1943), scholars have viewed Deuteronomy 1 through 2 Kings 25 as a continuous narrative, displaying via stories and speeches the theme that obedience to the Torah brings blessings on Israel while disobedience invokes divine curses. In this manner the historian can explain the exile of the Jews as a part of God's plan rather than a consequence of his inability to protect the nation. Furthermore, if Israel repents, God will restore previous fortunes (Deut 29:28; cf. 1 Kings 8:46 with Deut 30:1; 2 Kings 25:27). More-

over, such a theme of sin-exile-restoration also informs Israel's preexilic history (the periods of the conquest, the judges and the monarchy), adumbrating
the exile itself.

[4]On this point see Carey A. Moore, "Toward the Dating of the Book of
Baruch," *CBQ* 36 (1974): 312-20, esp. p. 315.

[5]In chapter four of this work, which treats the subject of messianic hope in
early Judaism, I will show that the prophet-like-Moses factors heavily in the
DSS and in the NT.

[6]Gerhard von Rad calls these passages "doxologies of judgment." See his
"Gerichtsdoxologie" in *Gesammelte Studien zum Alten Testament Band II*, ed.
Rudolf Smend; TBS: AT 48 (Munich: Kaiser, 1973), pp. 246-47; cf. Christian
Müller, *Gottes Gerechtigkeit und Gottes Volk: Eine Untersuchungen zu Römer 9-11*,
FRLANT 86 (Göttingen: Vandenhoeck & Ruprecht, 1964), pp. 59-64, 108-9. M.
A. Knibb's discussion of *Damascus Document* 1:3—2:4 from the Deuteronomis-
tic perspective (*The Qumran Community: Cambridge Commentaries on Writings
of the Jewish and Christian World—200 B.C. to A.D. 20* [Cambridge: Cambridge
University Press, 1987], p. 20) is helpful. Scott's application of the Deutero-
nomic curses to 1 Thessalonians 2:15-16 ("Paul's Use," pp. 651-57) is illuminating. For a comprehensive attempt to look at Luke-Acts from the perspective of the Deuteronomistic tradition, see David P. Moessner, *Lord of the
Banquet: The Literary and Theological Significance of the Lucan Travel Narrative*
(Minneapolis: Fortress, 1989).

[7]Steck, *Israel und das gewaltsame Geshick der Propheten*; N. T. Wright, *The New Tes-
tament and the People of God* (Minneapolis: Fortress, 1992); Moessner, *Lord of the
Banquet*; Scott, "Paul's Use"; Frank Thielman, *Paul and the Law: A Contextual
Approach* (Downers Grove, Ill.: InterVarsity Press, 1994).

[8]M. A. Knibb, "The Exile in the Literature of the Intertestamental Period,"
HayJ 17 (1976): 253-72; esp. pp. 271-72.

[9]Jacob Neusner, *Self-Fulfilling Prophecy: Exile and Return in the History of Judaism*
(Boston: Beacon, 1987).

[10]See Wright's development of this theme in *New Testament and the People*, pp.
152-66.

[11]Steck divides the restoration into two elements: Israel has the opportunity to
repent and upon taking that opportunity will be restored (*Israel und das
gewaltsame Geshick der Propheten*). Scott ("Paul's Use") follows Steck in this
regard. I think, however, we may just as well combine the two, for Israel's restoration necessarily involves Israel's opportunity to repent.

[12]George W. E. Nickelsburg, *Jewish Literature Between the Bible and the Mishnah:
A Historical and Literary Introduction* (Philadelphia: Fortress, 1981), p. 18. Nickelsburg's work (like Steck's) emphasizes the influence of Deuteronomistic tra-
dition(s) on the literature of early Judaism.

[13]Regarding these two points, see my forthcoming work, *The Reverse of the
Curse: Paul, Wisdom and the Law*, WUNT II (Tübingen: J. C. B. Mohr [Paul Sie-
beck]).

[14]E. P. Sanders called attention to covenantal nomism in his watershed book *Paul and Palestinian Judaism: A Comparison of Patterns of Religion* (Philadelphia: Fortress, 1977).

[15]Thielman highlights this aspect of Deuteronomy in his work *Paul and the Law,* pp. 64-65. Compare the earlier remarks on the theology of Deuteronomy by Otto Kaiser, *Introduction to the Old Testament: A Presentation of Its Results and Problems,* trans. John Sturdy (Minneapolis: Augsburg, 1975), p. 133.

[16]Annie Jaubert, *La notion d'alliance dans le judaïsme aux abords de l'ère chrétienne,* Patristica Sorbonesia 6 (Paris: Éditions du Seuil, 1963), p. 44.

[17]Daniel 9:4-19, especially its pattern of sin-exile-restoration, exerted influence on passages like 2 *Maccabees* 1:10—2:18; the DSS (4QDibHam; 1QS 1:24--2:1; CD 20:28-30); *Psalms of Solomon* 2; 8:23-32; 9; 11; 17; Ezra 9; Nehemiah 1:5-11; 9:5-37; *Testament of Moses.* See the discussion of Peter Stuhlmacher, *Gerechtigkeit Gottes bei Paulus,* FRLANT 87, 2nd ed. (Göttingen: Vandenhoeck & Ruprecht, 1966), p. 160 (on the DSS); George W. E. Nickelsburg and M. E. Stone, *Faith and Piety in Early Judaism: Texts and Documents* (Philadelphia: Fortress, 1983), p. 127 (for *T. Moses*); James M. Scott, "'For As Many As Are of the Works of the Law Are Under a Curse' (Galatians 3:10)" in *Paul and the Scriptures of Israel,* ed. Craig A. Evans and James A. Sanders, Journal for the Study of the New Testament Supplement Series 83, Studies in Scripture in Early Judaism and Christianity 1 (Sheffield, U.K.: JSOT Press, 1993), pp. 187-221, esp. pp. 198-213 (on Daniel 9's influence in Second Temple Judaism).

[18]For the influence of Nehemiah 9:5-37 on the prayers of the postexilic synagogue, see Leon J. Liebreich, "The Impact of Nehemiah 9:5-37 on the Liturgy of the Synagogue," *Hebrew Union College Annual* 32 (1961): 227-37.

[19]Joseph Klausner, *The Messianic Idea in Israel from Its Beginning to the Completion of the Mishnah,* 3rd ed. (London: Allen & Unwin, 1956).

[20]Steck, *Israel und das gewaltsame Geshick der Propheten.*

[21]Geza Vermes, *The Dead Sea Scrolls in English,* 3rd ed. (New York: Penguin Books, 1987), p. xiii.

[22]Helpful introductions to the Scrolls include: John C. Trever, *The Untold Story of Qumran* (Westwood, N.J.; Fleming H. Revell, 1965); Miller Burrows, *The Dead Sea Scrolls* (New York: Viking, 1955); Frank Moore Cross, "The Development of the Jewish Scripts," in *The Bible and the Ancient Near East: Essays in Honor of William Foxwell Albright,* ed. G. E. Wright (Garden City, N.Y.: Doubleday, 1961), pp. 133-202; Todd Beall, *Josephus' Description of the Essenes Illustrated by the Dead Sea Scrolls,* SNTSMS 58 (Cambridge: Cambridge University Press, 1988); Krister Stendahl, ed., *The Scrolls and the New Testament* (New York: Harper & Row, 1957); Joseph A. Fitzmyer, "The Qumran Scrolls and the New Testament After Forty Years," *Revue de Qumran* 13 (1988): 609-20; *The Dead Sea Scrolls: Major Publications and Tools for Study,* Sources for Biblical Study 20, rev. ed. (Atlanta: Scholars Press 1990), pp. 180-86; *Responses to 101 Questions on the Dead Sea Scrolls* (New York: Paulist, 1992); Lawrence H. Schiffman, *Reclaiming the Dead Sea Scrolls: Their True Meaning for Judaism and*

Christianity, Anchor Bible Reference Library (New York: Doubleday, 1995); Robert Eisenman and Michael Wise, *The Dead Sea Scrolls Uncovered* (New York: Penguin Books, 1993); Florentino García Martínez, *The Dead Sea Scrolls Translated: The Qumran Texts in English* (Leiden: E. J. Brill, 1994).

[23]For this paragraph I am indebted to James C. VanderKam, *The Dead Sea Scrolls Today* (Grand Rapids, Mich.: Eerdmans, 1994), p. 4. His work demonstrates both soundness and nuance in his introduction to the DSS.

[24]The excavations of cave 1 took place from 1947-1952. The publication of the first seven scrolls was completed by 1956.

[25]VanderKam, *Dead Sea Scrolls Today*, p. 12, provides this encapsulation of the findings.

[26]For the overview in table 1.1 I am indebted to Fitzmyer, *Responses to 101 Questions*, pp. 22-25.

[27]A duplicate of this Hebrew text of *Sirach* was discovered in Cairo, Egypt, by Solomon Schechter. Until then, *Sirach* was known only in Greek and Latin.

[28]Wendell Jones, a self-styled archaeologist, has been using the Copper Scroll for years in an attempt to discover its purported treasures in the Judean wilderness. It has been said that the Indiana Jones films were inspired by his endeavors.

[29]VanderKam, *Dead Sea Scrolls Today*, p. 189.

[30]Fitzmyer observes that all of the manuscripts from caves 1-3 and 5-10 were eventually published, while most of the findings of cave 11 have been disclosed (*Responses to 101 Questions*, p. 12). The problem of publication concerned cave 4.

[31]Schiffman, *Reclaiming the Dead Sea Scrolls*, p. 17.

[32]Ibid., p. 21.

[33]The standard guide is that by Joseph Fitzmyer, *Dead Sea Scrolls*, pp. 3-8. A highly respected translation of the DSS is that by Florentino García Martínez, *The Dead Sea Scrolls Translated*.

[34]See Fitzmyer's discussion, *Responses to 101 Questions*, pp. 16-20.

[35]Schiffman, *Reclaiming the Dead Sea Scrolls*, p. 163.

[36]Unless otherwise specified, I am using García Martínez's translation, *The Dead Sea Scrolls Translated*.

[37]Actually the council at Jamnia seems to have been more of an attempt to confirm an already existing canon than to close it. Moreover, only a few books were questioned there with regard to their canonicity (e.g., Song, Eccles). For further discussion on this issue, see Schiffman, *Reclaiming the Dead Sea Scrolls*, pp. 162-69. The classic work on the topic of the canon, which happens to support the theory offered here, is by Roger Beckwith, *The Old Testament Canon of the New Testament Church and Its Background in Early Judaism* (Grand Rapids, Mich.: Eerdmans, 1985), pp. 234ff.

[38]See Schiffman, *Reclaiming the Dead Sea Scrolls*, pp. 171-73. The Hebrew text progressively became entrenched as the official Bible of Judaism as is clear from its development from the Qumran texts (A.D. 68) to those of Masada

(A.D. 73) and Bar Kokhba (A.D. 132-135).

[39]*Apocryphal* is the Protestant term for this material, whereas Roman Catholics prefer the word *deuterocanonical*. The collection consists of *Tobit, Judith, 1-2 Maccabees, Wisdom of Solomon, Sirach (Ecclesiasticus), Baruch, The Additions to Esther, Susanna,* the *Prayer of Azariah,* the *Song of the Three Young Men, Bel and the Dragon,* and the *Epistle of Jeremiah* (chap. 6 of *Baruch*).

[40]*Sirach* seems to have been the first of a number of Jewish works to equate God's preexistent wisdom with the Torah (see, e.g., *Sir* 24:1-34; *Bar* 4:1-4; *1 Enoch* 5:3-4).

[41]The name *pseudepigrapha* means "false writings" with reference to the pseudonymous nature of these materials. There are about fifty such Jewish works dating from 200 B.C. to A.D. 200. No religious tradition regards this literature as canonical, though its value is inestimable. The pseudepigraphical works, along with the Apocrypha, can be found in the two-volume set edited by James H. Charlesworth, *The Old Testament Pseudepigrapha* 1 (New York: Doubleday, 1983) and 2 (London: Darton, Longman and Todd, 1985).

[42]See VanderKam's list, *Dead Sea Scrolls Today,* pp. 42-43.

[43]Schiffman, *Reclaiming the Dead Sea Scrolls,* pp. 167-68.

[44]See Nickelsburg's treatment, *Jewish Literature Between the Bible and the Mishnah,* as well as my forthcoming work, *The Reverse of the Curse.*

[45]*Pesher* on Psalm 37, among others, should be included in this list.

[46]Fitzmyer, *Responses to 101 Questions,* pp. 29-30.

[47]Ibid., pp. 27-28.

[48]Michael O. Wise, *A Critical Study of the Temple Scroll from Qumran Cave 11,* Studies in Ancient Oriental Civilization 49 (Chicago: Oriental Institute of the University of Chicago, 1990).

[49]Vermes, *Dead Sea Scrolls in English,* p. 129.

[50]It was published by Eisenman and Wise, *Dead Sea Scrolls Uncovered,* pp. 188-200.

[51]Schiffman, *Reclaiming the Dead Sea Scrolls,* p. 322.

[52]VanderKam, *Dead Sea Scrolls Today,* p. 63.

[53]The classic study on this aspect of the DSS is by Heinz-Wolfgang Kuhn, *Enderwartung und gegenwärtiges Heil: Untersuchungen zu den Gemeindeliedern von Qumran,* Studien zur Umwelt des Neuen Testament 4 (Göttingen: Vandenhoeck & Ruprecht, 1966).

Chapter 2: Prelude to the Story

[1]J. Neusner, W. S. Green and E. Freirichs, eds., *Judaisms and Their Messiahs at the Turn of the Christian Era* (Cambridge: Cambridge University Press, 1987).

[2]N. T. Wright, *The New Testament and the People of God* (Minneapolis: Fortress, 1992), p. 203. For an early description of religious sectarianism, see Ernst Troeltsch, *The Social Teaching of the Christian Churches,* trans. Olive Wyon, 2 vols. (New York: MacMillan, 1931). For an application of Max Weber's sect typology (to which Troeltsch was indebted) to Qumran, see Shemaryahu Talmon,

"The Emergence of Jewish Sectarianism in the Early Second Temple Period,"
in *King, Cult and Calendar in Ancient Israel: Collected Studies* (Jerusalem: The
Magnes Press, 1986), pp. 165-211, esp. 192-201. See also Francis Watson, *Paul,
Judaism and the Gentiles: A Sociological Approach*, SNTSMS 56 (Cambridge:
Cambridge University Press, 1986), pp. 38-43.

[3]Roland de Vaux, *Archaeology and the Dead Sea Scrolls*, Schweich Lectures 1959,
rev. ed. (London: Oxford University Press, 1973). For a helpful summary of de
Vaux's findings, see Lawrence H. Schiffman, *Reclaiming the Dead Sea Scrolls:
Their True Meaning for Judaism and Christianity*, Anchor Bible Reference Library
(New York: Doubleday), pp. 37-61. (I reproduce his chart here from p. 40).

[4]See the article by Esther Eshel and Frank Moore Cross, "Ostraca from Khirbet," in *Israel Exploration Journal* 47 (1997): 17-28.

[5]For a statement of Norman Golb's view see, for example, his "The Problem of
Origin and Identification of the Dead Sea Scrolls," *Proceedings of the American
Philosophical Society* 124 (1980): 1-24; and "The Dead Sea Scrolls: A New Per-
spective," *The American Scholar* 58 (1989): 177-207; not to mention his full-scale
study, *Who Wrote the Dead Sea Scrolls? The Search for the Secret of Qumran* (New
York: Simon & Schuster, 1995).

[6]For a further description and criticism of the Donceel's theory, see James C.
VanderKam, *The Dead Sea Scrolls Today* (Grand Rapids, Mich.: Eerdmans,
1994), pp. 24-26, whose argumentation seems now confirmed by the *yaḥad*
inscription.

[7]These historical allusions are helpfully compiled by Michael Wise, Martin
Abegg and Edward M. Cook, *A Comprehensive Translation of the Dead Sea
Scrolls* (San Francisco: HarperCollins, 1997), pp. 15-16. Mention of the
Prayer for King Jonathan (with reference most likely to Alexander Jannaeus,
104-76 B.C.) calls for comment here because the positive statements made
about him, a Hasmonean ruler, are contrary to what one would expect
from an anti-Hasmonean community. Three answers have been offered to
explain this apparent anomaly: (1) Wise, Abegg and Cook argue that the
DSS people were pro-Hasmonean, not anti-Hasmonean, and that therefore
we are to look elsewhere than to the Essenes for the identity of the community, pp. 29-39; (2) Schiffman suggests as one possibility that this
pro-Hasmonean text simply got included in the DSS even though they are
decidedly anti-Hasmonean, a testimony to the heterogeneous nature of
the Qumran collection (Schiffman, *Reclaiming the Dead Sea Scrolls*, p. 240);
and most likely, (3) as VanderKam notes, a positive reference to Jannaeus
in the DSS is not unthinkable because, after all, he did crucify eight hundred Pharisees, the enemies of the DSS people. But this third suggestion
raises a question: Why, if they felt positively about Jannaeus, did the
Qumran community continue their separated existence? VanderKam's
reply is plausible: "The answer may be that their beliefs about living in the
last days and their stand on purity and separation from all impurity
caused them to remain apart" (*Dead Sea Scrolls Today*, p. 107). Schiffman

also allows for the last possibility (*Reclaiming the Dead Sea Scrolls,* p. 240).
[8]I should briefly evaluate here a recent attempt to refute the traditional viewpoint of the history of the DSS. Wise offers a different historical reconstruction of the origin of these materials, arguing that the events alluded to took place c. 76-63 B.C., about a century later than the conventional view. On this reading of things, the DSS community was mainline Jewish, approximating the beliefs and practices of the Sadducees. The group was pro-Hasmonean; the wicked priest was John Hyrcanus II (67-63 B.C.); and the DSS are not to be connected with Khirbet Qumran (Wise, Abegg and Cook, *Comprehensive Translation of the Dead Sea Scrolls,* pp. 29-39). This is an intriguing theory, but it suffers from its dependence on Golb's theory, a significant part of which the *yahad* inscription has now seriously called to question.
[9]VanderKam, *Dead Sea Scrolls Today,* p. 101.
[10]Schiffman, *Reclaiming the Dead Sea Scrolls,* p. 269.
[11]For further discussion of this point, see VanderKam, *Dead Sea Scrolls Today,* p. 102.
[12]Schiffman, *Reclaiming the Dead Sea Scrolls,* p. 270.
[13]Ibid., p. 234.
[14]Ibid., pp. 234-56. Another theory places this event at the time of John Hyrcanus (103 B.C.), whose two sons, Antigonus and Aristobulus, were seen as the fulfillment of Joshua's curse. During the period when Hyrcanus was rebuilding Jericho, Antigonus murdered his brother, Aristobulus I, and then shortly thereafter died himself.
[15]Joseph Fitzmyer, *Responses to 101 Questions on the Dead Sea Scrolls* (New York: Paulist, 1992), p. 56.
[16]Schiffman, *Reclaiming the Dead Sea Scrolls,* pp. 262-63. The name *Alexander Jannaeus,* adopted no doubt in honor of Alexander the Great (330 B.C.), itself bespeaks a certain amount of Hellenizing influence on the Hasmonean dynasty.
[17]Ibid., p. 269.
[18]Typical of this interpretation is the discussion of VanderKam, *Dead Sea Scrolls Today,* pp. 106-7.
[19]See note 8 above.
[20]Schiffman, *Reclaiming the Dead Sea Scrolls,* p. 75.
[21]See the discussion by Hartmut Stegemann, "The Qumran Essenes: Local Members of the Main Jewish Union in Late Second Temple Times," in *The Madrid Qumran Congress,* ed. J. T. Barrera and V. M. Montaner (Leiden: E. J. Brill, n.d.), 1:83-166; 146-66.
[22]Ibid., p. 106.
[23]For further discussion of this aspect of the debate, see VanderKam, *Dead Sea Scrolls Today,* pp. 93-95.
[24]Documentation for the view that the Zealots did not officially form a movement until the Jewish revolt is provided by David Rhoads, "Zealots," *Anchor Bible Dictionary* 6, ed. David Noel Freedman (New York: Doubleday, 1992),

pp. 1043-54.

[25]Schechter gathered this from the self-description of the community, "Sons of Zadok" (The Zadokite Fragments), connecting it to the Sadducean priestly group.

[26]J. M. Baumgarten, "The Pharisaic-Sadducean Controversies About Purity and the Qumran Texts," *JJS* 31 (1980): 157-70.

[27]Y. Sussmann, "The History of Halakha and the Dead Sea Scrolls: Preliminary Observations on *Miqsat Maase Ha-Torah* (4QMMT)," *Tarbiz* 59 (1989-1990).

[28]Schiffman, *Reclaiming the Dead Sea Scrolls.*

[29]Ibid., p. 87.

[30]Ibid., pp. 86-87.

[31]VanderKam, *Dead Sea Scrolls Today*, p. 94.

[32]Stegemann, "Qumran Essenes," p. 106.

[33]VanderKam, *Dead Sea Scrolls Today*, p. 94.

[34]Schiffman, *Reclaiming the Dead Sea Scrolls*, p. 75.

[35]Called Pliny the Elder (d. A.D. 79) in contrast to his nephew, Pliny the Younger (A.D. 61-114), who became the governor of the Roman province of Bithynia under Caesar Trajan.

[36]Quoted in VanderKam, *Dead Sea Scrolls Today*, p. 86.

[37]Ibid., pp. 75-86.

[38]Ibid., p. 86.

[39]Todd Beall, *Josephus' Description of the Essenes Illustrated by the Dead Sea Scrolls*, SNTSMS 58 (Cambridge: Cambridge University Press, 1988), pp. 123-28.

[40]VanderKam, *Dead Sea Scrolls Today*, p. 89.

[41]Ibid., p. 91.

[42]Ibid., pp. 91-92. For a summary of the possible meanings informing the name *Essene*, see Beall, *Josephus' Description of the Essenes*, pp. 35-36.

[43]VanderKam, *Dead Sea Scrolls Today*, p. 72.

[44]Ibid., pp. 73-74.

[45]For various attempts to explain the relationship between the Essenes at Qumran and other Essene branches, see the following: Geza Vermes, *The Dead Sea Scrolls in English*, 3rd ed. (New York: Penguin, 1987), pp. 15-17; H. Stegemann, "The Qumran Essenes"; Florentino García Martínez, *The Dead Sea Scrolls Translated: The Qumran Texts in English* (Leiden: E. J. Brill, 1994), pp. lv-lvi; see also his "Qumran Origins and Early History: A Gröningen Hypothesis," *FO* 25 (1988): 113-36.

[46]Frank M. Cross, "The Early History of the Qumran Community," in *New Directions in Biblical Archaeology*, ed. D. N. Freedman and J. C. Greenfield (Garden City, N.Y.: Doubleday, 1969), pp. 63-79; esp. 68-69.

[47]VanderKam, *Dead Sea Scrolls Today*, p. 159.

[48]J. Dupont-Sommer, *The Dead Sea Scrolls: A Preliminary Survey* (Oxford: Basil Blackwell, 1952), p. 99. He later qualified his assessment.

[49]Later incorporated into Edmund Wilson, *The Scrolls from the Dead Sea* (New York: Oxford University Press, 1955), p. 100.

[50]Ibid., pp. 82, 89.

[51]See, for example, Michael Baigent and Richard Leigh, *The Dead Sea Scrolls Deception* (London: Johnathan Cape, 1991).

[52]Quoted in Fitzmyer, *Responses to 101 Questions*, p. 163.

[53]Ibid., p. 164.

[54]Ibid., pp. 164-65.

[55]Robert Eisenman and Michael Wise, *The Dead Sea Scrolls Uncovered* (New York: Penguin, 1993), p. 29. It should be noted that the authors add a qualifying statement in the text: "This might also be read depending on the context, 'and the Leader of the Community, the Bran[ch of David], will put him to death'" (p. 29).

[56]Schiffman, *Reclaiming the Dead Sea Scrolls*, p. 346.

[57]California State University, Long Beach, news release, November 1, 1991, p. 1; quoted in Fitzmyer, *Responses to 101 Questions*, p. 158.

[58]See, for example, O. Betz, "Was John the Baptist an Essene?" *Bible Review* 6, no. 6 (1990): 18-25.

[59]VanderKam, *Dead Sea Scrolls Today*, p. 170.

[60]Barbara E. Thiering, *Redating the Teacher of Righteousness* (Sydney: Theological Explorations, 1979); *The Gospels and Qumran: A New Hypothesis* (Sydney: Theological Explorations, 1981); *The Qumran Origins of the Christian Church* (Sydney: Theological Explorations, 1983); *The Riddle of the Dead Sea Scrolls* (San Francisco: HarperCollins, 1992).

[61]Fitzmyer, *Responses to 101 Questions*, p. 110.

[62]Ibid., p. 108.

[63]Robert E. Eiseman, *James the Just in the Habakkuk Pesher* (Leiden: E. J. Brill, 1985); Robert E. Eiseman and Michael Wise, *The Dead Sea Scrolls Uncovered*. See Eiseman's recent work, *James, the Brother of Jesus: The Key to Unlocking the Secrets of Early Christianity and the Dead Sea Scrolls* (New York: Viking, 1997).

[64]See the critiques by Stegemann, "Qumran Essenes," p. 95; and Fitzmyer, *Responses to 101 Questions*, pp. 109-10.

[65]I owe the observations in this paragraph to Dan Reid, whose input on this project was invaluable.

Chapter 3: The Hermeneutic of Restoration

[1]For discussions of the DSS use of *pesher*, see W. H. Brownlee, "Biblical Interpretation Among the Sectaries of the Dead Sea Scrolls," *BA* 14 (1951): 54-76, which is expanded in his *The Midrash Pesher of Habakkuk*, SBLMS 24 (Missoula, Mont.: Scholars Press, 1979); F. F. Bruce (who traces the origin of *r'z* and *pesher* back to Daniel 2—7), *Biblical Exegesis in the Qumran Texts* (Grand Rapids, Mich.: Eerdmans, 1959); Krister Stendahl, *The School of Matthew and Its Use of the Old Testament*, 2nd ed. (Philadelphia: Fortress, 1968); Bert L. Gärtner, "The Habakkuk Commentary (DSH) and the Gospel of Matthew," *ST* 8 (1955): 1-24; George J. Brooke, *Exegesis at Qumran: 4 Florilegium in its Jewish Context*, Journal for the Study of the Old Testament Supplement Series 29

(Sheffield, U.K.: JSOT Press, 1985), pp. 36-44. G. Vermes lists four basic logical principles of *pesher*: "(i) the mysteriousness of the prophetic writings and their need of new revelation; (ii) the eschatological character of this new revelation; (iii) the imminence of the end of the world and hence the application of prophecy to the present generation; and (iv) the Teacher of Righteousness himself is the recipient of this revelation" ("The Qumran Interpretation of Scripture in Its Historical Setting," ALUOS 6 [1966-1968]: 84-97, esp. p. 91).

[2]Stendhal, *School of Matthew*.

[3]Gärtner, "Habakkuk Commentary."

[4]Joseph A. Fitzmyer, "The Use of Explicit Old Testament Quotations in Qumran Literature and in the New Testament," in *Essays on the Semitic Background of the New Testament*, Sources for Biblical Study 5 (Missoula, Mont.: Scholar's Press, 1974), pp. 3-58, esp. pp. 13-14.

[5]Michael Knowles, *Jeremiah in Matthew's Gospel: The Rejected Prophet Motif in Matthean Redaction*, Journal for the Study of the New Testament Supplement Series 68 (Sheffield, U.K.: JSOT Press, 1993), p. 26. Fitzmyer delineates the ways the DSS interpret the OT: (1) literally, in the same sense as the biblical source and with due respect to its original context; (2) in a modernizing sense, with the original meaning reapplied to an analogous contemporary situation (so "typologically"); (3) by accommodation, with the scriptural text "obviously wrested from its original context, modified or deliberately changed . . . in order to adapt it to a new situation or purpose"; and (4) eschatologically, with an eschatological threat or promise being understood to apply to the new eschaton of Qumran theology. As examples of similar modernizing or typological exegesis in Matthew, Fitzmyer cites Matthew 4:15-16; 8:17; 11:10; 13:35; 15:8 and 21:42; of accommodational exegesis, Matthew 3:3 (on Is 40:3, as in 1QS 8.13-16) and Matthew 12:32 (on Ex 3:6, 15-16), in Fitzmyer, "Use of Explicit Old Testament Quotations," pp. 17-51. Fitzmyer's third point, *accommodation*, allows for an important connection between Matthew and *pesherim*. Compare also a similar conclusion by R. S. McConnell, *Law and Prophecy in Matthew's Gospel: The Authority and Use of the Old Testament in the Gospel of Saint Matthew* (Basel: Friedrich Reinhardt, 1969), pp. 215-16. For an attempt to relate *pesher* to the Synoptics as a whole, see M. Black, "The Theological Appropriation of the Old Testament by the New Testament," SJT 39 (1986): 1-17. Compare also E. E. Ellis, "Biblical Interpretation in the New Testament Church," in *Mikra*, ed. Martin Jan Mulder (Minneapolis: Fortress, 1990), pp. 691-726.

[6]Odil H. Steck, *Israel und das gewaltsame Geshick der Propheten* (Neukirchen-Vluyn, Germany: Neukirchener, 1967), pp. 62-64, 122-24 (which provide a composite summary of the components of the Deuteronomistic tradition.)

[7]David P. Moessner, *Lord of the Banquet: The Literary and Theological Significance of the Lucan Travel Narrative* (Minneapolis: Fortress, 1989), pp. 87-90. He follows Steck, *Israel und das gewaltsame Geshick der Propheten*, pp. 165-70.

[8]See Steck, *Israel und das gewaltsame Geshick der Propheten*, p. 166.

[9]The *revealed things* (see 1QS 1:9; 5:9; 8:1, 15, etc.) refer to the general precepts of the Mosaic law known to all, while the *hidden things* (CD 3:13-16; 1QS 5:11; 8:11; 9:17; 11:16; 1QH 11:19, etc.) are those specific precepts known only to the Qumran community by revelation, namely, its *halakhah*.

[10]1QS agrees with CD on the nature of the Qumran community's *halakhah*, which consists of a different, more stringent interpretation of the Mosaic Law. Three comments are in order here regarding 1QS and this matter. First, the covenanter's sectarian understanding of the divine law pertains to stricter clean-unclean regulations, including food (1QS 5:13; 7:21) and drink (1QS 6:20). In actuality, the Qumran community viewed itself as the true priesthood, which represented the only legitimate means of finding forgiveness and which constituted the spiritual temple (1QS 5:6-12; 8:1-11; 9:3-6). As such, it refused to be contaminated by non-Qumranians (1QS 4:5, 22; 5:1-5). Second, the *halakhah* of 1QS was based on the solar calendar, which consequently called for the observance of sabbaths and other holy days at different times than did the majority of Judaism (1QS 1:8-9; 10:1-10). Third, because Qumran practiced this stricter observance of the law, it viewed itself as the true circumcision of the heart (1QS 5:4-5; cf. Deut 10:16). In essence, then, one can see that 1QS *redefines* the marks of the faithful Jew—dietary laws, sabbath-keeping, circumcision—in terms of its sectarian interpretation of the divine law.

[11]N. T. Wright, *Jesus and the Victory of God* (Minneapolis: Fortress, 1996), p. 261. Wright uses the following Jewish references in arriving at these characteristics of faith: Is 7:9; 28:16; 30:15; Jer 40:6 (LXX); Hab 2:4; 1QpHab 2:1-7; 7:18—8:3; 4QS 521 II.2.1-9; *Wis* 3:9; *T. Dan.* 5:13; 6:4; *T. Asher* 7:6-7; *Sir* 44:20; 4 *Macc* 15:24; 16:22 (see pp. 259-61).

[12]On the relationship between faith and faithfulness in both the OT and NT, Wright's discussion is useful; Wright, *Jesus and the Victory of God*, pp. 258-59.

[13]The author may be alluding to Jonathan's defeat by the Syrians.

[14]John J. Collins's summary of the identification of the *Kittim* in Jewish literature is helpful: *The Star and the Scepter: The Messiah of the Dead Sea Scrolls and Other Ancient Literature* (New York: Doubleday, 1995), pp. 58-59.

[15]N. T. Wright, *The New Testament and the People of God* (Minneapolis: Fortress, 1992), pp. 385-86.

[16]Chapter four, on messianism in the DSS and in the NT, more specifically deals with the figure of Moses in the Gospel of Matthew.

[17]Wright, *New Testament and the People of God*, pp. 386-87.

[18]Ibid, p. 387. Wright suggests this chiastic structure, but he does not offer any explanation of how "B, C, B'" are related.

[19]On the connection between the kingdom of God and the Deuteronomic blessings, see Marvin C. Pate, *The Reverse of the Curse: Paul, Wisdom and the Law*, (forthcoming), chap. 6.

[20]Chapter four considers with N. T. Wright how Jesus' death embraces the Deuteronomic curses.

[21]Wright, *New Testament and the People of God*, p. 388.

[22]It can also connote the place of danger and death or the place of rebellion and punishment. See my discussion of this in chapter five.

[23]For a composite description of these movements see Wright, *New Testament and the People of God*, pp. 170-81.

[24]See H. W. Brownlee's discussion, "John the Baptist in the New Light of Ancient Scrolls," in *The Scrolls and the New Testament*, ed. K. Stendahl (New York: Harper & Row, 1957), p. 44.

[25]Such a reversal is not unusual in *pesher* hermeneutics. See 1QpHab 3:1-7; 4QpIs 2:6-8; Acts 2:14-21; 4:10-11; 13:32-35.

[26]Donald Hagner's discussion of Matthew's phrase *with fire* is helpful. See Donald Hagner, *Matthew*, WBC 33A (Dallas: Word, 1993), 1:51, as is Robert A. Guelich, excursus in *Mark 1—8:26*, WBC 34A (Dallas: Word, 1989), pp. 27-28.

[27]See Guelich, *Mark 1—8:26*, pp. 28-29, for his treatment of this triad. It should be noted that while 1QS 4:20-21 uses the word *refine*, not *fire*, 1QH 16:11-12 does employ *fire* as connected with *spirit*.

[28]Ibid., p. 29.

[29]Compare here 1QS 8:14-16 and CD 1:1-21. The former applies Is 40:3 to the Qumran community, while the latter specifies the time in which the Essenes lived as the period of the exile. All of this indicates that the DSS people viewed the Judean wilderness in which they resided as the staging ground for the conquest of the land.

[30]This passage about the Branch of David occurs immediately before 4QpIsaiah 5, suggesting the interpretation I have offered here: The Qumran community is the true vineyard of God. In chapter four I will track the use of the Branch metaphor in the DSS, thereby highlighting its messianic significance.

[31]Wright provides an insightful treatment of this parable in the Gospels (especially Mark 12:1-9) relative to the story of Israel in *Jesus and the Victory of God*, pp. 497-501.

[32]Rendall Harris, *Testimonies* 1 (Cambridge: Cambridge University Press, 1916).

[33]C. H. Dodd, *According to the Scriptures* (London: Nisbet, 1952).

[34]For an excellent overview of the debate, see Joseph A. Fitzmyer, "4Q Testimonia and the New Testament," in *Essays on the Semitic Background of the New Testament*, Sources for Biblical Study 5, SBL (Missoula, Mont.: Scholars Press, 1974), pp. 59-89.

[35]Chapter four will investigate the role of the prophet-like-Moses (and his relationship with the Teacher of Righteousness) in the DSS and Matthew, as well.

[36]We will also look at the place of the messianic Levitic priest in the DSS and Hebrews in chapter four.

[37]Recall from chapter two the discussion of this text vis-à-vis the authorship of the Scrolls.

[38]A number of issues surround the Matthean OT fulfillment quotations that are not directly related to our purpose: Which OT text is Matthew quoting (Aramaic or a variant of the MT)? Do the quotations predate Matthew in the form of a testimonia collection (like 4QTestimonia)? One of the most thorough

examinations of these questions is the work by Raymond E. Brown, *The Birth of the Messiah* (Garden City, N.Y.: Image, 1977), pp. 96-121. I draw here on his chart identifying the quotations, (see his p. 98).

[39]Ibid., pp. 209-13. Brown evaluates the three theories of the meaning of *Nazarene* (Mt 2:23): Nazareth (the city), Nazirite (see Num 6:1-21; Judg 16:17), *Nezer* (Branch [of David], Is 11:1; 4:2), arguing that all are operative in the mind of Matthew. For our part, *Nezer* is definitely a part of Matthew's semantical field in Mt 2:23, even as it is in the DSS (see in chapter five the discussion of 4QpIs 8-10:3:11-19; 4QFlor 1-3:1:10-19; 4QpGen 5:1-7).

[40]Chapter four explores this perspective.

[41]There are obvious differences between 4QTestim and Matthew's OT fulfillment quotations, notably (1) They do not draw on the same OT verses and (2) the OT texts in 4QTestimonia are combined into one setting, whereas the OT verses Matthew quotes are scattered throughout his Gospel. Nevertheless, with regard to the second difference, it is quite possible that Matthew found the OT verses he employs in composite form and those he has broken up. Concerning the first difference, even though the OT substratum is not the same for 4QTestimonia and Matthew, the underlying motif is the restoration of Israel.

[42]Brooke divides this piece into two parts: 4QFlor 1:1-13 and 4QFlor 1:14—2:6. The first unit features a pun on the Hebrew *bet* ("house") from 2 Samuel 7, while the second unit focuses on Psalms 1—2 (Brooke, *Exegesis at Qumran*, pp. 129-59). Added to these main units are two fragments: 6—11 and 4, 5, 12, 15—26, which locate the trials of the author in the end times, probably the messianic woes.

[43]See Brooke, *Exegesis at Qumran*, pp. 34-37, for his analysis of this pun on "house." S. Aalen earlier provided a more general discussion of 2 Samuel 7 in this regard ("'Reign and House' in the Kingdom of God in the Gospels," *NTS* 8 [1961-1962]: 215-40).

[44]Brooke (*Exegesis at Qumran*, pp. 187-93), who combines two previous views: (1) that 4QFlor presents the DSS people as the present eschatological temple (so B. Gärtner, *The Temple and the Community in Qumran and the New Testament*, SNTSMS 1 [Cambridge: Cambridge University Press, 1965], pp. 30-42); (2) that it is the future eschatological temple, not present people, which is envisioned (so G. Klinzing, *Die Umdeutung des Kultus im der Qumrangemeinde und im Neuen Testament*, SUNT 7 [Göttingen: Vanderhoeck & Ruprecht, 1971], pp. 80-87).

[45]The reference to the sons of Zadok here in 4QFlor calls attention to the occurrence of that phrase in CD 3:12—8:20 (CD 4:3), a text that shares a number of parallels with 4QFlor. For example, the sons of Zadok are identified as the chosen ones (cf. CD 4:3-4 with 4QFlor 1:17-19); the community lives in the latter days (cf. CD 4:4; 6:11 with 4QFlor 1:2, 12, 15, 19); the house of Judah is mentioned (cf. CD 4:11; 7:12-13 with 4QFlor 1:16-17); the interpretation of the law appears (cf. CD 6:7; 7:18 with 4QFlor 1:11). These and other parallels

between CD 3:12-8:20 and 4QFlor suggest to Brooke that one is dependent on the other literarily (Brooke, *Exegesis at Qumran*, pp. 206-9).

[46]In particular, the Matthean text associates Jesus with God's wisdom, which is analogous to the connection of the Torah with Wisdom as found in *Sir* 51. See my discussion and extensive bibliography in Pate, *Reverse of the Curse*, chap. 8.

[47]See the allusions of Exodus 33 in Matthew 11:25-30 as spelled out by W. D. Davies and Dale C. Allison Jr., *Matthew*, ICC (Edinburgh: T & T Clark, 1988, 1991), 1:478-83; 2:283-87.

[48]See again Pate, *The Reverse of the Curse*, chap. 8.

[49]Jon Laansma, *I Will Give You Rest: The Rest Motif in the New Testament with Special Reference to Matthew 11 and Hebrews 3—4*, WUNT 98 (Tübingen: J. C. B. Mohr [Paul Siebeck], 1997): 209-51.

[50]Ibid., pp. 223-27.

[51]I reserve discussion of this aspect of the Matthean Jesus vis-à-vis the *halakhah* of the Pharisees for chapter four.

[52]Laansma, *I Will Give You Rest*, p. 226 n. 79; cf. p. 233 n. 118.

[53]I did not supply 4QFlor 1-3:2:1-5; 4:1-7 in my earlier quotation, but these two passages amplify the Scrolls' condemnation of the Hasmonean rulers (who were partial to the Pharisees). These will be defeated at God's appointed time.

Chapter 4: Messianism in the DSS & in the New Testament

[1]Research on messianic expectations in Second Temple Judaism falls roughly into two stages: An older approach tended to read the literature as presenting a rather uniform view. See, e.g.: Joachim Becker, *Messianic Expectations in the Old Testament*, trans. David E. Green (Philadelphia: Fortress, 1980); Joseph Klausner, *The Messianic Idea in Israel from Its Beginning to the Completion of the Mishnah*, trans. W. F. Stinespring (New York: Macmillan, 1955; 3rd ed., London: Allen & Unwin, 1956); Emil Schürer, *History of the Jewish People in the Age of Jesus Christ*, ed. Geza Vermes, 3 vols. (Edinburgh: T and T Clark, 1973-1987), 2:488-554; George A. Riggan, *Messianic Theology and Christian Faith* (Philadelphia: Westminster, 1967); Joseph Bonsirven, *Palestinian Judaism in the Time of Jesus Christ*, trans. William Wolf (New York: Holt, Rinehart & Winston, 1964), pp. 172-225; Sigmund Mowinckel, *He That Cometh: The Messianic Concept in Israel and Later Judaism*, trans. G. W. Anderson (New York: Abingdon, 1956); David Daube, *The New Testament and Rabbinic Judaism* (New York: Arno, 1973), pp. 3-51. Note the helpful discussion and bibliography in Julius Scott, *Customs and Controversies: Intertestamental Jewish Backgrounds of the New Testament* (Grand Rapids, Mich.: Baker, 1995), p. 308. More recently, the trend has been for scholars to read the literature of Second Temple Judaism as depicting diversified messianic expectations. See, e.g., James H. Charlesworth, ed., *The Messiah: Developments in Earliest Judaism and Christianity* (Minneapolis: Fortress, 1992); Jacob Neusner et al., eds., *Judaisms and Their Messiahs at the Turn of*

the Christian Era (Cambridge: Cambridge University Press, 1987); N. T. Wright, *The New Testament and the People of God* (Minneapolis: Fortress, 1992), pp. 280-338; *Jesus and the Victory of God* (Minneapolis: Fortress, 1996), pp. 147-97; Martin Hengel, *Studies in Early Christology* (Edinburgh: T & T Clark, 1995); John J. Collins, *The Star and the Scepter: The Messiah of the DSS and Other Ancient Literature* (New York: Doubleday, 1995).

[2]Wright, *New Testament and the People of God,* pp. 310-19.

[3]Ibid., pp. 312-14; cf. pp. 170-81, for arguments that Josephus is here alluding to Daniel, along with other references in Josephus to messianic claimants during late Second Temple Judaism.

[4]Ibid., p. 304. Wright calls attention to this interesting point.

[5]I will return to these apocalyptic writings and especially the DSS and Mark 13 later in this chapter when we discuss the influence of the Danielic Son of Man on late Second Temple Jewish literature.

[6]Collins, *Star and the Scepter,* pp. 3-14, esp. p. 12, though I have somewhat rearranged that author's categories—king, priest, prophet and heavenly Messiah.

[7]Ibid, chaps. 3—9.

[8]D. S. Russell, *The Method and Message of Jewish Apocalyptic* (Philadelphia: Westminster Press, 1964), pp. 304-23.

[9]Wright, *New Testament and the People of God,* pp. 308-10, though I have revised his presentation into a chronological order.

[10]Collins, *Star and the Scepter,* pp. 60-61.

[11]Ibid., p. 61.

[12]Ibid.

[13]Recall my earlier defense of this reading in chapter two.

[14]Collins, *Star and the Scepter,* pp. 60-67.

[15]Ibid., p. 67.

[16]Wright, *Jesus and the Victory of God,* p. 209.

[17]Ibid., pp. 536-37. On the historical reliability of the Gospels' presentations of the baptism of Jesus, see also Ben Witherington III, *The Christology of Jesus* (Minneapolis: Fortress, 1990), pp. 148-55; Robert H. Gundry, *Mark: A Commentary on His Apology for the Cross* (Grand Rapids, Mich.: Eerdmans, 1993), pp. 46-53.

[18]Wright, *Jesus and the Victory of God,* p. 537

[19]Ibid., pp. 528-29. For further discussion of first century A.D. would-be messiahs' journeys to Jerusalem to set up the kingdom, see Wright, *New Testament and the People of God,* pp. 170-81.

[20]Wright, *Jesus and the Victory of God,* pp. 533-34.

[21]Ibid., p. 535. On the Davidic Messiah and the rebuilding of the temple, see 4QFlor 1:1-12 and *Tg. Isa.* 53:5; cf. Zech 3:6-10; 4:5-14; 6:9-13.

[22]Wright, *Jesus and the Victory of God,* p. 535; cf. pp. 390-96.

[23]Ibid., pp. 507-9. For a discussion of Ps 110 in early Christianity, see David M. Hay, *Glory at the Right Hand: Psalm 110 in Early Christianity,* SBL Monograph Series 18 (Nashville: Abingdon, 1973); Donald Juel, *Messianic Exegesis: Christo-*

logical Interpretation of the Old Testament in Early Christianity (Philadelphia: Fortress, 1988), pp. 137-39, 162-64; Hengel, Studies in Early Christology, chap. 3; Collins, Star and the Scepter, pp. 142, 182. Pre-Christian Judaism, however, apparently did not read Ps 110 messianically (Wright, Jesus and the Victory of God, p. 508 n. 116).

[24]Wright, Jesus and the Victory of God, pp. 535-36.

[25]Although David is not mentioned in this work, the "branch of David" is, as we saw earlier in 4QpIs 8-10:3:18 on Isaiah 11:1-5 (cf. 4QFlor 1-3:1:12-13).

[26]Wright, Jesus and the Victory of God, pp. 229-30.

[27]Ibid., p. 191 n. 177. See, e.g., 1QSa 2:3-11, an expansion of Deut 23:1-6, which prohibits the physically challenged from worshiping with the community.

[28]Wright, Jesus and the Victory of God, p. 172 nn. 179-86. Wright collects references in the Gospels to the sightless (Mt 9:27-31; 12:22; 21:4; Mk 8:22; Mt 20:29-34/Mk 10:46-52/Lk 18:35-43); the deaf and dumb (Mt 9:32-33; 12:22/Lk 11:14; Mk 7:32); lepers (Mt 8:1-4/Mk 1:40-45/Lk 5:12-16; 17:11-14); a woman with a hemorrhage (Mt 9:20-22/Mk 5:24-34/Lk 8:48); a crippled woman (Lk 13:10); touching and raising of the dead (Mt 9:18-19, 23-26/Mk 5:21-24, 35-43/ Lk 8:40-42, 49-56; Lk 7:11-17); miracles for Gentiles (Mt 8:5-13/Lk 7:1-10; Mt 15:21-28/Mk 7:24-30) and a Samaritan (Lk 17:11-19).

[29]Wright, Jesus and the Victory of God, pp. 451-56.

[30]Ibid., p. 455 n. 48. Wright gives a bibliography of those supporting the view that the one who can kill the body is the Roman empire, not God (the traditional interpretation).

[31]Joseph Fitzmyer, The Gospel According to Luke X—XXIV, AB 28a (New York: Doubleday, 1985), pp. 1565-66.

[32]Wright, Jesus and the Victory of God, pp. 579-84. See, e.g., Wis 2:12-20; 3:1-19; 1QpHab 5:10-11, 8:1-3, 11:4-7; 1QS 5:6; 8:1-4; 9:4; 2 Macc 6:12-17, 27-29; 7:36-38; 4 Macc 17:20-22; 18:3-4.

[33]On this, see Pate, Reverse of the Curse, chaps. 5-6 and the extensive bibliography cited there.

[34]Ibid., chap. 5 and the bibliography.

[35]Wright's entire work Jesus and the Victory of God makes this point in one way or another. An encapsulation of it can be found on pp. 592-611.

[36]Collins, Star and the Scepter, p. 83.

[37]Lawrence Schiffman provides a significant modification of this conventional classification of the twofold messianic expectation in the DSS, arguing instead that the two ideas were competing. He writes, "What emerges . . . is that, contrary to the popular view, Qumran sectarian literature expressed two competing messianic ideas: the notion of a single, Davidic Messiah and the notion of two complementary Messiahs—the Aaronide, priestly leader and the lay Messiah of Israel. We must resolutely resist the temptation to conflate these two ideas by first trying to force all Qumran texts into the two-Messiah rubric and then falsely identifying the Messiah of Israel as Davidic. As in every religious group, sectarians did not always agree, and certainly not in the case of

messianic ideology" (*Reclaiming the Dead Sea Scrolls: Their True Meaning for Judaism and Christianity*, Anchor Bible Reference Library [New York: Doubleday, 1995], p. 326). One wonders, however, whether Schiffman's formulation is not a revival of R. H. Charles's old theory, now refuted, that the two-Messiah concept evident in *T. 12 Patr.* is contradictory, not complementary. Schiffman seems to have applied such a notion to the DSS. For a refutation of Charles's theory, see Karl George Kuhn, "The Two Messiahs of Aaron and Israel," in *The Scrolls and the New Testament*, ed. Krister Stendahl (New York: Harper & Row, 1957), pp. 54-64; esp. pp. 57-58.

[38]Collins, *Star and the Scepter*, pp. 114-15.

[39]Ibid., pp. 111-12, on the debate of whether or not the Teacher of Righteousness is distinct from the coming interpreter of the law, with convincing evidence that the two are not the same. The two seem to be distinguished, e.g., in CD 6:11 and in 4QpHab 1:5.

[40]So Paul Kobelski, *Melchizedek and Mechirěsa*, CBQMS 10 (Washington, D.C.: Catholic Biblical Association of America, 1981), p. 133. This author also factors into the discussion the equation of Michael (Dan 12:1-3) with the heavenly Son of Man (Dan 7:13-14) and also with the Melchizedek of 11QMelch. Kobelski believes these connections go back to Ps 110:4 (pp. 133-34).

[41]See Scott, *Customs and Controversies*, p. 318, esp. nn. 35, 36, his bibliography regarding the Moses typology.

[42]Schiffman, *Reclaiming the Dead Sea Scrolls*, pp. 248-49.

[43]While the Teacher of Righteousness could take on the role of the prophet-like-Moses (cf. CD 1:11-12 with 1QS 8:14-16), 1QS 9:11 seems to separate the two persons, indicating that the prophet-like-Moses will accompany the two Messiahs at the end of history.

[44]For a thorough and convincing defense of this thesis, see Dale C. Allison Jr., *The New Moses: A Matthean Typology* (Minneapolis: Fortress, 1993), pp. 137-328.

[45]For this last consideration, especially the relevance of Mark's Gospel, refer to Tremper Longman III and Daniel G. Reid, *God Is a Warrior* (Grand Rapids, Mich.: Zondervan, 1995), pp. 91-118.

[46]James C. VanderKam, *The Dead Sea Scrolls Today* (Grand Rapids, Mich.: Eerdmans, 1994), p. 167.

[47]Pate, *Reverse of the Curse*, chap. 8. Recall also chapter three of the current volume. For a more encompassing treatment of Matthew's use of the Deuteronomistic tradition, see Michael Knowles, *Jeremiah in Matthew's Gospel: The Rejected Prophet Motif in Matthaean Redaction*, Journal for the Study of the New Testament Supplement Series 68 (Sheffield, U.K.: JSOT Press, 1993).

[48]See Knowles's treatment of this theme, which locates the Matthean polemic against the Pharisees in the aftermath of the fall of Jerusalem in A.D. 70 (*Jeremiah in Matthew's Gospel*, pp. 265-311).

[49]*1 Enoch*, a composite work, dates to the first century B.C. Although J. T. Milik dated the *Similitudes of Enoch* (*1 Enoch* 37—71) to the third century A.D.

because, among other things, it did not surface in the DSS whereas the other components did (*Book of the Watchers* 1—36; *Book of Astronomical Writings* 72—82; *Book of Dream Visions* 83—90; *Epistle of Enoch* 91—107), most interpreters assign the *Similitudes* to the time of the rest of *1 Enoch*. See the discussion by E. Isaac, "1 Enoch," in *The Old Testament Pseudepigraphia*, ed. James H. Charlesworth (New York: Doubleday, 1983), 1:6-7. Milik's arguments were first presented in his article, "Problèmes de la littérature Hénochique à la lumière des Fragments Araméens de Qumrân," *HTR* 64 (1971): 333-78.

[50] Although *1 Enoch* 71:14 equates Enoch with the heavenly Son of Man, Collins carefully demonstrates that the identification should not be pressed, because the one—the Son of Man—is the heavenly counterpart of the other—Enoch (*Star and the Scepter*, p. 178).

[51] *Fourth Ezra* was written after the fall of Jerusalem in A.D. 70. See the discussion by B. M. Metzger in *TOTP* 517-24.

[52] The *collective entity* view is based on a comparison of Daniel 7:13-14 (an individual) with Daniel 7:18, 27 (the saints of God). See L. F. Hartman and A. A. DiLella, *The Book of Daniel*, AB 23 (Garden City, N.Y.: Doubleday, 1978), pp. 85-102, for this interpretation. The *angelic personage* most likely identified is Michael. See John J. Collins, *The Apocalyptic Vision of the Book of Daniel*, Harvard Semitic Monographs 16 (Missoula, Mont.: Scholars Press, 1977), pp. 144-46; *Daniel*, Hermeneia (Minneapolis: Fortress, 1993), pp. 304-10; A. Lacoque, *The Book of Daniel* (Atlanta: John Knox, 1979), p 133; C. Rowland, *The Open Heaven* (New York: Crossroads, 1982), p. 182. The traditional *messianic individual* interpretation has fallen into disfavor in recent times. Supporters of this view include A. J. Ferch, *The Son of Man in Daniel 7* (Berrien Springs, Mich.: Andrews University Press, 1979), pp. 4-12; G. R. Beasley-Murray, "The Interpretation of Daniel 7," *CBQ* 45 (1983): 44-58. Wright provides additional evidence for this viewpoint by factoring into the discussion Daniel 2, 9 (Wright, *New Testament and the People of God*, pp. 291-97, 304, 312-14; *Jesus and the Victory of God*, pp. 500-501).

[53] See Wright again for a comparative reading of Daniel 2; 7; 9:24-27 in terms of the Messiah's deliverance of Israel (Wright, *Jesus and the Victory of God*, pp. 514-15). See also Wright, *New Testament and the People of God*, pp. 291-97, 304, 312-14.

[54] The other two writings utilizing the Son of Man figure, *1 Enoch* 37-71 and *4 Ezra*, also are heavily influenced by the Deuteronomistic tradition. The former, in that it is sectarian in nature (much like the DSS writers), also reverses the story of Israel to wit that the elect are identified as those who follow the Enochian community's *halakhah* (e.g., solar calendar), not ethnic Israel per se. *Fourth Ezra*, however, adheres to more traditional categories: The wicked are the Gentiles and nonobedient Jews, whereas the righteous are those who follow the Torah of Moses. For further discussion, see Pate, *Reverse of the Curse*, chaps. 3, 4.

[55] Fitzmyer seems to have been one of the first scholars to call attention to this

text. For further discussion, see his *Responses to 101 Questions on the Dead Sea Scrolls* (New York: Paulist, 1992), pp. 112-13.

[56]Schiffman, *Reclaiming the Dead Sea Scrolls*, pp. 341-44.

[57]This manuscript is also entitled *Pseudo-Daniel* because of its perceived connections to Danielic thought. Its publication caused quite a stir in scholarly circles, not the least because of its correspondence with Lk 1:32, 35: "will be great"; "he will be called Son of the Most High" (Lk 1:32); "he will be called Son of God" (Lk 1:35). Fitzmyer has not missed the significance of these parallels between 4Q246 and Lk 1:32, 35: "No one who reads this text fails to see its importance. It not only shows that the title 'Son of God' was current in Palestine in the first century B.C. or A.D. (the text is written in Herodian script), but it uses the same titles 'Son of God' and 'Son of the Most High' with the same verb 'be called' that is used in the Lucan infancy narrative when Gabriel informs Mary of the birth of Jesus (1:32-35)" (Fitzmyer, *Responses to 101 Questions*, p. 113).

[58]Collins, *Star and the Scepter*, pp. 155-56.

[59]Martin Hengel, *The Son of God* (Philadelphia: Fortress, 1976), p. 44.

[60]Collins, *Star and the Scepter*, p. 161.

[61]This view gains strength if indeed in the DSS "Michael," "Melchizedek" and "the Prince of Light" refer to the same personage. See Florentino García Martínez, "The Eschatological Figure of 4Q246," in *Qumran and Apocalyptic: Studies on the Aramaic Texts from Qumran* (Leiden, The Netherlands: E. J. Brill, 1992), pp. 162-79.

[62]Kobelski, *Melchizedek and Mechirĕsa*, pp. 133-34. It should also be observed that in the OT *sons of God* could refer to angels (e.g., Gen 6; Deut 32:8-9 [LXX]; Ps 82; Dan 3).

[63]Collins, *Star and the Scepter*, p. 163.

[64]So T. N. D. Mettinger, *King and Messiah: The Civil and Sacral Legitimation of the Israelite Kings* (Lund: Gleerup, 1976), pp. 254-93. See also Collins, *Star and the Scepter*, pp. 163-67 and his bibliography.

[65]Note Collins's description in his *The Star and the Scepter*, p. 167; cf. *Pss. Sol.* 17:34; 4QpIsa 8-10:3:18-19.

[66]Collins (*Star and the Scepter*, pp. 157-60) calls attention to two echoes of 1QM in 4Q246, thereby indicating a literary relationship between the two: (1) Both refer to the king of Ashur and Egypt (cf. 4Q246 1:6 with 1QM 1:2, 4). (2) Both use the same word (*nhšr*, "carnage"); cf. 4Q246 1:5 with 1QM 1:9 for the destiny of the wicked.

[67]Ibid., p. 160.

[68]In Judaism the "messianic woes" refer to the time of great sorrow and tribulation to come upon God's people immediately prior to the coming of the Messiah. The concept is foreshadowed in the Old Testament in association with the day of Yahweh (see, for example, Is 24:17-23; Dan 12:1; Joel 2:1-11, 28-32; Amos 5:16-20; Zeph 1:14—2:3) and developed in Jewish apocalypticism (*4 Ezra* 7:37; *Jub.* 23:11; 24:3; *2 Apoc. Bar.* 55:6; *1 Enoch* 80:4-5). The term itself, however, does not occur until the writing of the Talmud (for example,

b. Shab. 118a; *b. Pes.* 118a). A number of events were often associated with the messianic woes, for example, wars, earthquakes, famines, the persecution of God's people, the apostasy of God's people and cosmic disturbances. Recall p. 237 n. 4.

[69]Wright, *Jesus and the Victory of God,* pp. 346-49. Wright, following C. H. Dodd, argues that Lk 21 (cf. Lk 19:42-44) was written before the fall of Jerusalem in A.D. 70. According to Dodd, those passages derive from an oracle predating the destruction ("The Fall of Jerusalem and the Abomination of Desolation," *JRS* 37 [1947], pp. 45-54, esp. p. 52).

[70]For a discussion of some late Second Temple writings that apocalypticize the Deuteronomic curses and blessings (the former characterizing this age and the latter the age to come, see *1 Enoch,* the DSS, *4 Ezra, 2 Apoc. Bar.*), consult Pate, *Reverse of the Curse,* chaps. 3, 4. A good example of this in the DSS can be found in 1QS 3—4.

[71]For a discussion of the various views of Daniel 9:24-27, with emphasis on its partial fulfillment during the Maccabean crisis, see C. Marvin Pate and Calvin B. Haines Jr., *Doomsday Delusions: What's Wrong with Predictions About the End of the World* (Downers Grove, Ill.: InterVarsity Press, 1995), pp. 69-75.

[72]Wright, *Jesus and the Victory of God,* pp. 349-54.

[73]Ibid., pp. 354-58.

[74]Ibid., p. 358.

[75]Ibid., pp. 361-62; though it must be said that I am not convinced that Jesus' judgment of Jerusalem was not without remainder, that is to say that apocalyptic statements about Jesus' return are more than symbolic. They will yet occur in history.

[76]Four key issues surface in discussions of the Son of Man: (1) the background; (2) whether or not there was a titular usage of the phrase in pre-Christian Judaism; (3) whether or not in the same period the Son of Man was associated with the Messiah; (4) the historicity of Jesus' application of the phrase to himself. Space permits only cursory remarks on these vast and vexing debates. First, for most of the twentieth century, the prevailing view of the background of the Son of Man figure was that it was rooted in the primordial myth of the ancient Near East (exemplified in Sigmund Mowinckel, *He That Cometh,* pp. 422, 425; cf. Norman Perrin, *A Modern Pilgrimage in New Testament Christology* [Philadelphia: Fortress, 1974], p. 24). But in the latter part of this century, the pendulum has swung away from that position to the view that there was no such encompassing myth informing ancient Judaism (thus R. Leivestad, "Der apokalyptische Menschensohn: ein theologisches Phantum," *Annual of the Swedish Theological Institute* 6 [1967-1968]: 49-109; "Exit the Apocalyptic Son of Man," *NTS* 18 (1971-1972): 243-67. Collins, however, seems closer to the truth in steering a middle course between the above extremes. On the one hand, he rightly discards the concept of "the Anthropos Myth," which is a post-first century A.D. mosaic, while on the other hand arguing that Daniel 7 is the key source for the later idea of an apocalyptic Son of Man (Collins, *Star and the*

Scepter, pp. 173-75). In other words, the primary stimulus for the development of the idea of a heavenly Son of Man is Judaism (e.g., Daniel 7).

Second, two comments may be made about whether or not "Son of Man" was a title in pre-Christian Judaism. First, the titular usage seems to first occur only with Jesus (so G. Vermes, *Jesus and the World of Judaism* [Philadelphia: Fortress, 1984], pp. 96-98; J. A. Fitzmyer, "The New Testament Title 'Son of Man' Philogically Considered," in *A Wandering Aramean: Collected Aramaic Essays*, SBLMS 25 [Missoula, Mont.: Scholars Press, 1979], pp. 143-60; Marinus de Jonge, *Christology in Context: The Earliest Christian Response to Jesus* [Philadelphia: Westminster Press, 1988], pp. 169-72). Nevertheless, even though it is now commonly recognized that "Son of Man" was not a title before Jesus, the whole debate, as Collins recognizes, has been too narrowly focused, since the idea of such a heavenly, apocalyptic figure is broader than just the terminology (Collins, *Star and the Scepter*, pp. 174-75). Related to this discussion, Judith L. Kovacs and Paul Kobelski have made a case for a rather fixed concept of the heavenly Son of Man in apocalyptic circles in the first century B.C. Kovacs's article (" 'Now Shall the Ruler of This World Be Driven Out': Jesus' Death as Cosmic Battle in John 12:2-26," *JBL* 114 [1995]: 227-47) culls the testimony from Dan 7, *1 Enoch*, *4 Ezra* and the NT (particularly the Gospels and Revelation). She provides the following thematic threads uniting the pertinent literature on the subject:

☐ *a heavenly, superhuman figure* (Dan 7:13; *1 Enoch* 48:2; 62:7; *4 Ezra* 13:3, 26; Mt 25:31; Mk 14:62; Rev 1:12-18; 14:14; cf. Jn 1:51)

☐ *a ruler who is given eternal dominion and authority* (Dan 7:14; *1 Enoch* 69:27-29; Mt 16:27; 25:34; cf. Rev 1:5; 3:21; 5:12-13; 17:14; *1 Enoch* 45:3; 49:2; 55:4; 61:8; cf. Jn 12:23)

☐ *a judge who executes the final, righteous judgment of God* (*1 Enoch* 62:7-14; 63:11-12; 69:27; *4 Ezra* 13:37-39; Mt 13:41-43; 16:27; 19:28; 25:31-46; Rev 1:18; 14:14 [as reaper], cf. Rev 2:22-23; 19:11; *1 Enoch* 45:3; 49:4; 55:4; 61:8-9; cf. Jn 3:16-21)

☐ *a warrior who is victorious over the forces of evil* (*1 Enoch* 46:3-6; 62:7-12; *4 Ezra* 13:4-11; cf. Rev 2:16; 3:21; 17:17; 19:11; cf. Jn 12:20-36; 14:30-31; 16:8-11)

The second author, Paul Kobelski (*Melchizedek and Melchiresa*, pp. 133-34), showed (as I noted earlier) that the Son of Man personage of Dan 7 corresponds to the presentation of Melchizedek in 11QMelch. Kobelski draws the following parallels:

Both Daniel 7 and 11QMelch describe the events of the final age in terms of a judgment and a military defeat of the enemy. Although the "one like a son of man" is not specifically presented as a judge of his opponents, he appears in a judicial context (Dan 7:10, 14; cf. Dan 7:24, 37) in which he is given the kingdom. In both cases, the "one like a son of man" (i.e., Michael in Dan 7:9-14) and Melchizedek are exalted to a place in the heavens (Dan 7:9, 13; 11QMelch 2:10-11), both triumph over the power of the enemy (Dan 7:23-27; 12:1; 11QMelch 2:13-16; 2;25). The "one like a son of man" is given an inde-

structible kingdom (Dan 7:14); Melchizedek is described as a king in the final
age (11Q Melch 2:7-8; 2:16; 2:23-25).

We may now filter Kobelski's correspondences between the Son of Man
and 11QMelch through the grid of Kovacs's four comparisons, thereby per-
mitting us to include the DSS in the tradition of the heavenly Son of Man:
☐ a heavenly, superhuman figure (11QMelch 2:10-11)
☐ a ruler who is given eternal dominion and authority (11QMelch 2:7-9,
23-25)
☐ a judge who executes the final, righteous judgment of God (11QMelch
2:9-14)
☐ a warrior who is victorious over the forces of evil (11QMelch 2:13-16, 25)

It would seem, then, that the evidence culled from the above materials
admits to the conclusion that there did exist in pre-Christian Judaism a concept of a heavenly, apocalyptic Son of Man.

Third, the previous point helps to solve the debate over whether late Second Temple Judaism associated the heavenly Son of Man with the messianic
hope (so according to, e.g., Bonsirven, *Palestinian Judaism*, p. 189) or not (so,
e.g., T. W. Manson, "The Son of Man in Daniel, Enoch and the Gospels," in
Studies in the Gospels and Epistles [Philadelphia: Westminster, 1982], pp.
123-45), in favor of the first option (see again Jn 12:34). Fourth, the issue of
whether or not the historical Jesus employed "Son of Man" as a self-designation need not detain us, for of the three types of Son of Man sayings in the
Gospels (the Son of Man on earth, the suffering Son of Man, the exalted Son
of Man), the authenticity of the exalted Son of Man category has been the
least disputed, which is the type of saying occurring in the Olivet discourse.

[77]Wright, *Jesus and the Victory of God*, p. 363.

[78]Ibid., p. 363.

[79]See Pate and Haines, *Doomsday Delusions*, chap. 2.

Chapter 5: Story, Symbol & Praxis

[1]N. T. Wright, *The New Testament and the People of God* (Minneapolis: Fortress,
1992), p. 243. In his sequel *Jesus and the Victory of God* (Minneapolis: Fortress,
1996), pp. 467-72, Wright adds another question to the mix: "What time is it?"
In that work, the author answers the query in terms of Jesus' announcement
of the kingdom of God. (Wright chooses to refer to God using a lowercase *g*.)

[2]Wright, *New Testament and the People of God*, pp. 215-23.

[3]Ibid., pp. 224-32.

[4]Ibid., pp. 233-41.

[5]Ibid. My list proceeds along somewhat different lines than Wright's, which is
made up of worship and festivals as well as the study and practice of the
Torah, though we both make the same basic points.

[6]For a discussion of the origin, structure and meaning of the Lucan birth
hymns, the reader can consult C. Marvin Pate, *Luke: Moody Gospel Commentary* (Chicago: Moody Press, 1995), pp. 46-92.

[7]The classic analysis of the hymnic features of the *Hôdāyôt* is that by G. Jeremias, *Der Lehrer der Gerechtigkeit* (Göttingen: Vanderhoeck & Ruprecht, 1963). Yigael Yadin provides a helpful study on the War Scroll that touches on its character as a Divine Warrior hymn (Yigael Yadin, *The Scroll of the War of the Sons of Light against the Sons of Darkness* [Oxford: Oxford University Press, 1962]). Other hymns in the Qumran library include the Apocryphal Psalms, the Hymns Against the Demons and the Hymns of the Poor, which provides an interesting background to the Lucan concept of poverty-piety; see below.

[8]So according to Robert A. Guelich, *The Sermon on the Mount: A Foundation for Understanding* (Waco, Tex.: Word Books, 1982), pp. 68ff.

[9]Ibid., p. 69. I am drawing here on Guelich's remarks. He offers an important qualification at this point, noting that although the term *'nwm* is significant for the Qumran community, it is not the only self-designation of the group.

[10]This theme, as I have noted before, forms an important part of the fabric of Qumranic self-understanding, particularly as it viewed itself as the true Israel, the faithful remnant who awaited the restoration of the land. A similar idea informs Luke's perspective, as I have argued in elsewhere (Pate, *Luke*, pp. 27-29, 56-57, 88).

[11]Ibid., p. 71. In my commentary on Luke 1 I have analyzed the structure of the *Benedictus,* suggesting that a chiastic arrangement informs the hymn:

A vv. 68-69: redemption/horn of salvation (Messiah)
  B v. 70: prophet's prediction (Isaiah?)
    C v. 71: salvation of Israel from enemies
      D v. 72: mercy to the patriarchs and the covenant
      D' v. 73: faithfulness to the covenant with Abraham
    C' vv. 74-75: deliverance of Israel from her enemies
  B' v. 76: prophet's prediction (Is 40:3)
A' vv. 77-79: salvation/sunrise on high (Messiah)

Our concern here is with vv. 78-79, in particular the meaning of *anatolē,* v. 78. The proposed chiastic structure between v. 78 and vv. 68-69 helps solve the difficulty of this word. While the term is used generically in the Septuagint to translate Malachi 3:20 ("For you who fear my name the sun of righteousness shall rise [anatelei] with healing in its wings"), it was also used to translate the word *shoot* or *branch* with reference to the Davidic messianic heir (Is 11:1; Jer 23:5; Zech 3:8). Moreover, the verb *anatelō* is used of Jacob's seed in Num 24:17, which was later interpreted messianically (CD 7:18; 1QM 11:6; *T. Levi* 18:3; etc.). On balance, then, given the messianic connotation of the term in the OT as well as in early Judaism, along with the chiastic correlation of Lk 1:68-69 and Lk 1:77-79, *anatolē* most probably should be interpreted messianically as the shoot of David, not just generically for the rising of the sun. For further discussion, see Pate, *Luke,* pp. 70-74.

[12]The reader is referred to Ernest Vogt's note on this debate, "'Peace Among Men of God's Good Pleasure': Luke 2:14," in *The Scrolls and the New Testament,* ed. Krister Stendahl (New York: Harper & Row, 1957), pp. 114-17, esp. p. 117.

[13]Ibid., pp. 114-17.

[14]Ibid., p. 117.

[15]Herman Ridderbos, *Paul: An Outline of His Theology,* trans. John Richard Dewitt (Grand Rapids, Mich.: Eerdmans, 1975), p. 215.

[16]George Ladd, *A Theology of the New Testament* (Grand Rapids, Mich.: Eerdmans, 1974), pp. 453-84.

[17]French L. Arrington, *Paul's Aeon Theology in 1 Corinthians* (Washington, D.C.: University Press of America, 1978), pp. 132-35.

[18]J. Christiaan Beker, *Paul the Apostle: The Triumph of God in Life and Thought* (Philadelphia: Fortress, 1980), pp. 281-82.

[19]David Ewert (*The Holy Spirit in the New Testament* [Scottdale, Pa.: Herald, 1983], p. 25) makes this point.

[20]Scholars have differed in their opinions as to whether the Qumran community viewed the Spirit as a present eschatological reality within it. For example, W. D. Davies argues against this perspective in his "Paul and the Dead Sea Scrolls: Flesh and Spirit," in *The Scrolls and the New Testament,* ed. Krister Stendahl (New York: Harper & Brothers, 1957), pp. 157-82, esp. pp. 173-77. H. W. Kuhn, however, in his monumental study *Enderwartung und gegenwärtiges Heil: Untersuchungen zu den Gemeindeliedern von Qumran,* Studien zur Umwelt des Neuen Testament 4 (Göttingen: Vandendoeck & Ruprecht, 1966), concluded from the *Hôdāyôt* that its twofold claim—the Spirit belonged to the whole community, and it was there the Spirit produced a special manifestation of divine power (cf. Joel 2:28-32)—indicates that the DSS people did indeed believe themselves to possess the eschatological Spirit (pp. 137ff.). For a superb survey of the debate as a whole, see Arthur Everett Sekki, *The Meaning of* Ruach *at Qumran,* SBLDS 110 (Atlanta: Scholars Press, 1989), pp. 7-69.

[21]Kuhn, *Enderwartung und gegenwärtiges Heil,* pp. 130ff.

[22]See the very helpful treatment by Robert M. Menzies, *The Development of Early Christian Pneumatology, with Special Reference to Luke—Acts,* Journal for the Study of the New Testament Supplement Series 54 (Sheffield, U.K.: Sheffield Academic Press, 1991), pp. 87-89.

[23]Ibid., pp. 224ff.

[24]Ibid., pp. 224-25. Menzies demonstrates this to be the case throughout Luke—Acts.

[25]Lincoln convincingly shows that *Tg. Ps.-J.*68:18 is utilized in Eph 4:7-10. See Andrew T. Lincoln, *Paradise Now and Not Yet,* SNTSMS 43 (Cambridge: Cambridge University Press, 1981), pp. 155-63.

[26]Lincoln, *Paradise Now and Not Yet,* pp. 157-58; Robert Eisenman and Michael Wise, *The Dead Sea Scrolls Uncovered* (New York: Penguin, 1993), pp. 214-17.

[27]Lincoln, *Paradise Now and Not Yet,* pp. 157-58.

[28]Eisenman and Wise, *The Dead Sea Scrolls Uncovered,* pp. 213-19.

[29]Ibid., pp. 218-19. The text, 4Q266, is from Eisenman and Wise.

[30]For a summary of this position, see the survey by Menzies, *Development of Early Christian Pneumatology,* pp. 229-44, though he opposes the view.

[31]This comment by Luke is often thought to be in tension with Paul's writings. See C. Marvin Pate, *The Reverse of the Curse: Paul, Wisdom, and the Law* (forthcoming), chap. 9.

[32]Ibid. The two communities, however, obviously interpreted the Torah differently. The DSS demanded strict observance of the letter of the law; not so Luke—Acts (see, e.g., Acts 15:10). Jesus had reduced the Torah to its moral summary and by his Spirit now empowered believers to follow the divine intent of the commandments.

[33]For helpful treatments of the organization of the DSS as compared to early Christianity, see Sherman E. Johnson, "The Dead Sea Manual of Discipline and the Jerusalem Church of Acts," and Bo Reicke, "The Constitution of the Primitive Church in Light of Jewish Documents," in *The Scrolls and the New Testament,* ed. Krister Stendahl (New York: Harper & Brothers, 1957), pp. 129-42, 143-56. For a more recent discussion, see Richard A. Horsley, *Jesus and the Spiral of Violence: Popular Jewish Resistance in Roman Palestine* (San Francisco: Harper & Row, 1987), pp. 200-201.

[34]James C. VanderKam, *The Dead Sea Scrolls Today* (Grand Rapids, Mich.: Eerdmans, 1994), p. 170. It should also be noted that, although the Essenes took ritual baths regularly, an initiate's admission into the community was probably celebrated by a bath that marked his separation to Qumran from society, as has been argued in W. H. Brownlee, "John the Baptist in the New Light of Ancient Scrolls," in *The Scrolls and the New Testament,* ed. Krister Stendahl (New York: Harper & Brothers, 1957), pp. 33-53, esp. p. 39.

[35]For further discussion, see Karl George Kuhn, "The Lord's Supper and the Communal Meal of Qumran," in *The Scrolls and the New Testament,* ed. Krister Stendahl (New York: Harper & Brothers, 1957), pp. 65-93, esp. p. 68. Lawrence H. Schiffman, *Reclaiming the Dead Sea Scrolls: Their True Meaning for Judaism and Christianity,* Anchor Bible Reference Library (New York: Doubleday, 1995), pp. 335-37, seems forced in his attempt to deny the sacral actions of the priest's blessings.

[36]VanderKam, *Dead Sea Scrolls Today,* p. 175.

[37]Schiffman provides a more nuanced reading of the data of the DSS on this point, concluding that upon entrance into the Qumran sect, members made their property available for common use but did not fully surrender private ownership of it (*Reclaiming the Dead Sea Scrolls,* pp. 106-10). This conclusion is in keeping with the Lucan perspective, especially since Acts 5:1-11 specifies that the sin of Ananias and Sapphira was that they had lied about the proceeds of the sale of their property, not that they had kept part of the money from the sale. Brian Capper also provides insight into the communal sharing of the early church as compared with the Essenes, concluding, like Schiffman, that there were two stages in the process of transferring one's possessions over to those respective communities (thus compare the incident of Ananias and Sapphira in Acts 5:4 with 1QS 6:20). Moreover, Capper identifies certain connections between the early church and the Essenes: they both labeled

themselves as the "community" precisely over the point of sharing their possessions (cf. Acts 2:44, 47 and 1QS 6:18-23); they both supported a daily distribution of food to their communities (cf. Acts 6:1 with Philo's description of the Essenes [Philo *Hypothetica* 11.4-11]); the early church grew in the area next to the Essene quarter in southwest Jerusalem (Brian Capper, "The Palestinian Cultural Context of the Earliest Christian Community of Goods," in *The Book of Acts in Its First Century Palestinian Setting,* ed. Richard J. Bauckham [Grand Rapids, Mich.: Eerdmans, 1995], 4:323-56).

[38]Recall the earlier discussion concerning the hymns of the two communities, especially the connection between the *'nwm* tradition and those who numbered themselves among the remnant of true Israel. Such a relationship can be stated axiomatically: Blessed are the poor, for they will inherit the land.

[39]A convenient summary chart of the nature of Qumranic offenses and punishments can be found in Schiffman, *Reclaiming the Dead Sea Scrolls,* p. 109.

[40]Wright, *New Testament and the People of God,* p. 226.

[41]W. D. Davies, *The Gospel and the Land: Early Christianity and Jewish Territorial Doctrine* (Berkeley: University of California Press, 1974), pp. 76-77, 83-85.

[42]Tremper Longman III and Daniel G. Reid, *God Is a Warrior* (Grand Rapids, Mich.: Zondervan, 1995), p. 92 n. 2.

[43]Ibid., pp. 99 n. 20, 101 n. 25, 102. As is noted by Longman and Reid, Luke, following Mark, frequently uses the verb *epitimaō* ("rebuke") of demons with the connotation of divine warfare (e.g., Lk 4:35 = Mk 1:25; Lk 4:41 = Mk 3:12; Lk 9:42 = Mk 9:25). Luke also uses *epitimaō* with reference to Jesus' driving away sickness (Lk 4:39; 13:10-16), suggesting that author wished to extend the activity of Satan beyond demon possession into the broader field of disease.

[44]Ibid., p. 105 and n. 36.

[45]Odil H. Steck, *Israel und das gewaltsame Geshick der Propheten* (Neukirchen-Vlyun, Germany: Neukirchener, 1967). See his composite summary of the components of the Deuteronomistic tradition, pp. 62-64, 122-24.

[46]David P. Moessner, *Lord of the Banquet: The Literary and Theological Significance of the Lucan Travel Narrative* (Minneapolis: Fortress, 1989), pp. 87-90. Recall also the discussion by Steck, *Israel und das gewaltsame Geshick der Propheten,* pp. 165-70.

[47]C. F. Evans, "The Central Section of St. Luke's Gospel," in *Studies in the Gospels: Festschrift to R. H. Lightfoot,* ed. D. E. Nineham (Oxford: Blackwell, 1955), pp. 37-53. Those endorsing this theory include J. D. M. Derrett, *Law in the New Testament* (London: Darton, Longman & Todd, 1970), pp. 100, 126-55; J. Bligh, *Christian Deuteronomy: Luke 9—18* (Langley: St. Paul, 1970); J. A. Sanders, "The Ethic of Election in Luke's Banquet Parable," in *Essays in Old Testament Ethics: J. Philiip Hyatt in Memoriam,* ed. J. L. Crenshaw and J. T. Willis (New York: Ktav, 1974), pp. 247-71; J. Drury, *Tradition and Design in Luke's Gospel: A Study in Early Christian Historiography* (London: Darton, Longman & Todd, 1976), pp. 138-64; M. D. Goulder, *The Evangelist's Calendar* (London: SPCK, 1978), pp. 95-101; C. A. Evans, "Luke's Use of the Elijah/Elisha Narratives

and the Ethic of Election," *JBL* 106 (1987): 75-83; Robert W. Wall, "'The Finger of God': Deuteronomy 9.10 and Luke 11.20," *NTS* 33 (1987): 144-45. Those rejecting this view include J. A. Fitzmyer, *Luke I-IX*, p. 826; C. L. Blomberg, "Midrash, Chiasmus, and the Outline of Luke's Central Section," in *Studies in Midrash and Historiography*, ed. R. T. France and D. Wenham, Gospel Perspectives 3 (Sheffield, U.K.: Sheffield Academic Press, 1983), pp. 228-33; T. L. Brodie, *Luke the Literary Interpreter: Luke—Acts as a Systematic Rewriting and Updating of the Elijah-Elisha Narrative in 1 and 2 Kings* (Rome: Pontifical University of St. Thomas Press, 1987), pp. 410-11. Craig A. Evans has, in my opinion, successfully answered the objections of those dismissing the Deuteronomy hypothesis in his "Luke 16:1-18 and the Deuteronomy Hypothesis," in *Luke and Scripture: The Function of Sacred Tradition in Luke—Acts*, ed. Craig A. Evans and James A. Sanders (Minneapolis: Fortress, 1993), pp. 121-39.

[48]Moessner, *Lord of the Banquet*, pp. 211.

[49]Ibid., p. 211.

[50]Horsley, *Jesus and the Spiral of Violence*, p. 285.

[51]The remark is by Johnson, "Dead Sea Manual of Discipline," p. 137.

[52]Because this information provides the reader with insight into the heart of Luke's message, it is listed here: Lk 1:5—2:52; 3:10-14, 23-38; 4:17-21, 23, 25-30; 5:4-9, 39; 7:12-17; 8:1-3; 9:52-55, 61-62; 10:17-20, 25-28; 12:13-15, 16-21, 35-38, 47-48, 49, 54-56; 13:1-9, 16-17, 30, 31-33; 14:1-6, 7-14, 28-32; 15:8-10, 11-32; 16:1-8, 8-12, 14-15, 19-31; 17:7-10, 12-18, 20-21, 28-32; 18:2-8, 10-14; 19:1-10, 39-40, 41-44; 20:18; 21:8, 21-22, 24, 28, 34-36, 37-38, 39; 22:15-18, 19-20, 27, 31-33, 35-38, 44-49, 63-71; 23:1-12, 27-32, 35, 36-37, 39-43.

[53]Wright, *Jesus and the Victory of God*, pp. 592-611.

[54]Ibid., pp. 579-91. Though Wright has called attention to certain individuals in Judaism whose sufferings were perceived to embrace the covenantal curses and thereby motivate Israel to obey God in order to receive the Deuteronomic blessings (e.g., Is 53; Wis 2:1-20; 3:1-6, 7-9; 1QpHab 5a:10-11; 8:1-3; 11:4-7; 1QM 1:11-12; 1QS 8:1-4; 2 Macc 6:27-29; 7:36-38; 4 Macc 9:23-24), Wright himself acknowledges that such a concept should not be equated with a suffering or cursed Messiah.

[55]It may be that Acts 1:6-11 and 3:20-21 hold out the hope for a future restoration of Israel. If so, then Luke, like Rom 11:25-27, will have reversed the order of things in the end times: not the restoration of Israel and then conversion of the Gentiles but the opposite.

[56]Scott McKnight, *A Light Among the Gentiles: Jewish Missionary Activity in the Second Temple Period* (Minneapolis: Fortress, 1991), p. 21.

[57]Wright, *New Testament and the People of God*, p. 375. At this point, we should acknowledge a collection of essays edited by Richard Bauckham that attempts to overthrow the traditional view that the Gospel authors (including Luke) wrote to specific communities under their care. Rather, argues this work, the four Gospels were directed to the *whole* church, not specific audi-

ences (Richard Bauckham, ed., *The Gospels for All Christians* [Grand Rapids, Mich.: Eerdmans, 1998]). While there is much in this book that provides a healthy corrective to the conclusions of form and redaction criticisms, it has gone too far in the opposite direction, bordering on an ahistorical reading of the Gospels. I thus affirm what I have referred to throughout this chapter, namely Luke wrote his two volumes to a specific congregation—the Lucan community.

Chapter 6: The Reverse of the Curse

[1]Millar Burrows, *The Dead Sea Scrolls* (New York: Viking, 1955), p. 334.

[2]Siegfried Schulz, "Zur Rechtfertigung aus Gnaden in Qumran und bei Paulus," *ZTK* 56 (1959): 155-85, esp. p. 184. See the recent article by Martin Abegg, "Paul, Works of the Torah and MMT," *Biblical Archaeology Review* 20, no. 6 (November-December 1994): 52-55. Abegg's article shows that "Works of the Torah" is the correct translation of the phrase in 4QMMT (not "some words about the Torah") and that Paul diametrically opposes such a concept because it conveys the idea that salvation can be earned.

[3]E. P. Sanders, *Paul and Palestinian Judaism: A Comparison of Patterns of Religion* (Philadelphia: Fortress, 1977), esp. pp. 239-328 with regard to the DSS. Sanders's student Benno Przybylski applied the concept of covenantal nomism to the DSS more extensively, arguing that the sectarians did not equate salvation (entrance into the covenant based on divine grace) with righteousness (remaining in the covenant through human works). The author rather maintains that righteousness in the DSS is to be equated with "truth" (Benno Przybylski, *Righteousness in Matthew and His World of Thought*, SNTSMS 41 [Cambridge: Cambridge University Press, 1980], pp. 13-38). There are two problems, however, with Przybylski's thesis. First, as we will see later in this chapter, righteousness in the DSS is ethical in nature, thus assigning soteric value to human conduct which, in effect, negates the concept of salvation by grace. Second, as Mark A. Seifrid (*Justification by Faith: The Origin and Development of a Central Pauline Theme*, Supplements to Novum Testamentum LXVIII [Leiden: E. J. Brill, 1992], p. 97 n. 93) writes, "The emphasis in 1QS upon 'truth' as faithfulness to the covenant, used as an equivalent to righteousness (cf. Is 48:1, Jer 4:2, Zech 8:8), is probably motivated by the attempt of the community to place a clear demarcation between its participation in salvation and Jews on the outside (n.b. the stress which the polarity of truth and error receives in the teaching on the two spirits). Contra B. Przybylski, *Righteousness in Matthew and His World of Thought*, p. 28, it is not clear that the concept of righteousness is subordinate to that of truth in 1QS." In other words, the emphasis on truth in the DSS and its close association with righteousness therein, in good sectarian fashion, became the touchpoint of salvation.

[4]J. Becker, *Das Heil Gottes. Heils und Sündenbegriffe in den Qumrantexten und im Neuen Testament*, SUNT 3 (Göttingen: Vanderhoeck und Ruprecht, 1964), p. 125.

⁵Sanders, *Paul and Palestinian Judaism*, pp. 305-16.

⁶Two comments are in order here about righteousness/justification. The Hebrew term for "righteous" is *tsaddiq*. Its Greek counterparts are *dikaios*, which means "righteous" or "just," and *diakaioun*, which means to "justify." The fact that the same root word informs *righteousness* and *justification* is obscured in the English translation.

The second consideration, the meaning of the words *righteousness of God*, is a controversy-laden issue. As a thumbnail sketch, we may consider four interpretations of the phrase in the order of their appearance in the history of the debate.

1. The phrase is a possessive genitive—"God's own righteousness," with reference to divine distributive justice. This was the pre-Reformation understanding of the idea, which lent itself to the possibility that human works could merit one's standing before God.

2. Martin Luther came to disagree strongly with the first perspective, claiming instead that the phrase is a genitive of origin: God's righteous standing is imputed to sinners through Christ. In his classic statement on the subject, Luther writes of Rom 1:17,

> For, however irreproachably I lived as a monk, I felt myself before God to be a sinner with a most unquiet conscience, nor could I be confident that I had pleased him with my satisfaction. I did not love, nay, rather I hated this righteous God who punished sinners. . . . At last, God being merciful, . . . I began to understand the justice of God as that by which the righteous man lives by the gift of God, namely by faith. . . . This straightway made me feel as though reborn and as though I had entered through open gates into Paradise itself. . . . And now, as much as I hated the word 'justice of God' before, so much the more sweetly I extolled this word to myself." (Lewis W. Spitz, ed., *Luther's Works* 34 [Philadelphia: Muhlenburg, 1960], pp. 336-37)

3. The righteousness of God is a subjective genitive which encompasses both God's gift of righteousness and his power. This was the novel view offered by Ernst Käsemann, who claimed that "righteousness of God" was a technical term of late-Jewish apocalypticism for God's saving justice. As such, it reveals God's sovereign faithfulness to his covenant with Israel and to his creation by which he brings Jews back to himself in obedience (see Deut 33:21; 1QS 10:25; 11:12; 1QM 4:6; *T. Dan* 6:10; *1 Enoch* 71:14; 99:10; 101:3). Thus the righteousness of God expresses both his gift of forgiveness and his power for obedience toward his people, the new creation. Käsemann claimed that Paul inherited this conceptual background of the phrase and redefines it in terms of God's present reign over the world through Jesus. See Ernst Käsemann, "The Righteousness of God in Paul," in *New Testament Questions of Today*, trans. W. J. Montague (Philadelphia: Fortress, 1969), pp. 168-82. But see Mark Seifrid's critique of Käsemann's theory in his *Justification by Faith*, pp. 99-108. N. T. Wright also criticizes this view as failing to note the covenantal nuance of righteousness in Sec-

ond Temple Judaism (N. T. Wright, *What Saint Paul Really Said* [Grand Rapids, Mich.: Eerdmans, 1997], p. 103).

4. Wright's view is that the phrase is a possessive genitive but with reference to God's faithfulness to his covenant with Israel. More specifically, Paul's understanding of the righteousness of God is that God has brought Israel's sin and exile to a close at the cross of Christ so that through his resurrection the covenantal blessings can now be appropriated by Jews and Gentiles alike (Wright, *What Saint Paul Really Said*, chaps. 5—7).

For excellent summaries of the debate as a whole, see C. E. B. Cranfield, *Romans I—VIII*, ICC (Edinburgh: T & T Clark, 1975), pp. 99-102; Manfred Brauch, "Perspectives on 'God's Righteousness' in Recent German Discussions," in *Paul and Palestinian Judaism: A Comparison of Patterns of Religion*, ed. E. P. Sanders (Philadelphia: Fortress, 1977), pp. 523-42; Wright, *What Saint Paul Really Said*, pp. 100-103.

[7]Sanders, *Paul and Palestinian Judaism*, pp. 306-7.

[8]This conviction that humans are sinful should not be confused with the Protestant doctrine of total depravity. According to the latter, humans are sinful in every aspect of their beings and therefore are incapable of good acts before God. Judaism, however, including the DSS, allows for good in humans. This is so because in every person there exists the good inclination and the bad inclination, and the law empowers the individual to choose the good inclination. See 1QS 3—4 for the classic expression of this perspective.

[9]Sanders cites this text, but he does not call attention to the covenantal framework of it as I am doing here.

[10]See Sanders, *Paul and Palestinian Judaism*, pp. 307-10.

[11]Ibid., p. 312.

[12]Seifrid (*Justification by Faith*, p. 97 nn. 90, 91) supplies these references.

[13]Sanders, *Paul and Palestinian Judaism*, p. 313, follows Bertil Gärtner, *The Temple and the Community in Qumran and the New Testament*, SNTSMS 1 (Cambridge: Cambridge University Press, 1965), p. 5; and Georg Klinzing, *Die Umdeutung des Kultus in der Qumrangemeinde und im Neuen Testament*, SUNT 7 (Göttingen: Vanderhoeck & Ruprecht, 1971), pp. 106-43. Ezek 43:18—44:26 factors heavily in the Essenes' priestly self-understanding.

[14]Abegg, "Paul, Works of the Torah and MMT."

[15]It can be seen from these foundational documents that this perspective of the DSS on justification remains a constant. Sanders earlier argued that, similarly, covenantal nomism is the consistent mindset of the Qumran community, despite the diversity of the group (*Paul and Palestinian Judaism*, pp. 319-20).

[16]Frank Thielman, *Paul and the Law: A Contextual Approach* (Downers Grove, Ill.: InterVarsity Press, 1994), p. 78.

[17]Thomas R. Shreiner, *The Law and Its Fulfillment* (Grand Rapids, Mich.: Baker, 1993), p. 44.

[18]That Paul was not unique in applying Deut 21:23 to crucifixion is now clear,

for the DSS did the same. See 4QpNah 1:7-8 and 11QTemple 64:6-13; see also J. A. Fitzmyer, "Crucifixion in Ancient Palestine, Qumran Literature and the New Testament," *CBQ* 40 (1978): 493-513.

[19]Richard B. Hays, *Echoes of Scripture in the Letters of Paul* (New Haven, Conn.: Yale University Press, 1989), p. 43; James M. Scott, "Paul's Use of the Deuteronomic Tradition(s)," *JBL* 112 (1993): 660 n. 64.

[20]That the divine condemnation for disobedience described in Rom 1:18-32 is intended by Paul to apply to both Gentile and Jew because it is rooted in Adam's sin is demonstrated by Cranfield, *Romans I-VIII*, pp. 106ff.; Morna Hooker, "Adam in Romans 1," *NTS* 6 (1960): 297-306; James D. G. Dunn, *Romans 1-8* (Waco, Tex.: Word, 1988), pp. 60ff. The upshot of the passage is that Paul is indicating that Israel is still in Adam and therefore fares no better than Gentiles in terms of obedience to God.

[21]Neither Hays *(Echoes of Scripture)* nor Scott ("Paul's Use of the Deuteronomic Tradition(s)") mentions this reversal motif in treating Romans 1—3.

[22]Hays, *Echoes of Scripture*, pp. 36-41.

[23]N. T. Wright, *The Climax of the Covenant: Christ and the Law in Pauline Theology* (Edinburgh: T & T Clark, 1991), pp. 193-219.

[24]Ibid., p. 195.

[25]Frank Thielman, "The Story of Israel and the Theology of Romans 5—8," in *Pauline Theology*, ed. David M. Hay and E. Elizabeth Johnson (Minneapolis: Fortress, 1995), 3:169-95.

[26]Cf. Num 6:22-27; Ps 55:18-19; Is 9:6, 7; 48:17-22; 54:10; Jer 14:19-22; Ezek 34:25-31; 37:26; Mic 5:4; Hag 2:9; Zech 8:12; *Sir* 47:13; *2 Macc* 1:2-4; *1 Enoch* 5:7-9; 10:17; 11:2. Refer to Dunn, *Romans 1—8*, p. 264.

[27]See also remarks on Rom 5:1-11 in Thielman, "Story of Israel," pp. 177-79.

[28]See Dunn, *Romans 1-8*, p. 255. Compare N. T. Wright, *Jesus and the Victory of God* (Minneapolis: Fortress, 1996), pp. 582-85.

[29]Dunn, *Romans 1-8*, p. 255.

[30]Refer to a more extensive discussion of this point in C. Marvin Pate, *The Reverse of the Curse: Paul, Wisdom and the Law* (forthcoming), chap. 7.

[31]Wright, *Climax of the Covenant*, p. 39; cf. p. 198.

[32]Ibid., p. 195. Recall Wright's suggestion along this line of thinking.

[33]Thielman, *Paul and the Law*, p. 202; Wright, *Climax of the Covenant*, pp. 210-11.

[34]Thielman, *Paul and the Law*, pp. 201-2; Wright, *Climax of the Covenant*, p. 211.

[35]Hays, *Echoes of Scripture*, p. 164.

[36]Scott, "Paul's Use of Deuteronomic Tradition(s)," pp. 659-65.

[37]Hays, *Echoes of Scripture*, p. 163.

[38]This section is indebted to Pate, *Reverse of the Curse*, chap. 7.

[39]Thielman *(Paul and the Law*, pp. 148-49) persuasively identifies Paul's opponents at Philippi as Judaizing Christians.

[40]Peter T. O'Brien, *The Epistle to the Philippians: A Commentary on the Greek Text*, NIGTC (Grand Rapids, Mich.: Eerdmans, 1991), p. 355.

[41]Ibid., p. 357.

[42]Ibid., p. 356.

[43]For support that Paul alludes to his Damascus road conversion in Phil 3:7-11, see Seyoon Kim, *The Origin of Paul's Gospel*, WUNT 24 (Tübingen: J. C. B. Mohr [Paul Siebeck], 1981), p. 66.

[44]This last paragraph is more fully developed in Pate, *Reverse of the Curse*, chap. 7.

[45]Ibid., chap. 6.

[46]Lincoln plausibly defends the view that the phrase "whose god is their belly" refers not to libertine conduct but to the Judaizers' boast in their food laws (cf. a similar use of "belly" in Rom 16:18). See Lincoln, *Paradise Now and Not Yet*, p. 96.

[47]Ibid., p. 96. The phrase "whose glory is their shame," argues Lincoln, is sarcastic, predicting future judgment (not glory) on those who practice circumcision as a means of salvation. (The "shame" alluded to the nakedness required for circumcision.)

[48]This phrase is reminiscent of Paul's reference to present (earthly) Jerusalem in Gal 4:25 which, as I have argued elsewhere, represents the Judaizers' aspirations for the restoration of Israel (Pate, *Reverse of the Curse*, chap. 5).

[49]Ibid., chap. 7.

[50]See, e.g., Lincoln, *Paradise Now and Not Yet*, pp. 87-89; Hawthorne, *Philippians*, p. 169.

morphē (2:6) *morphēn* (2:7)	*symmorphon* (3:21)
hyparchōn (2:6)	*hyparchei* (3:20)
schēmati (2:7)	*metaschēmatisei* (3:20)
etapeinōsen (2:8)	*tapeinōseōs* (3:21)
epouraniōn (2:10)	*ouranois* (3:20)
pan gony kampsē . . . kai pasa kai glōssa exomologēsetai (2:10-11)	*tou dynasthai auton hypotaxai autō ta panta* (3:21)
kyrios Iēsous Christos (2:11)	*kyrion Iēsoun Christon* (3:20)
doxan (2:11)	*doxēs* (3:21)

Links between passages

[51]Morna Hooker, "Interchange in Christ," *JTS* (1971): 349-61.

[52]Thielman, *Paul and the Law*, p. 157.

[53]Ibid., p. 155.

[54]Sanders, *Paul and Palestinian Judaism*, pp. 442ff., see esp. p. 514.

[55]Frank Thielman, *From Plight to Solution*, Supplement to *Novum Testamentum* 61 (Leiden: E. J. Brill, 1989).

[56]Thielman registers a change of perspective between his first book (*From Plight*

to Solution) and his second book *(Paul and the Law).* The former argued for the continuing role of the law in the Christian life. What was removed in Christ's death and resurrection was the *curse* of the Torah, not the law itself. In his next work, Thielman argues that the Torah itself is ended.

[57]N. T. Wright, *What Saint Paul Really Said* (Grand Rapids, Mich.: Eerdmans, 1997).

[58]We eagerly await Wright's volume on Paul to be included as the third work alongside his *New Testament and the People of God* and *Jesus and the Victory of God.*

Chapter 7: The Agony of the Ecstasy

[1]The title is adapted from the chapter in Ben Witherington III, *Conflict and Community in Corinth: A Socio-Rhetorical Commentary on 1 and 2 Corinthians* (Grand Rapids, Mich.: Eerdmans, 1995), p. 274.

[2]Alan F. Segal, "Paul and Ecstasy," in *Society of Biblical Literature 1986 Seminar Papers*, ed. Kent Harold Richards (Chico, Calif.: Scholars Press, 1986), pp. 550-80, esp. p. 558. Segal later developed this mixture of apocalypticism and mysticism in his *Paul the Convert: The Apostolate and Apostasy of Saul the Pharisee* (New Haven, Conn.: Yale University Press, 1990).

[3]Pioneering studies in this area include W. D. Davies, *Paul and Rabbinic Judaism,* 2nd ed. (New York: Harper & Brothers, 1955), pp. 198, 210ff.; 317ff. Lincoln, *Paradise Now and Not Yet,* addressed this topic thoroughly, as did James Tabor, *Things Unutterable: Paul's Ascent to Paradise in Its Graeco-Roman, Judaic, and Christian Context* (Lanham, Md.: University Press of America, 1986). Other works comparing 2 Cor 12:1-10 with Jewish *merkabah* and/or Jewish Hellenistic mystic ascent texts include William Baird, "Visions, Revelations, and Ministry: Reflections on 2 Corinthians 12:1-5 and Galatians 1:11-17," *JBL* 104, no. 4 (1985): 651-52; J. W. Bowker, "'Merkabah' Visions and the Visions of Paul," *JJS* 16 (1971): 157-73; Mary Dean-Otting, *Heavenly Journeys: A Study of the Motif in Hellenistic Jewish Literature* (Frankfort, N.Y.: Peter Lang, 1984); Gershom Scholem, *Jewish Gnosticism, Merkabah Mysticism, and Talmudic Traditions* (New York: Jewish Publication Society, 1960). More recently, Thomas J. Sappington has utilized this concept to meticulously explore the Colossian heresy in his *Revelation and Redemption at Colossae,* Journal for the Study of the New Testament Supplement Series 53 (Sheffield: JSOT Press, 1991). Regarding the debate whether the descriptions found in the Jewish and Christian literature cited represent real mystic experiences (with an answer in the affirmative), see Sappington, *Revelation and Redemption at Colossae,* pp. 76-88.

[4]The following description is adapted from F. F. Bruce, *The Epistles to the Colossians, to Philemon and to Ephesians,* NICNT (Grand Rapids, Mich.: Eerdmans, 1984), pp. 17-26; cf. Peter T. O'Brien, *Colossians, Philemon,* WBC 44 (Waco, Tex.: Word, 1982), pp. xxx-xli.

[5]John Strugnell, "The Angelic Liturgy at Qumran—4Q Serek Širŏt 'ōlat Haššabāt," *Congress Volume, Oxford, 1959,* VTSupp7 (Leiden: Brill, 1960):

318-45, esp. p. 320.

[6]Neil S. Fujita, *A Crack in the Jar: What Ancient Jewish Documents Tell Us About the New Testament* (Mahweh: N.J.: Paulist, 1986), p. 162. On pages 162-63, Fujita characterizes this type of experience as "literary mysticism." However, in light of the belief of the Qumran community that it joined the angels in heavenly worship when the sectaries met in a cultic setting, it is difficult to restrict such a phenomenon to mere literary device.

[7]Four of the dominant interpretations of the Colossian heresy are Judaizers, Gnosticism, mystery religions and Jewish *merkabah* mysticism. The scholarly opinion today is leaning toward the last of these options. See O'Brien, *Colossians*, pp. xxx-xli; F. F. Bruce, *Epistles*, pp. 17-26; F. O. Francis, "Humility and Angelic Worship in Colossians 2:18," in *Conflict at Colossae*, ed. F. O. Francis and Wayne Meeks, SBLMS 4 (Missoula, Mont.: Scholars Press, 1975), pp. 163-95; Sappington, *Revelation and Redemption at Colossae*; James D. G. Dunn, *The Epistles to the Colossians and to Philemon*, NIGTC (Grand Rapids, Mich.: Eerdmans, 1996), pp. 20-35 (though this author is hesitant to label the Colossian teaching "heresy" or "error," preferring rather the term *philosophy*). The view of Morna D. Hooker that there was no Colossian heresy as such has not met with scholarly approval (Morna D. Hooker, "Were There False Teachers in Colossae?" in *Christ and Spirit in The New Testament*, ed. B. Lindars and S. S. Smalley [Cambridge: Cambridge University, 1973], pp. 315-31). For a convincing refutation of Hooker's view, see O'Brien, *Colossians*, pp. xxx-xli.

[8]For a general discussion of the theme of angels and mystic worship in Jewish apocalyptic texts, see Sappington, *Revelation and Redemption at Colossae*, pp. 90-110. For discussions of angelic worship and the Colossian heresy, see Dunn, *Epistles to the Colossians and to Philemon*, e.g., pp. 33-35, 48, 76-78, 180-83, as well as the seminal work by Francis, "Humility and Angelic Worship in Colossians 2:18."

[9]For a defense of Pauline authorship of Colossians, see W. Kümmel, *Introduction to the New Testament*, trans. Howard Clark Kee (Nashville: Abingdon, 1973), pp. 240-41; O'Brien, *Colossians*, pp. xli-xlix; Donald Guthrie, *New Testament Introduction* (Downers Grove, Ill.: InterVarsity Press, 1970), pp. 551-54; Lincoln, *Paradise Now and Not Yet*, pp. 122-34.

[10]Those representing this view in one way or another include M. Dibelius and H. Greeven, *An die Kolosser, Epheser, an Philemon* (Tübingen: J. C. B. Mohr, 1953), p. 35; and G. Bornkamm, "The Heresy of Colossians," in *Conflict at Colossae*, ed. F. O. Francis and W. A. Meeks, SBLMS 4 (Missoula, Mont.: Scholars Press, 1975), pp. 123-45.

[11]The identification of the "rulers and authorities" here in Col 2:15 and in the parallel passage, 1 Cor 2:6-10, is hotly debated. Those identifying these rulers as demonic forces include C. K. Barrett, *Commentary on the First Epistle to the Corinthians*, HNTC (New York: Harper & Row, 1968), pp. 69-70; and Judith L. Kovacs, "The Archons, the Spirit and the Death of Christ," *Apocalyptic and the New Testament: Essays in Honor of J. Louis Martyn*, ed. Joel Marcus and Marion

Soards, Journal for the Study of the New Testament Supplement Series 24 (Sheffield, U.K.: JSOT Press, 1989), pp. 217-36. Those opting for the political interpretation only include A. Wesley Carr, *Angels and Principalities: The Background, Meaning, and Development of the Pauline Phrase Haï Archai kai Hai Exousia*, SNTSMS 42 (Cambridge: Cambridge University Press, 1981); and Gordon Fee, *The First Epistle to the Corinthians*, NICNT (Grand Rapids, Mich.: Eerdmans, 1987), pp. 103-4. Those combining the two previous views (demonic influence lies behind the governmental rulers) include Oscar Cullmann, *Christ and Time* (Philadelphia: Westminster Press, 1956), pp. 80-82; and G. H. C. MacGregor, "Principalities and Powers: The Cosmic Background of Saint Paul's Thought," *NTS* (1954): 17-28. Of the three views, the second view seems to have the least to commend itself. In particular, Martinus C. de Boer is unimpressed with Carr's thesis that the idea of suprahuman powers is not present in Paul's thought. He rejects that posture for three reasons: (1) Carr omits any discussion of the figure of Satan in Paul's letters (which is amply attested therein: Rom 16:20; 1 Cor 5:5; 7:5; 2 Cor 4:4; 11:14; 12:7; 1 Thess 2:18); (2) he fails to perceive that death for Paul is a personified, cosmic ruler (see especially Rom 5:12—6:23); (3) as a last resort to evade the evidence, Carr deems Eph 6:12 to be a later interpolation dating to the second century A.D. (Martinus C. de Boer, "The Defeat of Death: Apocalyptic Eschatology in 1 Corinthians 15 and Romans 5" [Ph.D. diss., Union Theological Seminary, 1983], pp. 23-24). The choice is therefore reduced to numbers one and three, the third of which seems to have the edge.

[12]For a convincing presentation of this viewpoint, see Francis, "Humility and Angelic Worship"; Sappington, *Revelation and Redemption at Colossae*, pp. 158-61; Dunn, *Epistles to the Colossians and to Philemon*, pp. 180-85.

[13]But see Dunn's critique of those passages as admitting to that meaning (Dunn, *Epistle to the Colossians and to Philemon*, pp. 179-80).

[14]First pointed out by Francis, "Humility and Angelic Worship."

[15]Dunn, *Epistles to the Colossians and to Philemon*, p. 181.

[16]W. Ramsay, *The Teaching of Paul in Terms of the Present Day* (London: Hodder, 1913), pp. 286-305.

[17]M. Dibelius, "The Isis Initiation in Apuleius and Related Initiatory Rites," in *Conflict at Colossae*, ed. F. O. Francis and W. A. Meeks, SBLMS 4 (Missoula, Mont.: Scholars Press, 1975), pp. 61-121. The argument was put forth by Dibelius in 1917.

[18]Francis, "Humility and Angelic Worship." See also his "The Background of Embateuein (Colossians 2:18) in Legal Papyri and Oracle Inscriptions," in *Conflict at Colossae*, ed. F. O. Francis and W. A. Meeks, SBLMS 4 (Missoula, Mont.: Scholars Press, 1975), pp. 197-208.

[19]For critiques of the theory that the mystery religions significantly influenced Paul's thought, the following two authors should be consulted: David Seeley, *The Noble Death: Graeco-Roman Martyrology and Paul's Concept of Salvation*, Journal for the Study of the New Testament Supplement Series 28 (Sheffield,

U.K.: Sheffield Press, 1990), pp. 67-82; and A. J. M. Wedderburn, *Baptism and Resurrection: Studies in Pauline Theology Against Its Graeco-Roman Background,* WUNT 44 (Tübingen; J. C. B. Mohr [Paul Siebeck], 1987). A somewhat dated but still useful investigation of the issue is that by Gunther Wagner, *Pauline Baptism and the Pagan Mysteries,* trans. J. P. Smith (Edinburgh: Oliver & Boyd, 1967). Furthermore, A. Wesley Carr (*Angels and Principalities,* chap. 1) has provided damaging evidence showing that the mystery religions were not all that influential until after the first century A.D.

[20]So Francis, "Background of Embateuein," pp. 198-99.

[21]Dunn, *Epistles to the Colossians and to Philemon,* p. 183; Sappington, *Revelation and Redemption at Colossae,* pp. 155-58.

[22]Dunn, *Epistles to the Colossians and to Philemon,* p. 183.

[23]Ibid.

[24]That the law of Moses is alluded to in Col 2:8-23 is common knowledge among interpreters of the letter. For the probability that the Colossian heresy equated wisdom and the law, see among others O'Brien, *Colossians,* p. 22, and Dunn, *Epistles to the Colossians and to Philemon,* pp. 71ff.

[25]C. Marvin Pate, *The Reverse of the Curse* (forthcoming), part 1.

[26]See, e.g., 1QS 2:2-3; 4:2-6; 9:9-11; 1QH 1:1-20; 4:9-11 and the thesis that these texts portray the Essenes as joining angelic worship, presented in David E. Aune, *The Cultic Setting of Realized Eschatology in Early Christianity,* Supp. NovT 28 (Leiden: E. J. Brill, 1972), pp. 37-44.

[27]Here we have to do with the themes of *merkabah* (throne) and *hekalot* (palaces).

[28]See, e.g., J. Gnilka, *Der Kolosserbrief,* HTKNT 10/1 (Freiburg: Herder, 1980), p. 41; O'Brien, *Colossians,* p. 22.

[29]See E. Lohse, *Colossians and Philemon,* Hermeneia (Minneapolis: Fortress, 1971), p. 25; Dunn, *Epistles to the Colossians and to Philemon,* p. 70.

[30]For a discussion of the hymnic nature of this piece, see Ernst Lohmeyer, *Die Briefe and die Philipper, an die Kolosser und an die Philemon* (Göttingen: Vandenhoeck & Ruprecht, 1956), pp. 41-42; Ernst Käsemann, "A Primitive Christian Baptismal Liturgy," in *Essays on New Testament Themes* (Naperville, Ill.: Alec R. Allenson, 1964), pp. 149-68, esp. pp. 150-52; Jean-Noël Aletti, *Colossiens 1:15-20: Genre et exégèse du texte, fonction de la thématicque Sapientielle,* An Bib 91 (Rome: Biblical Institute Press, 1981); N. T. Wright, "Poetry and Theology in Colossians 1:15-20," *NTS* 36 (1990): 444-68, esp. p. 449.

[31]For bibliography and further discussion, see Pate, *The Glory of Adam and the Afflictions of the Righteous: Pauline Suffering in Context* (New York: Edwin Mellen, 1993), pp. 214-27, where Paul's Adam theology is also brought into the discussion.

[32]N. T. Wright, *The Climax of the Covenant: Christ and the Law in Pauline Theology* (Edinburgh: T & T Clark, 1991), pp. 109-10, 118.

[33]Raymond E. Brown, *The Semitic Background of the Term "Mystery" in the New Testament,* Facet Books, Biblical Series 21 (Philadelphia: Fortress, 1968), pp.

22-29, is the seminal study on this topic.

[34]B. Rigaux provides a helpful analysis of this term as used in the NT and in the DSS in his "Révélation des Mystères et Perfection à Qumrân et dans le Nouveau Testament," *NTS* 4 (1957-1958): 237-62.

[35]J. Dupont, *Gnosis: La connaissance religieuse dans les épîtres de Saint Paul* (Paris: Gabalda, 1949), pp. 16-18.

[36]Dunn, *Epistles to the Colossians and to Philemon*, p. 34.

[37]W. Schenk, "Der Kolosserbrief in der neueren Forschung (1945-1985)," *ANRW* 2.25.4 (1987), pp. 3327-64; 3351-53.

[38]According to Sappington, *Revelation and Redemption at Colossae*, p. 163.

[39]The references are supplied by Dunn, *Epistles to the Colossians and to Philemon*, p. 175; and Sappington, *Revelation and Redemption at Colossae*, p. 163.

[40]For further discussion, see Sappington, *Revelation and Redemption at Colossae*, pp. 100-108; 216-20; Dunn, *Epistles to the Colossians and to Philemon*, pp. 164-65.

[41]The references come from Dunn, *Epistles to the Colossians and to Philemon*, p. 165, which suggests that behind natural law is the law of Moses.

[42]A. J. Bandstra, *The Law and the Elements of the World* (Kampen: KOK, 1964), pp. 5-30.

[43]E.g., W. M. L. de Wette, *Kurze Erklarung der Briefe an die Colosser, an Philemon, an die Ephesier und Philipper*, 2nd ed. (Leipzig: Weidmann, 1847), pp. 33-43; B. Weiss, *Biblical Theology of the New Testament*, trans. from the 3rd German ed. (Edinburgh: T & T Clark, 1882), 1:358, 372-73; J. B. Lightfoot, *Saint Paul's Epistle to the Galatians*, 10th ed., (1890; reprint London: Macmillan, 1986), p. 180.

[44]E.g., E. D. Burton, *A Critical and Exegetical Commentary on the Epistle to the Galatians*, ICC (Edinburgh: T & T Clark, 1921), pp. 215-16; W. L. Knox, *St. Paul and the Church of the Gentiles* (Cambridge: Cambridge University Press, 1939), pp. 108-9, 140-41.

[45]So according to B. Reicke, "The Law and This World According to Paul," *JBL* 70 (1951): 259-76, esp. pp. 261-63; Bruce, *Epistles*, pp. 99-100; E. Percy, *Die Problem Der Kolosser und Epheserbriefe* (Lund: Gleerup, 1946), pp. 160-67.

[46]Dunn, *Epistles to the Colossians and to Philemon*, p. 150.

[47]See the defense of this view in O'Brien, *Colossians*, pp. 129-32.

[48]Compare these references of Dunn, *Epistles to the Colossians and to Philemon*, pp. 150-51.

[49]Francis, "Humility and Angelic Worship," p. 168.

[50]Sappington, *Revelation and Redemption at Colossae*, pp. 65-70.

[51]Dunn, *Epistles to the Colossians and to Philemon*, pp. 191-92. Note also the discussion by M. Newton, *The Concept of Purity at Qumran and in the Letters of Paul*, SNTSMS 53 (Cambridge: Cambridge University Press, 1985), pp. 10-26.

[52]Refer to these respective references in Dunn, *Epistles to the Colossians and to Philemon*, pp. 48, 76-77, 125.

[53]Sappington, *Revelation and Redemption at Colossae*, p. 186.

[54]For a defense of this connection of the Deuteronomic curses with Galatians 1:8, see Pate, *Reverse of the Curse*, chap. 6.

Chapter 8: Monotheism, Covenant & Eschatology

[1]N. T. Wright, *The New Testament and the People of God* (Minneapolis: Fortress, 1992), pp. 244-79.

[2]Cited in ibid., p. 248, where Wright notes that similar statements abound in the Psalms and Is 40—55. For earlier treatments of Israel's monotheistic faith, see H. H. Rowley, *The Re-Discovery of the Old Testament* (Philadelphia: Westminster Press, 1946), chap. 5; Walter Eichrodt, *Theology of the Old Testament*, trans. J. A. Baker, The Old Testament Library, 2 vols. (Philadelphia: Westminster Press; 1961, 1967), 1:220-27; Gerhard von Rad, *Old Testament Theology: The Theology of Israel's Historical Traditions*, trans. D. M. G. Stalker (New York: Harper & Row, 1962), 1:210-12.

[3]Wright, *New Testament and the People of God*, pp. 248-52.

[4]Ibid., pp. 251-52.

[5]Ibid., pp. 261-62, and the references Wright lists.

[6]For a helpful presentation of this vantage point, see J. Julius Scott Jr., *Customs and Controversies: Intertestamental Jewish Backgrounds of the New Testament* (Grand Rapids, Mich.: Baker, 1995), esp. part 2.

[7]This is an advancement beyond earlier attempts to connect Hebrews in some way with the DSS, which I highlight here. In 1958, Yigael Yadin provided the first serious treatment of Hebrews and Qumran, which constituted a counter-argument to the previous theory of Philonic influence on the epistle that theretofore dominated scholarship. Yadin's hypothesis of a fourfold point of contact between the DSS and Hebrews has served as the framework for a comparative study between the two writings thereafter. I summarize his arguments here.

1. The Qumran sect assigned a superior status to angels, which Hebrews combats in Hebrews 1—2.

2. The sect held to a belief in two Messiahs, one priestly and one lay, which forms the backdrop of Hebrews' portrayal of Jesus as combining both offices in one person.

3. Hebrews 1:1, which juxtaposes the revelation of Jesus with that of the Prophets, is directed against the belief that in the eschatological era a prophet should appear—a prophet who is not to be identified with the Messiah himself. This figure is the Mosaic prophet of Deuteronomy 18:15-19, which accounts for much of the concentration on Moses in Hebrews.

4. The high degree of Pentateuchal quotations in Hebrews is the result of the sect's concentration on its wilderness calling and identity (Yigael Yadin, "The Dead Sea Scrolls and the Epistle to the Hebrews," *Scripta Hierosolymitana* IV [1958], pp. 36-53).

L. D. Hurst calls attention to other possible points of contact between the DSS and Hebrews: Qumran ritual baths and Hebrews 6:2; 9:10; 10:22; Qumran ritual meals and Hebrews 13:10; Qumran dualism and Hebrews; the focus on the wilderness period in both materials; the heavenly temple and sacrifice in both; the New Covenant; and Qumran discipline and the severity of

Hebrews' warnings (L. D. Hurst, *The Epistle to the Hebrews: Its Background of Thought*, SNTSMS 65 [Cambridge: Cambridge University Press, 1990], pp. 154-55). For his discussion as a whole, see pp. 43-85. Hurst's conclusion, which is that there is no real contact in thought between Hebrews and the DSS, seems to be hypercritical. The sheer volume of probable connections between the two materials is a formidable obstacle to explain away.

Perhaps the most intriguing comparison between the DSS and Hebrews is that of Melchizedek, regarding which there are at least four similarities between the two writings.

1. The Melchizedek of 11QMelch and Jesus in Hebrews 7 are both in some sense "heavenly" figures.

2. Both are "eschatological" figures.

3. Both achieve the salvation of the elect, possibly through the Day of Atonement.

4. Both wage a (final) conflict with the devil (Heb 1:13; 2:14-15; 10:12-13).

For this, see Hurst, *Epistle to the Hebrews*, p. 59. The two most thorough treatments of the traditions of Melchizedek, including the DSS and Hebrews, are those by Fred L. Horton Jr., *The Melchizedek Tradition*, SNTSMS 30 (Cambridge: Cambridge University Press, 1976); and Paul Kobelski, *Melchizedek and Melchirĕsa*, CBQMS 10 (Washington, D.C.: Catholic Biblical Association, 1981). The commentaries on Hebrews 5:5-10; 6:13—7:28 are also helpful in this regard, especially the comments by Philip E. Hughes, *A Commentary on the Epistle to the Hebrews* (Grand Rapids, Mich.: Eerdmans, 1977); Harold W. Attridge, *The Epistle to the Hebrews*, Hermeneia (Philadelphia: Fortress, 1989); William L. Lane, *Hebrews 1—8*, vol. 47a, WBC (Dallas, Tex.: Word, 1991); Paul Ellingworth, *The Epistle to the Hebrews: A Commentary on the Greek Text*, NIGTC (Grand Rapids, Mich.: Eerdmans, 1993). For other authors seeing a connection between the DSS and Hebrews consult Hans Kosmala, *Hebräer-Essener-Christen* (Leiden: E. J. Brill, 1971); R. E. Brown, "The Messianism of Qumran," *CBQ* 19 (1957): 53-82; G. W. Buchanan, "The Present State of Scholarship on Hebrews," in *Christianity, Judaism and other Greco-Roman Cults: Festschrift for Morton Smith*, ed. J. Neusner (Leiden: E. J. Brill, 1975), 1:299-330; B. Gärtner, "The Habakkuk Commentary (DSH) and the Gospel of Matthew," *ST* 8 (1955): 1-24; C. Spicq, "L'Epître aux Hébreux, Apollos, Jean-Baptiste, les Hellénistes et Qumran," *RevQ* 1 (1959): 365-90; Hughes, *Commentary on the Epistle to the Hebrews*, whose work sees the Essenes as the chief opponents of Hebrews.

[8]*Sirach* dates to c. 180 B.C., being reworked by his grandson in c. 130 B.C.

[9]The translations of the apocrypha and pseudepigrapha here and elsewhere in this work, unless otherwise specified, are from James H. Charlesworth, ed., *The Old Testament Pseudepigrapha*, 2 vols. (New York: Doubleday, 1983, 1985).

[10]See C. Marvin Pate, *The Reverse of the Curse: Paul, Wisdom and the Law* (forthcoming), chap. 4. For a groundbreaking study of law and wisdom in early Judaism and in Paul, see Eckhard J. Schnabel, *Law and Wisdom from Ben Sira to*

Paul, WUNT 2.16 (Tübingen: J. C. B. Mohr [Paul Siebeck], 1985).

[11]1QS 11:7-9 contains several ideas that have relevance for understanding Hebrews, especially the following: (1) the Qumran community is here portrayed as God's inheritor of wisdom (cf. Heb 1:1-4); (2) the covenanters perceive themselves as both united with angels in heavenly worship (cf. Heb 1:5—2:9) and (3) as the true habitation or temple of God (cf. Heb 3:1—4:13; 8:1-13). See the discussion below, along with the remarks by Attridge, *Epistle to the Hebrews,* p. 40. Recall also the earlier remarks on Melchizedek in chapter four.

[12]It is significant that Psalm 110:4 associates the Lord's anointed with the eternal priesthood of Melchizedek, a topic that is vital to both Qumran and Hebrews. See the discussion below, as well as Lane, *Hebrews 1—8,* p. 16.

[13]Hughes, *Commentary on the Epistle to the Hebrews,* p. 49, citing D. W. B. Robinson, "The Literary Structure of Hebrews 1:1-4," *The Australian Journal of Biblical Archaeology* 2 (1972): 178ff. The chart is my combination of the two.

[14]To my knowledge, this observation on Hebrews 1:1-4 has not been made by commentators.

[15]Early Jewish-Christian traditions believed that God gave the law to Moses via angels (e.g., *Jub.* 1:29; Josephus *Ant.* 15.5.3 [136]; Acts 7:38-39; Gal 3:19). A helpful discussion of this association is found in Lane, *Hebrews 1—8,* p. 17. The logical connection between Hebrews 1:1-2 and the prophets and Hebrews 1:4 and the angels is Moses, who is both the lawgiver and the greatest of the prophets (cf. Deut 18:15-22). In a sense, then, Moses was considered by some as the beginning (law) and end (prophets) of divine revelation.

[16]For a detailed analysis of the theme of Christ and the wisdom of God, refer to C. Marvin Pate, *The Glory of Adam and the Afflictions of the Righteous: Pauline Suffering in Context* (New York: Edwin Mellen, 1993), chap. 6, especially the treatment of Colossians 1:15-20 therein.

[17]Although angels are not specifically mentioned in Exodus 19—20 and Deuteronomy 33:2 with regard to the giving of the law, the phrase "myriad of holy ones" was interpreted as angels in the LXX of Psalm 68:17.

[18]Recall here the treatment of the Angelic Liturgy in chapter seven. Related to the exaltation of the angels is the DSS elevation of the covenanters themselves. Such a status of the sectaries may have been viewed by them as consisting of the earthly counterpart to the heavenly throng when the Essenes gathered for worship, or perhaps they believed themselves to be mystically raptured to heaven during worship (see, e.g., 1QH 3:20-22; 11:10-12; 1QSb 4:24-26). See chapter nine.

[19]Hughes, *Commentary on the Epistle to the Hebrews,* p. 77.

[20]For the significance of Adam Christology in general, see C. K. Barrett, *From First Adam to Last* (Edinburgh: Black, 1962); Robin Scroggs, *The Last Adam: A Study in Pauline Anthropology* (Oxford: Blackwell, 1966); Pate, *Glory of Adam*; James D. G. Dunn, *Christology in the Making: A New Testament Inquiry into the Origin of the Doctrine of the Incarnation* (Philadelphia: Westminster Press, 1980), pp. 114-21, esp. p. 117 on Hebrews 2:5-18.

[21]I have developed this proposal with regard to the Pauline passages referenced in *Glory of Adam*. Here I argue that the same concept applies to Hebrews 2:5-18 which, as far as I know, has not been suggested by other interpreters of this text. I first applied this twofold motif to 2 Corinthians 4:7—5:21 in C. Marvin Pate, *Adam Christology as the Exegetical and Theological Substructure of 2 Corinthians 4:7—5:21* (Lanham, Md.: University Press of America, 1991). There are at least two similarities between the *T. Levi* 18:2-14 and Hebrews 2:5-18: both portray the Messiah as a *priest* who *restores* Adam's lost dominion and glory. For the last point, see Pate, *Glory of Adam*, pp. 126-27.

[22]Pate, *Adam Christology*, chap. 2; *Glory of Adam*, pp. 69-71. These texts speak of the community of the DSS as being the true inheritor of the glory of Adam.

[23]In Hebrews 2:9-10, the apocalyptic concept of righteous suffering leading to glory (v. 9) is basically restated with the words "suffering leading to perfection" (v. 10). That the term *perfection* in Hebrews is eschatological in import has been shown to be the case by M. Silva, "Perfection and Eschatology in Hebrews," *WTJ* (1976): 60-71. For a detailed look at the apocalyptic background of suffering and Pauline theology, see Pate, *Glory of Adam*.

[24]Note the comments by Attridge, *Epistle to the Hebrews*, p. 126 n. 51.

[25]Ibid., p. 126 n. 52.

[26]The other two were monotheism and land. See Scott, *Customs and Controversies*, pp. 265-66.

[27]Susanne Lehne, *The New Covenant in Hebrews*, Journal for the Study of the New Testament Supplement Series 44 (Sheffield, U.K.: Sheffield Academic Press, 1990), pp. 47-48, cf. chap. 3.

[28]Ibid., p. 50. Lehne adds the point on page 51 that the DSS people perceived their reception of divine revelation to be qualitatively different from the old covenant, as well.

[29]As mentioned before, early Judaism, including the DSS, understood that the Mosaic law was the stipulation or requirement to be kept in order to maintain the covenant (1QS 8:8-27; 1QpHab 2:1-10). This positive view of the law in the DSS is no grounds for a conscious legalism, however, for the Qumran covenanters believed that the divine choice of them as the elect remnant was rooted in grace (1QH 10:5-7; cf. 1QS 11:7-9) as was their faithfulness to the law (1QH 6:34-37). More than that, the very knowledge of the law itself was God's gift to the Qumran sectaries (1QH 11:5-8). This idea that divine election is by grace and obedience to the law is for the purpose of maintaining, not entering, the covenant is called by E. P. Sanders "covenantal nomism."

> The pattern [of the religion of Judaism] is based on election and atonement for transgressions, it being understood that God gave commandments in connection with the election and that obedience to them, or atonement and repentance for transgression, was expected as the condition for remaining in the covenant community. The best title for this sort of religion is "covenantal nomism" . . . the covenant by God's grace and Torah obedience as man's proper response within the covenant. (*Paul and Palestinian Judaism*, pp. 236, 240)

   Be that as it may, however, the author of Hebrews would not have entertained the possibility that the Mosaic law is to be heeded to preserve the New
Covenant. According to Hebrews 7:11—8:13, the old covenant, the Mosaic
law and the Aaronic priesthood are all inferior and are passing away. In their
place is Christ, the New Covenant, received by faith. In this conviction
Hebrews resonates with Paul, as we saw in chapter six.

[30]Recall the earlier use of Kobelski's comparisons of Hebrews 7 and
Melchizedek (Kobelski, *Melchizedek and Mechiresa*).

[31]Lehne, *New Covenant in Hebrews*, p. 50.

[32]Wright, *New Testament and the People of God*, p. 410.

[33]Ibid., p. 218 n. 10. It should be noted that Wright makes a passing reference to
CD 2—6 as being one of a number of Jewish texts providing a summary of
Israel's history.

Chapter 9: Exile & Eschatology

[1]Rudolf Bultmann championed the theory that Gnosticism, especially as seen
in the *Odes of Solomon* and the Mandean writings, was the key background to
the prologue in particular and the Gospel in general. See J. Ashton, *The Interpretation of John* (Philadelphia: Fortress, 1986), pp. 18-35. See also Bultmann,
The Gospel of John: A Commentary (Philadelphia: Westminster Press, 1971), pp.
17-18; and "γινώσκω κτλ.," in *TDNT* 1:689-719, esp. pp. 708-13. For an older
commentary that understands the fourth Gospel from this perspective, see W.
Bauer, *Das Johannesevangelium*, HNT 6 (Tübingen: Mohr [Paul Siebeck], 3rd
ed., 1933). Bultmann (e.g., *Primitive Christianity in Its Contemporary Setting*
[New York: Meridian, 1955], p. 162) never doubted that Gnosticism was a
pre-Christian movement and a significant contributor to Christian theology.
Another alternative to the supposed Gnostic background of the Gospel of
John was proposed by C. H. Dodd, namely, the *Corpus Hermeticum*. See his
Interpretation of the Fourth Gospel (Cambridge: Cambridge University Press,
1953), pp. 34-35, 50-51. Two Hermetic trac-tates are among the writings of
Nag Hammadi (cf. *The Discourse on the Eighth and Ninth* [NHC 6:61] and *Ascl-
epius* 21-29 [NHC 6:8]). For penetrating critiques of these two theories, see
Craig A. Evans, *Word and Glory: On the Exegetical and Theological Background of
John's Prologue*, Journal for the Study of the New Testament Supplement
Series 89 (Sheffield, U.K.: JSOT Press, 1993), chap. 2. Closer to Jewish soil,
other scholars have posited Philonic influence on John, especially the pro-
logue; A. F. Segal, *Two Powers in Heaven: Early Rabbinic Reports about Christianity and Gnosticism*, SJLA 25 (Leiden: E. J. Brill, 1977), pp. 159-81; L. Hurtado,
One God, One Lord: Early Christian Devotion and Ancient Jewish Monotheism
(Philadelphia: Fortress, 1988), pp. 44-50. For a sketch of the Hellenistic ante-
cedents to Philo's *logos*, see H. Kleinknecht, "λέγω," TDNT 4:77-91; R. L. Dun-
can, "The Logos: From Sophocles to the Gospel of John," *Christian Scholar's
Review* 9 (1979): 121-30. See also T. H. Tobin, "The Prologue of John and Hellenistic Jewish Speculation," *CBQ* 152 (1990): 252-64. But see again Evans, who

concludes from his study of Philo and the Johannine prologue, rightly we believe, that the influence of the former on the latter is indirect, not direct (Evans, *Word and Glory*, pp. 100-113). The bibliography in this endnote comes from Evans, *Word and Glory*, pp. 13, 72, 100-101.

[2]The two usually go in hand in the scholarly literature, the one, the DSS, confirming the other, the Palestinian background. This is not to say, however, that the Gospel of John was composed on Jewish soil like the DSS were. Rather it is to make the point that the evangelist (who probably earlier lived in Palestine but moved outside it [to Ephesus?]), shared the same Jewish milieu as did the DSS. Those seeing this background as the formative influence on the Johannine corpus include J. H. Charlesworth, "A Critical Comparison of the Dualism in 1QS 3.13-4.26 and the 'Dualism' contained in the Gospel of John," *NTS* 15 (1969): 389-418; J. Becker, "Beobachtungen zum Dualismus im Johannesevangelium," *ZNW* 65 (1974): 71-87. For a broader study on Johannine dualism, see O. Böcher, *Der johanneische Dualismus im Zusammenhang des nachbiblischen Judentums* (Gütersloh: Gerd Mohn, 1965). See also W. F. Albright, "Recent Discoveries in Palestine and the Gospel of John," in *The Background of the New Testament and its Eschatology*, eds. W. D. Davies and D. Daube (Cambridge: Cambridge University Press, 1964), pp. 153-71; W. H. Brownlee, "Whence the Gospel According to John?" in *John and the Dead Sea Scrolls*, ed. James H. Charlesworth, (New York: Crossroad, 1990), pp. 166-94, esp. pp. 179-85; G. Quispel, "Qumran, John and Jewish Christianity," in *John and the Dead Sea Scrolls*, ed. Charlesworth, pp. 137-55; J. A. T. Robinson, "The New Look on the Fourth Gospel," in *Studia Evangelica: Papers Presented to the International Congress on The Four Gospels*, ed. K. Aland et al., TU 73 (Berlin: Akademie Verlag, 1959), pp. 338-50; K. Schubert, *The Dead Sea Community: Its Origin and Teachings* (London: A & C Black, 1959), pp. 151-54. This bibliography is indebted to Evans, *Word and Glory*, pp. 146-47, 148-49.

[3]D. S. Russell, *The Method and Message of Jewish Apocalyptic* (Philadelphia: Westminster Press, 1964), pp. 37-39, provides a convenient list of Jewish apocalyptic literature dating from this time period: *Daniel* (165 B.C., though one may wish to contest this date); *1 Enoch* (c. 164 B.C.); *Jubilees* (c. 150 B.C.); *Sibylline Oracles*, book 3 (from c. 150 B.C. onwards); *Testaments of the Twelve Patriarchs* (latter part of second century B.C.); *Psalms of Solomon* (c. 48 B.C.); *Assumption of Moses* (A.D. 6-30); *Martyrdom of Isaiah*; *Life of Adam and Eve* or *Apocalypse of Moses* (shortly before A.D. 70); *Apocalypse of Abraham* (c. A.D. 70-100); *Testament of Abraham* (first century A.D.); *2 Enoch* or *Book of the Secrets of Enoch* (first century A.D.); *Sibylline Oracles* book 4 (c. A.D. 80); *2 Esdras* or *4 Ezra* 3—14 (c. A.D. 90); *2 Apocalypse of Baruch* (after A.D. 90); *3 Apocalypse of Baruch* (second century A.D.); *Sibylline Oracles* book 5 (second century A.D.). Russell rightly also includes in this genre materials from the Dead Sea Scrolls discovered at Qumran (dating between 150 B.C. and A.D. 70): commentaries on Isaiah, Hosea, Micah, Nahum, Habakkuk, Zephaniah and Ps 37; the Zadokite Document; the Manual of Discipline; the Rule of the Congregation; a Scroll of Benedic-

tions; the Testimonies Scroll (or a messianic anthology); Hymns of Thanksgiving; the War of the Sons of Light Against the Sons of Darkness; the Book of Mysteries; a Midrash on the Last Days; a Description of the New Jerusalem; an Angelic Liturgy; the Prayer of Nabonidus; a Pseudo-Daniel Apocalypse; and the Genesis Apocryphon.

[4]Gordon Fee, *1 and 2 Timothy and Titus* (Peabody, Mass.: Hendrickson, 1988), p. 19.

[5]Lawrence H. Schiffman, *Reclaiming the Dead Sea Scrolls: Their True Meaning for Judaism and Christianity,* Anchor Bible Reference Library (New York: Doubleday, 1995), p. 322.

[6]These similarities are taken from the authors' references discussed in Evans, *Word and Glory,* pp. 146-47, 148-49, and elaborated in n. 2 above.

[7]As was mentioned in p. 253 n. 68, the technical term for the messianic woes refers to the time of great sorrow and tribulation to come upon God's people immediately prior to the coming of the Messiah. The concept is adumbrated in the OT in association with the Day of Yahweh (see, for example, Is 24:17-23; Dan 12:1; Joel 2:1-11, 28-32; Amos 5: 16-20; Zeph 1:14—2:3) and developed in Jewish apocalypticism (4 *Ezra* 7:37f.; *Jub.* 23:11; 24:3; 2 *Apoc. Bar.* 55:6; *1 Enoch* 80:4- 5). However, the term itself does not occur until the writing of the Talmud (e.g., *b. Shab.* 118a; *b. Pes.* 118a). Dale C. Allison has proved that the Gospel authors and Paul believed Jesus' death was part of the messianic woes (Dale C. Allison, *The End of the Ages Has Come: An Early Interpretation of the Passion and Resurrection of Jesus* [Philadelphia: Fortress, 1985], chaps. 3-5, 8).

    In this chapter I am following Vermes's numbering of the *Hôdāyôt,* as do the commentaries I draw upon. I still follow García Martínez's translation, however; he includes the newer and older numbering system (with the older in parentheses) in his text. Thus 1QH 3 is to be found under 1QH 11 in García Martínez.

[8]Allison, *End of the Ages,* p. 58.

[9]Ibid., p. 10.

[10]Matthew Black, *The Scrolls and Christian Origins: Studies in the Jewish Background of the New Testament* (New York: Charles Scribner's Sons, 1961), p. 150.

[11]Allison, *End of the Ages,* p. 10.

[12]Recall N. T. Wright, *Jesus and the Victory of God* (Minneapolis: Fortress, 1996), pp. 577-91.

[13]If the latter case is the reality, then the words of exaltation will have been placed on the lips of the Teacher of Righteousness by the Qumran community.

[14]Two scholars can be credited for alerting interpreters to the presence of inaugurated eschatology in the DSS: Heinz-Wolfgang Kuhn and David E. Aune. I provide here an overview of their respective contributions to the subject. Heinz-Wolfgang Kuhn, *Enderwartung und gegenwärtiges Heil: Untersuchungen zu den Gemeindeliedern von Qumran,* Studien zur Umwelt des Neuen Testaments 4 (Göttingen: Vandenhoeck & Ruprecht, 1966), seems to have been the first scholar to demonstrate that inaugurated eschatology is present in the

teachings of the DSS. His thesis is that, in addition to the customary future expectations characteristic of Jewish apocalypticism, the Qumran community was also conscious that eschatological salvation had already entered the present age in its history and experience (p. 11). Kuhn does so by examining 1QH 3:19-36; 11:3-14; 11:15ff.; 15. On the basis of 1QH 11:3-14; 3:19-36, Kuhn enumerates five eschatological acts which are thought to be actualized in the present age by the Qumran covenanters: (1) resurrection (1QH 11:12); (2) new creation (1QH 3:2; 11:13); (3) communion with angels (1QH 3:21-23; 11:13ff.); (4) deliverance from the final power of the realm of death (1QH 3:19); (5) proleptic eschatological transference to heaven (1QH 3:20; see Kuhn, *Enderwartung und gegenwärtiges Heil*, pp. 44-112). In a more general way, 1QH 11:15ff. depicts eschatological salvation as consisting of joy (cf. 1QH 3:23) and forgiveness of sins (cf. 1QH 3:21), both of which are perceived by the Qumran sectaries as present realities. Moreover, 1QH 15 portrays eschatological peace and the end of sorrow as having dawned in the Qumran community (1QH 15:15-17; see Kuhn, *Enderwartung und gegenwärtiges Heil*, p. 15). Added to the preceding, Kuhn also demonstrates that Qumran understood that the eschatological gifts of the Spirit (pp. 117-39)—knowledge and wisdom (pp. 139-75)—were also present possessions realized in its midst.

The second scholar who argues for the presence of realized eschatology in the DSS is David E. Aune, *The Cultic Setting of Realized Eschatology in Early Christianity*, Supp. NovT 28 (Leiden: E. J. Brill, 1972), pp. 37-44, whose thesis is that realized eschatology was thought by the Qumran community to be actualized in its cultic setting. This is especially clear when one realizes that the DSS portray worship as an end-time experience that recaptures paradise, particularly the restoration of Adam's lost glory (pp. 37-40). Furthermore, Aune demonstrates that the five eschatological acts Kuhn showed to be operative in 1QH are connected with the paradise motif: resurrection recovers the life Adam forfeited through disobedience and his subsequent death; communion with the angels reflects the restoration of Adam's lost heavenly status; the new creation recaptures Edenic conditions, which is realized in worship and the transference of the devotee to heaven (pp. 41-42). For Aune, it is the concept of the overlapping of the two ages that informs the combination of realized and futurist eschatologies in the DSS. Although this age is the time of the messianic woes, the Qumran members are delivered from it in their communal worship (pp. 42-44).

[15]Principally based on John 9:22, 34; 12:42; 16:2, texts which speak of being expelled from the synagogue, Recent Johannine scholarship has developed the theory that the setting of the Gospel of John was the aftermath of the expulsion of Jewish Christians from the synagogues. The method for doing so was to craft the Twelfth Benediction (one of the eighteen recited in the synagogue), which read: "Let the Nazarenes and the minim be destroyed in a moment, and let them be blotted out of the Book of Life."

[16]The quote comes from Evans, *Word and Glory*, p. 178.

[17]Ibid., pp. 178-80.

[18]Ibid., pp. 180-81.

[19]While I contend that John is, as tradition has it, the apostle of said name, such a position is not vital to the overall concern of this chapter.

[20]Wright discusses the interplay between the messianic woes and the Deuteronomic curses of Israel's exile, though he does not relate this dynamic to the Gospel of John, as we are attempting to do here. See his *Jesus and the Victory of God*, pp. 576-79; compare his *The New Testament and the People of God* (Minneapolis: Fortress, 1992), pp. 277f.

[21]Allison, *End of the Ages*, p. 57. For a discussion of the pervasiveness of realized eschatology in John, see C. K. Barrett, *The Gospel According to John*, 2nd ed. (Philadelphia: Westminster Press, 1972), p. 58, who follows the lead of C. H. Dodd, *The Apostolic Preaching and Its Developments* (New York: Harper, 1944), pp. 38-45.

[22]Allison, *End of the Ages*, p. 58.

[23]See the comments by Barnabas Lindars, *John* (Sheffield, U.K.: JSOT Press, 1990), pp. 81-82.

[24]I have interpreted the suffering-glory paradox apocalyptically elsewhere (C. Marvin Pate, *The Glory of Adam and the Afflictions of the Righteous: Pauline Suffering in Context* [New York: Edwin Mellen, 1993]).

[25]Recall the discussion in chapter four concerning the Son of Man. For a more thorough treatment of this and related topics, see C. Marvin Pate and Douglas Kennard, *The New Testament and the Messianic Woes* (forthcoming). Our working hypothesis in that study is that Christ endured the messianic woes on the cross so that the church will not have to undergo such affliction.

[26]Kovacs, "'Now Shall the Ruler of This World Be Driven Out': Jesus' Death as Cosmic Battle in John 12:2-26," *JBL* 114 [1995]: 228-35. The two other passages factoring into the discussion are Jn 14:30-31 and Jn 16:8-11. This perspective, as Evans argues, helped to deflect criticisms of early Christianity that it was insurrectionist in orientation, for, as John shows, the real enemy of Israel was not Rome but Satan (Evans, *Word and Glory*, pp. 178-79; cf. Wright, *Jesus and the Victory of God*, pp. 451-67).

[27]Wright, *Jesus and the Victory of God*, pp. 588-91.

[28]Ibid., p. 591.

[29]This section is a summation of Pate, *The Reverse of the Curse* (forthcoming), chap. 4.

[30]James D. G. Dunn: "Let John Be John: A Gospel for Its Time," in *Das Evangelium und die Evangelien*, ed. Peter Stuhlmacher, WUNT 28 (Tübingen: Mohr, 1983), pp. 309-39; p. 333; Martin Scott, *Sophia and the Johannine Jesus*, Journal for the Study of the New Testament Supplement Series 71 (Sheffield, U.K.: JSOT Press, 1992), pp. 88-170; see also Lindars, *John*, pp. 54-58; Evans, *Word and Glory*, 94-99.

[31]Evans provides numerous other contacts between the wisdom tradition and the Johannine prologue in his *Word and Glory*, pp. 84-92. The ones we identify

here are some of the more crucial comparisons. For a general discussion of the sapiential influence on John's prologue, the "I Am" sayings, the descending-ascending revealer motif and other matters, see Martin, *Sophia and the Johannine Jesus*, pp. 94-170.

[32]Pate, *Reverse of the Curse*, chaps. 1—4.

[33]Scott, *Sophia and the Johannine Jesus*, pp. 116-30.

[34]Ibid., pp. 94-170.

[35]Dunn, "Let John Be John," p. 333. This background sheds new light on the nature of "life" promised in John to followers of Jesus. It is the life of the covenant which the law was unable to provide but which is now possible through Christ. The key passages in this regard, as Evans shows, are Jn 3:15-16, 36; 5:39; 6:47, 51-52; 8:51-52; 10:28; 11:24-26 (Evans, *Word and Glory*, p. 151).

[36]James D. G. Dunn, *The Parting of the Ways: Between Christianity and Judaism and Their Significance for the Character of Christianity* (Philadelphia: Trinity International Press, 1991), p. 227.

Conclusion: The Real Story Behind the Story of Israel

[1]C. Marvin Pate and Calvin B. Haines Jr., *Doomsday Delusions: What's Wrong with Predictions About the End of the World* (Downers Grove, Ill.: InterVarsity Press, 1995), chap. 5.

[2]The next two pages come from ibid., pp. 115-17.

[3]Leon Festinger, *A Theory of Cognitive Dissonance* (Stanford, Calif.: Stanford University Press, 1957), pp. 1-3; cf. Leon Festinger, Henry W. Riecken and Stanley Schachter, *When Prophecy Fails* (Minneapolis: University of Minnesota Press, 1956). I should mention here that in a phone conversation Dr. Michael Douglas first called my attention to the possibility that cognitive dissonance is operative in the DSS. Moreover, I see now that Michael O. Wise explores that phenomenon relative to the Scrolls in his *The First Messiah: Investigating the Savior Before the Christ* (San Francisco: HarperCollins, 1999).

[4]Festinger et al., *When Prophecy Fails*, p. 3.

[5]Ibid., p. 4.

[6]Ibid.

[7]See Pate and Haines, *Doomsday Delusions*, pp. 93-94.

[8]Ibid., pp. 120-21.

[9]Ibid., p. 129.

Selected Bibliography

Aalen, S. "'Reign and House' in the Kingdom of God in the Gospels." *NTS* 8 (1961-1962): 215-40.

Allison, Dale C., Jr. *The End of the Ages Has Come: An Early Interpretation of the Passion and Resurrection of Jesus.* Philadelphia: Fortress, 1985.

———. *The New Moses: A Matthean Typology.* Minneapolis: Fortress, 1993.

Arrington, French L. *Paul's Aeon Theology in 1 Corinthians.* Washington, D.C.: University Press of America, 1977.

Barrera, J. Trebolle, and L. Vegas Montaner, eds. *The Madrid Qumran Congress: Proceedings of the International Congress on the Dead Sea Scrolls, Madrid, 18-21 March 1991.* Leiden: Brill, 1991.

Baumgarten, J. M. "The Pharisaic-Sadducean Controversies about Purity and the Qumran Texts." *JJS* 31 (1980): 157-70.

Beall, Todd. *Josephus' Description of the Essenes Illustrated by the Dead Sea Scrolls.* SNTSMS 58. Cambridge: Cambridge University Press, 1988.

Beasley-Murray, G. R. "The Interpretation of Daniel 7." *CBQ* 45 (1983): 44-58.

Beckwith, Roger. *The Old Testament Canon of the New Testament Church and Its Background in Early Judaism.* Grand Rapids, Mich.: Eerdmans, 1985.

Brooke, George J. *Exegesis at Qumran: 4 Florilegium in Its Jewish Context.* Journal for the Study of the Old Testament Supplement Series 29. Sheffield, U.K.: JSOT Press, 1985.

Brownlee, W. H. "Biblical Interpretation among the Sectaries of the Dead Sea Scrolls." *BA* 14 (1951): 54-76.

———. *The Midrash Pesher of Habakkuk.* SBLMS 24. Missoula, Mont.: Scholars Press, 1979.

Bruce, F. F. *Biblical Exegesis in the Qumran Texts.* Grand Rapids, Mich.: Eerdmans, 1959.

———. "Paul and the Law of Moses." BJRL 57 (1975): 259-79.

Burrows, Millar. *The Dead Sea Scrolls.* New York: Viking, 1955.

Charlesworth, James H., ed. *The Old Testament Pseudepigraph.* 2 vols. New York: Doubleday, 1983; London: Darton, Longman and Todd, 1985.

Collins, John J. *The Apocalyptic Vision of the Book of Daniel.* Harvard Semitic Monographs 16. Missoula, Mont.: Scholars Press, 1977.

———. *Daniel.* Hermeneia. Minneapolis: Fortress, 1993.

———. *The Star and the Scepter: The Messiah of the DSS and Other Ancient Literature.* New York: Doubleday, 1995.

Cranfield, C. E. B. *The Epistle to the Romans.* 2 vols. ICC. Edinburgh: T & T Clark, 1975, 1979.

Cross, Frank Moore. "The Development of the Jewish Scripts." *The Bible and the Ancient Near East: Essays in Honor of William Foxwell Albright.* Edited by G. E. Wright. Garden City, N.Y.: Doubleday, 1961.

———. "The Early History of the Qumran Community." *New Directions in Biblical Archaeology.* Edited by D. N. Freedman and J. C. Greenfield. Garden City, N.Y.: Doubleday, 1969.

Davies, Glenn N. *Faith and Obedience in Romans: A Study of Romans 1-4.* Sheffield: JSOT, 1990.

Dupont-Sommer, A. *The Dead Sea Scrolls: A Preliminary Survey.* Oxford: Basil Blackwell, 1952.

Eiseman, Robert E. *James, the Brother of Jesus: The Key to Unlocking the Secrets of Early Christianity and the Dead Sea Scrolls.* New York: Viking, 1997.

———. *James the Just in the Habakkuk Pesher.* Leiden: E. J. Brill, 1985.

Eisenman, Robert, and Michael Wise. *The Dead Sea Scrolls Uncovered.* New York: Penguin, 1993.

Ferch, A. J. *The Son of Man in Daniel 7.* Berrien Springs, Mich.: Andrews University Press, 1979.

Fitzmyer, Joseph A. *The Dead Sea Scrolls: Major Publications and Tools for Study.* Sources for Biblical Study 20. Rev. ed. Atlanta: Scholars Press, 1990.

———. *Essays on the Semitic Background of the New Testament.* Sources for Biblical Study 5. SBL. Missoula, Mont.: Scholars Press, 1974.

———. "Habakkuk 2: 3-4 and the New Testament." In *To Advance the Gospel: New Testament Studies.* New York: Crossroads, 1981.

———. "The Qumran Scrolls and the New Testament after Forty Years." *Revue de Qumran* 13 (1988): 609-20.

———. *Responses to 101 Questions on the Dead Sea Scrolls.* New York: Paulist, 1992.

Fujita, Neil S. *A Crack in the Jar: What Ancient Jewish Documents Tell Us About the New Testament.* New York: Paulist, 1986.

García Martínez, Florentino. *The Dead Sea Scrolls Translated: The Qumran Texts in English.* Leiden: E. J. Brill, 1994.

———. "The Eschatological Figure of 4Q 246." In *Qumran and Apocalyptic Studies on the Aramaic Texts from Qumran.* Leiden: E. J. Brill, 1992.

———. "Qumran Origins and Early History: A Gröningen Hypothesis." *FO* 25 (1988): 113-36.

Gärtner, Bert L. "The Habakkuk Commentary (DSH) and the Gospel of Matthew." *ST* 8 (1955): 1-24.

———. *The Temple and the Community in Qumran and the New Testament.* SNTSMS 1. Cambridge: Cambridge University Press, 1965.

Gundry, Robert H. *Mark: A Commentary on His Apology for the Cross.* Grand Rapids, Mich.: Eerdmans, 1993.

Hartman, L. F., and A. A. DiLella. *The Book of Daniel.* AB 23. Garden City, N.Y.: Doubleday, 1978.

Hay, David M. *Glory at the Right Hand: Psalm 110 in Early Christianity.* SBL Monograph Series 18. Nashville: Abingdon, 1973.

Hayes, Richard B. *Echoes of Scripture in the Letters of Paul.* New Haven, Conn.: Yale University Press, 1989.

Jaubert, Annie. *La notion d'alliance dans le judaïsme aux abords de l'ère chrétienne.*

Patristica Sorbonesia 6. Paris: Éditions du Seuil, 1963.

Juel, Donald. *Messianic Exegesis: Christological Interpretation of the Old Testament in Early Christianity.* Philadelphia: Fortress, 1988.

Klausner, Joseph. *The Messianic Idea in Israel from Its Beginning to the Completion of the Mishnah.* Translated by W. F. Stinespring. 3rd ed. New York: Macmillan, 1955; London: Allen & Unwin, 1956.

Klinzing, Georg. *Die Umdeutung des Kultus im der Qumrangemeinde und im Neuen Testament.* SUNT 7. Göttingen: Vandenhoeck & Ruprecht, 1971.

Knibb, M. A. "The Exile in the Literature of the Intertestamental Period." *Hay J* 17 (1976): 253-72.

————. *The Qumran Community: Cambridge Commentaries on Writings of the Jewish and Christian World—200 B.C. to A.D. 200.* Cambridge: Cambridge University Press, 1987.

Knowles, Michael. *Jeremiah in Matthew's Gospel: The Rejected Prophet Motif in Matthean Redaction.* Journal for the Study of the New Testament Supplement Series 68. Sheffield, U.K.: Sheffield Academic Press, 1993.

Kobelski, Paul. *Melchizedek and Mechirēsa.* CBQMS 10. Washington, D.C.: Catholic Biblical Association of America, 1981.

Kuhn, Heinz-Wolfang. *Enderwartung und gegenwärtiges Heil: Untersuchungen zu den Gemeindeliedern von Qumran.* Studien zur Umwelt des Neuen Testament 4. Göttingen: Vandenhoeck & Ruprecht, 1966.

Laansma, Jon. *I Will Give You Rest: The Rest Motif in the New Testament with Special Reference to Matthew 11 and Hebrews 3—4.* WUNT 2/98. Tübingen: Mohr/Siebeck, 1997.

Leivestad, R. "Exit the Apocalyptic Son of Man." *NTS* 18 (1971-1972): 243-67.

Liebreich, Leon J. "The Impact of Nehemiah 9: 5-37 on the Liturgy of the Synagogue." Hebrew Union College Annal 32 (1961): 227-37.

Locoque, A. *The Book of Daniel.* Atlanta: Knox Press, 1979.

Longman, Tremper, III, and Daniel G. Reid. *God Is a Warrior.* Grand Rapids, Mich.: Zondervan, 1995.

Mettinger, T. N. D. *King and Messiah: The Civil and Sacral Legitimation of the Israelite Kings.* Lund: Gleerup, 1976.

Moessner, David P. *Lord of the Banquet: The Literary and Theological Significance of The Lucan Travel Narrative.* Minneapolis: Fortress, 1989; reprint, Philadelphia: Trinity International Press, 1998.

Moore, Carey A. "Toward the Dating of the Book of Baruch." *Catholic Biblical Quarterly* 36 (1974): 312-20.

Mowinckel, Sigmund O. P. *He That Cometh: The Messianic Concept in Israel and Later Judaism.* Translated by G. W. Anderson. New York/Nashville: Abingdon, 1955.

Müller, Christian. *Gottes Gerechtigkeit und Gottes Volk: Eine Untersuchungen zu Römer 9-11.* FRLANT 86. Göttingen: Vandenhoeck & Ruprecht, 1964.

Neusner, Jacob. *Self-Fulfilling Prophecy: Exile and Return in the History of Judaism.* Boston: Beacon, 1987.

Neusner, Jacob, W. S. Green, and E. Freirichs, eds. *Judaism and Their Messiahs at the Turn of the Christian Era*. Cambridge: Cambridge University Press, 1987.

Nickelsburg, George W. E. *Jewish Literature Between the Bible and the Mishnah: A Historical and Literary Introduction*. Philadelphia: Fortress, 1981.

Nickelsburg, G. W. E., and M. E. Stone. *Faith and Piety in Early Judaism: Texts and Documents*. Philadelphia: Fortress, 1983.

Noth, Martin. *Überlieferungsgeschichtliche Studien*. Part 1. Halle, Germany: Niemeyer, 1943.

Pate, C. Marvin. *The Glory of Adam and the Afflictions of the Righteous: Pauline Suffering in Context*. New York: Edwin Mellen Press, 1993.

————. *The Reverse of the Curse: Paul, Wisdom, and the Law*. WUNT. Tübingen: J. C. B. Mohr (Paul Siebeck), forthcoming.

Pate, C. Marvin, and Calvin B. Haines Jr. *Doomsday Delusions: What's Wrong with Predictions About the End of the World*. Downers Grove, Ill.: InterVarsity Press, 1995.

Perrin, Norman. *A Modern Pilgrimage in New Testament Christology*. Philadelphia: Fortress, 1974.

Rad, Gerhard von. "Gerichtsdoxologie." *Gesammelte Studien zum Alten Testament Band II*. TBS: AT 48. Edited by Rudolf S. Mend. Munich: Kaiser, 1973.

Rhoads, David. "Zealots." *Anchor Bible Dictionary*. Edited by David Noel Freedman. New York: Doubleday, 1992.

Rhyne, C. T. *Faith Establishes the Law*. SBLDS 55. Chico, Calif.: Scholars Press, 1981.

Rowland, C. *The Open Heaven*. New York: Crossroads, 1982.

Russell, D. S. *The Method and Message of Jewish Apocalyptic*. Philadelphia: Westminster Press, 1964.

Sanders, E. P. *Paul and Palestinian Judaism: A Comparison of Patterns of Religion*. Philadelphia: Fortress, 1977.

Sandmel, Samuel. "Parallelomania." *JBL* 81 (1962): 1-13.

Schiffman, Lawrence H. *Reclaiming the Dead Sea Scrolls: Their True Meaning for Judaism and Christianity*. Anchor Bible Reference Library. New York: Doubleday, 1995.

Scott, James M. "'For As Many As Are of the Works of the Law Are Under a Curse' (Galatians 3:10)." *Paul and the Scriptures of Israel*. Journal for the Study of the New Testament Supplement Series 83. Studies in Scripture in Early Judaism and Christianity 1. Edited by Craig A. Evans and James A. Sanders. Sheffield, U.K.: JSOT Press, 1993.

————. "Paul's Use of the Deuteronomic Tradition(s)." *JBL* 112 (1993): 645-65.

Steck, Odil H. *Israel und das gewaltsame Geshick der Propheten: Untersuchungen zur Überlieferung des deuteronomistischen Geshichtsbildes im Alten Testament, Spätjudentum und Urchristentum*. Wissenschaftliche Monographien Zum Alten und Neun Testament 23. Neukirchen-Vluyn, Germany: Neukirchener, 1967.

Stegemann, Harmut. "The Qumran Essenes—Local Members of the Main Jewish Union In Late Second Temple Times." *The Madrid Qumran Congress* 1. Edited by Barrera, Montaner. Leiden: E. J. Brill.

Stendahl, Krister, ed. *The Scrolls and the New Testament*. New York: Harper &

Row, 1957.

————. *The School of Matthew and Its Use of the Old Testament.* 2nd ed. Philadelphia: Fortress, 1968.

Stuhlmacher, Peter. *Gerechtigkeit Gottes bei Paulus.* 2nd ed. FRLANT 87. Göttingen: Vandenhoeck & Ruprecht, 1966.

————. "Das Ende des Gesetzes: Über ursprung und ansatz der paulinischen theologie," *ZTK* 67 (1970): 14-39.

Sussmann, Y. "The History of Halakha and the Dead Sea Scrolls." Appendix 1, Qumran Cave 4. Vol. 5, *Miqsat Ma'aśe Ha-Torah.* Edited by Elisha Qimron and John Strugnell. Oxford: Clarendon, 1994.

Thielman, Frank. *Paul and the Law: A Contextual Approach.* Downers Grove, Ill.: InterVarsity Press, 1994.

Thiering, Barbara E. *The Gospels and Qumran: A New Hypothesis.* Sydney: Theological Explorations, 1981.

————. *The Qumran Origins of the Christian Church.* Sydney: Theological Explorations, 1983.

————. *Redating the Teacher of Righteousness.* Sydney: Theological Explorations, 1979.

————. *The Riddle of the Dead Sea Scrolls.* San Francisco: HarperCollins, 1992.

Trever, John C. *The Untold Story of Qumran.* Westwood, N.J.: Fleming H. Revell, 1965.

Troeltsch, Ernst. *The Social Teaching of the Christian Churches.* 2 vols. Translated by Olive Wyon. New York: MacMillan, 1931.

VanderKam, James C. *The Dead Sea Scrolls Today.* Grand Rapids, Mich.: Eerdmans, 1994.

Vermes, Geza. *The Dead Sea Scrolls in English.* 3rd ed. New York: Penguin, 1987.

Watson, Francis. *Paul, Judaism and the Gentiles: A Sociological Approach.* SNTSMS 56. Cambridge: Cambridge University Press, 1986.

Wilson, Edmund. *The Scrolls from the Dead Sea.* New York: Oxford University Press, 1955.

Wise, Michael O. *A Critical Study of the Temple Scroll from Qumran Cave 11.* Studies In Ancient Oriental Civilization 49. Chicago, Ill.: Oriental Institute of the University of Chicago, 1990.

Witherington, Ben, III. *The Christology of Jesus.* Minneapolis: Fortress, 1990.

Wright, N. T. *The Climax of the Covenant: Christ and the Law in Pauline Theology.* Edinburgh: T & T Clark, 1991.

————. *Jesus and the Victory of God.* Minneapolis: Fortress, 1996.

————. *The New Testament and the People of God.* Minneapolis: Fortress, 1992.

Subject Index

Scripture & Ancient Texts Index

105, 106
12:3-4, *115*
12:6, *102, 105, 106*
12:22-32, *117*
12:23, *116*
12:41-42, *115*
12:43-45, *117*
13, *94, 117*
13:11, *94*
13:14-15, *94, 101*
13:35, *101*
15:22, *116*
16:13-20, *114*
18, *94*
18:12-14, *114*
18:15-17, *145*
18:21-22, *145*
20:30-34, *116*
21:9, *116*
21:15, *116*
21:33-34, *98*
21:33-44, *97, 98*
21:33-46, *86, 97, 106*
21:34, *98*
21:35-39, *98*
21:40-44, *98*
21:43, *98*
21:45-46, *98*
22:41-45, *115*
23:1-28, *93*
23:1-39, *105*
23:23-39, *126*
23:29-30, *93*
23:31-34, *93*
23:34, *93*
23:35-36, *93*
23:37, *93*
24, *130*
26:26-28, *126*
26:26-29, *142*
26:30, *114*
26:56, *101*
27:9-10, *102*
27:34, *193*

Mark
1:3, *81, 94*
1:9-11, *114*
2:25-28, *115*
3:20-30, *117*

4, *117*
6:34, *114*
8:27-30, *114*
8:31, *118*
9:31-32, *118*
10:32-34, *118*
12:1-8, *98*
12:35-37, *115, 116*
13, *127, 130, 131, 132*
13:2, *130*
13:5-23, *130, 131*
13:12, *130*
13:14, *131*
13:17, *130*
13:19, *224*
13:20, *130*
13:22, *130*
13:24, *224*
13:24-31, *130, 131, 132*
13:26, *224*
13:26-27, *127*
14:22-25, *142*
14:27, *114*
14:58, *151*

Luke
1:46-53, *135*
1:48-49, *135*
1:48-53, *147*
1:50-53, *135*
1:54-55, *135*
1:68-79, *136*
1:72-73, *136*
1:78, *135, 136*
1:80, *81*
2:14, *136, 147, 183*
2:29-35, *136*
2:30-31, *136*
2:32, *137*
3, *141*
3:1-20, *81*
3:2, *81*
3:3, *141, 148*
3:3-6, *81, 148*
3:4, *147*
3:4-6, *94*
3:4-8, *145*
3:4-14, *141*
3:7-8, *141, 147*

3:10-14, *144*
3:16, *81*
3:21-22, *114, 148*
4:1-13, *148*
4:18-19, *144*
4:18-21, *115, 116*
5, *140*
6:3-5, *115*
6:20-23, *144*
6:20-24, *135, 147*
6:24-25, *144*
7:31, *24*
8:1-3, *144*
9:1-3, *144*
9:18-21, *114*
9:23-27, *144, 145*
9:51-18:14, *149*
9:51-19:44, *153*
9:57-58, *144*
10, *148*
10:3, *114*
10:10-12, *144*
10:19-31, *144*
10:25-28, *151*
11:24-26, *118*
11:29, *24*
11:31, *115*
12:4-7, *117*
12:13-21, *135, 147*
12:22-34, *144*
12:32, *114*
13:34-35, *25*
14:7-14, *147*
14:7-24, *135*
14:24, *193*
15, *117*
15:3-7, *114*
16:1-13, *144*
16:19-31, *135*
17:3-4, *145*
17:22, *224*
18:18-26, *144*
18:28, *144*
19:1-10, *135*
19:44, *149*
20:9-19, *98*
20:41-44, *115*
21, *130*
22:14-20, *143*
22:17-20, *142*

22:20, *147*
24:32, *39*
24:44-45, *39*

John
1, *224*
1:1, *227*
1:1-3, *227*
1:1-18, *227*
1:4, *227*
1:5, *227*
1:9, *227*
1:10, *227*
1:10-13, *229*
1:11, *227*
1:12, *227*
1:14, *227*
1:14-18, *229*
1:17-18, *229*
1:23, *94*
1:29-34, *114*
1:47-51, *228, 229*
2:9, *193*
2:19-21, *151*
2:22, *217*
3:1-14, *229*
3:3-8, *217*
3:12-13, *228, 229*
3:31-36, *229*
4:3, *217*
5:24-30, *217*
6, *229*
6:35, *228*
6:61-62, *228, 229*
6:70, *217*
8:12, *217, 228*
10, *114*
10:7, *228*
10:11, *228*
10:14, *228*
11:25, *228*
12, *224*
12:1, *217*
12:20-24, *229*
12:23, *223*
12:23-36, *225*
12:28, *223*
12:30-33, *225*
12:32, *229*
12:35-36, *225*

DATE DUE